Animal Worlds

Animal Worlds

Film, Philosophy and Time

Laura McMahon

University Press

Edinburgh University Press is one of the leading university presses in the UK. We publish academic books and journals in our selected subject areas across the humanities and social sciences, combining cutting-edge scholarship with high editorial and production values to produce academic works of lasting importance. For more information visit our website: edinburghuniversitypress.com

© Laura McMahon, 2019, 2021

First published in hardback by Edinburgh University Press 2019

Edinburgh University Press Ltd
The Tun – Holyrood Road
12 (2f) Jackson's Entry
Edinburgh EH8 8PJ

Typeset in 11/13 Monotype Ehrhardt by
Manila Typesetting Company

A CIP record for this book is available from the British Library

ISBN 978 1 4744 4638 9 (hardback)
ISBN 978 1 4744 4639 6 (paperback)
ISBN 978 1 4744 4640 2 (webready PDF)
ISBN 978 1 4744 4641 9 (epub)

The right of Laura McMahon to be identified as author of this work has been asserted in accordance with the Copyright, Designs and Patents Act 1988 and the Copyright and Related Rights Regulations 2003 (SI No. 2498).

Contents

List of Figures vii
Acknowledgements ix

Introduction: Unfurling Worlds 1
1 Cinematic Time and Animal Worlds 42
2 Still/Moving: *Bestiaire*'s Lives in Limbo 66
3 *The Turin Horse*: Animal Labour and Lines of Flight 95
4 *Leviathan*, Meat and the Annihilation of Worlds 134
5 Actual/Virtual: *Bovines ou la vraie vie des vaches* 161
Conclusion: Cinematic Worlds and Beyond 192

Bibliography 203
Filmography 217
Index 219

Figures

2.1	The animal displaced (*Bestiaire*)	74
2.2	The captive look (*Bestiaire*)	80
2.3	Alive and looking (*Bestiaire*)	81
2.4	The taxidermied look (*Bestiaire*)	82
2.5	Biopolitical governing (*Bestiaire*)	85
2.6	Intraspecies care and lines of flight (*Bestiaire*)	86
3.1	Equine labour (*The Turin Horse*)	103
3.2	Vulnerability and domination (*The Turin Horse*)	106
3.3	Refusing to work (*The Turin Horse*)	109
3.4	Exhaustion (*The Turin Horse*)	111
3.5	Animal resistance (*The Turin Horse*)	117
4.1	The seriality of slaughter (*Leviathan*)	143
4.2	Fragments underwater (*Leviathan*)	144
4.3	Massification (*Leviathan*)	146
4.4	Indistinct realms of life and death (*Leviathan*)	149
5.1	The inextricability of aesthetics and capital (*Bovines ou la vraie vie des vaches*)	162
5.2	Calling the calves (*Bovines*)	167
5.3	Animal capital (*Bovines*)	176
5.4	Becoming other (*Bovines*)	182
5.5	Rumination, life, *puissance* (*Bovines*)	185

Acknowledgements

This book has benefited from, and been decisively shaped by, an ongoing set of conversations with others. I am deeply indebted in particular to those who read and generously offered feedback on various parts of the book, including Jonathan Burt, Martin Crowley, Rhiannon Harries, Michael Lawrence, Robert McKay, Anat Pick and Emma Wilson. I am also hugely grateful for conversations about the project with many other colleagues and friends, including Georgina Evans, Katherine Groo, Nikolaj Lübecker, Karen Lury, David Martin-Jones, Isabelle McNeill, Matilda Mroz, John David Rhodes and Jacqui Stacey. My thanks also to the contributors to *Animal Life and the Moving Image* (BFI, 2015), a book that I co-edited with Michael Lawrence, for helping me to think further about the central concerns of this project and of the field more broadly. I am grateful to Gonville and Caius College, Cambridge, to Girton College, Cambridge, to the French Section at the University of Cambridge, and to the University of Aberdeen for providing vital support for my research during the development of the project. The writing of the book was also supported by an Early Career Fellowship at the University of Cambridge's Centre for Research in the Arts, Social Sciences and Humanities in 2015. I am deeply grateful as ever to Matthew Stephenson, and to my parents Eilleen and John McMahon. The book was completed just before the arrival of Anna Stephenson, to whom it is dedicated – with love, joy and hopefulness about the future.

Chapters 2, 4 and 5 revise material from, respectively, 'Animal Worlds: Denis Côté's *Bestiaire*', *Studies in French Cinema*, 14:3 (2014), 195–215, 'Film', in Ron Broglio, Undine Sellbach and Lynn Turner (eds), *The Edinburgh Companion to Animal Studies* (Edinburgh: Edinburgh University Press, 2018), and 'Cinematic Slowness, Political Paralysis? Animal Life in *Bovines*', *NECSUS*, Spring 2015, http://www.necsus-ejms.org/category/spring-2015-animals/. I am grateful to the editors for their kind permission to draw on this material here.

Introduction: Unfurling Worlds

The cinema does not just present images, it surrounds them with a world.[1]

Animals have been central to the histories and practices of the moving image, from the protocinematic studies of animal motion by Eadweard Muybridge and Étienne-Jules Marey to the proliferation of animal videos on YouTube. But in recent years a particular kind of philosophical reflection on animal life has emerged on our screens. Slow, contemplative films about animals represent a burgeoning trend in contemporary art cinema, involving recent releases such as *Bestiaire* (Denis Côté, Canada, 2012), *Bovines ou la vraie vie des vaches/A Cow's Life* (Emmanuel Gras, France, 2011) and *Le Quattro Volte* (Michelangelo Frammartino, Italy, 2010).[2] These works provide none of what Jonathan Burt calls 'the framing narrative structures of natural history films'.[3] Rather, they deploy particular forms of delay and temporal distension, combined with a lack of expository voiceover commentary, as a way of attending to animal worlds of sentience and perception. This patient mode of cinematic attentiveness – ranging across various sites and spaces, from the zoo in *Bestiaire* to the farm in *Bovines* – invites us to examine the material conditions of captive and domesticated animals, and the biopolitical regimes through which animal lives are regulated and reproduced under late capitalism. Yet, as I argue in this study, these films also open up paths of thought beyond those immediate material conditions, and beyond the critique of biopower that they invite, allowing cinematic time to envisage modes of becoming, lines of flight from fixed identities, and 'virtual' realms (the 'virtual' being, for Gilles Deleuze, the condition of the living yet to be actualised).

In this study, I offer a sustained analysis of the relations between cinema, philosophy and animal life. I focus in particular on interactions between cinematic time and animal worlds, making a detailed argument for the value of Deleuze's writings in these areas. While Deleuze's reflections, with Félix Guattari, on 'becoming-animal' have been extensively addressed in critical animal studies,[4] Deleuze's writings on cinema have received relatively little attention within the burgeoning body of scholarship on animals and film[5] in comparison to the field's sustained focus on the film theoretical work of André Bazin. In recent commentary on animals and cinema, by Anat Pick, Jennifer Fay and others, the work of Bazin – and the role played by animals in his model of cinematic realism – has provided a key point of reference.[6] But by following Deleuze's shift away from Bazin, which Deleuze signals above all by his reflection that what is at stake in cinema is not 'at the level of the real' but rather at the level of 'thought',[7] I seek to move beyond the Bazinian accounts (and their linking of the animal image to a particular kind of realism) that have dominated scholarship in this area thus far.

I aim to reconfigure and revitalise Deleuze's thought for critical animal studies, both by revisiting his writings on animals and by turning to his work on cinema, foregrounding in particular his account of cinematic time. As Raymond Bellour notes in *Le Corps du cinéma*, Deleuze develops his reflections on animals and on cinematic time quite separately, without addressing potential links between them.[8] I seek to bridge this gap by bringing these accounts together in a sustained manner for the first time, drawing on concepts such as the time-image and the virtual in order to trace relations between animal life and cinematic thought. At the same time, I place the work of Deleuze (with Guattari) in dialogue with a range of conceptual frameworks, from Nicole Shukin's theorisation of 'animal capital' and Jacques Derrida's reflections on the ethics and politics of animal life to Jean-Christophe Bailly's consideration of 'pensivity', as I seek to develop a form of film-philosophy that responds to the demands to thought posed by this recent wave of filmmaking.

What is an 'animal world'? The ethologist Jakob von Uexküll's concept of the *Umwelt* (or 'environment-world') has played a key role in philosophical reflection, by thinkers such as Martin Heidegger, Maurice Merleau-Ponty and Deleuze and Guattari, on the question of animal worlds.[9] Rejecting the Cartesian model of the animal as an instinctual machine without conscious reflection, Uexküll sees animals as engaged in perception and meaning-making, as 'subjects, whose essential activities consist in perception and production of effects'.[10] For Uexküll, each animal inhabits a realm simultaneously perceived and produced by that animal: 'These two worlds, of perception and production of effects, form one closed unit, the *environment*.'[11] Animal environments are thus shaped by 'purely subjective realities'[12] in a manner akin to human environments, though as Brett Buchanan observes, Uexküll's project is an 'attempt at articulating the meaning of the environment beyond a strictly human perspective [. . .]'.[13] I draw on Uexküll's reflections on animal worlds as realms of perception, sentience, thought, action and meaning-making, yet

I also follow the implications of Deleuze and Guattari's reworking of Uexküll's thought. In *A Thousand Plateaus*, Deleuze and Guattari suggest: 'Von Uexküll, in defining animal worlds, looks for the active and passive affects of which the animal is capable in the individuated assemblage of which it is a part.'[14] While invoking Uexküll, they shift away from his emphasis on the 'subject' – a term that, though important for redressing a tendency to present animals as 'objects', might be seen to remain too attached to a humanist tradition (even in the context of the nonanthropocentric dimensions of Uexküll's thought).[15] Deleuze and Guattari move towards a model of 'desubjectified'[16] affects and assemblages that I pursue in my readings by linking this to Deleuze's theorisation of cinematic worlds as reaching beyond any one subject position.

And while von Uexküll's animals – observed and imagined in their natural environments – seem abstracted from political realms, my study, following work by Shukin, Cary Wolfe and others, aims to remain grounded in the material realities of animal lives within the biopolitical regimes of late capitalism. From the animals on display at the zoo in *Bestiaire* to the cows farmed for meat in *Bovines*, these films diagnose the reduction of animal worlds to forms of 'bare life', that drastically eroded state of existence which, as Giorgio Agamben puts it, 'remains included in politics in the form of the exception'.[17] Tracing the mundane and the seemingly uneventful, these films unfold modes of political critique, deploying 'dead time'[18] in order to bear witness to animal lives suspended in captivity or endlessly reproduced. While Deleuze and Guattari offer resources for thinking through such forms of political critique, my readings of these films, particularly in Chapter 5, also probe the possible limitations of their approach in relation to the biopolitical regimes that manage animal life.

SLOW ANIMAL CINEMA

Critical commentary on wildlife documentary, including work by Gregg Mitman, Derek Bousé and Cynthia Chris,[19] has noted 'the resurgence of theatrical wildlife documentaries in recent years',[20] against the broader backdrop of a contemporary 'green wave' of film and television[21] and the rise of the 'ecodoc'.[22] Stephen Rust cites films such as *March of the Penguins* (Luc Jacquet, 2005), *Earth* (Alastair Fothergill and Mark Linfield, 2009) and *Being Caribou* (Leanne Allison, 2008), while pointing to *Microcosmos* (Claude Nuridsany and Marie Pérennou, 1996) and *Winged Migration* (Jacques Perrin, Jacques Cluzaud and Michel Debats, 2001) – both made in France[23] – as particularly important moments in the history of wildlife documentary: while the withdrawal of voiceover narration in these latter two films works to 'minimise' anthropomorphism, they also 'appeared to signal that the theatrical wildlife film [. . .] had broken free of the tendency to focus almost exclusively on mascot species'.[24]

The engagement with insects in *Microcosmos* and birds in *Winged Migration* seems a radical departure from the more usual focus on 'charismatic species'[25] in wildlife programming. The films I examine in this book extend this interest in less 'charismatic', less usually observed species: rather than elephants and cheetahs, we see cows (*Bovines*), fish (*Leviathan*, Lucien Castaing-Taylor and Véréna Paravel, 2012), a horse (*The Turin Horse*, Béla Tarr and Ágnes Hranitzky, 2011). The drive for megafauna spectacle and action often found in traditional wildlife programming is implicitly refused.[26]

Yet, while sharing some elements in common with these recent wildlife documentaries – particularly the absence of voiceover commentary that Rust identifies in *Microcosmos* and *Winged Migration* – the films I explore differ in two key ways: they adopt an extreme mode of temporal distension that is very different from the predominantly (or residually) action-orientated concerns and 'edutainment' values of these nature documentaries,[27] and they shift away from a focus on wildlife. In fact, wildlife does not really feature in these films at all (unless we include, from *Leviathan*, the fish before they have been caught or the gulls flying past the trawler). Instead, these films focus on zoo animals (*Bestiaire*), a labouring animal (*The Turin Horse*), farmed animals (*Bovines*) and 'food animals' (*Leviathan*) – that is, animals that are used, controlled and consumed in particular ways.[28] In these films, then, the 'use value' of the animal (as entertainment, labour or food) is set against a 'wasting' of cinematic time. While this use value has been theorised by Shukin as 'animal capital', this wasting of cinematic time has been conceptualised by Deleuze as the 'time-image' – two key concepts that I explore further below. In the insistence of these films on temporal dilation, biopolitical regimes of animal productivity are made to encounter, and opened to question by, cinematic strategies of non-productivity.

While this formal approach intersects to some extent with that of observational documentary (defined by Bill Nichols as an 'exhaustive depiction of the everyday'),[29] the extreme mode of temporal delay at work in these films, as well as their privileging of the nonverbal, suggests a particular affinity with forms of 'slow cinema' – a filmmaking tradition often seen to have emerged in the early 2000s, exemplified by the work of filmmakers such as Tarr, Chantal Akerman, Abbas Kiarostami, Tsai Ming-liang, Hou Hsiao-hsien and Lisandro Alonso. Slow cinema tends to be shaped by an extensive use of long takes, forms of 'de-dramatisation', and 'a diminution of pace' that 'serves to displace the dominant momentum of narrative causality'.[30] Like slow cinema, these experimental animal films adopt a de-dramatised, long-take aesthetic in order to probe questions of duration and eventhood (though it should be noted at this stage that *Leviathan* sits awkwardly in this tradition of 'slow cinema' – an anomalous position that I address below). Yet while one can trace a nascent interest in human–animal relations in the broad category of slow cinema,[31] the films I explore in this book radically extend this interest. While Alonso's *Freedom* (2001) and *The Dead* (2004), for example, adopt strategies of intermittently decentring the human and attending to nonhuman life, the focus of his films remains on the human protagonists. By contrast, the films I examine tend to shift the focus fully, rather than intermittently, from humans to animals in ways that have important aesthetic, ethical and political implications. (The continued occupation of screen time by the human in *The Turin Horse* can be seen as an exception here, but as is clear from the title, questions of animal life remain central to the film's concerns.)

As critical commentary on slow cinema has underlined, the relation between 'narratorial subject and duration' is key to the concept of cinematic slowness.[32] As Ivone Margulies puts it in her study of Akerman, the phrase 'nothing happens' is used to describe a film when 'the representation's substratum of content seems at variance with the duration accorded it'.[33] There is, of course, a long tradition of art cinema in which 'nothing happens', that comes to prominence with Italian neorealism (as celebrated by Bazin) and passes via modernist and experimental cinema in Europe (for example, Andrei Tarkovsky, Jean-Marie Straub and Danièle Huillet, Akerman) and in the United States (including the work of Michael Snow, Andy Warhol, Hollis Frampton).[34] As Margulies writes of Warhol in particular: 'interest is challenged on all fronts: the filmmaker is absent, the object is banal, the spectator is bored.'[35] The perception that 'nothing happens' in slow cinema is central to its various provocations, thus prompting the fundamental question, as Song Hwee Lim puts it, of 'what qualifies as a legitimate subject in film – the very notion of "thing," and what counts as "nothing" within a film's narrative'.[36]

For Mary Ann Doane, anxieties about uneventfulness shape cinema from its very beginnings. Early actualities, such as those filmed by the Lumières, document the contingent, seemingly uneventful wanderings of everyday time, but as early films develop narrative structures, alongside the rationalisation of time in industrial modernity, contingency is increasingly regulated in pursuit of coherent, linear narration.[37] For Doane, 'the cinema, together with other technologies of modernity, is instrumental in producing and corroborating an investment in events, in dividing temporality to elicit eventful and uneventful time.'[38] Significantly, Doane develops this theory of (un)eventful time in relation to Thomas Edison's *Electrocuting an Elephant* (1903), a film that documents the execution of an elephant, a circus performer named Topsy, putatively in order to demonstrate the deadly power of alternating current electricity. Though this film occupies an important place in theorisations of cinema's relation to animals,[39] Doane reads it not from a critical animal studies perspective but rather as a film that activates questions of cinematic eventhood. Observing a jump cut in the film, an elision, during which Topsy must have been strapped down and bound to the electrodes, she notes: 'That break functions to elide time that is perceived as "uneventful" – the work of situating the elephant and binding her in the electrical apparatus.'[40] 'Dead time' is excluded or elided in what Doane describes as a 'denial of process'. Here animal action, including gestures of animal resistance, have been edited out, suggesting a hierarchisation of eventhood constituted by the film.[41] *Electrocuting an Elephant* resists representing events deemed to be insignificant, time in which, according to its anthropocentric focus, 'nothing happens' – 'time which is in some sense "wasted", expended without product'.[42] What is privileged in *Electrocuting an Elephant* is the event of animal death itself, while paradoxically the lived time of the animal is considered 'dead time'.

Yet 'dead time' is precisely what is embraced by slow cinema. Drawing on Doane, Lim notes:

> Rather than construct a narrative in which many events happen, a cinema of slowness chooses to dwell instead on the interstices between events or on moments within events during which nothing much happens. Indeed, it uses so-called dead time to create non-events as events through which a different temporality, meaning, and value can come into being, thereby questioning the notion of 'event' or 'happening' and unsettling the very foundation of what constitutes a film's narrative.[43]

Thought along these lines, a cinema of slowness destabilises and reconfigures understandings of the 'event' in cinema, proposing an alternative model of eventhood. In works of 'slow animal cinema', this allows for a renewed mode of attentiveness to the time of animals – to mundane and apparently insignificant gestures – and thus a different register of meaning and value, in ways that *Electrocuting an Elephant* forecloses.

In the context of slow animal cinema, this alternative model of eventhood has particular political implications. Karl Schoonover has emphasised a politics of 'wasted time and uneconomical temporalities' that issues forth from slow cinema's 'unproductive episodic meandering'.[44] If the 'politics of slow cinema' can be understood, in broad terms, as an interrogation of the speed of 'late capitalism's economic labour systems, social values and the contemporary audiovisual and cultural regimes',[45] as Tiago de Luca and Nuno Barradas Jorge suggest, then the 'unproductive' or 'uneconomical' wanderings of films such as *Bestiaire* and *Bovines* function as a way of examining the place of animals within such systems. Through a focus on 'dead time' – on the banal, the everyday, the seemingly insubstantial – this recent wave of filmmaking proposes a mode of sustained engagement with the time of animals in which supposedly 'nothing happens', asking us to see these lives anew, beyond their reduction to resource and capital. Though one would want to avoid an uncritical, universalising valorisation of slowness as resistance to capitalism (accelerationist theories, for example, offer a very different approach),[46] I make a particular case in this study for the ways in which slow cinema can resist the material specificities of an all-too-efficient conversion of animal life into capital.

At the same time, slow, de-dramatised animal cinema intensifies the stakes of the debate that Lim identifies around 'what qualifies as a legitimate subject in film'. If, as Richard Misek observes, spectatorial boredom occurs 'when there is a mismatch between our time and an object's time',[47] to what extent is this exacerbated by the species gap? Some viewers, even enthusiasts of slow cinema, may consider animals to be illegitimate subject matter for such durational attention. The contingent wanderings of the animals in films such as *Bovines* and *Bestiaire* usher in a particular kind of nonlinearity, of unregulated action, that seems to radicalise slow cinema's challenge to causal narrative structure (while also upsetting a long tradition of directed, regulated animal acting onscreen). And if slow cinema tends to minimalise dialogue, slow animal cinema takes this to an extreme. Or, at least, these films are largely devoid of languages that humans can understand. Instead of human speech, we hear untranslatable animal sounds, sometimes amplified by the film as though to emphasise their simultaneous invitation and resistance to meaning (one thinks, for example, of the strident mooing at the beginning of *Bovines*). Recalling the gaze of Derrida's cat and its indexing of an existence that 'refuses to be conceptualised',[48] the animals in these films offer an extreme illegibility of expression that works to resist psychological narrative and spectatorial identification. This is exacerbated by the durational aesthetic, particularly the long take and the lack of cuts. Whereas the conventional wildlife film, for example, deploys fast editing, point-of-view and shot-reverse-shots to invite spectatorial identification, such techniques are largely refused in the slow animal films that I study here. Also refused here (as noted above) is the voiceover commentary of the wildlife film that works to narrate feelings and motivations, anthropomorphically projecting psychology onto the animal. While the films I explore can offer particular forms of viewing pleasure (*Bovines* was described by *Télérama*, for example, as a 'surrealist, philosophical story', and by *Les Inrockuptibles* as 'a pure trip'),[49] spectatorial anxiety about uneventfulness – cinematic time in which supposedly 'nothing happens' – seems likely to be especially intensified by slow cinema about animals.

Yet it is also necessary to bear in mind the ways in which contemporary technologies and media platforms are changing the ways in which we watch animals and our relations to animal (un)eventfulness. The increasing popularity of ZooCams (streaming live feeds of zoo animals), for example, radically reconfigures spectatorial expectations in relation to animals onscreen. As Andrew Burke argues, the ZooCam 'enables, even encourages, a mode of watching that is at least in part liberated from the desire for drama that distorts the conventional wildlife documentary'; indeed, 'part of the attraction is the uneventfulness'.⁵⁰ Burke suggests that this may be because the ZooCam is part of a viewing ecology in which spectatorial attention is already radically dispersed: 'such viewing usually takes place as part of an array of digital activities, with the ZooCam being one window among many open on my desktop [. . .] the streaming live feed is a broadcast form tailor-made for an era defined by "continuous partial attention" [. . .]'.⁵¹ Burke proposes a very different model of spectatorship here, one in which the ZooCam is 'something to be checked in on occasionally rather than watched continuously [. . .]'.⁵² Burke does not connect his insights to Doane or other film theoretical accounts of the event, but his analysis indicates ways in which new media contexts – and the particular role of the animal within those contexts – ask us to rethink certain assumptions, such as those about spectatorial anxiety in encounters with uneventfulness.⁵³ Burke's account does not replace film theory's conceptualisation of eventfulness onscreen (and animal eventfulness in particular), then, but it supplements it in ways that attend to the specificities of online media and to what it means to look at animals now.⁵⁴

THE TIME-IMAGE

Interestingly, Burke points to certain parallels between ZooCams and slow cinema, not only in their formal approaches – '[t]he absence of cuts, the fixity of perspective, the lack of music, and the relative stasis of the scene' – but also in relation to the question of what happens when 'nothing happens'.⁵⁵ While acknowledging such echoes between different formats and modes of address, I seek to trace what might still be specific – in philosophical, political and aesthetic terms – about the particular configurations of uneventful time offered up by these slow animal films, given that, as De Luca and Jorge note, 'when watched under fixed-time conditions cinema strictly enforces its own temporality'.⁵⁶ It is here that Deleuze's theorisation of cinematic time devoid of ostensible action becomes particularly apposite.

For one of the central claims of this study is that, beyond the more immediate connections to slow cinema and ZooCams traced above, the animal films that I explore belong to a broader aesthetic and political lineage – that of the cinema of the 'time-image'. This is the concept created by Deleuze in order to characterise works of postwar cinema (by directors such as Akerman, Tarkovsky, Alain Resnais and Marguerite Duras) that develop a 'direct' presentation of time, untied from a narrative logic of cause and effect (as opposed to the cinema of the 'movement-image', in which the presentation of time is 'indirect', that is, subordinated to a causal chain of narrative development). Reflecting on the collective disorientation of perception articulated by cinematic works in the aftermath of the Second World War and the decades that followed,[57] Deleuze writes:

> If all the movement-images, perceptions, actions and affects underwent such an upheaval, was this not first of all because a new element burst on to the scene which was to prevent perception being extended into action in order to put it in contact with thought, and, gradually, was to subordinate the image to the demands of new signs which would take it beyond movement?[58]

The delayed, wandering representations of animal life offered up by films such as *Bovines*, *Bestiaire* and *The Turin Horse* constitute another upheaval, another set of 'new signs'. Indeed, in the unharnessing of animal time from spectacle and narrative we see a contemporary, non-anthropocentric reworking of what Deleuze discerns in the cinema of postwar Europe. Deleuze locates the emergence of the time-image in Italian neorealism in particular: in films such as *Germany, Year Zero* (Roberto Rossellini, 1948), characters drift among the ruins of the postwar city; unable to act, they can only bear witness to the lack of political alternatives – '[t]his is a cinema of the seer and no longer of the agent'.[59] In the animal films that I discuss here, particularly in relation to the biopolitical regimes that they explore, there is also a striking lack of agency at stake – an absence of political alternatives for the animals onscreen, to which an often delayed, directionless aesthetic seems to bear witness. Yet at the same time, for Deleuze, drawing on Henri Bergson's model of the perpetual splitting of time, such a 'direct' presentation of 'time itself, pure virtuality'[60] opens onto realms of becomings, to that which is yet to be actualised (as I discuss in Chapter 1). Moving between the actual and the virtual, these animal films envisage deterritorialising lines of 'flight from established identity',[61] even from within the realms of territorialisation, captivity and instrumentalisation that they register. I develop the political implications of this question of the virtual – a time of differing and becoming – throughout the book.[62]

If Deleuze finds that in the cinema of postwar Europe 'a new race of characters was stirring, kind of mutant', then in this recent trend of slow animal cinema we also sense 'a new race of characters [. . .] stirring' – 'mutant', perhaps, in their possible flights and transformations, and in their troubling of borders between the human and the animal, a troubling accentuated by cinema's growing attentiveness to them. Thus to what Elena Gorfinkel describes as art cinema's catalogue of 'dilated temporality', to 'Vittorio De Sica's slowly stretching maid Maria [. . .] Robert Bresson's dedramatized "models," [. . .] Andy Warhol's diffident portrait subjects' and 'Tsai Ming-Liang's itinerant sleepy drifters',[63] we now add an emerging set of apparently uneventful, wandering portraits of animal life.

WHY NOW?

While such art cinema precedents range over a period of more than sixty years, the animal films that I focus on have all emerged at a particular historical moment. The clustering of the dates of release – *Bestiaire* (2012), *The Turin Horse* (2011), *Leviathan* (2012), *Bovines* (2011) – is striking. There are other recent 'slow animal films' that might have been included here too, such as *Le Quattro Volte* (Frammartino, 2010), *Les Hommes* (Ariane Michel, 2006) and *Sweetgrass* (Ilisa Barbash and Lucien Castaing-Taylor, 2009).[64] Recent reflections on the nonhuman more broadly – on ecologies, environment and sustainability – can also be found in experimental work by filmmakers such as James Benning and Rose Lowder.[65] While these waves of filmmaking recall earlier independent art film and video work interested in links between duration, animals and ecologies – for example, Bill Viola's *I Do Not Know What It Is I Am Like* (1986)[66] – there has been a noticeable surge of interest in questions of the nonhuman in independent filmmaking in recent years.

Why might these slow animal films have emerged now? On one level, my corpus of films work through a set of age-old fascinations with human–animal commonalities and differences: while interested in the blurring of perceived boundaries between the human and the animal, these films also reflect on ways in which animals have represented, throughout the ages, what Erica Fudge describes as 'the limit case [. . .] of all of our structures of understanding'.[67] But these films are also shaped by their particular historical moment, and by a set of contemporary cultural trends that point to what might be broadly described as an increased sensitivity to animal life. A wide range of factors has contributed to this development. One might note the confluence of such phenomena as the threat of environmental crisis and related anxieties about ever-accelerating losses in biodiversity,[68] a surge of interest in vegetarianism and veganism (linked also to issues of 'ethical consumption', resource scarcity and environmental crisis), the continued rise of animal rights activism (for which Peter Singer's *Animal Liberation* (1975) remains a key point of reference),[69] and recent discoveries in the biological, zoological and ethological sciences, providing further evidence of our genetic proximity to animals and of the complexity of animal language, cognition and social behaviour.[70] Such cultural, scientific and epistemological shifts bear witness to what Wolfe has described as 'a broad reopening of the question of the ethical status of animals in relation to the human'.[71]

Specific 'crisis' events, such as the cloning of Dolly the sheep in 1996 and the bovine spongiform encephalopathy epidemic (BSE or 'mad cow disease') of 1986–96, have contributed further to the development of a certain set of anxieties around animal life. As Matthew Senior, David L. Clark and Carla Freccero suggest:

A new threshold seemed to be crossed with these two crises, raising the specter, simultaneously, of a lethal epidemic and the end of natural reproduction in both animals and humans. Psychologically, 'mad cow disease' [...] and cloning were last straws, apocalyptic events, states of exception, that led to the dismantling of the traditional concepts of the human and the animal.[72]

Indeed, zoonotic diseases such as BSE, and also, more recently, the H5N1 avian flu virus, provoke a particular set of cultural anxieties. As Shukin suggests of the recent 'fixation on zoonotic diseases', 'human–animal intimacy is one of the most ideologically and materially contested sites of postmodernity as formerly distinct barriers separating humans and other species begin to imaginatively, and physically, disintegrate.'[73] Such insights help us to discern some of the reasons why a wave of films meditating on animal life might be appearing now. In their patient, wordless engagements with animal worlds, these films anxiously work through 'ideologically and materially contested' sites of 'human–animal intimacy' in the wake of such crises, and in an era in which the question of the animal, and that of technologies of life more broadly, is perpetually 'reopening'.

In dialogue with such contexts, the humanities have witnessed, in recent years, an increased interrogation of categories of the human and the animal, and the development of the field now described as 'critical animal studies' (against the backdrop of a broader interest in ecocriticism, and in questions of the Anthropocene and the posthuman). Work in contemporary philosophy (a context that I foreground here), by thinkers such as Derrida, Haraway, Bailly, Agamben, Jean-Luc Nancy, Michel Serres and Florence Burgat – following, yet also diverging from, Deleuze and Guattari before them – has turned to address questions of animal life, and of human–animal relations more broadly. This 'animal turn' has been shaped not only by the cultural contexts signalled above but also by a specific network of intellectual developments, such as the crisis of humanism prompted by structuralism and poststructuralism – genealogies that have been richly traced elsewhere.[74] One might also point to an intensifying interest in animal life in contemporary literature. In the UK, 'new nature-writing', epitomised by works by Robert Macfarlane, Helen Macdonald and Michael McCarthy, is on the rise.[75] In French and Francophone contexts, animals proliferate in texts such as Yves Bichet's *La Part animale* (1994), Noëlle Revaz's *With the Animals* (2002), Tristan Garcia's *Mémoires de la jungle* (2010) and Jean-Baptiste Del Amo's *Règne animal* (2016),[76] against a broader backdrop of interest in ecologies, as evidenced by such works as the 'ecopoetic' writings of Michel Deguy and Philippe Jaccottet.[77] One might also think of the increasing visibility of animals in contemporary art, ranging from the drawings of Sue Coe to the reworked taxidermic sculptures of Angela Singer and the performance art of Kira O'Reilly.[78]

But there is arguably something specific about this cultural moment that shapes, and is shaped by, the interrelations between animals and moving images. This is in part because of a history of fascination with moving images of animal life that dates back to the protocinematic studies of Muybridge and Marey and persists today in the proliferation of wildlife television programming and animal videos online. It is also related to the archival, testimonial and indexical dimensions of photography and cinema, that is, their capacity to record and document – this archival impetus seems particularly relevant in relation to animal life as certain species become increasingly more precarious and less visible.[79] More than thirty years ago, John Berger argued that with the rise of industrial capitalism, animals began to disappear from public life, while 'coopted into the *family*' (as domestic pets) and 'into the *spectacle*',[80] proliferating in commodified forms: 'Zoos, realistic animal toys and the widespread commercial diffusion of animal imagery, all began as animals started to be withdrawn from daily life [. . .] Everywhere animals disappear.'[81] Writing twenty years later, Akira Mizuta Lippit pursues the spectralising logic of Berger's thesis: 'the cinema developed, indeed embodied, animal traits as a gesture of mourning for the disappearing wildlife'; 'Technology and ultimately cinema came to determine a vast mausoleum for animal being.'[82] But Lippit updates Berger's thesis too, his conceptual emphasis being more ecological than economic: 'No longer a sign of nature's abundance, animals now inspire a sense of panic for the earth's dwindling resources.'[83] While Burt usefully critiques the melancholia that subtends Lippit's thesis, this cinematic 'gesture of mourning'[84] – and the phenomena of precarious life to which it is attached – remains a suggestive way to think through a particular testimonial and archival fascination with animal life onscreen in our current historical moment.[85]

Yet the predominant focus on captive and domesticated animals in the films I consider brings with it a particular dimension that suggests something different from Lippit's melancholy, nostalgic mode and the threat of extinction subtending his thesis. Indeed, the status of these animals in various domesticated forms – as 'food', as farmed, or as 'available' to the spectator in a zoo – is key (even if some of the species appearing in the zoo are 'exotic' and/or also under the threat of extinction). Rather than operating as a 'vast mausoleum for animal being', cinema appears to have a different role here, and it is one that seems more aligned with the economic conditions identified by Berger – a bearing witness to the intensified instrumentalisation of animal life under capitalism. That these films explore such an intensification often through a delayed, contemplative aesthetic suggests an interest in interrogating the accelerated speeds of cinema and technologies, and of late capitalism more broadly – an interest that they share with slow cinema (as noted above). But this interrogation assumes particular dimensions in the context of animal life's specific entanglements with modes of neoliberal capitalist (re)production, as indicated by a range of practices, from the history of Dolly the sheep and the proliferation of related (though much less visible, less publicised) forms of genetic experimentation, to the intensification of mass industrialised slaughter across the globe.

THE BIOPOLITICS OF ANIMAL LIFE

Animal life becomes a particular kind of 'object' within an era of rapidly expanding, globalised networks of biopower, defined by Michel Foucault as *'the right to make live and let die'*.[86] This is the realm of what Michael Hardt and Antonio Negri, following Foucault, refer to as the 'production and reproduction of life itself'.[87] Biopower not only controls but also (re)produces life, shaping it across a network of political, economic and technological domains. But, as Shukin points out, the lives of animals are governed by biopolitical regimes in very particular ways. Derrida sees our era as one of an unprecedented instrumentalisation of, and intervention in, animal life:

> It is all too evident that in the course of the last two centuries [. . .] traditional forms of treatment of the animal have been turned upside down by the joint developments of zoological, ethological, biological, and genetic forms of *knowledge*, which remain inseparable from *techniques* of intervention *into* their object, from the transformation of the actual object, and from the milieu and world of their object, namely, the living animal. This has occurred by means of farming and regimentalization at a demographic level unknown in the past, by means of genetic experimentation, the industrialization of what can be called the production for consumption of animal meat, artificial insemination on a massive scale, more and more audacious manipulations of the genome, the reduction of the animal not only to production and overactive reproduction (hormones, genetic crossbreeding, cloning, etc.) of meat for consumption, but also of all sorts of other end products, and all of that in the service of a certain being and the putative human well-being of man.[88]

In this book, I seek to remain grounded in the material realities of animal lives that Derrida signals here. In so doing, I aim to avoid abstracted, 'idealist', timeless invocations of animal being or animal otherness (what Bailly calls the 'vast concept-spaces from which [animals] are not supposed to be able to exit').[89] This focus on material realities is invited by the films themselves, by their emphasis, as noted above, on the ways in which animals are used, controlled and consumed. These are films that are reflecting – in patient, contemplative, sustained terms – on the ways in which certain animals live not in the 'wild' but in modes and environments overtly engineered, managed, transformed by humans, by '*forms of knowledge*' and '*techniques* of intervention'.

Yet, despite animal life becoming a particular point of focus for biopower, reflections on biopolitics have often privileged the metaphorical figure of 'animality' or 'the animal' while tending to overlook 'actual animals', as Shukin suggests:

> Actual animals have already been subtly displaced from the category of 'species' in Foucault's early remarks on biopower, as well as in the work of subsequent theorists of biopower [such as Agamben], for whom animality functions predominantly as a metaphor for that corporeal part of 'man' that becomes subject to biopolitical calculation.[90]

While Agamben himself configures 'bare life' as a 'socially stripped-down figure of *Homo sacer* that he traces back to antiquity', he overlooks the place of actual animals – that is, historical, situated beings – within this model of 'bare life'.[91] For as Shukin points out:

> the theorization of bare life as 'that [which] may be killed and yet not sacrificed'[92] – a state of exception whose paradigmatic scenario in modernity is, for Agamben, the concentration camp – finds its zoopolitical supplement in Derrida's theorization of the 'non-criminal putting to death' of animals,[93] a related state of exception whose paradigmatic scenario is arguably the modern industrial slaughterhouse.[94]

But in Agamben and elsewhere, conceptions of *zoe*, or 'bare life', become abstracted from the material conditions of animal lives and deaths. As Shukin argues, various strands of critical theory seeking to focus on animals have 'tended to sidestep materialist critique in favor of philosophical, psychoanalytical, and aesthetic formulations of animal alterity'.[95] Frequent invocations of 'animality' or 'the Animal' (a monolithic term critiqued by Derrida)[96] often have nothing to do with the lives of actual animals as 'historically situated' beings.[97] As Bailly suggests in *Le Parti pris des animaux*, 'animality [...] does not speak, or hardly ever speaks, of animals'.[98] Animality, or 'the Animal', becomes, as Burt puts it in his critique of Lippit, 'an overly free-floating signifier'.[99]

Agamben's work reveals what Wolfe describes as a 'flattening of the category of "the animal" itself' in two particular ways that Wolfe delineates by drawing on LaCapra's critique of Agamben.[100] First, as LaCapra suggests: animals in Agamben's thought 'are not figured as complex, differentiated living beings but instead function as an abstracted philosophical topos'.[101] And secondly,

Agamben's approach is thus unable to address 'the extent to which certain animals, employed in factory farming or experimentation, may be seen in terms of the concept of bare or naked, unprotected life'.[102] Drawing on these aspects of LaCapra's critique, Wolfe suggests:

> What gets lost, in other words, is our ability to think a highly differentiated and nuanced biopolitical field, and to understand as well that the exercise of violence on the terrain of biopower is not always, or even often, one of highly symbolic and sacrificial ritual in some timeless political theater, but is often – indeed, maybe usually – an affair of power over and of life that is regularized, routinized, and banalized in the services of a strategic, not symbolic, project.[103]

Following Shukin, Wolfe and LaCapra, I aim to avoid any 'idealist' invocations of the timeless alterity of the Animal.[104] Rather, this study seeks to remain grounded in the material realities of animal lives within the biopolitical regimes of late capitalism. From the reflections on captivity in *Bestiaire* to the scenes of industrialised slaughter in *Leviathan*, these films chart the ways in which animal life is put, in these various contexts, to the service of what Derrida calls 'the putative human well-being of man'. The temporal dilation of the films allows for a durational form of bearing witness to the 'banalized' routines of biopower.

If it is often overlooked that biopolitics involves 'an affair of power over and of life that is regularized, routinized, and banalized', it is important to add that a particular blindspot within contemporary philosophical reflections on 'The Animal' is arguably that of animal labour (a question that I address in particular in Chapter 3, on *The Turin Horse*). The work of the historian Jason Hribal has been fundamental in drawing attention to this blindspot – as Hribal notes: 'The unpaid labor of animals has [. . .] provided the structural conditions for the rise of capitalism.'[105] Hribal argues that farmed animals belong to the working class: 'They work for humans, who extract a surplus from their labor for the purposes of use, exchange, and/or accumulation.'[106] In contradistinction to the focus by Haraway and others on the collaborative dimensions of animal labour – a focus that often seems to overlook the question of exploitation – Hribal's focus is firmly on exploitation: animals who work 'are treated as property to be bought and sold. They are not waged.'[107] To draw attention to the labouring lives of animals – such as the horse in *The Turin Horse*, or the zoo animals in *Bestiaire* – is to push once more against the abstraction of the figure of 'the Animal'. As Jocelyne Porcher suggests: 'The question of work is not a theoretical anecdote, it is at the heart of our lives and of the relations that we maintain with domestic animals [. . .], and with certain "wild" animals, at work in animal parks, zoos, and circuses.'[108] Yet this question of animal labour has frequently been neglected by contemporary philosophies of the animal by Derrida, Bailly and others – a lacuna that I seek to address in this study, and one that seems indicative of the broader tendency to dematerialise or abstract animal life identified by Shukin and others.

Certainly cinema featuring animals may seem better placed than philosophy to avoid the abstract, homogenising logic of references to the Animal.[109] The 'live action' dimension of the films in this study means that they necessarily engage with 'actual animals', with singularities, in indexical, material, situated ways that it can be difficult for philosophy to do (even in spite of the emphasis on singularity in reflections on animals by Derrida, Bailly and others).[110] This is not to dismiss philosophy – philosophical thought provides much of the theoretical framework that I develop throughout the book. Indeed, these films arguably undertake their own styles of philosophy: here cinema becomes a mode of thinking, for, as Deleuze suggests, the time-image 'bring[s] the emancipated senses into direct relation with time and thought'.[111] But given the philosophical tendency to abstract animal life into figurations of the Animal, it also seems important to bear in mind the ways in which in these films, 'actual animals' are inescapably present before the camera, as cinema makes manifest a particular desire to bear witness to the lived, embodied, material conditions of animal lives.

In *When Species Meet*, Haraway emphasises the need to focus on mundane, ordinary, 'earthly' interactions with animals rather than idealised figures. In her reading of Derrida's encounter with his cat (an oft-cited scene within critical animal studies), Haraway critiques Derrida for not being curious enough about 'what the cat might actually be doing, feeling, thinking, or perhaps making available to him in looking back at him that morning'.[112] Here, for Haraway, Derrida 'missed a possible invitation, a possible introduction to other-worlding'.[113] But, as in a number of other critiques of this passage, Haraway focuses on this one part of Derrida's *The Animal That Therefore I Am* to the near-exclusion of the rest of the text. Though Derrida's reflections on his cat can certainly be criticised along the lines suggested by Haraway, his engagement elsewhere in the text with biopolitical regimes and '*techniques* of intervention' is indicative of an attentiveness to the material realities of animal lives, as we saw above.

Nevertheless, Haraway's emphasis on 'other-worlding' is particularly relevant here, given my focus on animal worlds. The term is a translation of *autre-mondialisation*, a word 'invented by European activists to stress that their approaches to militarized neoliberal models of world building are not about antiglobalization but about nurturing a more just and peaceful other-globalization'.[114] For Haraway: 'There is a promising *autre-mondialisation* to be learned in retying some of the knots of ordinary multispecies living on earth [. . .] I think we learn to be worldly from grappling with, rather than generalizing from, the ordinary.'[115] Affirming the entangled agencies of animals and humans, she writes of 'companion species' – animals that accompany our everyday lives as 'messmates' – and of 'the flesh of mortal world-making entanglements' that she calls 'contact zones'.[116] Haraway looks back at the animal 'figures' that have populated her work: cyborgs, monkeys, apes, oncomice, dogs; these 'figures are at the same time creatures of imagined possibility and creatures of fierce and ordinary reality; the dimensions tangle and require response.'[117]

Haraway's entanglements of the ordinary and 'imagined possibilities', of lived realities and *autre-mondialisation*, speak to my interest in the coexistence of the actual and the virtual, and in slow animal cinema's attentiveness to the mundane and the everyday. Emphasising 'a subject- and object-shaping dance of encounters' between humans and animals, Haraway writes of:

> ordinary beings-in-encounter in the house, lab, field, zoo, park, office, prison, ocean, stadium, barn, or factory. As ordinary knotted beings, they are also always meaning-making figures that gather up those who respond to them into unpredictable kinds of 'we.'[118]

Like Haraway, the films I explore are interested in ordinary rather than exotic animal sites – the farm, the zoo (which is a place of banal encounters despite housing exotic creatures) – and in the 'unpredictable kinds of "we"' that respond to these sites (both inside and outside the films).

Yet if the question of the mundane, the ordinary and the everyday functions as a blindspot in certain philosophical engagements with animals, Haraway might be critiqued for an idealisation of 'a subject- and object-shaping dance of encounters' that, while acknowledging questions of suffering and killing, also seeks to move beyond them.[119] Reflecting on Jeremy Bentham's question about animals ('Can they suffer?') and Derrida's privileging of that question ('The *first* and *decisive* question would rather be to know whether animals *can suffer*'),[120] Haraway suggests that while she does not deny the importance of animal suffering ('and the criminal disregard of it throughout human orders'), she does not see it as 'the decisive question, the one that turns the order of things around, the one that promises an autre-mondialisation'.[121] She recognises the importance of the question of pity that Bentham's question motivates in Derrida's text but argues that things such as 'work and play, and not just pity' should be taken into account.[122] Haraway's point, in particular the emphasis on labour, is a useful one: as noted above, work does appear to be something of a blindspot in reflections on animals by Derrida and the continental tradition more broadly. Yet I also want to keep the asymmetries of power and force that shape animal labour in view,[123] which means keeping the question of suffering foregrounded here too. While understandably keen to affirm the role of animals as agents, Haraway appears to place suffering and 'autre-mondialisation' in opposition, her methodology suggesting implicitly (even if inadvertently) that the former aligns more easily with passivity, the latter with activity. For Haraway, 'work and play' are more obviously, more actively, world-making. Haraway's implicit dichotomy between suffering and *autre-mondialisation* seems to rely on her understanding of *autre-mondialisation* as 'nurturing a more just and peaceful other-globalization'. Yet, as the films I consider here suggest, animal suffering remains a key context for foregrounding *why* such alternative, more just and peaceful worlds need to be imagined. *Autre-mondialisation* involves, vitally, envisaging the world otherwise, imagining what the world *might be* (this resonates with my emphasis in this volume on the virtual, and on lines of flight through the biopolitical matrix of 'bare life'). Yet a focus on animal suffering remains key to documenting how the world *is*. What is needed, alongside Haraway's rich reflections on *autre-mondialisation*, is an analysis of the ideological and material organisation of animal life and attendant asymmetries of power and vulnerability that appear to be underplayed at times in her thought.[124] For this, I turn to the work of Shukin, a key point of reference throughout my study.

RENDERING

Attentive to the 'use value' of animals as both bodies and signs – that is, to the ways in which animal life is biopolitically governed in both material and representational terms – Shukin's *Animal Capital* highlights the double meaning of 'rendering': '*Rendering* signifies both the mimetic act of making a copy [. . .] *and* the industrial boiling down and recycling of animal remains' (in which the remains of slaughter are converted into an array of products and thus back into capital).[125] The term 'animal capital' thus 'signals a tangle of biopolitical relations within which the economic and symbolic capital of animal life can no longer be sorted into binary distinction'.[126] In the co-implicated dynamics of animal rendering, the material is entangled with the semiotic, the literal with the representational:

> Such an interimplication of representational and economic logics is pivotal to biopolitical critique, since biopower never operates solely through the power to reproduce life literally, via the biological capital of the specimen or species, nor does it operate solely through the power to reproduce it figuratively via the symbolic capital of the animal sign, but instead operates through the power to hegemonize both the meaning and matter of life.[127]

Within the broader dynamics of rendering that Shukin identifies here, she indicates the particular role of cinema, pointing to the use of gelatin ('a protein extracted from the skin, bones, and connective tissues of cattle, sheep, and pigs') in the production of celluloid film stock.[128] Cinema is thus not only attracted to animals as onscreen figures of animation and vitality; in the age of celluloid, it is 'materially contingent' on animal life and death, thereby embodying the 'double logic of rendering' – of bodies and signs – to which Shukin points: 'The rendered material [. . .] archives an "unconscious" death wish on animal life that is radically, yet productively, at odds with the fetishistic signs of life.'[129] As cinema moves into the age of the digital, it distances itself from this literal, industrial link to the materiality of animal bodies, but the history of this deathly relation remains, alongside cinema's continued exploitation of 'photogenic' animal vitality. Cinema's conflicted relation to animal life – its (extradiegetic) domination and (diegetic) celebration of animals – can thus be read as indicative of what Shukin describes, drawing on Michael Taussig's work on mimesis, as 'a "two-layered" logic of reproduction involving "sympathetic" technologies of representation and "pathological" technologies of material control'.[130]

Yet in this study I also want to consider the ways in which cinema can move beyond this 'double bind' of animal rendering. Shukin undertakes a 'critical practice of rendering', a form of critique positioned as immanent to the field of symbolic-material processes of rendering that it interrogates.[131] But in Shukin's analysis, there is a risk that, while engaging with 'the role that symbolic power plays in the reproduction of market life',[132] cinema itself is reduced and 'boiled down' to the material and economic dynamics underpinning its discursive and symbolic operations. This is a risk that Shukin herself acknowledges with reference to the broader methodological approach of her study: 'Rendering's evocation of a literal scene of industrial capitalism is constantly at risk of implying recourse to an economic reality underlying the ideological smokescreen of animal signs; that is, it is at risk of sliding back into an essentialist Marxist materialism.'[133] It is a risk that she takes strategically, in order to avoid 'the alternate pitfall' of reducing 'social space' – and specifically here, animal life – to 'a linguistic model of discourse'.[134] But what this means is that, in Shukin's study, cinema itself is 'rendered' as, and limited to, an 'ideological smokescreen of animal signs': it finds itself reduced to a practice that hides the material operations of power to which animal life is subjected – operations that then need to be revealed through the workings of ideology critique. In her powerful analysis of Edison's *Electrocuting an Elephant*, Shukin sees the elephant as a 'sacrificial subject' and the film as 'spectacle' and 'technological monstration'.[135] Such readings are urgently needed: they demonstrate the ways in which, as Shukin puts it, 'animal sacrifice constituted something of a founding symbolic and material gesture of early electrical and cinematic culture'.[136] But in her drive to expose ideological mechanisms, Shukin arguably misses the opportunity to attend to cinema as a realm in which animal life might be engaged with differently, both within and beyond the saturated field of biopolitical domination.

This entails imagining cinema otherwise, that is, as something other than 'spectacle', 'technological monstration' and an (albeit complex, contradictory) ideological machine. It entails, for example, envisaging cinema as a medium that might open up – through the use of time, as I argue in this study – ethical and political attention to animal realms of perception, sentience and meaning-making. This is why I shift the conceptual emphasis here from 'animal capital' to 'animal worlds'. While Shukin's focus on material animal bodies has been key in redressing a critical tendency to configure the animal as a sign without a body, she tends to see the animal as a body subject to power rather than a being with a life-world. The questions of capital, ideology and biopower that Shukin raises remain central to my analyses, but while drawing on her vital ideological critique of rendering, I seek to reconfigure interactions between animal life and cinema otherwise, in order to attend more generatively to cinema's ethical and political potentialities. In other words, I seek out the philosophical and cinematic remainders that resist the 'closed loop'[137] of rendering in its various incarnations (both as hegemonic symbolic-material practices and as counterhegemonic immanent critique of those practices).[138]

In so doing, I return to some of the philosophical frameworks that Shukin is critical of, especially the work of Deleuze and Guattari, in order to reconsider them anew. While Shukin criticises Deleuze and Guattari's concept of becoming-animal for its investment in 'a virtual state of pure potential as opposed to a state of historical actuality',[139] I am interested in precisely this 'virtual state of pure potential' – that is, in that which takes place within and alongside the realm of the 'actual', in an imagining of escape routes through the matrices of biopower. Deleuze and Guattari's thinking of *puissance* (power as potential), following Spinoza, insists that there is something other than the saturated field of power as domination (*pouvoir*). This resonates with Wolfe's emphasis, in his reading of Foucault (who shares Deleuze's debt to Nietzsche), on 'a potentially creative, aleatory element that inheres in the very gambit of biopower, one not wholly subject to the thanatological drift of a biopolitics subordinated to the paradigm of sovereignty'.[140] Wolfe cites Jeffrey Nealon's reading of Foucault here: 'the power relation names not "a 'negative' relation of domination between *concrete objects, institutions, or persons*, but a 'positive' relation among *virtual forces*"'.[141] Across the chapters that follow, I trace cinema's articulations of a 'potentially creative, aleatory element' via its engagement with such '*virtual forces*'. In particular, I argue that the cinematic splintering of time into the actual and the virtual, in the manner described by Deleuze, works as a mode of deterritorialisation that gestures both to and beyond the biopolitical grid of 'bare life' to which certain animals are consigned. Thus, in place of

Shukin's corrective project of favouring 'historical actuality' over the virtual, I seek to think these two dimensions together. While these films evoke the actual, the material and the embodied, they also extend beyond the phenomenologically-lived situations that they frame, bringing virtual worlds and planes of becoming into view.

FURTHER CONTEXTS AND CHAPTER OUTLINES

The wave of films I examine here have emerged alongside 'the animal turn' in the humanities outlined above; as I trace in each chapter, interviews with and essays written by the filmmakers reveal a range of implicit and explicit engagements with these philosophical developments. For example, in his essay 'The Animal Equation' (2012), Côté cites a number of works of 'contemplative cinema' about animals, including Gras's *Bovines*, Castaing-Taylor and Barbash's *Sweetgrass* and Frammartino's *Le Quattro Volte*, demonstrating a heightened awareness of the areas of filmmaking and thought in which his own film *Bestiaire* is intervening.[142] Certainly the films I study here are in dialogue with the broader cultural currents of growing interest in, and anxieties around, animal life that I have signalled above. While indicating a fascination with the possibilities of non-anthropocentric cinema (a position explicitly articulated by Côté, Gras, and Castaing-Taylor and Paravel in interviews), these films also work through a nexus of underlying concerns about biopower and its management of nonhuman lives.

Surveying the recent wave of documentary work about animals, from films such as *Darwin's Nightmare* (Hubert Sauper, 2004), *Our Daily Bread* (Nikolaus Geyrhalter, 2005) and *Sweetgrass*, to Disney's *Arctic Tale* (Adam Ravetch and Sarah Robertson, 2007) and the BBC television series *Frozen Planet* (2011), Belinda Smaill usefully suggests that 'one of the most striking features of these films is the growing emphasis on paradigmatic debates about anthropogenic knowledge or use of animal life, whether it concerns food, agriculture, science, exploration, or species loss'.[143] Given this burgeoning terrain of documentary filmmaking, and the developing corpus of scholarship devoted to it,[144] it is worth underlining a little further how I see the corpus of films that I address in this book as particularly distinctive. Unlike Smaill and others focusing on this recent wave of documentaries about animals, I consider fiction (*The Turin Horse*) alongside nonfiction, and the putatively nonfiction films – *Bestiaire, Leviathan, Bovines* – do not sit neatly within the category of documentary either: while Côté rejects the term 'documentary' as a description of *Bestiaire*,[145] Castaing-Taylor and Paravel position *Leviathan* as a work of 'sensory ethnography'. My attention to nonfiction, fiction and hybrid forms thus seeks to consider representations of animal life in cinema in a broad sense (rather than viewing these films, for example, predominantly through the lens of wildlife documentary-making and its associated histories and theories).

As set out above, I link these films above all through a shared aesthetic approach: the privileging of the long take, the absence of voiceover, and the distension of non-narrative time. Yet as I have already suggested, these films also share thematic interests, particularly in their focus on animals instrumentalised by humans (as food, entertainment) and their sensitivity to the 'broad reopening of the question of the ethical status of animals in relation to the human' identified by Wolfe. This turn towards domesticated animals and their place within networks of production, labour and consumerism[146] intersects, to some extent, with the recent surge of documentary filmmaking about food (especially meat) production, from the impassive long-take aesthetic of *Our Daily Bread* to more mainstream, investigative films such as *Food, Inc.* (Robert Kenner, 2008).[147] Yet the films I trace in the book also move beyond such examples by focusing almost exclusively on the lived time of animals, rather than tracing the broader systems of production in which they are involved. My chosen corpus also intersects to some extent with the focus on the 'human management of animal lives' in films such as *Grizzly Man* (Werner Herzog, 2005) and *Blackfish* (Gabriela Cowperthwaite, 2013),[148] yet the films I explore stage questions of human–animal relations in less dramatic and investigative forms. While implicitly attentive to the biopolitical instrumentalisation of animal life, my corpus also differs from the kinds of investigative exposure and activist impulses found in recent documentaries such as *The Cove* (Louie Psihoyos, 2009), *Fowl Play* (Adam Durand, 2009) and *Cowspiracy: The Sustainability Secret* (Kip Andersen and Keegan Kuhn, 2014).

And while there has been a growing interest in mainstream nonfiction's representations of animal life threatened by climate change, as signalled by recent documentaries such as *March of the Penguins*, *Earth* and *Arctic Tale*,[149] engagement with questions of ecological crisis in the films I explore is implicit rather than explicit. These films do not focus on endangered species (with the exception of some of *Bestiaire*'s zoo animals), and they pursue less dramatic, less spectacular histories. As Smaill notes in her discussion of archival footage of the last known thylacine (or Tasmanian tiger) and the use of this footage in the Channel 4 documentary *Extinct: The Tasmanian Tiger* (2001), there is often a mode of mythologisation and idealisation at work in the focus on such endangered megafauna. Drawing on Ursula K. Heise, Smaill suggests that 'animals become projections of human conceptions of crisis in modernity in accounts of species loss'.[150] In the films I study here, the animals function less overtly, less 'charismatically' (than a Tasmanian tiger, penguin or polar bear, for example), to signal an engagement with ecological concerns. But such concerns remain implicitly present in these films, from the resource scarcity staged by *The Turin Horse* to the apocalyptic aesthetic of *Leviathan* (and latent issues such as the depletion of fish stocks – left unarticulated by the film but described by Castaing-Taylor and Paravel in interview).[151]

I draw in the book on a number of key texts on animals and film, including works by Burt, Pick and Lippit that have emerged as part of the recent 'animal turn' in the humanities. I also draw in particular on philosophical thought in French and Francophone contexts because these contexts have been especially generative for the developing field of critical animal studies.[152] As Senior, Clarke and Freccero note, '[t]here has been a long tradition of reflection on the human–animal relationship in modern French thought', which passes via Alexander Kojève's lectures on Hegel in the 1930s and the antihumanist tradition that developed in response to those lectures (including the radical anthropology of Marcel Mauss and Georges Bataille, and the work of Foucault, Deleuze and Jean Baudrillard), through to Élisabeth de Fontenay's *Le Silence des bêtes* (1998),[153] the work of Derrida (including *The Animal That Therefore I Am* and also the two volumes of *The Beast and the Sovereign*),[154] the critiques of science developed by Bruno Latour and Isabelle Stenghers (whose works have in turn influenced thinkers such as Vinciane Despret and Haraway), and also, in relation to the visual in particular, recent works such as Bellour's *Le Corps du cinéma* and Bailly's writings on animals, which range across literature, painting, photography and film.[155]

Emerging via the work of Derrida in particular is an emphasis on an exposure to finitude shared by humans and animals. In a key passage in *The Animal That Therefore I Am*, Derrida writes:

> Mortality resides there as the most radical means of thinking the finitude that we share with animals, the mortality that belongs to the very finitude of life, to the experience of compassion, to the possibility of sharing the possibility of this nonpower, the possibility of this impossibility [. . .].[156]

Derrida draws here on Heidegger's conceptualisation of human death as 'the possibility of impossibility' but extends this to include animal life within a model of shared finitude (or what he refers to as '*being-with*').[157] Key to this passage, and running through Derrida's text, is an emphasis on the vulnerability and suffering of animals, to which we (humans) are asked to respond, and the ethical and political responsibilities that arise from this.[158] Reflecting on the mass industrialised slaughter of animals, Derrida suggests that the collective disavowal that allows such killing to continue on a global scale bears comparison with the worst cases of genocide. Sensitive to the problematic nature of such a comparison, he adds carefully: 'One should neither abuse the figure of genocide nor too quickly consider it explained away.'[159] If such comparisons are judged to fall merely into pathos, then, Derrida urges, this signals the need to reconsider:

the immense question of pathos and the pathological, precisely, that is, of suffering, pity, and compassion; and the place that has to be accorded to the interpretation of this compassion, to the sharing of this suffering among the living, to the law, ethics, and politics that must be brought to bear upon this experience of compassion.[160]

Though not always directly referenced in each chapter, Derrida's reflections on animal vulnerability and mortality – and attendant ethical and political demands – implicitly inform my readings, from the experience of captivity and 'nonpower' at stake in *Bestiaire* and the scenes of slaughter in *Leviathan*, to the animal vulnerabilities and deaths registered by *The Turin Horse* and *Bovines*.[161] As noted in the discussion of Haraway's work above, the question of suffering is, I argue, necessarily central to any reflection on the life-worlds of animals (despite this question seeming largely absent from Uexküll's considerations).[162]

At the same time, I seek to draw on areas of thought that have received less attention within the field of critical animal studies thus far – particularly Deleuze's reflections on film, as set out above, but also the work of Bailly.[163] While Bailly's thought remains relatively underexplored in critical animal studies,[164] it has received even less attention in film studies, despite his engagement with questions of film and visual culture in texts such as *The Animal Side*. Bailly's work provides a range of useful resources for considering cinema's ethical and political engagements with animal lives – I draw in particular on his reflections on animal worlds, on the connections between the animal gaze and the political (in which Bailly is in dialogue with Derrida), and on 'pensivity'. For Bailly, the gaze of an animal opens up a 'pathway of thought, or at least of a thinking that is not uttered, not articulated'[165] – a challenge to thought that my study pursues throughout.

Referencing the allegorical networks of meaning through which animal life has often been viewed, Bailly argues that:

> we have to abandon, despite its richness and exuberance, the extraordinary material offered by the allegorical and mythical power of the animal world; in other words, we have to force ourselves to remain on a threshold that precedes all interpretation. A threshold where, prior to any definition, animals are no longer reducible to a body of knowledge that localizes them or to a legend that traverses them; they are perceived in their pure singularity, as distinct beings that participate in the world of the living and that regard us in the same light.[166]

Bestiaire, *Bovines* and *The Turin Horse* respond to Bailly's philosophical demand, particularly through their sustained attentiveness to the singularities of the lives that they frame. Of course, interpretation – and the various symbolic and allegorical modes mobilised by representations of animals – cannot be evacuated from the scene.[167] And I wish to avoid the idealisation of a 'prediscursive' animal[168] – an idealisation that is implicitly at work in Bailly's reflection here. But in the paring away of narrative and of overtly symbolising frameworks, enacted in particular by the refusal of voiceover commentary, the films I study largely seek to attend to 'a threshold that precedes all interpretation'. In its minimalist structure and durational aesthetic, the slow animal film works to intensify the resistance of animal expression and gesture to projected significations. Yet we feel the force of these animal presences (or what Bailly calls their 'power of impregnation')[169] – they *endure*, they impress upon us, reminding us that, as Pick observes, 'the powerlessness of those who do [not] or cannot participate in a given discourse paradoxically carries its own inalienable force'.[170] (The key exception to the pattern I outline here is *Leviathan*, a film that overtly mobilises the allegorical and the mythical, and that fails to attend in meaningful ways to the singularities of the lives it frames.)

Citing as the epigraph to *The Animal Side* the observation by Plotinus that '[e]very life is some form of thought, but of a dwindling clearness like the degrees of life itself', Bailly develops the concept of animal 'pensivity' – a term that he uses to describe each animal being as a form, or movement, of thought.[171] Animal pensivity is 'made manifest in a thousand different ways, according to species, individuals, and circumstances'.[172] For Bailly, each animal 'adheres to its being and slips that adhesion into the world like a thought [. . .] Thoughts, not as signs whose meaning would be reduced to us, for us [. . .] but in an entirely different contemplation, an entirely different dispatch, that of signs gone away [. . .]'.[173] Bailly's aim of resisting the allegorical pull of animal figures through the concept of pensivity has an overtly political dimension:

> The pensivity of animals, or at least what I am trying to designate and grasp with this term, is neither a diversion nor a curiosity; what it establishes is that the world in which we live is gazed upon by other beings, that the visible is shared among creatures, and that a politics could be invented on this basis, if it is not too late.[174]

This final phrase is punctuated by a reference, in a footnote, to Derrida's *The Animal That Therefore I Am*, which Bailly sees as announcing 'the project of such a politics'. Bailly points to the importance in Derrida's text of 'an act of gazing – his cat contemplating him naked in the bathroom' via which 'Derrida unfurls the entire reflection through which he displaces and reconsiders the "abyssal limit" between humans and animals.'[175] One might ask why the gaze should necessarily be privileged by both Derrida and Bailly (a question that I take up in Chapter 2 on *Bestiaire*). Both Derrida and Bailly risk a certain fetishisation of the animal gaze and thus perhaps an anthropocentric logic that remains tied to the coordinates of a particularly human sensorium.[176] At the same time, as I argue in the chapters that follow, animal acts of looking can be thought otherwise, beyond the terms of (anthropocentric) fetishism and its economy of disavowal.

Bailly's crucial point, here and elsewhere in *The Animal Side*, is that we share the world with animals, a world that they also look upon (the animal gaze being something that for Bailly distinguishes animal life from objects or plants).[177] At one point, he refers to this as a 'community of the sense of sight' that 'makes us alike and relates us', without any 'solidarity' necessarily following from this.[178] If there are forms of solidarity to be forged here – 'a politics [. . .] if it is not too late' – they will have to be worked at, Bailly suggests. Indeed, in these reflections on animal pensivity, Bailly brings together the various notions of animal worldhood and thought, politics, the visible and the urgency of contemporary contexts that I seek to hold together in this study. In each chapter, I trace the particular contribution that cinema might make in its conjugation of these terms, through its encounters with the lives of animals, through its openings to what Bailly, following Uexküll, describes as animal worlds that 'unfurl',[179] spreading out before us while also slipping away.

Chapter 1 develops in detail the key aspects of the book's theoretical framework, moving between philosophies of animal worlds and Deleuze's account of cinematic time. I draw on the concept of the *Umwelt* developed by Uexküll, and the different responses to this concept offered by Heidegger and Deleuze and Guattari. Focusing in particular on Deleuze and Guattari's reworking of the concept of the *Umwelt* as a process of 'desubjectified' assemblages and becomings, I link this to Deleuze's thinking of the time-image as a shift from subject to world, and as a realm that is intricately bound up with questions of differing, becoming and the virtual. While Deleuze is often invoked as a key reference in critical commentary on slow cinema, in such works his conceptualisation of the time-image tends to remain fairly briefly outlined and without detailed exploration.[180] Addressing this gap, this chapter suggests particular ways of thinking through links between Deleuze, cinema and the slow animal film. At the same time, I turn to recent accounts of the relation between animals and film, including work by Pick, Burt, Lippit, Sobchack and others. Engaging with yet also moving beyond the recourse to Bazin that has tended to shape the field thus far, I emphasise what Deleuze's theory of cinematic time can add to this developing body of work, as well as what a more detailed and wide-ranging account of Deleuze and Guattari's model of animal worlds can contribute to the field of critical animal studies. This chapter makes a case for the time-image's pluralisation of worlds and for its opening up of the virtual in its capacity to gesture to realms beyond biopolitical domination (even from within the regimes of biopower registered by the films that I consider). Yet, as the final stages of this chapter suggest, questions of animal suffering and exploitation remain at the heart of each of these films and of my analyses throughout the book.

In Chapter 2, I explore Côté's *Bestiaire*, an experimental documentary about a zoo that initially seems in thrall to Bazin's idea that the onscreen animal reveals cinematic specificity. Exploring the exhibition of animals both living and dead, still and moving, Côté's film invokes two key metaphorical positionings (cinema as zoo, cinema as taxidermy), privileging a self-reflexive form of ontological investigation. I trace these ontological investments by drawing on accounts such as Lippit on the 'electric' animal, Bellour on hypnotic animal images and Haraway on taxidermy. Folded into *Bestiaire*'s set of somewhat essentialising, ontologising reflections, however, is an implicit questioning of the politics of the zoo and its links to biopower, neocolonialism, captivity and suffering. Structured by these tensions between the ontological, the aesthetic and the political, *Bestiaire* reflects on the zoo both as a metaphor for cinematic 'animality' *qua* cinematic specificity and as a set of material conditions in which these animals live. While *Bestiaire*'s distension of 'dead time' keeps the focus above all on questions of captivity – its durational aesthetic bearing witness to lives left in limbo, to beings made to survive yet reduced to 'bare life' – its Deleuzian time-images also invite attentiveness to animal worlds of embodiment, perception and meaning-making that reach beyond the biopolitical grid of imprisoned life.

Resonating with *Bestiaire*'s temporal drift and images of captivity, Tarr and Hranitzky's *The Turin Horse*, explored in Chapter 3, also uses cinematic forms of extended duration in order to bear witness to lives left in limbo. But it does so in a very different setting, and in a way that extends these reflections across the human–animal divide. The film opens with a voiceover recounting Nietzsche's apocryphal encounter with animal suffering – a horse being beaten in the street in Turin on 3 January 1889. Tarr and Hranitzky's film approaches this history obliquely, through the fictional story of another horse – a horse kept by a man, Ohlsdorfer, and his daughter, in a desolate, inhospitable part of Hungary, in an unidentified time. As the horse increasingly resists eating or moving, the film traces human lives of routine pitted against a nonhuman life refusing to submit to routine any longer. While critical commentary on *The Turin Horse* has tended to emphasise an existentialist, Beckettian focus on the inescapability of death and an apocalyptic 'end time', I read *The Turin Horse* as a film about labour, and about animal labour in particular. Alongside the work of Deleuze, I draw on Jacques Rancière's discussions of duration in Tarr's work (in *Béla Tarr, The Time After* (2011)), while engaging critically with Rancière's apparent neglect of questions of animal labour. While bearing witness to modes of exhaustion and precarity that reach across human and animal worlds, *The Turin Horse* is a quietly revolutionary film that patiently documents an animal's revolt through her withdrawal of labour – a deterritorialising line of flight.

Chapter 4 develops questions of animal labour, but it extends this line of inquiry by looking in particular at the aesthetic and affective labour extracted from documentary animal death in film. Castaing-Taylor and Paravel's *Leviathan* documents the daily activities of a commercial fishing boat, captured on multiple GoPro cameras. Its radically mobile, unstable audiovisual world represents a striking contrast to the long takes and static shots that shape the other films discussed in this book. I focus on *Leviathan* here in order to diagnose the way in which this absence of durational attentiveness can lead to a closing down – rather than an opening up – of animal worlds. While much attention has been devoted to *Leviathan*'s sensory, immersive aesthetics, commentary has tended to elide questions of industrialised slaughter. This elision is striking given the celebratory framing of the film as non-anthropocentric by critical commentary and by the filmmakers themselves. Drawing on Shukin, I trace how the 'carnal traffic' of *Leviathan*'s dying animals is simultaneously disavowed and exploited – by the film and its critical reception – as a form of theoretico-aesthetic capital that frames the film's immersive, visceral vision as a return to a prediscursive 'real'. While critical commentary on *Leviathan* has invoked Deleuzian concepts of folds and assemblages, I argue that these particular uses of Deleuze overlook the workings of biopower. In place of the durational attentiveness to animal lives that I trace elsewhere in the book, *Leviathan*'s flitting, indiscriminate vision reduces the fish to undifferentiated matter, the film's deathly, fusional logic refusing the possibility of singularity or what Nancy calls the 'spacing' of the world. In contrast to *The Turin Horse*, which makes visible the dynamics of animal labour, *Leviathan* thus disavows the affective labour extracted from its dying animals.

Explored in Chapter 5, Gras's *Bovines ou la vraie vie des vaches*, a contemplative documentary reflection on a herd of Charolais cows, is also interested in animals that are killed for food, but in approaching this question the film unfolds a series of delayed, wandering images of bovine life. I read *Bovines* as a film that, on one level, invites us to seek out further fertile connections between Deleuze's cinema books and his reflections, with Guattari, on animal worlds, enabling particular links to be made, for example, between the 'pure optical and sound situations' of the Deleuzian time-image and the account of animal art and expressive territory given in *What is Philosophy?* Building also on Bailly's notion of pensivity, while moving beyond his privileging of the gaze through particular attention to bovine sounds in the film, this chapter allows for further, still more textured development of dynamics of worlding traced in previous chapters. Yet I also read *Bovines* as a film that allows us to probe the possible limitations of Deleuze and Guattari's thought. In risking a privileging of what Peter Hallward calls, in his critique of Deleuze, 'virtual creations' over 'actual creatures',[181] the film's time-images might be seen as aestheticising political paralysis over political action, favouring a celebration of biovitality over a critique of biopolitics. While *Bovines*'s pastoral setting and lingering, durational aesthetic thus stage a set of ambivalences and contradictions, the film also points to the limitations, as well as the ongoing possibilities, of a Deleuzo-Guattarian engagement with cinema's animal worlds.

In Foucault's analysis of biopolitics, 'life as a political object' can be 'turned back against the system [. . .] bent on controlling it'.[182] Reflecting on this moment in Foucault, and the potent affirmation of life that Foucault's thought inherits from Nietzsche, Deleuze summarises: 'Life becomes resistance to power when power takes life as its object.'[183] In the chapters that follow, I seek to remain attentive both to the material workings of biopower addressed by Derrida, Shukin and others, and to the ways in which animal lives might be seen to resist or escape those workings – a resistance or escape that can be envisaged by cinema in its movements between the actual and the virtual, and in its durational openings to modes of differing and becoming. The films that I explore do not concretely depict sustained acts of animal resistance (apart from in *The Turin Horse*). But in aesthetic terms, through their attentiveness to animal worlds, they open up ways, even from within the regimes of exploitation portrayed, of imagining animal lives differently, tracing what Martin Crowley describes in another context as 'a line of flight rejecting the crushing of life beneath the project of accumulation, investment, and return'[184] – a residual mode of resistance to capitalist reterritorialisation.[185]

Reflecting on the paintings of Francis Bacon, Deleuze writes: 'The phenomenological hypothesis is perhaps insufficient because it merely invokes the lived body. But the lived body is still a paltry thing in comparison with a more profound and almost unliveable power [*puissance*].'[186] In spite of Deleuze's reference here to the 'lived body' as a 'paltry thing', I want to stay with the lived, the material and the phenomenological, particularly in relation to the questions of animal suffering that I have signalled above. At the same time, I seek out cinema's engagements with that 'almost unliveable power' to which Deleuze points here – the *puissance* (power as potential) that might exceed the grid of biopolitics and its instrumentalisation of animal lives, envisaging lines of flight and political futures yet to come.

NOTES

1. Gilles Deleuze, *Cinema 2: The Time-Image*, translated by Hugh Tomlinson and Robert Galeta (London and New York: Continuum, 2005), p. 66.
2. Daniel Walber notes the emergence of this 'mini-genre' in his review of *Bovines*. Walber, 'Pastoral: Emmanuel Gras's *Bovines* at Rooftop Films', *The Brooklyn Rail*, 2012. Available

at http://www.brooklynrail.org/2012/08/film/pastoral-emmanuel-grass-bovines-at-rooftop-films (last accessed 14 September 2018).
3. Jonathan Burt, 'Morbidity and Vitalism: Derrida, Bergson, Deleuze and Animal Film Imagery', *Configurations*, 14:1–2 (2006), 157–79 (p. 177).
4. Most conspicuously and critically by Donna Haraway's *When Species Meet* (Minneapolis: University of Minnesota Press, 2007). See also discussions of 'becoming-animal' in Steve Baker, *The Postmodern Animal* (London: Reaktion, 2000), Derek Ryan, *Animal Theory: A Critical Introduction* (Edinburgh: Edinburgh University Press, 2013), Jon Roffe and Hannah Stark (eds), *Deleuze and the Non/Human* (New York: Palgrave Macmillan, 2015), and Colin Gardner and Patricia MacCormack (eds), *Deleuze and the Animal* (Edinburgh: Edinburgh University Press, 2017). For an overview of the field of critical animal studies, see Dawn McCance, *Critical Animal Studies: An Introduction* (New York: SUNY Press, 2013).
5. For recent summaries of the field, see Anat Pick and Guinevere Narraway (eds), *Screening Nature: Cinema Beyond the Human* (Oxford: Berghahn, 2013), and Michael Lawrence and Laura McMahon (eds), *Animal Life and the Moving Image* (London: BFI, 2015).
6. Anat Pick, *Creaturely Poetics: Animality and Vulnerability in Literature and Film* (New York: Columbia University Press, 2011); Jennifer Fay, 'Seeing/Loving Animals: André Bazin's Posthumanism', *Journal of Visual Culture*, 7:1 (2008), 41–64; Seung-hoon Jeong, 'Animals: An Adventure in Bazin's Ontology', in Dudley Andrew (ed.), *Opening Bazin* (New York: Oxford University Press, 2011), pp. 177–86.
7. Deleuze, *Cinema 2*, p. 1.
8. Raymond Bellour, *Le Corps du cinéma: hypnoses, émotions, animalités* (Paris: POL, 2009), p. 431. A translation of the relevant extract can be found in Bellour, 'From Hypnosis to Animals', edited and translated by Alistair Fox, *Cinema Journal*, 53:3 (2014), 8–24. As Bellour notes, animals and cinema fleetingly come into contact in the tenth plateau of *A Thousand Plateaus*, 'Becoming-intense, becoming-animal, becoming-imperceptible . . .', which opens with a discussion of human–animal relations in the film *Willard* (Daniel Mann, 1971). However, Deleuze and Guattari treat the film's philosophical dimensions only briefly and in exclusively narrative terms. On Deleuze, animals and cinema, see also Burt, 'Morbidity and Vitalism'.
9. On the influence of Jakob von Uexküll's work on these thinkers, see Brett Buchanan, *Onto-Ethologies: The Animal Environments of Uexküll, Heidegger, Merleau-Ponty, and Deleuze* (New York: SUNY Press, 2008).
10. Jakob von Uexküll, *A Foray into the Worlds of Animals and Humans, with A Theory of Meaning*, translated by J. D. O'Neil (Minneapolis: University of Minnesota Press, 2010), p. 42.
11. Ibid., p. 42; original emphasis.
12. Ibid., p. 125. Here Uexküll's debt to Kant's understanding of *a priori* forms determining what presents itself to sense experience is evident, though as Geoffrey Winthrop-Young notes, Uexküll's adoption of Kant is very loose. Winthrop-Young, 'Afterword – Bubbles and Webs: A Backdoor Stroll Through the Readings of Uexküll', in *A Foray into the Worlds of Animals and Humans*, pp. 209–43 (p. 231).
13. Buchanan, *Onto-Ethologies*, p. 1.
14. Gilles Deleuze and Félix Guattari, *A Thousand Plateaus: Capitalism and Schizophrenia*, translated by Brian Massumi (Minneapolis: University of Minnesota Press), p. 257.
15. See Ryan, *Animal Theory*, p. 73.
16. Deleuze and Guattari, *A Thousand Plateaus*, p. 261.
17. Giorgio Agamben, *Homo Sacer: Sovereign Power and Bare Life*, translated by Daniel Heller-Roazen (Stanford: Stanford University Press, 1998), p. 13. Agamben

later transposes this anthropocentric model of the 'state of exception' to address the question of the animal in particular: 'precisely because the human is already presupposed every time, the [anthropological] machine actually produces a kind of state of exception, a zone of indeterminacy in which the outside is nothing but the exclusion of an inside and the inside is in turn only the inclusion of an outside' (Agamben, *The Open: Man and Animal*, translated by Kevin Attell (Stanford: Stanford University Press), p. 37). Yet here the discussion remains focused on the human – the animal hovers as an abstract category, incorporated by Agamben's thinking via a form of exclusion that mimes the structure of the 'anthropological machine'. Following Shukin's critique of Foucault and Agamben, I seek to transpose Agamben's formulations of 'bare life' and exception to the realm of 'actual animals' here – that is, the lived, material conditions of animal life.
18. The term is used by Mary Ann Doane. See Doane, *The Emergence of Cinematic Time: Modernity, Contingency and the Archive* (Cambridge, MA: Harvard University Press, 2002), especially Chapter 5, 'Dead Time, or the Concept of the Event', pp. 140–71.
19. Gregg Mitman, *Reel Nature: America's Romance with Wildlife on Film*, 2nd edn (Cambridge, MA: Harvard University Press, 2009); Derek Bousé, *Wildlife Films* (Philadelphia: University of Pennsylvania Press, 2000); Cynthia Chris, *Watching Wildlife* (Minneapolis: University of Minnesota Press, 2006).
20. Stephen Rust, 'Ecocinema and the Wildlife Film', in Louise Westling (ed.), *The Cambridge Companion to Literature and the Environment* (Cambridge: Cambridge University Press, 2013), pp. 226–40 (p. 231). Ecocinema is a broader field that intersects with, yet also reaches far beyond, my focus on animals here. See, for example, Scott MacDonald, 'Toward an Eco-Cinema', *ISLE: Interdisciplinary Studies in Literature and Environment*, 11:2 (2004), 107–32; Sean Cubitt, *EcoMedia* (Amsterdam and New York: Rodolfi, 2005); Paula Willoquet (ed.), *Framing the World: Explorations in Ecocriticism and Film* (Charlottesville: University of Virginia Press, 2010); Rust, Salma Monani and Cubitt (eds), *Ecocinema Theory and Practice* (New York: Routledge, 2012); Pick and Narraway (eds), *Screening Nature*.
21. Mitman, *Reel Nature*, p. 214.
22. Belinda Smaill notes the rise of the term 'eco-doc', 'which describes a broader body of films that critique corporate dominance and investigate and advocate on issues concerning the destruction of the environment and natural resources'. Smaill, 'Documentary Film and Animal Modernity in *Raw Herring* and *Sweetgrass*', *Australian Humanities Review*, 57 (2014), 61–80 (p. 65).
23. One thinks here in particular of the surrealist animal films of Jean Painlevé and their influence in shaping a more avant-garde nature documentary tradition in France.
24. Rust, 'Ecocinema and the Wildlife Film', p. 233.
25. Ibid., p. 231.
26. Mainstream wildlife documentaries, such as Attenborough's BBC series, increasingly include a focus on less obviously 'charismatic' species, including a wide range of insects. But they seek to render them more interesting, charismatic and spectacular through the voiceover narration, and they tend to balance such a focus with the usual megafauna stars.
27. Though within this body of mainstream documentary, *Microcosmos* is rather an exception in terms of its more experimental dimensions. On *Microcosmos*, see Georgina Evans, 'A Cut or a Dissolve? Insects and Identification in *Microcosmos*', and Pick, 'Animal Life in the Cinematic Umwelt', both in Lawrence and McMahon (eds), *Animal Life and the Moving Image*, pp. 108–20; pp. 221–37.

28. On the recent surge of non-narrative documentaries featuring agriculture, see Robert Koehler, 'Agrarian Utopias/Dystopias', *Cinema Scope*, 40 (2009), 12–15. Available at http://cinema-scope.com/features/features-agrarian-utopiasdystopias-the-new-nonfiction/ (last accessed 14 September 2018). In a discussion of recent nonfiction films about human–animal relations, including *Grizzly Man* (Werner Herzog, 2005) and *Sweetgrass* (Ilisa Barbash and Castaing-Taylor, 2009), Jennifer K. Ladino explores a disruption of 'expectations about wildlife films' and an opening to what Haraway describes as forms of 'worlding' and 'becoming with'. Ladino, 'Working with Animals: Regarding Companion Species in Documentary Film', in Rust, Monani and Cubitt (eds), *Ecocinema Theory and Practice*, pp. 129–48.
29. Bill Nichols, *Representing Reality: Issues and Concepts in Documentary* (Bloomington: Indiana University Press, 1991), p. 39.
30. Matthew Flanagan, 'Towards an Aesthetic of Slow in Contemporary Cinema', *16:9*, 29 (November 2008). Available at http://www.16-9.dk/2008-11/side11_inenglish.htm (last accessed 14 September 2018).
31. As Tiago de Luca has observed, slow cinema frequently engages with 'nature and animal life'; he cites work by Carlos Reygadas, Lisandro Alonso, Apichatpong Weerasethakul, Béla Tarr and Michelangelo Frammartino, among others. De Luca, 'Natural Views: Animals, Contingency and Death in Carlos Reygadas's *Japón* and Lisandro Alonso's *Los Muertos*', in De Luca and Nuno Barradas Jorge (eds), *Slow Cinema* (Edinburgh: Edinburgh University Press, 2016), pp. 219–30 (p. 219).
32. Song Hwee Lim, *Tsai Ming-liang and a Cinema of Slowness* (Honolulu: University of Hawai'i Press, 2014), p. 16. See also De Luca and Jorge, 'Introduction: From Slow Cinema to Slow Cinemas', in De Luca and Jorge (eds), *Slow Cinema*, pp. 1–21 (p. 5).
33. Ivone Margulies, *Nothing Happens: Chantal Akerman's Hyperrealist Everyday* (Durham, NC and London: Duke University Press, 1996), p. 21.
34. See De Luca and Jorge, 'Introduction', p. 9. Yet they also note the limitations of such traditional genealogies and their teleological and Eurocentric dimensions.
35. Margulies, *Nothing Happens*, p. 39.
36. Lim, *Tsai Ming-liang and a Cinema of Slowness*, p. 16.
37. Doane, *The Emergence of Cinematic Time*, pp. 140–5.
38. Ibid., p. 144.
39. For Nicole Shukin, 'Edison's electrical and cinematic execution of Topsy [. . .] makes visible the often overlooked fact that animal sacrifice constituted something of a founding symbolic and material gesture of early electrical and cinematic culture.' Shukin, *Animal Capital: Rendering Life in Biopolitical Times* (Minneapolis: University of Minnesota Press, 2009), pp. 150–2.
40. Doane, *The Emergence of Cinematic Time*, p. 159.
41. As Pick argues in her reading of Edison's film, drawing on Doane, the 'denial of process' here has a political dimension: the cut is 'censorious, and it works to reinforce certain ontological assumptions about animal life (and death). The cut does not merely secure, however failingly, the experience of continuous time but defines what we *should* or should not perceive as an event in the first place – what counts as "happening" on screen.' Pick, '"Sparks Would Fly": Electricity and the Spectacle of Animality', in Michael Lundblad (ed.), *Animalities: Literary and Cultural Studies Beyond the Human* (Edinburgh: Edinburgh University Press, 2017), pp. 104–26 (p. 110); original emphasis.
42. Doane, *The Emergence of Cinematic Time*, p. 160.
43. Lim, *Tsai Ming-liang and a Cinema of Slowness*, p. 30.

44. Karl Schoonover, 'Wastrels of Time: Slow Cinema's Laboring Body, the Political Spectator, and the Queer', *Framework: The Journal of Cinema and Media*, 53:1 (2012), 65–78 (p. 65).
45. De Luca and Jorge, 'Introduction', p. 15.
46. Accelerationist theories suggest that 'the only radical political response to capitalism is not to protest, disrupt, or critique [. . .] but to accelerate its uprooting, alienating, decoding, abstractive tendencies'. Robin Mackay and Armen Avanessian, 'Introduction', in Mackay and Avanessian (eds), *#Accelerate: The Accelerationist Reader* (Falmouth: Urbanomic, 2014), pp. 1–46 (p. 4).
47. Richard Misek, 'Dead Time: Cinema, Heidegger, and Boredom', *Continuum: Journal of Media and Cultural Studies*, 24:5 (2010), 777–85 (p. 781).
48. Jacques Derrida, *The Animal That Therefore I Am*, edited by Marie-Louise Mallet, translated by David Wills (New York: Fordham University Press, 2008), p. 9.
49. Quotations from the publicity poster for *Bovines*; translations mine.
50. Andrew Burke, 'ZooTube: Streaming Animal Life', in Michael Lawrence and Karen Lury (eds), *The Zoo and Screen Media: Images of Exhibition and Encounter* (New York: Palgrave Macmillan, 2016), pp. 65–83 (pp. 73–4).
51. Ibid., p. 74.
52. Ibid., p. 67.
53. And as Burke points out, the attraction of uneventfulness is not limited to animal content – it extends to other modes such as reality TV, slow television and slow cinema: '[t]he ZooCam participates in this wider deceleration of the image'. Ibid., p. 76.
54. There is another trajectory that could be traced here: the influence of YouTube on how we watch animals. On this, see James Cahill, 'A YouTube Bestiary: Twenty-six Theses on a Post-cinema of Animal Attractions', in Paul Flaig and Katherine Groo (eds), *New Silent Cinema* (New York: Routledge, 2015), pp. 263–93. A key popular form that has reconfigured ways of watching animals is of course the (viral) cat video. But rather than forms of de-dramatisation, a dominant pattern in cat videos is that they build towards a particular event, as discussed by Leah Shafer in terms of Tom Gunning's concept of a 'cinema of attractions'; see Shafer, 'Cat Videos and the Superflat Cinema of Attractions', *Film Criticism*, 40:2 (2016). Available at http://dx.doi.org/10.3998/fc.13761232.0040.208 (last accessed 14 September 2018). And cat videos are of course usually short, offering the kind of immediate gratification and eventfulness from which zoocams and naturecams diverge. On cat videos, see also: Rosalind Galt, 'Cats and the Moving Image: Feline Cinematicity from Lumière to Maru', in Lawrence and McMahon (eds), *Animal Life and the Moving Image*, pp. 42–57; Radha O'Meara, 'Do Cats Know They Rule YouTube? Surveillance and the Pleasures of Cat Videos', *M/C Journal: A Journal of Media and Culture*, 17:2 (2014). Available at http://journal.media-culture.org.au/index.php/mcjournal/article/view/794 (last accessed 14 September 2018).
55. Burke, 'ZooTube', p. 75. Stephanie Lam has similarly traced parallels between nature cam videos and slow cinema, particularly what she calls 'slow experimental ecocinema', including work by James Benning and Bill Viola. See Lam, 'It's About Time: Slow Aesthetics in Experimental EcoCinema and Nature Cam Videos', in De Luca and Jorge (eds), *Slow Cinema*, pp. 207–18.
56. De Luca and Jorge, 'Introduction', p. 5.
57. It is important to note that Deleuze's privileging of the Second World War in his account of the emergence of the time-image has been criticised for its Eurocentrism. See, for example, David Martin-Jones's critical engagement with Deleuze and his recasting of the time-image, in broader geopolitical terms, as a '*re-activation of world memory*'.

Martin-Jones also draws on Deleuze to explore cinema's archiving of nonhuman time (especially in relation to landscape and 'the memory of the Earth'). Martin-Jones, *Cinema Against Doublethink: Ethical Encounters with the Lost Pasts of World History* (New York: Routledge, 2018), p. 74; p. 92.
58. Deleuze, *Cinema 2*, p. 1.
59. Ibid., p. 2.
60. Ibid., p. 80.
61. Joanna Bednarek, 'The Oedipal Animal? Companion Species and Becoming', in Gardner and MacCormack (eds), *Deleuze and the Animal*, pp. 52–74 (p. 55).
62. On the time-image specifically in relation to documentary film, see Laura U. Marks, 'Signs of the Time: Deleuze, Peirce, and the Documentary Image', in Gregory Flaxman (ed.), *The Brain is the Screen: Deleuze and the Philosophy of Cinema* (Minneapolis: University of Minnesota Press, 2000), pp. 193–214, and Rhiannon Harries, 'The Future of Documentary: Time, Ethics and Politics in Recent European Documentary Film', PhD thesis, University of Cambridge, 2016.
63. Elena Gorfinkel, 'Weariness, Waiting: Endurance and Art Cinema's Tired Bodies', *Discourse*, 34:2/3 (2012), 311–47 (p. 325; p. 311).
64. One could also cite other recent independent films focusing on animals that diverge from the characteristics of slow cinema, particularly in their more conventional use of narrative, editing, dialogue and often comedy too; see, for example, two recent Icelandic films, *Of Horses and Men* (Benedikt Erlingsson, 2013) and *Rams* (Grímur Hákonarson, 2015).
65. For studies of both Benning and Lowder, see Pick and Narraway (eds), *Screening Nature*. On Benning, see also Nikolaj Lübecker and Daniele Rugo (eds), *James Benning's Environments: Politics, Ecology, Duration* (Edinburgh: Edinburgh University Press, 2017); on Lowder, see also MacDonald, *The Garden in the Machine: A Field Guide to Independent Films About Place* (Berkeley: University of California Press, 2001), pp. 82–7.
66. Drawing on notions of worlds in Heidegger and von Uexküll, Kari Weil develops a rich reading of duration and what she calls an 'aesthetics of attunement' in *I Do Not Know What It Is I Am Like*. Weil, *Thinking Animals: Why Animal Studies Now?* (New York: Columbia University Press, 2012), pp. 35–44.
67. Erica Fudge, *Animal* (London: Reaktion, 2002), p. 8.
68. As Smaill notes: 'Paleoanthropologists Richard Leakey and Roger Lewin project that one-half of the animal and plant species existing today will have vanished in the next one hundred years [. . .] The reasons for this decline range from habitat destruction, invasive species, pollution, human population growth, and over-harvesting.' Smaill, 'Tasmanian Tigers and Polar Bears: The Documentary Moving Image and (Species) Loss', *NECSUS: European Journal of Media Studies*, Spring 2015. Available at http://necsus-ejms.org/tasmanian-tigers-and-polar-bears-the-documentary-moving-image-and-species-loss/ (last accessed 14 September 2018).
69. Peter Singer, *Animal Liberation* (New York: Avon Books, 1975).
70. Cary Wolfe, 'Introduction', in Wolfe (ed.), *Zoontologies: The Question of the Animal* (Minneapolis: University of Minnesota Press, 2003), pp. ix–xxiii (p. xi).
71. Ibid., pp. xi–xii.
72. Matthew Senior, David L. Clark and Carla Freccero, 'Editors' Preface: *Ecce animot*: Postanimality from Cave to Screen', in Senior, Clark and Freccero (eds), '*Animots*: Postanimality in French Thought', *Yale French Studies*, 127 (2015), 1–18 (p. 3).
73. Shukin, *Animal Capital*, p. 205.

74. See, for example, Wolfe, 'Introduction' in Wolfe (ed.), *Zoontologies*; Rosi Braidotti, *The Posthuman* (Cambridge: Polity, 2013); Senior, Clark and Freccero, 'Editors' Preface: *Ecce animot*'.
75. For a critique suggesting that recent nature-writing risks becoming a 'literature of consolation', see Mark Cocker, 'Death of the Naturalist: Why is the "New Nature-Writing" So Tame?', *The New Statesman*, 17 June 2015. Available at http://www.newstatesman.com/culture/2015/06/death-naturalist-why-new-nature-writing-so-tame (last accessed 14 September 2018).
76. Yves Bichet, *La Part animale* (Paris: Gallimard, 1994); Noëlle Revaz, *With the Animals*, translated by W. Donald Wilson (Champaign, Dublin and London: Dalkey Archive Press, 2012); Tristan Garcia, *Mémoires de la jungle* (Paris: Gallimard, 2010); Jean-Baptiste Del Amo, *Règne animal* (Paris: Gallimard, 2016). A number of these texts are referenced in Anne Simon's 'Animality and Contemporary French Literary Studies: Overview and Perspectives', in Louisa MacKenzie and Stephanie Posthumus (eds), *French Thinking about Animals* (East Lansing: Michigan State University Press, 2015), pp. 75–88.
77. See Emily McLaughlin, 'The Practice of Writing and the Practice of Living: Michel Deguy's and Philippe Jaccottet's Ecopoetics', *Fixxions*, 11 (2015). Available at http://www.revue-critique-de-fixxion-francaise-contemporaine.org/rcffc/issue/view/21 (last accessed 14 September 2018).
78. On contemporary art's engagements with animal life, see Baker, *The Postmodern Animal*; Ron Broglio, *Surface Encounters: Thinking with Animals and Art* (Minneapolis: University of Minnesota Press, 2011), which includes a chapter on 'worlding' in the works of Bryndís Snæbjörnsdóttir and Mark Wilson; Giovanni Aloi, *Art and Animals* (London: I.B. Tauris, 2011); Baker, *Artist Animal* (Minneapolis: University of Minnesota Press, 2012).
79. As Rust reminds us: 'Throughout the twentieth century, many wildlife species experienced sharp declines attributable to such factors as exploding human populations, deforestation, pesticides, and lax environmental regulations. By the time stricter laws protecting air, water, and threatened species were enacted in the United States and elsewhere in the 1970s, humanity had already instigated what scientists are now calling the Sixth Extinction.' Rust, 'Ecocinema and the Wildlife Film', p. 230. On the relation between species loss and the film archive, see Smaill, *Regarding Life: Animals and the Documentary Moving Image* (Albany: SUNY Press, 2016), especially Chapter 4, pp. 71–95.
80. John Berger, 'Why Look at Animals?', *About Looking* (London: Bloomsbury, 1980), pp. 3–28 (p. 15); original emphasis. For useful critical engagements with Berger's foundational essay, see Burt, 'John Berger's "Why Look at Animals?": A Close Reading', *Worldviews*, 9:2 (2005), 203–18; Pick, 'Why Not Look at Animals', *NECSUS: European Journal of Media Studies*, Spring 2015. Available at http://www.necsus-ejms.org/why-not-look-at-animals/ (last accessed 14 September 2018).
81. Berger, 'Why Look at Animals?', p. 26.
82. Akira Mizuta Lippit, *Electric Animal: Toward a Rhetoric of Wildlife* (Minneapolis: University of Minnesota Press, 2000), p. 196; p. 187.
83. Ibid., p. 1.
84. Burt, *Animals in Film*, p. 29.
85. In an article in the *Cahiers du cinéma*, Cyril Béghin traces connections between the material realities of 'the animal condition (suffering, extinction, cloning)' and the increasing appearance of digitally created animals in cinema, in recent mainstream films such as *Life of Pi* (Ang Lee, 2012) and *Noah* (Darren Aronofsky, 2014): 'animals

have become unstable figures, simultaneously hyperpresent and on the verge of disappearance'. And while these new digital, composite images 'open up formal possibilities', they are founded on an 'absence of accident and alliances', that is, a further distancing from animals and the 'singularity of their drives'. Béghin, 'L'animal sans image', *Cahiers du cinéma*, 701 (June 2014), 74–7 (p. 75; p. 77); translation mine.
86. Michel Foucault, *Society Must Be Defended: Lectures at the Collège de France, 1975–76*, translated by David Macey, edited by Mauro Bertani and Alessandro Fontana (New York: Picador, 2003), p. 241; original emphasis.
87. Michael Hardt and Antonio Negri, *Empire* (Cambridge, MA: Harvard University Press, 2000), p. 24; cited in Shukin, *Animal Capital*, p. 7.
88. Derrida, *The Animal That Therefore I Am*, p. 25; original emphasis.
89. Jean-Christophe Bailly, *The Animal Side*, translated by Catherine Porter (New York: Fordham University Press, 2011), p. 4.
90. Shukin, *Animal Capital*, pp. 9–10. See also Fudge: 'Foucault and many of his followers do not go beyond the human. Strategies of othering are examined, but only in terms of othering humans; the animal is a powerful rhetorical category into which some humans – the mad, the criminal – are placed. Real animals are not the issue.' Fudge, 'A Left-Handed Blow: Writing the History of Animals', in Nigel Rothfels (ed.), *Representing Animals: Theories of Contemporary Culture* (Bloomington: Indiana University Press, 2002), pp. 3–18 (p. 14). John Mullarkey also addresses this tendency in contemporary philosophy to co-opt the category of 'the animal': 'Too often [. . .] the animal does indeed appear as an avatar of one or other such philosopheme.' Mullarkey, 'Animal Spirits: Philosomorphism and the Background Revolts of Cinema', *Angelaki: Journal of the Theoretical Humanities*, 18:1 (2013), 11–29 (p. 11).
91. Shukin, *Animal Capital*, p. 10.
92. Agamben, *Homo Sacer*, p. 8.
93. Derrida, '"Eating Well," or the Calculation of the Subject: An Interview with Jacques Derrida', translated by Peter Connor and Avita Ronell, in Eduardo Cadava, Peter Connor and Jean-Luc Nancy (eds), *Who Comes After the Subject?* (New York: Routledge, 1992), pp. 96–119 (p. 112).
94. Shukin, *Animal Capital*, p. 10.
95. Ibid., p. 10.
96. For Derrida, 'the strict enclosure of this definite article' reduces 'a heterogeneous multiplicity of the living'. Derrida, *The Animal That Therefore I Am*, p. 15.
97. I borrow the term 'historically situated animals' from Haraway, *When Species Meet*, p. 16.
98. Bailly, *Le Parti pris des animaux* (Paris: Christian Bourgois, 2013), p. 36; translation mine.
99. Burt, *Animals in Film*, p. 27.
100. Wolfe, *Before the Law: Humans and Other Animals in a Biopolitical Frame* (Chicago: University of Chicago Press, 2013), p. 27.
101. Dominick LaCapra, *History and Its Limits: Human, Animal, Violence* (Ithaca and London: Cornell University Press, 2009), p. 166; cited in Wolfe, *Before the Law*, p. 27.
102. LaCapra, *History and Its Limits*, p. 172.
103. Wolfe, *Before the Law*, p. 27.
104. Or what Shukin refers to as 'a mythopoetic invocation of animal signs as a universal lingua franca transcending time and space'. Referring to 'the question of the animal', Shukin sets out her aim of 'challenging its predominantly idealist treatments in critical theory and animal studies by theorizing the ways that animal life gets culturally and carnally rendered as capital at specific historical junctures'. Shukin, *Animal Capital*, p. 7.

105. Hribal, 'Animals Are Part of the Working Class Reviewed', *Borderlands*, 11:2 (2012), 1–37 (p. 24). Available at http://www.borderlands.net.au/vol11no2_2012/hribal_animals.pdf (last accessed 14 September 2018).
106. Ibid., p. 25.
107. Ibid., p. 25.
108. Jocelyne Porcher, 'The Work of Animals: A Challenge for Social Sciences', *Humanimalia*, 6:1 (2014). Available at http://www.depauw.edu/humanimalia/issue%2011/porcher.html (last accessed 14 September 2018). Like Haraway, Porcher emphasises the need to move beyond ways in which 'domestication is still analyzed for the most part as the process of appropriation and exploitation of nature and animals'. But this affirmative investment in the idea of farming as a form of 'co-operation' seems problematic. Porcher seeks to 'transform [animal] work in a liberating direction' but does not acknowledge, at least in this essay, that this labour is enforced and unpaid.
109. A notable example of philosophical thought refusing to homogenise animal life can be found in Tom Tyler's *Ciferae: A Bestiary in Five Fingers* (Minneapolis: University of Minnesota Press, 2012).
110. Derrida writes, for example, of the 'unsubstitutable singularity' of his cat (*The Animal That Therefore I Am*, p. 9). Bailly suggests: 'animality does not speak of animals; that's why instead of generalities, which are obviously necessary and possible, I will start with a case of a species, a story' (*Le Parti pris des animaux*, p. 36). It is still possible, of course, for the singularity of an animal to come forth in philosophy, but it arguably surfaces more forcefully in film, given the movement, materiality and indexicality of 'live action' cinema.
111. Deleuze, *Cinema 2*, p. 17. On the relation between film and philosophy, including the work of Deleuze, see Mullarkey, *Refractions of Reality: Philosophy and the Moving Image* (New York: Palgrave Macmillan, 2009).
112. Haraway, *When Species Meet*, p. 20.
113. Ibid., p. 20.
114. Ibid., p. 3.
115. Ibid., p. 3.
116. Ibid., p. 4.
117. Ibid., p. 4.
118. Ibid., p. 5.
119. Haraway writes: 'Maybe if we take seriously encounter value as the underanalyzed axis of lively capital [. . .] we can see how something more than the reproduction of the same and its deadly logics-in-the-flesh of exploitation might be going on in what I call "making companions."' Ibid., p. 65. Yet Haraway arguably moves too far in this other direction, allowing 'encounter value' to obscure the fact of exploitation and suffering – a trajectory that appears to continue in her more recent reflections on 'multispecies flourishing' in *Staying with the Trouble: Making Kin in the Chthulucene* (Durham, NC and London: Duke University Press, 2016), p. 40.
120. Derrida, *The Animal That Therefore I Am*, p. 27; original emphasis.
121. Haraway, *When Species Meet*, p. 22.
122. Ibid., p. 22. On animal play and thought, see also Brian Massumi's *What Animals Teach Us about Politics* (Durham, NC: Duke University Press, 2014).
123. As Ryan suggests, referring to Haraway's account in *When Species Meet* of her dog's collaborative work on agility training exercises: 'We need to be careful not to train ourselves in reassurance regarding our relations with domestic animals to the point where we obscure the power dynamics implicit in the relation.' Ryan, *Animal Theory*, p. 98.

124. For Dinesh Joseph Wadiwel, 'the danger of Haraway's approach is to side-step the question of violence, particularly manifold forms of violent domination that are the mainstay of our relations with animals and form the context for companion animal relations.' Wadiwel, *The War against Animals* (Leiden and Boston: Brill Rodopi, 2015), p. 61.
125. Shukin, *Animal Capital*, p. 20; original emphasis.
126. Ibid., p. 7.
127. Ibid., p. 20.
128. Ibid., p. 104.
129. Ibid., p. 91.
130. Ibid., p. 22.
131. Ibid., pp. 24–8.
132. Ibid., p. 25.
133. Ibid., pp. 25–6.
134. Ibid., p. 26.
135. Shukin, pp. 152–3. Shukin briefly considers questions of animal subjectivity and agency here by recounting biographical details of Topsy's life (pp. 153–5), but, significantly, these are actions that take place offscreen, and before the time of the film itself, reinforcing the sense that cinema itself fails to open up such questions.
136. Shukin, pp. 150–2.
137. Ibid., p. 16. Shukin is pessimistic about the possibilities of resistance: 'Caught in the double binds of animal capital, there seem to be few modes of political intervention capable of breaking its material-semiotic loops to produce other signs of nature and culture.' Shukin, *Animal Capital*, p. 232. Hribal critiques Shukin's 'emphasis on the supremacy of capitalism': 'instead of breaking free from the capitalist circuit, or, as she puts it, "animal become capital, capital become animal", she reproduces it'. Hribal, 'Animals Are Part of the Working Class Reviewed', p. 21. Yet Hribal's discussion of Shukin's work is relatively brief, and it somewhat flattens her thesis without attending to its nuances.
138. On this distinction, see Shukin: 'Rendering as critical practice, no less than rendering as hegemonic logic, is a discursive mode of production, with the difference that it seeks to produce counterhegemonic rather than hegemonic relationships and effects.' Shukin, *Animal Capital*, p. 28.
139. Ibid., p. 29.
140. Wolfe, *Before the Law*, p. 32.
141. Ibid., p. 32. The embedded quotation is from Jeffrey Nealon, *Foucault Beyond Foucault: Power and Its Intensifications since 1984* (Stanford: Stanford University Press, 2007), p. 46.
142. Denis Côté, 'The Animal Equation', *Cinema Scope*, 14 (2012), 10–12.
143. Smaill, *Regarding Life*, p. 2.
144. See the examples already cited in the Introduction, including work by Rust, Ladino and Smaill.
145. Côté, 'Interview with the Filmmaker Denis Côté', 12 October 2012, *Bestiaire* DVD, The KimStim Collection.
146. This recent focus on animal labour also intersects with a broader contemporary turn in recent documentary filmmaking to engage with representations of work in a particularly contemplative, durational register; see, for example, *C'est quoi ce travail?* (Luc Joulé and Sébastien Jousse, 2015) and the eight-hour-long *Park Lanes* (Kevin Jerome Everson, 2015).

147. On recent documentaries investigating meat production, see Smaill, *Regarding Life*, especially Chapter 3, pp. 45–70. At times, Smaill's readings seem to underplay questions of animal suffering and biopolitical violence. For example, scenes of fishing in *Raw Herring* (Leonard Retel Helmrich and Hetty Naaijkens-Retel Helmrich, 2013) are described in terms of the flow of 'energy and life', as '[t]he world of the fishermen is posed visually in a symbiotic relationship with the world of the fish' (p. 30). Yet Smaill's study remains an important wide-ranging reflection on recent documentary engagements with animal life.
148. Smaill, 'Documentary Film and Animal Modernity in *Raw Herring* and *Sweetgrass*', p. 61.
149. In 'Ecocinema and the Wildlife Film', Rust notes varying levels of engagement with issues of environmental crisis in these films – in *March of the Penguins*, for example, such issues are implicit rather than explicitly addressed.
150. Smaill, 'Tasmanian Tigers and Polar Bears'.
151. Anya Jaremko-Greenwold, 'Véréna Paravel and Lucien Castaing-Taylor by Anya Jaremko-Greenwold', *BOMB Magazine*, 1 March 2013. Available at http://bombmagazine.org/article/7084/v-r-na-paravel-and-lucien-castaing-taylor (last accessed 14 September 2018). Though not explicitly explored by my corpus of films, there are of course direct links to be drawn between animal agriculture and environmental crisis. As Jonathan Safran Foer notes: 'Animal agriculture makes a 40% greater contribution to global warming than all transportation in the world combined' and is therefore 'the number one cause of climate change'. Foer, *Eating Animals* (London: Penguin, 2009), p. 43.
152. On these genealogies, see Senior, Clarke and Freccero, 'Editors' Preface: *Ecce animot*'; Mackenzie and Posthumus (eds), *French Thinking about Animals*; and Jean-Paul Engélibert, Lucie Campos, Catherine Coquio and Georges Chapouthier (eds), *La Question animale: entre science, littérature et philosophie* (Rennes: Presses Universitaires de Rennes, 2011).
153. Élisabeth de Fontenay, *Le Silence des bêtes: La Philosophie à l'épreuve de l'animalité* (Paris: Fayard, 1999).
154. Derrida, *The Beast and the Sovereign*, Vol. 1, translated by Geoffrey Bennington (Chicago: University of Chicago Press, 2009); Derrida, *The Beast and the Sovereign*, Vol. 2, translated by Geoffrey Bennington (Chicago: University of Chicago Press, 2011).
155. Senior, Clarke and Freccero, 'Editors' Preface: *Ecce animot*', pp. 2–5. They point to a further strand of philosophical thought that focuses on intersections between race and the human/animal borderline, citing works by Frantz Fanon and Achille Mbembe (p. 6). Yet this strand of thought is understandably more tied to a critique of racist figurations of 'animality' rather than to an engagement with actual animals. For excellent, probing and critical discussions of the connections and tensions between animal studies, race studies and queer studies, see Mel Y. Chen and Dana Luciano (eds), 'Queer Inhumanisms', *GLQ: A Journal of Lesbian and Gay Studies*, 21:2–3 (2015).
156. Derrida, *The Animal That Therefore I Am*, p. 28.
157. Ibid., p. 10; original emphasis.
158. Critiquing what he sees as the residual humanism and anthropocentrism of Emmanuel Levinas's thinking of the ethical, Derrida writes that 'a thinking of the other, of the infinitely other who looks at me, should [. . .] privilege the question and the request of the animal'. Ibid., p. 113.
159. Ibid., p. 26.
160. Ibid., p. 26.

161. See also Pick's important work on animal life and vulnerability in cinema, literature and philosophy, particularly in *Creaturely Poetics*, and in 'Vulnerability', in Lori Gruen (ed.), *Critical Terms for Animal Studies* (Chicago: University of Chicago Press, forthcoming in 2018).
162. Uexküll reflects on animal suffering only briefly, and in relation to violence between animals rather than between humans and animals, for example in his example of the fly caught in a spider's web (*A Foray into the Worlds of Animals and Humans*, p. 182).
163. Bailly's recent writings on animals include *The Animal Side* (2011), *Le Parti pris des animaux* (2013) and (with Éric Poitevin) *Le Puits des oiseaux* (Paris: Seuil, 2016).
164. A key exception here is Pick's valuable work on Bailly. See Pick, 'Some Small Discrepancy: Jean-Christophe Bailly's Creaturely Ontology', *Journal of Animal Ethics*, 3:2 (2013), 176–87; and Pick, 'Reflexive Realism in René Clément's *Forbidden Games*', in Senior, Clark and Freccero (eds), '*Animots*: Postanimality in French Thought', *Yale French Studies*, 127 (2015), 205–20.
165. Bailly, *The Animal Side*, p. 14.
166. Ibid., p. 13.
167. This also raises the issue of anthropomorphism and its various uses and abuses. On the value of anthropomorphism, see Lorraine Daston and Gregg Mitman (eds), *Thinking with Animals: New Perspectives on Anthropomorphism* (New York: Columbia University Press, 2006).
168. Shukin, *Animal Capital*, p. 141.
169. Bailly, *The Animal Side*, p. 57.
170. Pick, *Creaturely Poetics*, p. 189.
171. For Pick, this is an 'ontological mode of animal life-thought'; Pick, 'Reflexive Realism in René Clément's *Forbidden Games*', p. 206.
172. Bailly, *The Animal Side*, p. 15.
173. Ibid., p. 57.
174. Ibid., p. 15.
175. Ibid., p. 80n4. The embedded quotation is from Derrida, *The Animal That Therefore I Am*, p. 30.
176. As Wolfe argues: 'Freud's valorization [in *Civilization and Its Discontents*] of the human who sees at the expense of the animal who smells is sustained (even if transvalued) in the figure of vision that runs from Sartre's discourse on the look in *Being and Nothingness* through Foucault's anatomy of panopticism in *Discipline and Punish*. This critical genealogy tells us that the figure of vision is indeed ineluctably tied to the specifically human [. . .]'. The task then for critical animal studies is to 'resituate' vision 'as only one sense among many in a more general – and not necessarily human – bodily sensorium'. Wolfe, *Animal Rites: American Culture, the Discourse of Species, and Posthumanist Theory* (Chicago: University of Chicago Press, 2003), p. 3. See also Pick's critique of Bailly's privileging of 'the paradigm of exchanged looks', and 'its latent narcissism and frequent oversights'; Pick, 'Some Small Discrepancy', p. 183.
177. Bailly writes: 'it is through sight that we recognize that we are not the only ones who see, that we know that others see us, look at us, contemplate us'. Bailly, *The Animal Side*, p. 27.
178. Ibid., p. 16.
179. Ibid., p. 49; p. 55.
180. See, for example, De Luca and Jorge, 'Introduction', pp. 8–9.
181. Peter Hallward, *Out of this World: Deleuze and the Philosophy of Creation* (London and New York: Verso, 2006), p. 163.

182. Foucault, cited in Deleuze, *Foucault*, translated and edited by Seán Hand (London and New York: Continuum, 2006), p. 76.
183. Deleuze, *Foucault*, p. 77. And as Deleuze suggests in his reflections on 'societies of control' (responding to Foucault's mapping of the shift from the disciplinary to the biopolitical), 'liberating and enslaving forces confront one another' within each biopolitical regime (p. 4). Animals are explicitly present in this analysis – not only figuratively ('The old monetary mole is the animal of the spaces of enclosure, but the serpent is that of the societies of control' (p. 5)) but literally, when Deleuze cites instances of different 'control mechanisms', referring to the 'animal in a reserve or human in a corporation' (p. 7). Deleuze, 'Postscript on the Societies of Control', *October*, 59 (1992), 3–7.
184. Martin Crowley, 'No Futures (Duras 72/77)', *Qui parle*, 24:2 (2016), 109–36 (p. 118).
185. Deleuze and Guattari address capitalism's deterritorialising and reterritorialising effects in *Anti-Oedipus: Capitalism and Schizophrenia*, translated by Robert Hurley, Mark Seem and Helen R. Lane (Minneapolis: University of Minnesota Press, 1983).
186. Deleuze, *Francis Bacon: The Logic of Sensation*, translated by Daniel W. Smith (London and New York: Continuum, 2003), p. 44.

CHAPTER 1

Cinematic Time and Animal Worlds

In this chapter I explore some key strands of philosophical thought in relation to the question of animal worlds, passing principally via Uexküll, Heidegger, and Deleuze and Guattari. While Deleuze and Guattari draw on Uexküll's model of the *Umwelt*, they move away from his emphasis on subjective worlds in order to elaborate processes of assemblages and becomings.[1] I argue that this theory of animal worlds as becomings, as decentred compositions extending beyond any one subject position, can be related to what Deleuze sees as cinema's opening to the virtual as a time of differing and becoming. I am also interested in the ways in which Deleuze's theorisation of the shift from the movement-image to the time-image in the *Cinema* books denotes a shift of emphasis from 'subject' to 'world'. As we will see, this emphasis on worlding within the realm of the time-image allows for a reconfiguration of relations between animals and cinema beyond a (humanist) logic of subjecthood.

Yet I also seek in this chapter to attend to recent accounts of the relation between animals and film, including work by Burt, Pick, Lippit, Sobchack and others. I highlight what Deleuze's theory of cinematic time, and of the coexistence of the actual and the virtual, might contribute to this developing body of work in which, up until now, Bazin has emerged as the dominant film theoretical reference.[2] Shifting the emphasis away from Bazin and towards Deleuze, whose writing on cinema has received comparatively little attention in the field of animals and film,[3] I move from Bazin's phenomenological model of lived, subjective time towards what might be seen as Deleuze's post-phenomenological account of cinematic time, in which questions of worldhood and duration are reconfigured beyond categories such as the subject and the 'real'. As Claire Colebrook suggests, the Deleuzian time-image denotes not subjectively lived time but 'a presentation of time itself, which forces us to confront the very becoming and dynamism of life'.[4]

Thus, while proposing a Deleuzian account of cinema that might supplement current film theoretical work on animals, I also seek to draw out a Deleuzo-Guattarian model of animal worlds that might contribute to the field of critical animal studies. Deleuze and Guattari's work has been frequently addressed within the field but in a fairly narrow way that has often focused on the well-known concept of becoming-animal.[5] While I briefly address this debate, the main aim of this chapter is to look elsewhere in Deleuze's work, expanding the range of reference by moving from Deleuze and Guattari's reflections on animal worlds to Deleuze's conceptualisation of the time-image and its concomitant pluralisation of worlds of becoming. At the same time, I seek to remain attentive to the issues of biopolitics explored in the Introduction. As the final turn of this chapter indicates, questions of the 'real' – of animal suffering and exploitation – still need to be grappled with, both by film theory and by philosophies of animal worlds.

ANIMAL WORLDS

For Uexküll, the *Umwelt* denotes what is accessible, perceptible and meaningful to the animal. Uexküll demonstrates this, famously, in his discussion of the female tick in her quest to suck the blood of a mammal: blind and deaf, she extracts from her otherwise meaningless surroundings meaningful 'perception signs' transmitted via smell, temperature and touch.[6] Uexküll proposes that animal environments are shaped by such 'purely subjective realities'[7] – or what Bailly describes in evocative terms, reflecting on Uexküll's model, as 'the skein that every animal forms for itself by winding itself into the world according to its means, with its nervous system, its senses, its shape, its tools, its mobility'.[8]

Though these 'purely subjective realities' constitute enclosed worlds of biosemiotic meaning (what Uexküll refers to metaphorically as 'soap bubbles'), these worlds can also intersect. As Buchanan notes, a tick and a human would perceive the same mammal, for example, via a different set of signs: 'the *Umwelten* of different organisms may overlap with one another', 'in the form of interlacing and contrapuntal relationships'.[9] Here Buchanan draws on Uexküll's understanding of nature 'as a harmony composed of different melodic and symphonic parts'.[10] Understood thus, Uexküll's model suggests a multiplicity of coexisting spatio-temporal worlds (or what Crowley has described as a 'pluralist ontology').[11] What Uexküll proposes, then, is 'a wide diversity of *Umwelten*, rather than just one real world',[12] or, as Senior, Clarke and Freccero put it, 'something like a non-anthropocentric semiotics that would [. . .] open up the human to an understanding of the myriad worlds that are in existence in and around "our" world'.[13]

The influence of Uexküll's project on Heidegger's thought has been well documented. In *The Fundamental Concepts of Metaphysics: World, Finitude, Solitude*, Heidegger writes that Uexküll's work offers important insights into how 'the animal is bound to its environment',[14] thereby diverging from the Darwinist views of the time, which posited 'the animal and the environment as two distinct entities that happen to come together'.[15] Like Uexküll, Heidegger is interested in 'the relational structure between the animal and its environment'.[16] As Buchanan observes, 'Heidegger is drawn to Uexküll's research because he finds in him an accomplice in biology in order to think through the concept of world.'[17] But there are clear differences between their accounts, with Heidegger reserving a privileged relation to worldhood for the human. And thus, 'whereas Heidegger emphasises the particular comportment of human *Dasein* as being-in-the-world, the behaviour specific to animals is less clear'.[18] Indeed, Heidegger's reflections on the question of animal worlds often seem conflicted and ambiguous.[19] In *The Fundamental Concepts of Metaphysics*, he writes:

> Man has world. But what then about the other beings which, like man, are also part of the world: the animals and plants, the material things like the stone, for example [. . .]? Are they merely parts [*Stücke*] of the world, as distinct from man who in addition *has* world? Or does the animal too have world, and if so, in what way? In the same way as man, or in some other way? And how would we grasp this otherness? And what about the stone? However crudely, certain distinctions manifest themselves here. We can formulate these distinctions in the following three theses: [1.] the stone (material object) is *worldless*; [2.] the animal is *poor in world*; [3.] man is *world-forming*.[20]

Heidegger's concluding tripartite thesis appears to posit a clear distinction between human and animal being. This distinction stems from his model of human *Dasein* (being-there), in its world-forming and language-making capacities, as involving an ability to apprehend the world *as* world – the world 'disclosed in its worldhood',[21] the world 'as such'. Heidegger sees the animal, by contrast, as deprived of such linguistic, world-forming capacities. The animal for Heidegger is absorbed in the environment in a state of captivation (*Benommenheit*), lacking in any relation to the world 'as such': 'Captivation is the condition of possibility for the fact that, in accordance with its essence, the animal *behaves within an environment* [*Umgebung*] *but never within a world* [*Welt*].'[22] As Agamben observes, Heidegger thus borrows the idea of the animal's *Umwelt* from Uexküll only to invert it,[23] emptying that world of its perceptual richness and meaningfulness in order to assert what he sees as the animal's 'poverty' in world.[24]

Yet we note the questions and openings that precede and trouble Heidegger's concluding thesis above. Before the assertion that 'the animal is *poor in world*', Heidegger wonders if the animal has a world, 'and if so, in what way?'. As Derrida observes, this thesis seems anything but stable in Heidegger's text. Indeed, this uncertainty gradually seems to overtake Heidegger's thinking of worldhood: 'this question of the animal will – by means of a very strange process, for, although it is a guiding thread, it will finally invade the whole space – come to specify the question of world.'[25] Heidegger appears troubled, haunted, by the thought of animal worlds. The matter is not quite as closed as his oft-cited tripartite thesis might have us believe.[26]

In the work of Deleuze and Guattari, we find another ambiguous relation to the question of animal worlds, but in ways that are markedly different from Heidegger's position.[27] Indeed, they refuse the human exceptionalism of Heidegger's thesis, affirming relations between animal and world; as Deleuze puts it, 'an animal [. . .] is never separable from its relations with the world'.[28] The influence of Uexküll can be discerned here too, both in Deleuze's individual writings and in his work with Guattari, though as Buchanan suggests of Deleuze: 'rather than concerning himself with the animal–environment relation, he is more interested in the virtual and intensive processes that create actual beings and their relations.'[29] While Uexküll's theory of animal worlds is grounded in concepts such as 'body, environment, behaviour, organism',[30] Deleuze and Guattari recast this approach, seeing animal life 'as a continual process of becoming, where bodies are always changing, and entities like the organism represent not life but life's imprisonment'.[31]

Rejecting the organisational properties of the organism and its 'imprisonment' of life, Deleuze and Guattari disrupt the 'ring around organisms'[32] posited in different ways by Uexküll's model of the 'soap bubble' and Heidegger's theory of animal captivation. Deleuze and Guattari do this above all through an emphasis on affective *assemblages*: 'Von Uexküll, in defining animal worlds, looks for the active and passive affects of which the animal is capable in the individuated assemblage of which it is a part.'[33] Thus, as noted in the Introduction, while in dialogue with Uexküll, Deleuze and Guattari shift away from his emphasis on subjective worlds, moving towards a model of 'desubjectified' affective assemblages – a model that aligns with what Buchanan describes as Deleuze and Guattari's broader interest in a 'pre-individual plane of immanence'.[34] This form of worlding attests to a logic of the impersonal that extends beyond the enclosed subjective 'bubbles' of Uexküll's theory (though if we were to follow Bailly's reading of the *Umwelt* as 'prodigious', as 'pure unfolding',[35] then Deleuze and Guattari's notion of worlding might be seen as radicalising the infinite movement of this unfolding). For Deleuze and Guattari, worlding is a form of conjugation 'with others': 'becoming-everybody/everything, making the world a becoming, is to world, to make a world or worlds, in other words, to find one's proximities and zones of indiscernibility.'[36] Their emphasis is on worlding as an intensive, affective, conjugating process.

Deleuze and Guattari thus destabilise the place of 'the subject' in ways that might seem counterproductive at first, particularly in relation to questions of political agency. However, while there may be good reasons for seeking to remake a postanthropocentric subject 'rather than necessarily wanting to dispense with the subject altogether', as Ryan observes, it is important to acknowledge that 'the subject' is 'a term so thoroughly bound up with humanist discourses.'[37] And as Joanna Bednarek notes, drawing on Deleuze and Guattari's *Anti-Oedipus*:

> Because the unconscious is, according to Deleuze and Guattari, impersonal and structured primarily not by the logic of the signifier (as in Lacan), but by the machinic processes of flows and cuts of desiring production [. . .], becoming as the process of dismantling Oedipal structures brings the subject into contact with the material forces that underlie and condition its functioning.[38]

Attentive to these 'material forces', and in line with the poststructuralist, antihumanist tradition in which their thought is embedded, Deleuze and Guattari seek to move beyond the logic of a 'subject' who might 'have' or possess a world. Thus they destabilise the link between world and subject in Uexküll (and indeed *Dasein* and world-forming in Heidegger's residual humanism). For Deleuze and Guattari, to 'make a world' is a process of becoming rather than a state of 'having'; it is a mode of conjugating rather than possessing.

Animals occupy a particular place in Deleuze and Guattari's discussions of becoming. In *A Thousand Plateaus*, they distinguish between three kinds of animals (the first two kinds being anthropomorphic figurations): the individuated (pets, 'sentimental, Oedipal animals each with its own petty history, "my" cat, "my" dog', inviting regression and 'narcissistic contemplation'; this is 'the only kind of animal psychoanalysis understands'); animals 'with characteristics or attributes; genus, classification, or State animals, animals as they are treated in the great divine myths' (that is, as archetypes, symbols); and finally, their favoured category: 'more demonic animals, pack or affect animals that form a multiplicity, a becoming, a population, a tale . . .'.[39] Deleuze and Guattari have been critiqued for their apparent dismissal of pets (and human relations with those pets), most notably by Haraway,[40] but they do acknowledge in the same passage that 'it is also possible for any animal to be treated in the mode of the pack or swarm [. . .]'.[41] For Deleuze and Guattari, what matters above all are not fixed characteristics (the 'molar unities' of the domesticated or mythic animal) but ever-changing relations and zones of indiscernibility ('molecular multiplicities').[42]

Deleuze and Guattari's concept of 'becoming-animal', in which (predominantly human) beings enter into zones of indiscernibility with animals, is central to this processual thinking of becoming. They specify that 'becoming-animal' is not a mimetic, identificatory, phantasmatic or imaginary operation: becomings are 'perfectly real',[43] occurring when beings are involved in processes of mutual transformation. They suggest:

> There is no longer man or animal, since each deterritorializes the other, in a conjunction of flux, in a continuum of reversible intensities. [. . .] there is a circuit of states that forms a mutual becoming, in the heart of a necessarily multiple or collective assemblage.[44]

Crucially, Deleuze and Guattari link this idea of 'real' becomings, via Bergson, to the question of time:

> This is the point to clarify: that a becoming lacks a subject distinct from itself; but also that it has no term, since its term in turn exists only as taken up in another becoming of which it is the subject, and which coexists, forms a block, with the first. This is the principle according to which there is a reality specific to becoming (the Bergsonian idea of a coexistence of very different 'durations', superior or inferior to 'ours', all of them in communication).[45]

Here, via the invocation of Bergsonian duration, we see a potential link between becoming and the coexistence of different durations (and therefore coexisting multiple worlds, as I will suggest below).

In recent work on animals and film, the notion of 'becoming-animal' has often been affirmatively adopted,[46] as exemplified by readings of Herzog's *Grizzly Man* focusing on Timothy Treadwell's 'becoming-animal'.[47] Yet within the field of critical animal studies, the concept of 'becoming-animal' has frequently been criticised for its apparent abstractions.[48] Entailing 'a pack, a gang, a population, a peopling, in short multiplicity', becoming-animal seems to relate to all kinds of transformative, rhizomatic processes that often have very little to do with actual animals. And while Deleuze points to 'a *zone of indiscernibility or undecidability* between man and animal',[49] becoming-animal is something that appears to be open only to the human and not the animal: Deleuze and Guattari refer, for example, to the 'becoming-animal of the human being', while gesturing to the 'becoming-other of the animal'.[50] While this notion of the animal's 'becoming-other' has also been criticised for its lack of specificity,[51] I find this idea more productive than the concept of 'becoming-animal', precisely because it pertains to how animals might be open to various kinds of becomings and transformations.[52] There is no doubt there are still limitations to Deleuze and Guattari's approach here (not least the often non-specific reference to 'the animal'), but the notion of the 'becoming-other of the animal' retains a certain promise.

Indeed, by connecting this idea of 'becoming-other' to Deleuze and Guattari's discussion of animal worlds in *A Thousand Plateaus*, we can further understand the relation between animals and assemblages in their thought. Coining the phrase 'the animal-stalks-at-five-o'clock', they sketch a chain of deterritorialising assemblages:

> Climate, wind, season, hour are not of another nature than the things, animals, or people that populate them, follow them, sleep and awaken within them. This should be read without a pause: the animal-stalks-at-five-o'clock. The becoming-evening, becoming-night of an animal, blood nuptials. Five o'clock is this animal! This animal is this place![53]

The 'animal-stalks-at-five-o'clock' denotes a composition, a becoming and a decentring of any one apparently privileged term. As emphasised by Deleuze and Guattari's instruction that the phrase 'be read without a pause', 'the animal-stalks-at-five-o'clock', Buchanan suggests, 'has an inherent, one should even say intensive, immediacy to it': 'the contents cannot be broken up into parts unless one wanted to risk changing the very composition in question'.[54] Reflecting on the singularising yet impersonal qualities of such a composition, Deleuze and Guattari propose: 'There is a mode of individuation very different from that of a person, subject, thing, or substance. We reserve the name *haecceity* for it.'[55] Derived from Duns Scotus's conceptualisation of the singularity of 'this thing [*haec*]',[56] the term *haecceity* is used to describe 'the intensive processes that compose a given body, all the while being irreducible to *this* body [. . .]'.[57] Each (animal) body, then, in alliance with its surroundings, is becoming-other. And it is in this sense that, as we saw above, Deleuze and Guattari refer to Uexküll's concept of the *Umwelt* as 'the individuated assemblage of which [the animal] is a part'. They understand animal worlds as 'individuated' (that is, singularised) yet 'desubjectified' affective assemblages. For as Buchanan puts it: 'The animal is not the centre around which the assemblage "the animal-stalks-at-five-o'clock" turns. The hour, the weather, hunger – it all goes into this assemblage.'[58]

In what follows, I want to suggest that this mode of decentring, of assemblage, can be related to the virtual worlds of cinema proposed by Deleuze. Indeed, reflecting further on the phrase 'the animal-stalks-at-five-o'clock', Buchanan writes that it pertains to 'a relation with everything that might be found within a virtual plane capable of becoming actualized. Thus, it is the passing that occurs between virtual intensities and their actualizations into individuated beings that is of greater importance.'[59] In the next section, then, I want to consider how this model of animal worlds might relate to what Deleuze sees as the coexistence of the actual and the virtual within the worlds of cinema. But I wish first to address some key lines of thought within current scholarship on animals and film before turning to explore what Deleuze's theory of cinematic time might contribute to this.

ANIMALS IN FILM THEORY

Studies of animals and film have often tended to remain within frameworks that read 'the animal' onscreen in terms of an opening to the real that tests out the limits of representation. As Burt notes, a particular cultural sensitivity to what happens to animals onscreen (that is, the indexical reality of their treatment) is demonstrated by the history of specific legislation in this area, such as the American Humane Association's disclaimer 'No animals were harmed during the making of this film' – a phrase that, according to Lippit, 'attempts to frame the picture and limit the responsibility of the film and its fictions'.[60] As Burt observes, however, 'the fact that the animal image can so readily point beyond its significance on screen to questions about its general treatment or fate in terms of welfare suggests that the boundaries of film art [. . .] cannot easily delimit the meaning of the animal within its fictions.'[61] The presence of an animal onscreen often confounds clear distinctions between the diegetic and the extradiegetic, introducing a 'rupturing effect',[62] a radical instability in cinema's own acts of framing. Questions of coercion, cruelty, violence and harm become particularly urgent in such contexts; for as Pick observes, 'when it comes to animals, power operates with the fewest of obstacles'.[63] And thus, Burt suggests, the animal image's 'vulnerability to ambiguity says a great deal about the position of the animal in our culture'.[64] This vulnerability to ambiguity is linked to the vulnerability of animal life itself. The ways in which animal lives can be made to mean (onscreen) and put to use (offscreen) are inextricably and violently connected.[65]

Indeed, there is a long history of violence and cruelty to animals in cinema.[66] For Shukin, Edison's 1903 film *Electrocuting an Elephant* (discussed in the Introduction) 'makes visible the often overlooked fact that animal sacrifice constituted something of a founding symbolic and material gesture of early electrical and cinematic culture'.[67] This sacrificial economy of animal life and death, initiated by early documentary cinema, extends throughout the history of fiction film too: in works such as *The Rules of the Game* (Jean Renoir, 1939), *Apocalypse Now* (Francis Ford Coppola, 1979), *Weekend* (Jean-Luc Godard, 1967) and *Benny's Video* (Michael Haneke, 1992), documentary animal death ushers into the space of human fiction the particular charge of the real.[68] As Vivian Sobchack writes of one of the rabbits killed onscreen during the hunt scene in Renoir's *The Rules of the Game*:

> its quivering death leap transformed fictional into documentary space, symbolic into indexical representation, my affective investment in the irreal and fictional into a documentary consciousness charged with a sense of world, existence, bodily mortification and mortality, and all the rest of the real that is in excess of fiction.[69]

This logic of the animal image in film, particularly the animal dying onscreen, as denotation of the real has decisively shaped film theory in this area. For Bazin, as Pick suggests, animals function 'as the markers of film's representational limits: death, contingency, and temporality'.[70] Drawing on Bazin's work, De Luca suggests that 'non-human creatures – and in a more radical form, their death – have come to embody one of the strongest markers of contingency in the filmic image'; animals offer up an 'intractable reality surplus'.[71] In his analysis of *Blood of the Beasts* (Georges Franju, 1949), Lippit describes animal death as 'animetaphoric'[72] – a term he glosses elsewhere as 'a metaphor made flesh' that 'marks a limit of figurability'.[73] Lippit situates animal death as a form of excessive literality – a marker of the real – that overwhelms the film's allegorical content. Thus while Heidegger views animals as 'undying', consigning their deaths to a realm of impossibility (animals 'perish' rather than die; they do not experience death *as* death),[74] film theory has often regarded animal death onscreen as a particular marker of the real.[75] The animal death that is 'inauthentic' for Heideggerian philosophy thus becomes authenticating for film theory.

But in the conceptual frameworks drawn by, and inspired by, Bazin and Lippit in particular, the limit position of the animal risks being essentialised: the animal is equated with the real/contingency/excess/the impossible/the 'essence' of cinema itself.[76] These theoretical moves inevitably flatten out the question of animal worlds because animals are seen only to make meaning for the cinema rather than for themselves (via the kinds of biosemiotic processes set out by Uexküll, for example). When Sobchack writes of a 'documentary consciousness charged with a sense of world', we note that the world of the dying animal here is elided. Despite Sobchack's attention to questions of ethics, her reading inadvertently replicates the extinguishing of animal world effected (diegetically and extradiegetically) by the film itself in the killing of the rabbit. Animal consciousness disappears (note that the emphasis is on 'bodily mortification'), only to be replaced by 'documentary consciousness', as the 'quivering death leap' initiates a thesis about the ontological categories of film. This echoes the move made by Bazin in his discussion of Pierre Braunberger's

Bullfight (1951): writing that '[d]eath is surely one of those rare events that justifies the term [...] *cinematic specificity*',[77] Bazin seems more interested in what the animal's death means for cinema rather than what it means for the animal.[78]

Yet Pick draws out the ways in which, beyond a fascination with animal death onscreen, Bazin is also intrigued by cinema's ability to bear witness to 'life time', including the lived time of the animal. Here the long take, that privileged signifier of the real for Bazin, is key. Describing Vittorio De Sica's *Umberto D.* (1952), Bazin writes: 'I have no hesitation in stating that the cinema has rarely gone such a long way toward making us aware of what it is to be a man. (And also, for that matter, of what it is to be a dog).'[79] Here, Pick suggests (the embedded citations are from Bazin):

> equality between man and animal derives from fidelity to reality, in this case achieved through the cinema of pure duration: 'the sequence of events which De Sica reports obey a necessity that has nothing to do with dramatic structure'.[80] De Sica makes no concessions to 'classical dramaturgy.' He allows his camera to capture time as it passes, subjecting the 'plot' of *Umberto D* to the plotlessness of everyday life: duration. The profilmic 'event' of De Sica's neorealist films is thus time itself. The ruptures, discontinuities – what in narrative terms is called drama – are identical to the actual passing of time. Bazin calls this 'making "life time"'.[81]

Duration is key here, allowing for a patient tracing of the contingent wanderings of the everyday – a form of uneventfulness that eschews dramatic structure – and an asymptotic relation between the filmic and the profilmic, between the film's time and the lived time of Bergsonian *durée*.[82] Uneventfulness is linked to a 'fidelity to reality' and to an equitability of presentation across species divisions, in the absence of the peaks and troughs of dramatic structure.

Within Pick's framework, Bazin's conception of 'making "life time"' is particularly suggestive in indicating ways in which cinema might bear witness to the everyday details of lives, both human and animal (while still avoiding naive investments in classical realism).[83] This is certainly more fertile ground than the closing down of animal worlds that occurs in theoretical fixations on animal death onscreen and in essentialising alignments of the animal with the real (or indeed with the 'essence' of cinema itself). The idea of cinematic 'life time' underlined by Pick's reading of Bazin is particularly apt in relation to the 'plotlessness', and attendant unfolding of animal worlds, at stake in the films I examine (recalling also their connection to the uneventfulness of slow cinema, as detailed in the Introduction). Yet while drawing on this reading, I also seek to shift the frame of reference away from Bazin's phenomenological model of lived, subjective time, of duration as *durée*, towards a post-phenomenological theorisation of cinematic time, in which questions of worldhood and temporality are recast, via Deleuze, beyond categories such as the subjective and the 'real'.

DELEUZE, CINEMA, TIME

Deleuze writes that, for Bazin, neorealism 'was a matter of a new form of reality, said to be dispersive, elliptical, errant or wavering, working in blocs, with deliberately weak connections and floating events'.[84] Deleuze, like Bazin, sees neorealism as an important turning point in the history of cinema, with Deleuze viewing it as marking the break between the classical cinema of the 'movement-image' and the postwar cinema of the 'time-image'.[85] Yet Deleuze suggests that the limitations of Bazin's conceptualisation of the transformation of cinema brought about by neorealism lie in the 'posing of the problem at the level of reality'; neorealism is seen to produce 'a formal or material "additional reality"'.[86] Questioning Bazin's thesis, Deleuze writes: 'we are not sure that the problem arises at the level of the real, whether in relation to form or content. Is it not rather at the level of the "mental", in terms of thought?'[87] Deleuze's model shifts away from a Bazinian phenomenology of lived time, and beyond a necessarily asymptotic relation between filmic and profilmic worlds. Moving away from the adherence of Bazin's conceptual horizon to 'the real', Deleuze points to a reconfiguration of perception, thought and time in cinema, one that oscillates between the 'actual' and the 'virtual', as we shall see below.

In contrast to the movement-image (in which, via the sensory-motor schemata of realism, perception extends into action), in the realm of the time-image, perception is prevented from 'being extended into action in order to put it in contact with thought'.[88] Turning to Luchino Visconti's *Rocco and His Brothers* (1960), Deleuze describes 'the arrival of the family who, with all their eyes and ears, try to take in the huge station and the unknown city'; what the scene enacts is an '"inventory" of a setting – its objects, furniture, tools, etc.'. Here, Deleuze suggests:

> the situation is not extended directly into action: it is no longer sensory-motor, as in realism, but primarily optical and of sound, invested by the senses, before action takes place in it, and uses or confronts its elements. Everything remains real in this neo-realism (whether it is film set or exteriors) but, between the reality of the setting and that of the action, it is no longer a motor extension which is established, but rather a dreamlike connection through the intermediary of the liberated sense organs. It is as if the action floats in the situation, rather than bringing it to a conclusion or strengthening it.[89]

Deleuze is interested in what happens in this space before the setting is instrumentalised by action. If action is suspended, this is because cinematic space and time are given over to perception. No longer beholden to the 'motor extension' demanded by realism, the senses are 'liberated'.

For Deleuze, the suspension of action, the interruption of the sensory-motor schemata, allows for a layering of time, or what we might call a 'pluralisation' of the event:

> what we call temporal structure, or direct time-image, clearly goes beyond the purely empirical succession of time – past-present-future. It is, for example, a coexistence of distinct durations, or of levels of duration; a single event can belong to several levels: the sheets of past coexist in a non-chronological order.[90]

As Deleuze elucidates later on in *Cinema 2*, this idea of coexisting levels of duration is informed by the thought of Bergson. In Chapter 4, Deleuze sketches Bergson's philosophy of time as follows (a schematic summary but useful for our purposes here): 'the past coexists with the present that it has been; the past preserved in itself, as past in general (non-chronological); at each moment time splits itself into present and past, present that passes and past which is preserved.'[91] Thus we understand time as constituted by a process of perpetual splitting. For Deleuze, the 'present that passes' is the *actual*, the 'past which is preserved' is the *virtual*. Yet, as Deleuze underlines, this bifurcation of time never fully concludes – 'this splitting never goes right to the end'.[92] Rather than a fixed binary division between the actual and the virtual, there is a perpetual exchange between these realms – captured by Deleuze's model of the 'crystal of time': 'the crystal constantly exchanges the two distinct images which constitute it, the actual image of the present which passes and the virtual image of the past which is preserved: distinct and yet indiscernible [. . .].'[93] This is a 'perpetual *self-distinguishing*, a distinction in the process of being produced'.[94]

Within Deleuze's Bergsonian framework, anything that happens is already plural, distributed as it is between the actual and the virtual. The event is not just doubled (as the model of the actual and the virtual might appear, at first glance, to suggest) but multiplied, through an endless splitting. In relation to cinema, the event 'suddenly "multiplies" and "proliferates" in the new world of the time-image', as Tom Conley suggests.[95] Each cinematic event is self-differing, opening up 'distinct and yet indiscernible' layers of the virtual and the actual.

It is thus that cinematic images and sounds are freed from being harnessed to any one subject or point of view. For once movement has been released from the 'sensory-motor schema', cinema's dynamics of indetermination are more fully embraced. As Deleuze puts it:

every image reacts with every other one, on all their sides and in all their parts. This is the regime of universal variation, which goes beyond the human limits of the sensory-motor schema towards a non-human world where movement equals matter [. . .].[96]

Here the cinema of the time-image is no longer tied to a human subject but to a 'regime of universal variation', a realm of indetermination, in which 'every image reacts with every other one'. As Colebrook suggests, in her reflections on Deleuze and cinema: 'Only with cinema can we think of a mode of "seeing" that is not attached to the human eye. Cinema, then, offers something like a "percept": a reception of data that is not located in a subject.'[97] What Deleuze describes as a 'percept' is a realm of perception freed from any one perceiving subject. Thus, as he writes: 'Instead of going from the acentred state of things to centred perception', the cinema 'could go back up towards the acentred state of things, and get closer to it'.[98] Here Deleuze sees in cinema 'the capacity of life to go beyond its human, recognisable and already given forms'.[99]

Thus in the realm of the time-image, a time of 'pure virtuality', of indetermination, differing and becoming, there is, as Deleuze puts it, 'a coexistence of distinct durations' through which plural worlds come into view. Reflecting on the films of Luis Buñuel, Deleuze writes of:

a plurality of simultaneous worlds [. . .] a simultaneity of presents in different worlds. These are not subjective (imaginary) points of view in one and the same world, but one and the same event in different objective worlds, all implicated in the event, inexplicable universe.[100]

What is being described here by Deleuze is cinema's opening to a plurality of coexisting worlds reaching beyond any one subjective point of view. Within Deleuze's model, as Colebrook puts it:

There is not a world that contains time; there is a flow of time, which produces 'worlds' or durations. Time is a virtual whole of divergent durations: different rhythms or pulsations of life which we can think or intuit.[101]

Indeed, as Colebrook specifies further, emphasising the place of the nonhuman: 'The durations of different becomings produce different worlds – including the inhuman worlds of plants and animals.'[102] Deleuze thus indicates the kinds of openings that allow us to glimpse, through cinema, the possibility of different worlds, including animal worlds, without cinema necessarily having to frame those worlds in terms of subjecthood or 'point of view'. Through its attention to time as 'a virtual whole of divergent durations', cinema offers a particularly powerful way of envisaging the coexistence of plural worlds.

Crucially, this idea of plural worlds coexisting within the realm of the time-image takes place against the backdrop of a broader shift of emphasis from 'subject' to 'world' as Deleuze moves from *Cinema 1* to *Cinema 2*. In the latter, Deleuze writes:

> it is no longer the character who reacts to the optical-sound situation, it is a movement of world which supplements the faltering movement of the character. There takes place a kind of worldizing [*mondialization*] or 'societizing' [*mondianization*], a depersonalizing, a pronominalizing of the lost or blocked movement.[103]

> The world takes responsibility for the movement that the subject can no longer or cannot make. This is a virtual movement, but it becomes actual at the price of an expansion of the totality of space and of a stretching of time.[104]

Deleuze's model of worlding in cinema as a 'depersonalizing' movement recalls the reflections by Deleuze and Guattari on animal worlds as 'desubjectified' assemblages and becomings above. The worlding (or 'worldizing') envisaged by cinema is similarly an intensive process that extends beyond the subject, and beyond the human. Here in cinema, rather than the action of the sensory-motor schemata, there is a 'virtual movement', which comes to the fore in the 'stretching of time' at work in the realm of the time-image.

Thus when Deleuze writes of the 'movement of the world' to which the cinema of the time-image bears witness, we understand this 'world' as encompassing 'a virtual whole of divergent durations' – in other words, plural worlds (human and nonhuman). Bearing in mind the multiplicity of spatio-temporal worlds also at stake in Uexküll's model, as we saw above, this also returns us to the question of the *Umwelt*. For there is a rich set of resonances to be traced between Uexküll's 'pluralist ontology' and Deleuze's thinking of the time-image. Deleuze writes, in *Cinema 2*, of cinema's opening to 'a pluralist cosmology, where there are not only different worlds [. . .], but where one and the same event is played out in these different worlds, in incompatible versions'.[105] Though the connection is not made explicit, this 'pluralist cosmology' speaks to (and is possibly even shaped by) Uexküll's 'pluralist ontology' and the coexistence of different *Umwelten*.[106] When Buchanan describes how a tick and a human would perceive the same mammal, for example, via a different set of signs, this idea seems echoed by Deleuze's theory of 'the same event [. . .] played out in these different worlds, in incompatible versions'. Where the key difference lies, however, as we have seen, is in Deleuze's shift, via his theorisation of the time-image, beyond the model of 'subjective reality' to which Uexküll's conceptualisation of the *Umwelt* remains attached.

BEYOND THE (ANIMAL) SUBJECT

In 'Animal Life in the Cinematic Umwelt', Pick draws connections between Uexküll's model of the *Umwelt* and Bazinian realism in order to explore how cinema envisages different yet coexisting 'dwelling-worlds'.[107] Focusing on Nuridsany and Perennou's *Microcosmos* (1996) and Robert Bresson's *A Man Escaped* (1956), Pick is interested in how films address 'interior animal worlds, rendered, as far as possible, from the perspective of the creature itself' (which includes the human).[108] Here again, Bazinian realism is linked to subjective point of view, the lived space-time of each perceiving subject. If, as Pick suggests, Uexküll's model suggests 'the copresence of different spatiotemporal worlds', then this is a copresence that cinema can evoke:

> In life, as in film, there is not one but a proliferation of worlds, since what a world is can only be thought as a relationship between the perceiving being and the world it perceives. There is, then, the world (space-time) of the dog, of the beetle, or of the human being, which cinema can attune to and attempt to convey.[109]

As indicated above, Pick's key theoretical points of reference here are Uexküll and Bazin. However, these reflections also resonate suggestively with Deleuze's conception of the plural worlds and the 'coexistence of distinct durations' registered by the time-image. Yet while for Pick, following Uexküll, 'what a world is can only be thought as a relationship between the perceiving being and the world it perceives', for Deleuze, 'world' indicates something that seems more far-reaching, as we have seen. For Deleuze, each 'world' must be thought as part of a 'pluralist cosmology' that extends beyond subject positions (and beyond a Bazinian emphasis on lived, subjective time). Worlding for Deleuze, both in the cinema and beyond, pertains rather to a more general structure of the splitting of time. It is not just that any one particular event is perceived differently by different beings (as in Uexküll's model), but rather that the structure of time itself is self-differing. For Deleuze, it is this structure of implicated yet 'incompatible' presents, of pluralised events, that the cinema of the time-image brings to the fore.[110]

As Colebrook suggests, Deleuze's conception of cinema thus marks a radical difference from our everyday visions of the world: 'Our everyday seeing of the world is always a *seeing from* our interested and *embodied* perspective. I organise the flow of perceptions into "my" world.'[111] (Indeed, this would align with

Uexküll's model of subjective perception.) By contrast, Deleuze's approach suggests, as Colebrook indicates, that cinema 'can present images or perception liberated from the organising structure of everyday life and it does this by maximising its own internal power'.[112] And thus: 'What makes cinema *cinematic* is this liberation of the sequencing of images from any single observer.'[113]

Indeed, the films discussed in this book often present perceptual worlds ambiguously, refusing to locate or *actualise* them exactly (whereas wildlife films try to reduce or structure this ambiguity, for example through narrative framing and techniques of identification).[114] In *Bovines*, *Bestiaire* and *The Turin Horse*, there is a general avoidance, for example, of point-of-view shots. Often the images and sounds in these films are not framed distinctly as either human or animal perception, or as constituting distinct human or animal worlds. In this sense, there is a structure of 'implicated presents',[115] a thickened yet indeterminate texture of heterogeneous times and spaces. In the time-image, as Colebrook suggests, 'we see imaging as such, not yet incorporated into a viewpoint, not yet ordered into a line of time'.[116] And thus: 'This is not a cinema of the actual – the world as it is – but of the virtual; it presents the imaging and connection processes from which any world could be perceived [. . .].'[117]

THE RETURN OF THE REAL?

For Deleuze, cinema thus opens to dynamics of becoming and realms of the virtual, as we have seen.[118] Where, then, does this leave the place of the real within theorisations of the relations between animals and film? Here it is instructive to return to Burt's work, for if the animal onscreen introduces an 'extreme collapse between the figural and the real',[119] then this points to something very particular about animal images in film:

> the power of the animal film image stems from the fact that, because it is more prone to collapse the boundary of representation and reality than other forms of imagery, it threatens to reveal not just the isolated fact of coercion or cruelty but the whole system by which such coercion and cruelty are reproduced.[120]

What this means, as Burt argues, is that:

> animal imagery cannot be subsumed under a general and abstract theory of semiotics, as if the animal is a sign easily interchangeable with other kinds of signs, because for historical reasons the visual animal carries specific connotations particularly in relation to questions of treatment and welfare.[121]

As noted above, issues of coercion, cruelty, violence and harm become particularly significant in such contexts (as made evident, for example, by the exploitation of real animal death in cinema).

This is the challenge of animal images in particular. Yet it also points to ways in which animal images might challenge a Deleuzian film theoretical approach. Because contra Deleuze's desire to shift beyond the Bazinian real, when it comes to animal images, we still need to get entangled with questions at the level of the real. We may invoke here Cora Diamond's emphasis, in her reading of J. M. Coetzee's *The Lives of Animals* (1999), on the 'difficulty of reality', the difficulty of grappling with 'the horror of what we do to animals' (a view represented by Coetzee's character Elizabeth Costello).[122] Here we face the difficulty of grappling with animal images, and the particularities of their inescapable relations to power, passivity and domination. As I trace the emergence of animal worlds in various films in this book, I thus seek to remain attentive to the 'difficulty of reality' – to the issues of violence, power and biopolitics signalled in the Introduction.

Yet, as I suggested there, and as I explore throughout this study, there are resources in Deleuze's thought for thinking through these questions of power. As Deleuze writes in his reflections on Foucault, 'power is not essentially repressive' – it is 'a relation between forces'.[123] Foucault is close to Nietzsche, Deleuze observes, in recognising that 'the relation between forces greatly exceeds violence and cannot be defined by the latter'.[124] In the biopolitical regimes identified by Foucault, 'it is indeed life that emerges as the new object of power'.[125] But as Deleuze argues, following Foucault, 'when power in this way takes life as its aim or object, the resistance to power already puts itself on the side of life, and turns life against power [. . .]'.[126] And thus: 'When power becomes bio-power, resistance becomes the power of life, a vital power that cannot be confined within species, environment or the paths of a particular diagram [. . .] Is not life this capacity to resist force?'.[127]

For the captured, captive or domesticated animals living under the biopolitical regimes of the zoo, the farm and the trawler in the films I discuss, options for resistance to power are limited. While I attend to the animals' own gestures of resistance in my readings of the films (such as the horse's suicidal act in *The Turin Horse*), I also seek to delineate how the relation between animal worlds and the virtual realms envisaged by cinema opens up, in *aesthetic* terms, modes of resistance to force. For the realm of the time-image at work in these films ushers in the coexistence of the actual and the virtual – a time of indetermination, differing and becoming, as we have seen. This is the domain of *puissance* (power as potential), distinguished by Deleuze and Guattari, following Spinoza, as something other than the field of power as domination (*pouvoir*). As these films move between the actual and the virtual, they open a time and a space in which to consider the powers and capacities of animal life otherwise, beyond the operations of *pouvoir*. Through the interaction between cinema and life, these films deterritorialise diagrammatic lines of force, gesturing to modes of resistance and possible lines of flight. This recalls what Deleuze and Guattari describe, in reflecting on the place of animals in Kafka, as 'the way out, the line of escape, even if it takes place in place, or in a cage. *A line of escape, and not freedom.*'[128]

This relation between *puissance* and *pouvoir* is evocatively registered by Bailly's reading of a painting by Paolo Uccello, *Hunt in the Forest* (c. 1470). Bailly writes:

> in dark green undergrowth gilded by late-afternoon sunlight, the very flight of the prey (doe of some sort) organizes among the vertical tree trunks the vanishing point, the perspective of *fuite*, as if each animal is producing a link in the very optical network from which it is seeking to escape.[129]

For Bailly, the painting is beautiful because:

> it shows, right in the field of vision (the forest), by way of the animals that have come from there and are trying to return, the full power of what lies outside the field [*la puissance du hors-champ*]: the forest, still, but as a world beyond, a *selva obscura* [. . .] the animals' rightful place, the place where they have shelter and where they are, properly speaking, at home.[130]

Bailly's reading of Uccello's image highlights the way in which, from within a scene of hunting – a saturated field of domination – animal lines of flight can be traced. While the figures of flight (*fuite*) and power (*puissance*) implicitly invoke a Deleuzo-Guattarian context, Bailly's reference to the *hors-champ* (the French term used to designate off-screen space) resonates with the various cinematic inflections that run through his text. In evoking visual articulations – an 'optical network' – of animal lines of flight that emerge from within fields of power (as *pouvoir*), Bailly's reading chimes with my own emphasis in this study. Yet it also implicitly indicates the tensions that will remain at play throughout this study. For these are lines of flight envisaged from within – indeed, *made visible by* – a scene of hunting and violent appropriation, of animal terror and desperation. Such are the tensions at stake in the films I consider: they trace scenes of capture, domestication and instrumentalisation – in the hunt (*Leviathan*), in the zoo (*Bestiaire*), on the farm (*Bovines*, *The Turin Horse*) – while simultaneously registering, 'right in the field of vision', 'the full power of what lies outside the field' – 'a world beyond' (*un outre-monde*).

NOTES

1. Deleuze and Félix Guattari, *A Thousand Plateaus*, p. 261.
2. For example, De Luca describes Bazin as 'an obligatory starting point for meditations on the cinematic animal and film's relationship with the non-human world more generally'. De Luca, 'Natural Views', p. 220.
3. Key exceptions can be found in Bellour, *Le Corps du cinéma*, and Burt, 'Morbidity and Vitalism'.
4. Claire Colebrook, *Gilles Deleuze* (London: Routledge, 2002), p. 30.
5. Baker addresses the concept of becoming-animal in a usefully wide-ranging manner in 'What Does Becoming-Animal Look Like?', in Rothfels (ed.), *Representing Animals*, pp. 67–98.
6. Uexküll, *A Foray into the Worlds of Animals and Humans*, p. 47.
7. Ibid., p. 125.
8. Bailly, *The Animal Side*, p. 48.
9. Buchanan, *Onto-Ethologies*, pp. 25–6. In what follows, I am particularly indebted to Buchanan's study, while drawing also on Ryan's very useful account of animal worlds in Uexküll, Heidegger, Husserl and Merleau Ponty; Ryan, *Animal Theory*, pp. 99–110.
10. Buchanan, *Onto-Ethologies*, p. 25.
11. Crowley, 'The Many Worlds of Jean-Luc Nancy', *Paragraph*, 42:1 (2019), 22–36.
12. Buchanan, *Onto-Ethologies*, p. 23.
13. Senior, Clark and Freccero, 'Editors' Preface: *Ecce animot*', p. 12.
14. Martin Heidegger, *The Fundamental Concepts of Metaphysics: World, Finitude, Solitude*, translated by William McNeill and Nicholas Walker (Bloomington: Indiana University Press, 1995), p. 261.
15. Ryan, *Animal Theory*, p. 104.
16. Heidegger, *The Fundamental Concepts of Metaphysics*, p. 263.
17. Buchanan, *Onto-Ethologies*, p. 38.
18. Ibid., p. 38.
19. Not least because Heidegger claims in his earlier writings (1925–6) that animals do indeed have a world. Buchanan traces a significant shift in Heidegger's thought: 'In 1925, the essential thing is that animals have a world. By 1929, however, the essential thing is that animals are poor-in-world due to their being captivated by their surroundings.' Buchanan, *Onto-Ethologies*, p. 93.
20. Heidegger, *The Fundamental Concepts of Metaphysics*, p. 177; original emphasis.
21. Buchanan, *Onto-Ethologies*, p. 62.
22. Heidegger, *The Fundamental Concepts of Metaphysics*, p. 239; original emphasis.
23. Agamben, *The Open*, p. 51.
24. Heidegger himself claims that the relation between human world-forming and animal poverty in world is non-hierarchical. As Derrida observes, '[t]his is very difficult to defend', given the logic of human exceptionalism that structures Heidegger's thesis. Derrida notes further: 'Heidegger consistently says deliberately contradictory things, namely, that the animal has a world in the mode of "not having."' Derrida, *The Animal That Therefore I Am*, pp. 155–6.
25. Ibid., p. 149. It is also worth noting Derrida's critique of the term 'world' and its conceptualisation as that to which the human has privileged access in *The Beast and the Sovereign*, Vol. 2, pp. 265–6.
26. As Buchanan suggests, Heidegger 'circle[s] continuously' around the question of the animal, '[b]ut when the dizzying ambiguity becomes too vertiginous, Heidegger tends to

pull back, and, just like an intrepid explorer who marks a particular crossing with a flag, he leaves a mark for future retracing: "insoluble difficulty", "enigmatic", "impenetrable", "these questions remain to be asked"'. Buchanan, *Onto-Ethologies*, pp. 88–9.
27. As Jon Roffe and Hannah Stark suggest, Deleuze's approach to the question of the nonhuman can be broadly described as a 'resituation of the human in a univocal ontology, and a concomitant affirmation of the rich plurality within which the human is contextualized'. Roffe and Stark, 'Introduction: Deleuze and the Non/Human', in Roffe and Stark (eds), *Deleuze and the Non/Human*, pp. 1–16 (p. 6).
28. Deleuze, *Spinoza: Practical Philosophy*, translated by Robert Hurley (San Francisco: City Lights Books, 1988), p. 125.
29. Buchanan, *Onto-Ethologies*, p. 6.
30. Ibid., p. 6.
31. Ibid., p. 6.
32. Ibid., p. 100.
33. Deleuze and Guattari, *A Thousand Plateaus*, p. 257.
34. Buchanan, *Onto-Ethologies*, p. 168.
35. Bailly, *The Animal Side*, p. 43.
36. Deleuze and Guattari, *A Thousand Plateaus*, p. 280.
37. Ryan, *Animal Theory*, p. 73. Ryan's comment is in the context of his reflection on forms of 'post-anthropocentric' subjectivity in Braidotti's work.
38. Bednarek, 'The Oedipal Animal?', p. 55.
39. Deleuze and Guattari, *A Thousand Plateaus*, pp. 240–1.
40. Haraway, *When Species Meet*, pp. 27–30. Haraway accuses Deleuze and Guattari of a 'scorn for all that is mundane and ordinary and the profound absence of curiosity about or respect for and with actual animals' (p. 27) – a claim that I test out and challenge at various points in the book, especially in Chapter 3, with reference to their reflections on horses in *A Thousand Plateaus*.
41. Deleuze and Guattari, *A Thousand Plateaus*, p. 241. As Ryan points out, here Deleuze and Guattari are implicitly in dialogue with Bergson, particularly his *Creative Evolution*, in which he seeks to move beyond 'the quantitative classification of animals to an exploration of qualitative differences'; Ryan, *Animal Theory*, p. 60. As Bergson writes: 'There is no manifestation of life which does not contain, in a rudimentary state – either latent or potential – the essential characteristics of most other manifestations.' Bergson, *Creative Evolution*, translated by Arthur Mitchell (New York: Dover, 1998), p. 106.
42. Deleuze and Guattari, *A Thousand Plateaus*, p. 27. This raises questions about whether there is at times a certain neglect of species specificities in Deleuze and Guattari's considerations of animal life. Yet this is to be balanced with moments in which they display an acute attentiveness to species characteristics, for example in their discussion of the bower bird, or 'stagemaker', in *What is Philosophy?*, translated by Graham Burchell and Hugh Tomlinson (London and New York: Verso, 1994), p. 184; I discuss this example in Chapter 5.
43. Ibid., p. 238.
44. Deleuze and Guattari, *Kafka: Toward a Minor Literature*, translated by Dana Polan (Minneapolis: University of Minnesota Press, 1986), p. 22.
45. Deleuze and Guattari, *A Thousand Plateaus*, p. 238.
46. See, for example, Adrian Ivakhiv's discussion of becoming-animal, citing films such as *The Fly* (David Cronenberg, 1986) and *Tropical Malady* (Apichatpong Weerasethakul, 2004), in Ivakhiv, *Ecologies of the Moving Image: Cinema, Affect, Nature* (Waterloo:

Wilfred Laurier University Press, 2013), pp. 239–44. However, this interest in humans mutating into animals diverges from the focus of my study.
47. See, for example, Seung-hoon Jeong and Dudley Andrew, 'Grizzly Ghost: Herzog, Bazin and the Cinematic Animal', *Screen*, 49:1 (2008), 1–12.
48. As exemplified by Haraway's critique. Susan McHugh suggests that Deleuze and Guattari's model of 'becoming-animal' has been 'distorted, even explicitly disowned, within animal studies'; McHugh, *Animal Stories: Narrating Across Species Lines* (Minneapolis: University of Minnesota Press, 2011), p. 13.
49. Deleuze, *Francis Bacon*, p. 21; original emphasis.
50. Deleuze and Guattari, *A Thousand Plateaus*, p. 238.
51. See, for example, Mullarkey, 'Animal Spirits', pp. 15–16; and Bednarek, 'The Oedipal Animal?'.
52. Burt sees Deleuze and Guattari's notion of the animal becoming 'something else' as a usefully asymmetrical approach: 'Such an irreducibility and asymmetry seem crucial within the terms of this vitalist thinking; in other words, to conceive human–animal relations under the rubric "attention to life" would require that this asymmetry be taken into account not as an obstacle, but as the very condition of its representation. The sense of livingness requires the asymmetries of species difference, as it is the obstacles and resistances of this difference that give the necessary "intervals," the signs of life, their shape.' Burt, 'Morbidity and Vitalism', p. 174.
53. Deleuze and Guattari, *A Thousand Plateaus*, p. 238.
54. Buchanan, *Onto-Ethologies*, p. 183.
55. Deleuze and Guattari, *A Thousand Plateaus*, p. 261.
56. Ibid., pp. 540–1n33.
57. Buchanan, *Onto-Ethologies*, pp. 183–4.
58. Ibid., p. 185.
59. Ibid., p. 185.
60. Akira Mizuta Lippit, 'The Death of an Animal', *Film Quarterly*, 56:1 (2002), 9–22 (p. 10).
61. Burt, *Animals in Film*, p. 11.
62. Ibid., p 12.
63. Pick, *Creaturely Poetics*, p. 15.
64. Burt, *Animals in Film*, p. 11.
65. I draw here on material from McMahon, 'Introduction', in McMahon (ed.), 'Screen animals dossier', *Screen*, 56:1 (2015), 81–7 (p. 82).
66. As Mullarkey notes, 'cinematic history displays a persistent recourse to pained and dying animals in films ranging from the sensationalist – *Cannibal Holocaust* (1980); to the artful – *Apocalypse Now* (1979), *Heaven's Gate* (1980), or *Caché* (2005): each record of violence serves to heighten the "authenticity" of their spectacle.' Mullarkey, 'Animal Spirits', p. 21.
67. Shukin, *Animal Capital*, pp. 150–2.
68. On animal death in film, see, for example: Vivian Sobchack, 'Inscribing Ethical Space: Ten Propositions on Death, Representation and Documentary', and 'The Charge of the Real: Embodied Knowledge and Cinematic Consciousness', in *Carnal Thoughts: Embodiment and Moving Image Culture* (Berkeley: University of California Press, 2004), pp. 226–57; pp. 258–85; Lippit, 'The Death of an Animal'; Michael Lawrence, 'Haneke's Stable: the Death of an Animal and the Figuration of the Human', in Brian Price and John David Rhodes (eds), *On Michael Haneke* (Detroit: Wayne State University Press, 2010), pp. 63–84.
69. Sobchack, *Carnal Thoughts*, p. 269.

70. Pick, *Creaturely Poetics*, p. 110.
71. De Luca, 'Natural Views', p. 220.
72. Lippit, 'The Death of an Animal', p. 16.
73. Lippit, *Electric Animal*, p. 165; p. 163.
74. In *The Animal That Therefore I Am*, Derrida critiques a lineage of philosophical thought in which animals have been traditionally denied a relation to death – a denial that reaches its apotheosis in Heidegger's exclusion of the animal from the realm of language and therefore also *Dasein*'s finitude or 'being-towards-death'. See Heidegger, *Being and Time*, translated by John Macquarrie and Edward Robinson (New York: Harper, 1962). Derrida also develops a critique of Heidegger's reflections on animal death, including a deconstruction of the idea that the human might experience death 'as' death; see Derrida, *Aporias*, translated by Thomas Dutoit (Stanford: Stanford University Press, 1993), especially pp. 74–8.
75. Positioning animal death as the real beyond language, Lippit writes: 'If, according to the strained logic of Western metaphysics, the animal cannot die [. . .] then the death of the animal in film, on film, marks a caesura in the flow of that philosophy of being. The animal dies, is seen to die, in a place beyond the reaches of language.' Lippit, 'The Death of an Animal', p. 18.
76. Indeed, Lippit goes as far as to claim that 'cinema is an animal, animality a form of technology, technology an aspect of life'. Ibid., p. 20.
77. Bazin, 'Death Every Afternoon', translated by Mark A. Cohen, in Ivone Margulies (ed.), *Rites of Realism* (Durham, NC: Duke University Press, 2003), pp. 27–31 (p. 30).
78. Bazin writes: 'Animal films reveal the cinema to us.' Bazin, 'Les Films d'animaux nous révèlent le cinéma', *Radio Cinéma Télévision*, 285:2–3 (1955), p. 8; cited in Bellour, *Le Corps du cinéma*, p. 537; translation mine. Serge Daney suggests that for Bazin 'the essence of cinema becomes a story about animals'. Daney, 'The Screen of Fantasy (Bazin and Animals)', translated by Mark A. Cohen, in Margulies (ed.), *Rites of Realism*, pp. 32–41 (p. 32).
79. Bazin, 'De Sica: Metteur en scène', in *What is Cinema?*, Vol. 2, edited and translated by Hugh Gray (Berkeley: University of California Press, 2005), pp. 61–78 (p. 78).
80. Bazin, '*Umberto D*: A Great Work', *What is Cinema?*, Vol. 2, pp. 79–82 (p. 80).
81. Pick, *Creaturely Poetics*, pp. 115–16. The final embedded quotation is from Bazin, 'De Sica', p. 76.
82. '[T]he cinema only attains and constructs its aesthetic time based on lived time, Bergsonian "*durée*", which is in essence irreversible and qualitative.' Bazin, 'Death Every Afternoon', p. 30. C. Scott Combs notes affinities between Bazin and Bergson's notion of *durée*, as well as the 'asymptotic relation of unedited long takes to lived time' that pervades Bazin's work. Combs, *Deathwatch: American Film, Technology, and the End of Life* (New York: Columbia University Press, 2014), p. 16.
83. Conventional readings of Bazin as a naive realist have been questioned; see, for example, Philip Rosen, *Change Mummified: Cinema, Historicity, Theory* (Minneapolis: University of Minnesota Press, 2001).
84. Deleuze, *Cinema 2*, p. 1.
85. On points of convergence between Bazin and Deleuze, see Jon Beasley-Murray, 'Whatever Happened to Neorealism? Bazin, Deleuze and Tarkovsky's Long Take', *Iris*, 23 (Spring 1997), 37–52. As Beasley-Murray observes: 'Each equally offers an anti-representational analysis of the cinema [. . .] in that the cinema viewer is maintained as part of an immanent functional (and corporeal) effect of the film's unfolding through time; the cinema *is* before it *means* or signifies' (p. 39); original emphasis. However, this

article seems to neglect a key point of divergence – Deleuze's shift from 'the real' to thought itself – that I trace here.
86. Deleuze, *Cinema 2*, p. 1.
87. Ibid., p. 1.
88. Ibid., p. 1.
89. Ibid., p. 4.
90. Ibid., p. xii.
91. Ibid., p. 80.
92. Ibid., p. 79.
93. Ibid., p. 79.
94. Ibid., p. 79; original emphasis.
95. Tom Conley, 'The Film Event: From Interval to Interstice', in Gregory Flaxman (ed.), *The Brain is the Screen: Deleuze and the Philosophy of Cinema* (Minneapolis: University of Minnesota Press, 2000), pp. 303–25 (p. 307). In his discussion of 'cinematic world-making', Daniel Yacavone draws on Deleuze's discussion of Welles, Resnais and Robbe-Grillet to point to ways in which '[t]he *same* (or similar) subject, event, or reality' can be 'organized, arranged, and presented in multiple and different ways within the *same* film world [. . .]'. Yacavone, *Film Worlds: A Philosophical Aesthetics of Cinema* (New York: Columbia University Press, 2015), p. 97; original emphasis.
96. Deleuze, *Cinema 2*, p. 38.
97. Colebrook, *Gilles Deleuze*, p. 29.
98. Deleuze, *Cinema 1: The Movement-Image*, translated by Hugh Tomlinson and Barbara Habberjam (London and New York: Continuum), p. 60. As Gregory Flaxman suggests: 'Deleuze begins from an entirely different, acentered, and one could say "nonhuman" perspective within which the human emerges as a center of indetermination. Because this center is not presupposed and does not exist prior to the world, the possibility exists that the cinema may allow us to return to an acentered perception. For this reason, Deleuze constantly gravitates in the cinema books to moments, "as for example in Renoir, when the camera leaves a character," because such moments reveal a movement-image unfastened from any center of action. This cleavage of camera and character (center) suggests the way the cinema surpasses human perception [. . .].' Flaxman, 'Cinema Year Zero', in Flaxman (ed.), *The Brain is the Screen*, pp. 87–108 (p. 96).
99. Colebrook, *Gilles Deleuze*, p. 30.
100. Deleuze, *Cinema 2*, p. 103.
101. Colebrook, *Gilles Deleuze*, p. 42.
102. Ibid.
103. Deleuze, *Cinema 2*, p. 56.
104. Ibid., p. 57.
105. Ibid., p. 99.
106. As Buchanan puts it, Uexküll seeks to '*multiply* the world into infinite animal environments'. Buchanan, *Onto-Ethologies*, p. 2; my emphasis.
107. See also Pick's discussion of 'the worldhood (*Weltlichkeit*) of film' and 'the ways in which films construct their own worlds' (in her 'Three Worlds: Dwelling and Worldhood on Screen', in Pick and Narraway, *Screening Nature*, pp. 21–36 (p. 21)), as well as her suggestion elsewhere that: 'As a capturing and enframing device, cinema is both a revealer and creator of worlds. This "worlding" function, to use Donna Haraway's term in another context, allows cinema to actively make (or make up) multiple worlds that for Bailly come into being at the point of liminal difference between human and nonhuman being, where an opening is present at the very point of hermetic enclosure.'

Pick, 'Reflexive Realism in René Clément's *Forbidden Games*', p. 217. Relevant here too is Ivakhiv's discussion of cinema as '*cosmomorphic*', as 'a form of world-production'. Ivakhiv, *Ecologies of the Moving Image*, p. 6; original emphasis.
108. Pick, 'Animal Life in the Cinematic Umwelt', p. 222.
109. Ibid., p. 223.
110. Drawing on the work of Elizabeth Grosz (which is in turn inspired by Deleuze), De Luca and Jorge suggest that '[d]urational slowness' can be 'a means to ponder over the co-existence of multiple temporalities', including 'what it means to live in the midst of today's wildly entangled temporal configurations as well as non-human conceptions of time'. De Luca and Jorge, 'Introduction', p. 15.
111. Colebrook, *Gilles Deleuze*, p. 31; original emphasis.
112. Ibid., p. 31.
113. Ibid.; original emphasis. As noted above, along with Bellour, Burt is one of the few scholars to date to have offered a sustained reading of relations between Deleuze, animals and film. Drawing on both Bergson and Deleuze, Burt writes of the ways in which cinematic time interacts with the emergence of life, or 'livingness': 'Film makes livingness apparent to us in some of its most important forms as a temporal, material state that is felt or perceived by the intervals among beings.' Burt, 'Morbidity and Vitalism', p. 179. Burt's emphasis on the interval or spacing between beings seems to dovetail with Deleuze's focus (in the comments I cite above) on cinema's opening beyond a subjective point of view.
114. We might also note how in Uexküll's *A Foray into the Worlds of Animals and Humans*, the drawings of objects perceived from different (animal and human) points of view work to actualise worlds, to subjectivise them, fixing each image as viewed from a particular perspective. Deleuze's approach, by contrast, seeks to move beyond such subjectivisation and fixing of images.
115. Deleuze, *Cinema 2*, p. 98.
116. Colebrook, *Gilles Deleuze*, p. 53.
117. Ibid., p. 53.
118. Though differentiated from the 'actual' in Deleuze, the virtual is not to be understood as in opposition to the 'real' (though it clearly contrasts with representational 'realism', as we have seen). See Keith Ansell-Pearson, 'The Reality of the Virtual', *MLN*, 120:5 (2005), 1112–27. My approach here appears to intersect with Ansell-Pearson's observation that Deleuze 'wants to show that there is a being of the virtual which, although peculiar to a complex, individuated form of life such as us, is not reducible to a psychological consciousness' (p. 1120).
119. Burt, *Animals in Film*, p. 44.
120. Ibid., pp. 140–1.
121. Ibid., p. 30.
122. Cora Diamond, 'The Difficulty of Reality and the Difficulty of Philosophy', *Partial Answers: Journal of Literature and the History of Ideas*, 1:2 (2003), 1–26 (p. 3); J. M. Coetzee, *The Lives of Animals*, edited by Amy Gutmann (Princeton: Princeton University Press, 1999).
123. Deleuze, *Foucault*, pp. 59–60.
124. Ibid., p. 59.
125. Ibid., p. 76.
126. Ibid., p. 76.
127. Ibid., p. 77.
128. Deleuze and Guattari, *Kafka*, p. 35; original emphasis.
129. Bailly, *The Animal Side*, p. 7.
130. Ibid., p. 7.

CHAPTER 2

Still/Moving: *Bestiaire*'s Lives in Limbo

Horses congregate outside a snow-covered shed in winter, moving slowly in and out of the static frame. A white bull with curved horns stares at the camera. A young gazelle moves frantically in circles in a confined space indoors. A macaque, glimpsed through blurred lines of wire meshing, sits in a tyre swing. A lion, mostly obscured by bars, bangs on a cage door.

Denis Côté's *Bestiaire* (2012) largely takes place at the Parc Safari in Hemmingford, Quebec. Through a series of static long takes, it presents the zoo without any voiceover commentary or interviews, focusing predominantly on the animals kept there but also a handful of zookeepers, workers and visitors. The film's structure loosely follows the zoo's seasonal cycle: it begins in the winter months, with animals indoors or outside in the snow, and progresses to the summer months constituting the zoo's peak season.[1] But as *Bestiaire* moves episodically from one tableau to another, time drifts: as Deleuze writes of the time-image, 'situations no longer extend into action or reaction in accordance with the requirements of the movement-image'.[2] Cinematic time is left to wander in ways that allow the film to attend patiently to the situatedness of the animals onscreen (their gestures, their movements) and the interplay between the animals and their environment. In this way, from within the constricted spaces of the zoo and the flattened contours of the film's static frames, *Bestiaire* opens up questions about the affective and perceptive worlds of its animals.

While *Bestiaire* is shot mostly in the zoo, it also includes a sequence at a taxidermist. In reflecting on the display of animals both living and dead, still and moving, the film thus mobilises two key metaphors – cinema as zoo, and cinema as taxidermy – that seem to function, in a heightened mode of self-reflexivity, to probe the ontology of film. *Bestiaire* seems in thrall to Bazin's idea that the onscreen animal reveals cinematic specificity:[3] on one level, rather like Nicolas Philibert's *Nénette* (2010), a documentary about an orangutan in the menagerie at the Jardin des Plantes in Paris, *Bestiaire* is a film about looking, and about film spectatorship in particular. Côté suggests that 'the project proposed itself as a will to look, to show without telling'.[4] Yet folded into this set of ontological reflections is an implicit questioning of the politics of the zoo, which manifests itself in *Bestiaire* through various strategies of framing and 'witnessing'. These strategies constitute the political impetus of the film as it poses questions about zoo biopower and neocolonialism, captivity and suffering. *Bestiaire* pulls awkwardly in these different directions, reflecting on the zoo both as a set of material conditions in which these animals live and as a metaphor for cinematic animality *qua* cinematic specificity. Yet *Bestiaire* also extends beyond this potential conflation of cinema and the animal: through the 'pure optical and sound situations' of its time-images, the film invites spectatorial attunement to nonhuman perceptual and affective worlds in ways that cannot be reduced to an ontological convergence of cinema and the animal. What I want to argue here is that *Bestiaire*'s static framing of docile bodies, which works to reflect the biopolitical regime of the zoo, also opens up modes of worlding, becoming and, to invoke Bailly, 'pensivity'. *Bestiaire* thus explores two different concepts of life: the 'bare life' of zoopolitics and the animal worlds that expand, and make meaning, beyond this.

AESTHETICS AND POLITICS

Bestiaire is fascinated by notions of animal visibility and exhibition as they emerge through an interplay between the cinema and the zoo.[5] In interview, Côté suggests that 'the zoo is a very, very cinematic place',[6] gesturing to parallels between these two visual institutions and technologies. As Sabine Nessel argues, the cinema and the zoo both came to the fore in the nineteenth century as technologies of putting life on display, institutionalising (predominantly voyeuristic) ways of looking at animals.[7] In our contemporary era, moving images of animals are ubiquitous, particularly on video-sharing platforms such as YouTube. As Pick suggests: 'Now, more than ever before, zoos converge with and complement a plethora of media platforms of wildlife exhibits, primarily in film and television.'[8] Pick's argument is informed here by Berger's well-known essay, 'Why Look at Animals?', in which he discusses the disappearance of animals from public life in modernity and their increasing relegation to the representational realms of '[z]oos, realistic animal toys and the widespread commercial diffusion of animal imagery'.[9] Though Berger's essay has been critiqued for its nostalgic romanticisation of premodern human–animal relations and its reductive account of the complexities of animal visibility,[10] his argument about the increasing spectacularisation of animals remains compelling. As Pick suggests:

> It is difficult [. . .] to ignore the inverse relation between diminishing wildlife and animals' enhanced visual presence. Fussed over, tagged, screened, projected, and surveyed, exhibited, simulated, incarcerated, conserved, even manufactured and invented, nature and animals are gaining an exclusive kind of cultural visibility.[11]

Côté is clearly sensitive to these contemporary contexts of heightened visibility and the increasing dissemination of animal images across various media platforms. Speaking of our 'mania for anthropomorphising', he gestures to a saturation of the visual field by representations of animals: 'We've seen everything.' *Bestiaire* is motivated, he suggests, by 'an attempt at rejecting anthropomorphism'. The film seeks to ask, he says: 'Is it still possible today to film animals in an original way?'; 'Is it possible to film an animal for what it is: an animal?'.[12] This idea of the 'unmediated' animal – in the zoo, on film – is an impossible fantasy,[13] yet Côté's comments usefully signal a desire to move beyond more mainstream forms of animal representation.

In 'The Animal Equation', an essay published in *Cinema Scope* in 2012, Côté positions *Bestiaire* as an intervention in a cultural field of animal representation dominated by YouTube videos and nature documentaries:

> where is the salvation between the puppies on YouTube and a boa constrictor's reproductive cycle narrated in eight chapters? How should one look at an animal (and find a cinematic language specific to this act)? Is it possible to shoot animals other than through the lens of entertainment or for a non-educational purpose? Neither actor nor story catalyzer, cannot an animal be contemplated and filmed simply for what it is?[14]

Côté positions *Bestiaire* as a search for a mode of presentation that might bear witness to animals beyond the usual trappings of spectacle, narrative and 'psychologisation'.[15] He writes of being inspired by other works of 'contemplative cinema', citing a range of influences, from Robert Bresson's *Au hasard Balthazar* (1966)[16] and Artavazd Pelechian's *The Seasons* (1975), to Geyrhalter's *Our Daily Bread* (2005) and *Abendland* (2011), Castaing-Taylor and Barbash's *Sweetgrass* (2009), Frammartino's *Le Quattro Volte* (2010) and Gras's *Bovines* (2011).[17] Côté is less approving of Philibert's *Nénette*: 'the orangutan serves to reveal the comments and reflections of those who paid a sum to temporarily flee the boredom of their human condition'.[18] Yet, though it is without the off-screen voices deployed by Philibert, *Bestiaire* is perhaps closer to *Nénette* – and to the scenes of taxidermy in Philibert's accompanying film, *Animals* (1996) – than Côté may wish to admit, particularly in its use of long takes and 'dead time' (to which I return below).[19]

However, while these films by Philibert sit fairly comfortably in the category of documentary, the status of *Bestiaire* is perhaps more ambiguous. Côté describes the film as 'experimental', rejecting terms such as 'documentary' or 'cinéma vérité' as 'romantic', explaining that he is not interested in a faithfulness to reality; indeed, at one point in interview, he describes *Bestiaire* as 'fiction'.[20] His commitment to troubling the boundaries of documentary is evidenced by previous works such as *Carcasses* (2009), a film detailing the daily routine of a man who collects old cars; the film disrupts its documentary, observational approach with narrative, fictional elements, when a group of young people turn up unexpectedly in the car yard. *Bestiaire* contains less overtly fictionalised aspects. Yet the film's static framing, which it shares with *Carcasses*, connotes a stylised approach, which is further underscored by the sense that some of these scenes are staged, particularly those in which the animals stare directly at the camera (I return to these scenes below). In interview, Côté emphasises other dimensions of stylisation, describing *Bestiaire*'s soundtrack as 'very manipulated'.[21] This suggests, for example, that the loud clanking sounds evoking gates closing shut, and accompanying a number of the scenes of animals indoors, may be extradiegetic. Such sounds invoke forms of imprisonment, gesturing to a critique of these spaces of confinement. Yet, while Côté reports that *Bestiaire* is often received by audiences as a critique of the zoo, he has been keen in interviews to emphasise the film's neutral stance towards its subject matter: 'I didn't want to make a manifesto against the zoo';[22] '*Bestiaire* takes pleasure in being neither for nor against – in just being.'[23] What principally motivates the film, he says, is a sense in which 'the zoo is above all a place shaped by a dimension of absurdity.' For Côté, the film elaborates what he calls a 'mechanics of the absurd' rather than any particular 'argument' or 'judgment'.[24]

Indeed, in many ways, *Bestiaire* seems more interested in aesthetics than politics, privileging in particular the 'cinematic' quality of the animals and their surroundings through a self-consciously stylised, formalist presentation of bodies in space. Recounting the development of his ideas for the film, Côté remarks: 'in the beginning there was a purely aesthetic desire to create cinema'.[25] The first two images introducing the Parc Safari are noticeably devoid of animals. The first image shows a corrugated metal wall, the shot held long enough to observe steam emerging from the building (as though distilling the basic element of cinema itself: movement). The second shot is similarly mundane, framing a snow-covered road lined by a fence. Both shots instantiate a pattern of horizontal and vertical lines and a subdued colour scheme of cold grey and blue that will be repeated throughout the film. The animals finally 'arrive' in the third shot, which frames a group of wildebeest in a fenced area outside. The delayed 'reveal' of the living animal has encouraged the viewer to attend first and foremost to the *mise-en-scène* – to the environment of the zoo, its colours, its shapes.[26]

This formal attentiveness to colour and shape continues in the following scene with the wildebeest. The distant framing, the 'crepuscular' light and subdued colour palette encourage visual indistinction between the dark hairy bodies of the animals.[27] As their bodies seem to merge, they become dark, almost abstract shapes. A few scenes later, a group of horses – starkly shot against frost-covered corrugated metal, the whiteness of their manes echoing that of the frost – move in and out of frame: as the static shot registers the spatial interplay and visual overlapping of bodies, the animals lower their heads out of frame, becoming anonymous shapes, colours, movements. *Bestiaire* returns compulsively to this figure of the animal as abstract shape – perhaps most strikingly in the image of a row of antlers (the rest of the animals' heads and bodies, huddled in an indoor space, are out of frame). The elegant curved shapes of the antlers overlap, visually intertwining, gently shifting. Such moments suggest that the film is shaped above all by an interest in plasticity and formal patterns:[28] to some extent, animal images become merely matter to be manipulated.[29] And on this reading, the zoo simply offers the film a self-reflexive opportunity to reflect on, as one review puts it, 'the figure of the cinematic frame as a virtual prison'.[30] This might seem, on one level, incompatible with political critique. There is certainly a risk of abstraction here, and of tensions between Côté's avowed intention 'to film the animals as they are' and his pursuit of an overtly stylised cinematic formalism.

Yet a history of experimental filmmaking reminds us that formalism and political engagement are far from mutually exclusive. *Bestiaire*'s durational aesthetic and 'exaggerated focus on apparently mundane details of reality' echoes in particular the 'dry, cumulative intensity' of long, static shots in works such as *Jeanne Dielman, 23 quai du Commerce, 1080 Bruxelles* (1975), Akerman's study of a (fictional) woman's daily domestic, affective and sexual labour.[31] As in *Jeanne Dielman*, *Bestiaire* deploys extended takes in order to reflect on lived time, routine and a particular kind of imprisonment. Both films draw cinematic time into a project of estrangement and critical reflection, and like Akerman's 'antinaturalistic' approach, *Bestiaire* introduces a 'distancing effect' through 'the excess of detail resulting from a fixed stare'.[32] Yet, as Margulies suggests of Akerman, this is more than a question of formal estrangement:

> Within the minimalist mise-en-scene and under the camera's fixed stare, specific profilmic elements become heightened foci: the sound of footsteps, soapsuds, a reddish wrapping paper. The effect is more than a feeling of formal estrangement: the sharpened materiality of cinematic elements such as light, pattern, and color suggests the 'existential' materiality of a character's environment.[33]

In *Bestiaire*, the heightened 'materiality' of light, pattern, colour and sound similarly works to foreground the 'existential' situation of these bodies, these lives. The film makes stubbornly material the environment of the zoo, persistently focusing on the concrete walls, bars and fences framing the various enclosures. As Gailleurd suggests: 'Everything emphasises a carceral space: the omnipresence of bars, the predominance of grey colours and the confined spaces in which the animals collide with one another'.[34] The carceral logic of the zoo's own *mise-en-scène* arguably makes it impossible for the film to separate aesthetics and politics. But it is above all the heightened materiality at work in *Bestiaire*, foregrounded through the extended duration of the camera's 'fixed stare', that allows the referentiality of these images – particularly the conditions of captivity – to come to the fore.[35]

Bestiaire's strategy of defamiliarisation, its emphasis on a 'mechanics of the absurd', thus appears to function, despite Côté's claims to the contrary, as a form of political critique. It does this, on one level, by raising questions about the histories and modes of animal display with which the film is simultaneously fascinated. In line with the tradition of the bestiary, the film presents a cornucopia of different animal species, including lions, tigers, wolves, hyenas, bears, macaques, wildebeest, antelope, llamas, zebras, Watusi cattle and ostriches. In so doing, *Bestiaire* instantiates a cataloguing of animal bodies that recalls traditions of animal collection and menageries. As Yi-Fu Tuan suggests, in the nineteenth century a menagerie was a powerful expression of imperialism, 'a tool of high civilisation, combining the desire for order with the desire to accommodate the heterogeneous and the exotic'.[36] In presenting such a range of non-native species, many of them collected from Africa, *Bestiaire* evokes this imperialist ordering and display of 'the heterogeneous and the exotic'. Indeed, the tagline on Parc Safari's website – 'Africa in the heart of Quebec' – signals the neocolonialist dimensions of this zoo in particular. If, as Randy Malamud suggests, a zoo animal 'semiotically describes a power relationship between the spectator and the culture from which the animal was taken', connoting an opposition between 'advanced' and 'primitive' cultures,[37] then Parc Safari's spectacular staging of the 'exotic' suggests forms of neoimperialist exhibition (in excess of the conservationist and educational values that the zoo ostensibly promotes). *Bestiaire* accentuates these neocolonial dimensions through its serial construction: presenting the animals within a range of *tableaux vivants*, the film contributes to a sense of cataloguing and collection, evoking an imperialist, scopophilic ordering of animal life.

Yet the zoo's taxonomical drive is undercut by *Bestiaire*'s withholding of information about the animals onscreen. The lack of voiceover or any other informational cues hinders identification of the animals, certainly the less well-known species. This strategy of not identifying what we see works against documentary's general 'epistephilia'.[38] It also subverts the informative and educational framing of conventional wildlife film and the putative pedagogical mission of the zoo itself. As Malamud suggests: 'Historically, the zoo had presented itself as a scientific archive [. . .] Scientific compendia of animals bestow a sense – a false sense – of ownership, control, mastery over nature.'[39] Interrupting the logic of the scientific compendia, and undermining positions of knowledge, *Bestiaire* works against the viewer's mastery of these animal presences onscreen. What we see and hear cannot simply be reduced to a taxonomy of species. Our attention is thus directed elsewhere, beyond a concern with identificatory categories and towards the material situatedness – in space and time – of the animals onscreen.

REALM OF WITNESSING

Though Côté rejects a description of *Bestiaire* as an observational documentary, the film's strategy of mute observation resonates in particular with Frederick Wiseman's documentaries, particularly his explorations of the institutionalisation of animal life in *Primate* (1974) and *Zoo* (1993).[40] In her reading of Wiseman's *Primate*, a documentary observing laboratory practices at the Yerkes National Primate Research Centre in Atlanta, Pick reflects on the function of the lack of voiceover: the film '*refuses to speak*'; it belongs to 'the realm of *witnessing*'.[41] Pick argues that *Primate* reveals a traumatic dimension by privileging acts of bearing witness over verbal exposition: the absence of any rationalising voiceover allows the violent irrationality of what we see to come into focus.[42] Such a reading is also apt for Wiseman's *Zoo*, which presents without voiceover, among various events, the castration of a wolf and the post-mortem dissection of a stillborn rhinoceros calf. What *Primate* and *Zoo* reveal about the penetrative workings of biopower occupies the realm of the violent and the traumatic more overtly than what we see of the lives of animals in *Bestiaire*; however, Côté's film also denies the rationalising power of a human (and humanist) commentary, allowing the film to inhabit a 'realm of *witnessing*', as it works implicitly to reveal links between zoo space, biopolitics, power and violence.

Modern biopower, as Foucault argues, moves beyond the disciplining of individual bodies ('anatomo-politics') and extends to a management of life as species (biopolitics).[43] The modern zoo combines these dimensions, enacting both the anatomo-political disciplining of animal bodies (through, for example, caging and surveillance) and the production and management of life as species (via breeding and birth control, for instance). However, in the context of modern ethological standards, the biopolitical management of animals is less legible because, as Shukin notes, modern biopower 'denounces physical violence and operates, instead, through sympathetic investments in animal communication'.[44] While *Bestiaire* displays no physical violence as such, through scenes such as those of zookeepers feeding animals and children petting fawns, the film captures the kind of 'sympathetic animal management' and 'fervor for interspecies intimacy' that are the embodiments of modern biopower applied to animal life.[45] Some animals in *Bestiaire* express overt physical resistance – for example, the lion violently rattling and banging against the door of a cage. Yet much of the film focuses on what Shukin calls the 'obedient body content' upon which the zoo's regime of biopolitical management, spectacle and profit relies.[46] In one scene, bears stand on their hind-legs as a zookeeper throws food towards them, her hand playfully circling as she takes aim; while the image recalls a cruel history of dancing bears, the obedience on display – and the proximity of the zookeeper (with no substantial fence for protection) – marks out the status of the animals as 'docile bodies'.[47] Another scene, accompanied by the sounds of a fair offscreen, shows an elephant dutifully carrying an adult and three children (while one of the children pulls a face at the camera). Here the application of biopower is implicitly linked to 'entertainment capital' in ways that echo through the film: belying the zoo's conservationist ethos, animals become 'subject to biopower, to forms of positive economic and emotional investment designed to mold them into docile, willing performers of capitalist spectacles'.[48]

Relations between anatomo-politics, vision and technology are signalled explicitly by the surveillance camera images of cages shown briefly in the film at one point. *Bestiaire* emphasises the ways in which the zoo entails for animals what Bailly describes as an 'exile in visibility'.[49] In *Bestiaire*, this 'exile' is foregrounded in particular by scenes featuring glass tunnels in which visitors stand in order to view lions and tigers from various angles. The zoo's website advertises a fantasy of omnipotent vision: 'The glass tunnels are designed so that you can watch these majestic felines from three different angles – above, beside and below – for an experience you'll never forget.'[50] As one lion, asleep, lies on top of a glass tunnel while visitors take pictures below, we are reminded of the ways in which the privacy of zoo animals is perpetually denied, their bodies made endlessly available to sight.

Yet, counteracting the totalising gaze of zoo surveillance and capitalist spectacle, *Bestiaire* unfolds an implicit ethically and politically questioning vision. The film adopts modes of visual fragmentation throughout, interrupting the smooth visual consumption of species that the zoo's own conditions of display typically invite. *Bestiaire*'s images are frequently striated by cage bars and wire meshes. While the framing of the image accentuates the confines of zoo space, fragmentary close-ups, positioning the animals only partially within the frame, suggest the decontextualisation of the animal, a displacement from natural habitats, a truncation of life-worlds. This visual strategy of decentring the animal literalises Berger's reading of the position of the zoo visitor:

'*you are looking at something that has been rendered absolutely marginal*; and all the concentration you can muster will never be enough to centralise it.'[51] The film's aesthetic of visual fragmentation is reminiscent of the photographic work of Britta Jaschinski, particularly her series *Zoo* (1996), which deploys, as Malamud describes it, 'blurry, dark images of caged animals, chopped and cropped out of her photographic frame to signify their cultural dismemberment'.[52] As Malamud suggests, 'Jaschinski shows us that animals are misplaced, and displaced, in our sight lines.'[53] In many of *Bestiaire*'s scenes, animals are similarly misplaced, displaced and decentred. One image shows just the top of a tiger's head; the ear sits in the lower half of the frame. In another scene, we see in close-up several pairs of antlers moving but no heads. Later, paws appear through a wire mesh where a man is feeding apples to monkeys, yet the paws are all we see of the animals. Accompanying this scene are incongruous sounds of howling offscreen, as though the film has temporarily entered the realm of horror. While sounds intimate terror, the visual emphasis on physical barriers between humans and animals works to foreground not only the anatomo-political disciplining of bodies but also the biopolitical governing of species borders. *Bestiaire*'s ethical and political vision lies implicitly in the ways in which it makes manifest such framing, disciplining and governing.

While reflecting metaphorically on what Malamud calls the 'cultural dismemberment' of zoo animals, *Bestiaire*'s visual fragmentation of the animal body evokes more literal forms of dismemberment, anticipating the disembodied animal heads and other body parts that we will see in the film's taxidermy sequence. In visually articulating links between the zoo cage and the

Figure 2.1 The animal displaced (*Bestiaire*).

taxidermist's table, *Bestiaire* signals the workings of biopower – '*the right to make live and let die*'.[54] What we witness in *Bestiaire*'s zoo spaces are images of lives suspended, in limbo. *Bestiaire* attends to beings made to survive yet reduced to 'bare life', a drastically eroded state of existence.[55] *Bestiaire*'s durational aesthetic is key to this elucidation of biopolitical suspension. Its long takes interrupt the accelerated visual consumption of animal life associated both with zoo spectatorship[56] and wildlife film and television; the lack of focus on 'charismatic' animal activity confounds narrative conventions of animal film spectatorship in particular.[57] Often framing inactive animals, such as the baby llama near the end of the film, who stands completely still, *Bestiaire* reveals the torpor of the zoo.[58] Occupying a 'realm of *witnessing*', *Bestiaire* focuses on animals *enduring* time, on lives suspended in captivity. In this sense, it reveals biopolitical violence as 'constituted by the power to keep animal life in a limbo economy of interminable survival'.[59] Here cinema discloses something of the time of that interminable survival, of the relentless duration of being made to live.

Bestiaire's investment in apparently 'dead time', in banality, and in the apparently directionless gestures and wanderings of captive animals, recalls the 'everyday situations' of modern cinema from which Deleuze sees the time-image emerging. If the 'insignificant', mundane gestures documented by Italian neorealism, and exemplified by the maid in De Sica's *Umberto D.* (1952), can be understood as 'pure optical situations', as Deleuze suggests, then *Bestiaire* offers a non-anthropocentric reworking of this investment in the uneventful time of the everyday:

> In everyday banality, the action-image and even the movement-image tend to disappear in favour of pure optical situations, but these reveal connections of a new type, which are no longer sensory-motor and which bring the emancipated senses into direct relation with time and thought.[60]

For Deleuze, such moments in film often reveal something 'intolerable which is simply [. . .] everydayness itself'.[61] This intolerability is at stake in *Bestiaire*, as the film tracks affects of boredom, disorientation and distress among the zoo's inhabitants. The interminable duration of captivity is starkly communicated by such moments as the lion violently rattling the door of a cage or the young gazelle moving frantically in circles (as seen above). Yet it is also made felt – more subtly, more mundanely – by other gestures: the repetitive motion of a llama trotting to and fro (framed by fences and electricity pylons); an ape sitting on a bridge, looking listless (while two visitors embrace in the background); a bird with only one wing, pacing back and forth in a cage, trying in vain, in the cramped space, to extend the wing (while a mirror in the cage, to which the bird turns, threatens to evoke the question of animal self-reflection).

These images of listlessness, boredom and entropy remind us of *Nénette*, while also evoking the threat of unstructured time that Doane detects in early cinema.[62] Here, as Deleuze puts it, beings are 'condemned to wander about'; 'the sensory-motor schema is no longer in operation [. . .] [i]t is shattered from the inside'.[63] Through static poses and repetitive rhythms, *Bestiaire* puts the viewer's senses 'into direct relation with time and thought', the cumulative intensity of its time-images staking out the everyday in all its intolerability.

Yet *Bestiaire*'s attachment to dead time needs to be read not only via the time-images of modern(ist) cinema but also in relation to contemporary media contexts, particularly cultures of viewing animals online. As Burke has suggested, *Bestiaire*'s 'fixed camera perspectives' and extended takes evoke the primary characteristics of ZooCam live feeds; like the ZooCam, *Bestiaire* offers predominantly dead time, uneventfulness and de-dramatisation.[64] However, as Burke points out, ZooCam viewing tends to be habitually part of an online culture in which spectatorial attention is radically dispersed: 'such viewing usually takes place as part of an array of digital activities'.[65] Though of course not always viewed at the cinema, *Bestiaire* imposes extended duration in a way that marks it out as different from the intermittent 'checking in' that typically characterises a viewer's relationship to the ZooCam live feed.[66] Inadvertently or not, *Bestiaire* taps into this post-televisual mode of watching animals doing very little (and in this sense it evokes 'the latent presence of one regime of expression in another' that Rancière sees as characteristic of the 'pensive image').[67] But *Bestiaire* imposes time on the viewer in ways that are distinct: it uses cinematic duration (and enduring), and the possibility of spectatorial boredom, in order to allow for the dead time of the lives that it frames to be sensed.[68]

STILL / MOVING

Bestiaire's reflections on lives in limbo, on stillness and movement, and on visual dismemberment, culminate in the extended sequence set in the taxidermist's practice (positioned in the middle of the film). Here the film reflects on a mode of animal display that relies on the petrification of the animal body yet also the mimesis of livingness. As such, this sequence engages self-reflexively with the stakes of the film's own project of putting life on display, in particular the static framing that brings a dimension of immobility to every living body that it exhibits. Yet in the taxidermy sequence, *Bestiaire* also invites critical reflection on the stakes of the zoo's project of animal visibility – taxidermy is thought through here as the horrifying apotheosis of the 'obedient body content' of public zoos, and thus part of the biopolitical regimes governing animal life and death, and the 'interminable survival' of animals produced by biopower, that the film implicitly questions.[69] *Bestiaire* invites us to read the zoo in taxidermic terms from the opening scene set in the art class, in which students sketch a taxidermied deer. These sequences at the art class and at the taxidermist's work to activate further relations between vision, animal bodies and the intertwined histories of cinema and taxidermy. As 'a primary technology for making creaturely life visible', taxidermy played a key role in developments in natural history in the eighteenth and nineteenth centuries, offering a form of visual realism that anticipated the advent of photography and cinema.[70] These visual technologies share an archival function as well: Haraway describes taxidermy as a 'craft of remembering'.[71] Like cinema, taxidermy preserves and reanimates animal being. Unlike taxidermy, however, cinema does not necessarily rely on the death of the animal.

The lengthy taxidermy sequence is meticulously attentive to the details of the taxidermist's labour, laying bare the illusion of liveness that the stuffed animal supposedly connotes. We see the hands of two taxidermists at work on dead animal bodies: fur is scraped away, and bloodied bones and limbs are exposed, inviting uncanny associations between taxidermy and meat-eating. Though these animal bodies are inanimate, tactile close-ups persist in evoking – however counter-intuitively – a sense of corporeal vulnerability. The sequence reveals the various stages of the preparation of a bird in particular: the pelt and feathers are pulled down over a polyurethane foam model; the bird's skull is attached with a long pin; the feathers are blow-dried and preened. Putting the finishing touches to his model, the taxidermist turns the bird around to face the camera; glassy eyes look directly at the camera. Slightly shuddering at first from the gesture of the taxidermist's hands, the bird's body then comes to a standstill – a transition from moving to still that redoubles the animal's petrification. Yet this is arguably an instance of 'botched taxidermy' (to invoke Steve Baker's term): the film has rendered the animal too *'abrasively visible'*; it has shown us too much.[72] At the same time, its invocation of corporeal vulnerability, fleshed out by the tactile close-ups, threatens to unsettle the human–animal boundary on which the practice of taxidermy relies.[73]

Yet while playing with these ambiguities, the sequence posits the taxidermied animal as a privileged figure through which cinema might self-reflexively attend to its own mode of re-presenting and reanimating the living. Recalling the presence of taxidermied animals in the natural history museum in Chris Marker's *La Jetée* (1962), and their connection to the film's broader reflections on stillness and movement, time and memory, and the ontology of film itself,[74] here petrified animal bodies are central to *Bestiaire*'s investigation of cinema's being. Yet, in contrast to *La Jetée*, *Bestiaire* needs its animals to be moving as well as still in order to probe cinematic essence. The film explores the interlocked relations between animal *kinesis* and cinematic animation in a striking scene featuring zebras. In a medium shot, a group of zebras move agitatedly in a small enclosed space; seemingly panicked, they push into one another with increasing force and aggression, their legs scrabbling. Clanking sounds offscreen contribute again to a sense of imprisonment. The scene cuts to a static close-up focusing on the frantic movement of their legs; objects in the foreground, at either side of the frame, narrow the field of vision. Zebra legs flit back and forth in a blur of animal motion, as though suddenly disconnected from the rest of their bodies, recalling the aesthetic of dismemberment and fragmentation at work in other scenes. The focus on the movement of animal legs recalls Muybridge's protocinematic studies of animal motion and his well-known series of horse movement in particular. By representing animal movement as a series of static frames, and by measuring that movement through a system of numbered scales and grids, Muybridge sought to dissect and master animal motion; photography configured the animal body as an object of knowledge.[75] *Bestiaire* simultaneously recalls Muybridge's photographic studies and troubles this inheritance. It offers bodily fragments rather than whole bodies, and the zebras' movements are so frantic that, apart from a brief moment in which their legs come to a standstill, these blurred images defy measurement and mastery. The positioning of the animal as an object of (taxonomical) knowledge is undercut. Blurred and confusing, these images move beyond the sphere of epistemological inquiry into the realm of visual hypnotics, recalling Bellour's exploration of the relations between cinema, hypnotism and animal motion. In his reading of Hitchcock's *The Birds* (1963), Bellour is interested in the intimation of stillness in the midst of animal motion: the bird wings beating frantically figure 'the indivisible but perceptible intervals' of illusory cinematic motion (that is, motion reliant on still photographic images) with terrifying, hypnotic effects.[76] Bellour draws attention to the stilled image at the heart of animal motion onscreen – though he does not articulate it in such terms, his reflections frame moving images of animals as shaped by a taxidermic unconscious, a will to stillness masked by the liveliness of animal motion.

Bestiaire's blur of animal movement similarly invokes a taxidermic unconscious – in the stopping and starting legs of the zebras, and in the scene's appeal to a photographic history of the animal, one senses 'the indivisible but perceptible intervals' of Muybridgean optics, and of stillness within motion. This taxidermic unconscious extends to the following scene, which cuts directly to an image of corrugated iron, before an ostrich head bobs into view. Setting up a clear visual resonance between zebra stripes and corrugated iron – between the animate and the inanimate – through the doubled pattern of striated lines, the cut itself is taxidermic, stilling animal bodies while visually invoking a human predilection for curating and coordinating animal patterns and skins. The formal patterning effected by the cut, and the ontological reflections suggested by the preceding scene, sit uneasily with what we might read as the uncertainty, panic, even terror of the zebras. Yet this sequence holds these ontological, aesthetic, affective and political threads together, in tension. Here

Bestiaire reveals a fascination with animal movement and the animal origins of cinema that coexists with a set of implicit reflections on the brutalising effects of animal captivity.

THE TELEPATHIC LOOK

Bestiaire's exploration of cinematic ontology comes to the fore above all in the film's obsessive return to the motif of the animal look. Several sequences show animals, including cattle and antelope, looking directly and (mostly) soundlessly at the camera. The images are striking, particularly as the animals are usually positioned centrally within the frame. If, for Berger, the zoo visitor looks upon '*something that has been rendered absolutely marginal*', *Bestiaire* attempts, in these scenes, to retrieve that 'something' from the margins, and to centralise the animal looking back at us. But in so doing, it locks itself – on one level at least – into a fascinated stance that fetishistically configures the animal look captured by film in terms of a telepathic, transferential charge.[77] This gives cinematic form to Lippit's thesis of animal magnetism transferred to the technology of film. Lippit writes:

> In a radical departure from the framework of nature, the technological media commemorated and incorporated that which it has surpassed: the speechless semiotic of the animal look. Animal magnetism had moved from the hypnotist's eye to the camera eye, preserved in the emblematic lure of cinema.[78]

Here spectatorial desire, visual hypnotics and technological mediation converge in the figure of the mute, magnetic animal look encrypted by cinema. Shukin critiques Lippit's positioning of the animal, arguing that this technological or 'electric' animal becomes a fetishised site of vitalistic, 'transferential' communication. Similarly, here *Bestiaire* sets up a fantasy of transferential communication in its proliferation of animal looks direct to camera. It electrifies us with the charge of these looks (the sound edits jolt us too, for example, when a cut between gazes – of a bull and an antelope – coincides with the clanking of a gate). We feel the frisson of coming into contact with the animal, the kind of 'animal magnetism' of which Lippit writes, as animal and cinema converge here in their 'affective immediacy'.[79] *Bestiaire* mobilises an idea of animals – as Shukin puts it in her critique of Lippit – as 'monstrative', as 'eloquent in their mute acts of physical signing', according to a 'logic by which the animal body is rendered a transparent or demonstrative sign of technological communication'.[80] Recalling the question that, for Côté, motivates the film – 'Is it possible to film an animal for what it is: an animal?' – *Bestiaire* attempts to render the animal here, cinematically, in all its mutely transparent, monstrative self-evidence.

Yet, in line with the critique that Shukin makes of Lippit, this is paradoxically the point at which the film loses sight of the animal. Indeed, in these scenes *Bestiaire* seems to flatten the look of the animal into something that might – 'mimetically, magnetically'[81] – reveal the truth of cinema. As Libby Saxton suggests in a different context, the *regard caméra*/look to camera is 'privileged as an event which captures the essence of the medium'[82] – a relation exacerbated here by long-standing Cartesian associations between the animal and the machinic. As Burt writes in relation to the animal gaze in particular (and with reference to Lippit): 'Film fetishises the animal look to such a degree that it could be suggested that it is around the idea of visual communication that the animal figure comes closest to resembling the technology that produces it.'[83] In this fantasy of clairvoyant communication set up by *Bestiaire*, what is celebrated is the telepathic charge of the animal look conveyed to us by cinema (and, conversely, the hypnotic vitalism of cinema transmitted via the animal look); what is obscured are the material conditions of captivity and hierarchies of power that enable such a look to be captured.[84] We might note in particular how, in contrast to many of the other scenes in *Bestiaire*, none of the animals filmed staring at the camera are behind bars (for example, the bull and the antelope are filmed in a shed indoors). By privileging looks that appear unobstructed – and all the more electric for seeming so direct – *Bestiaire* problematically frames the zoo animal's gaze as transcending captivity. Though the concrete and metallic backdrops persist in recalling the context of the zoo, the

Figure 2.2 The captive look (*Bestiaire*).

hypnotic power of these extended looks also functions as a kind of temporary elision or disavowal of that material environment.

In an unsettling visual pattern, *Bestiaire* sets up echoes between live and taxidermied looks. The sequence at the taxidermist's is punctuated by static shots of taxidermied animals – many of the same species seen at the zoo – some whole, some dismembered. In a medium shot, we see the heads of antelopes and other animals mounted on the wall. The film moves in closer, capturing one antelope in extreme close-up, framing the base of the antlers, an ear and an eye, as though the animal were staring directly at the camera. The glass eye reflects the light, drawing our gaze. The film implicitly poses a connection between this dead eye and earlier living eyes and looks. In her analysis, in *Primate Visions*, of the exhibition of taxidermied animals in the Akeley African Hall in the American Museum of Natural History, Haraway reflects on the fetishistic, mystical encounter made possible by the stuffed animal's gaze:

> Each diorama has at least one animal that catches the viewer's gaze and holds it in communion. The animal is vigilant, ready to sound an alarm at the intrusion of man, but ready also to hold forever the gaze of meeting, the moment of truth, the original encounter. [. . .] The gaze holds and the wary animal heals those who will look [. . .] This is a spiritual vision made possible only by their death and literal re-presentation.[85]

In *Bestiaire*, taxidermied animal looks, captured by and for cinema, raise this spectre of eternal communion. Yet in the context of the film's implicit

Figure 2.3 Alive and looking (*Bestiaire*).

82 ANIMAL WORLDS

Figure 2.4 The taxidermied look (*Bestiaire*).

critique of human–animal relations, we are also invited to read these looks otherwise. Through a set of uncanny echoes, these petrified looks have a contaminating and deadening effect on the live animal gazes captured elsewhere in the film. The animal deaths engendering the eternal gaze, the 'original encounter', bleed across the spaces of the film, from the taxidermist's to the zoo, in a petrification of the living. This contaminating effect suggests the zoo's own taxidermic functions, in its exhibition of captive bodies and its promise of telepathic communion. The mystical encounter across species lines enabled by taxidermy, as Haraway frames it, converges with the 'fervor for interspecies intimacy' through which, as Shukin suggests, the biopower of the modern zoo is made manifest. Animating 'the speechless semiotic of the animal look',[86] taxidermied gazes in *Bestiaire* are ambiguous: in the context of the film's deconstruction of the labour of taxidermy, the images puncture the 'spiritual vision' of which Haraway writes; at the same time, these hypnotic looks suggest that the animal might function just as magnetically to reveal cinematic specificity whether alive or dead, as though the film were almost indifferent to the distinction between those realms.

WORLD, BECOMING, PENSIVITY

I suggested above that *Bestiaire* pulls awkwardly in various aesthetic and political directions.[87] Indeed, in other scenes the film shifts away from a self-reflexive investment in cinematic essence as the frenzy of animal kinetics or the electric, telepathic animal look, and allows for the terms of particular animal worlds to unfold. While the long takes and lack of voiceover in *Bestiaire* subvert zoo spectatorship, as suggested above, they also usher the film into a documentary, durational 'realm of *witnessing*', allowing for various perceptual and affective worlds to be made manifest.

Bestiaire deploys duration not only to trouble the ease of (zoological) viewing but in order to attend to modes of worlding that work against the film's taxidermic dimensions. Here, as Colebrook puts it, evoking the multiplicity of worlds to which Deleuze attends: 'The world is not something within which time takes place; there are flows of time from which worlds are perceived. The durations of different becomings produce different worlds – including the inhuman worlds of plants and animals.'[88] *Bestiaire*'s use of duration is a particularly important part of the film's dimensions of worlding. Refusing to subject these worlds to codes of narrative causality, what *Bestiaire* presents is a set of 'pure optical and sound situations' characteristic of the time-image, which work, as Deleuze suggests, 'to prevent perception being extended into action in order to put it in contact with thought [. . .]'.[89] *Bestiaire*'s setting – its constricted spaces – radicalises this non-extension of perception into action. From within these biopolitical schemata, and the static, flattened planes of the film itself, *Bestiaire*'s emergent time-images bear witness to the affective worlds of animals, to 'pensivity', to assemblages and becomings.

One extended shot lasting for almost three minutes shows a hyena being examined by a group of zookeepers. The hyena is held in a cage with movable barriers designed to position the animal tightly to enable close inspection. Offscreen sounds of cages rattling and animal cries invoke the institutionalisation of lives beyond the limits of the frame. We witness the hyena's apparent distress when the barriers shift, trapping the animal into a narrow section of the cage; the hyena moves warily back and forth, squeezing through this tight space – through a focus on physical gesture, the scene conveys a set of perceptual responses to this sudden shrinking of territory. Humans at ease, chattering to the hyena and among themselves and moving freely as they work, stand in stark contrast to the mute, anxious caged animal. When the inspection is over, the bars of the cage are moved back; the hyena glances repeatedly around the limits of this newly enlarged space. One of the keepers throws a piece of food into the cage, which the hyena quickly eats. The humans exit the frame. While the shot is held, the hyena looks towards the back of the cage.

The scene articulates the kind of 'sympathetic animal management' and 'fervor for interspecies intimacy' that is the embodiment of biopower applied to animal life.[90] Framing a hyena in a cage in a zoo in Quebec, the scene also reminds us of the neoimperialist dimensions of the management of this particular displaced, 'exotic' animal. The lack of voiceover, and the refusal to offer any information or explanation, allows for a foregrounding of the perverse, violent logic of the scene (echoing Pick's reading of *Primate*). Yet the withdrawal of any overt human interpretation also creates a time and a space in which multiple worlds are gradually made manifest. Alongside, and in excess of, its registering of the symptoms of neocolonialist biopower, the scene bears witness to what Burt calls 'livingness' as 'a mode of active coexistence' that takes places across the 'intervals' of species difference,[91] tracking the unfolding dynamics of response, power and action between the animal and the human. Here, '[t]he durations of different becomings produce different worlds'[92] – worlds that coexist, made plurally manifest by cinema.

Yet by focusing on the animal, remaining with her after the humans have exited the frame, what the scene allows to come into view above all is the world of the hyena. In line with Deleuze and Guattari's understanding of the *Umwelt* not as something that belongs to a subject but as a mode of assemblage (as seen in Chapter 1), this scene proposes a composition of affects, patiently charting the intensities that fluctuate as the animal's physical territory shrinks and expands. Those temporalised and spatialised intensities – tracked by the long take – are communicated to us via the gestures of the hyena, intimating response, anxiety and thought (yet all the while resisting anthropocentric interpretation). In the absenting of humans from the frame, the lack of any voiceover, and in the image's resistance to interpretative coding, the scene makes manifest a perceptual and affective world that, from within the space of captivity, extends beyond the human. Yet at the same time, across the intervals between animal onscreen and human viewer, meaningful realms of perception and sentience overlap. Deleuze and Guattari would describe this as a 'mutual becoming', a 'collective assemblage': 'There is no longer man or animal, since each deterritorialises the other, in a conjunction of flux, in a continuum of reversible intensities.'[93] And in this 'mutual becoming' – the culmination of a durational bearing witness – a set of ethical and political questions about captivity, suffering and 'sympathetic animal management' are implicitly posed.

Bestiaire also explores the unfolding of nonhuman worlds through instances of intraspecies exchange, in particular in a sequence featuring chimps that comprises three shots. In the first shot, we view, in close-up, a chimp lying down, alone, watchful and listening. The second shot, another close-up, shows two chimps together, one grooming the other. In the third shot, framed at a distance, a group of chimps wait patiently for food that they receive from a zookeeper through the gate of their enclosure (the composition of the image evoking a multiplication of constraints, compounding the sense of disciplinary control suggested by the surveillance camera images of the chimps that precede this sequence). An implicit political argument emerges here as the sequence juxtaposes the biopolitical reduction of the animal to 'obedient body content' in the third shot and the perceptual and experiential expansiveness of life-worlds suggested by the preceding shots. In these first two shots, we are offered an evocative glimpse of animal perception and exchange, as the scene lingers on the chimp's watchful, responsive registering of surroundings and then details of the grooming session, in which one chimp sucks and nibbles the other, lifting the lips of the fellow chimp to nibble further.[94] Unfolding these dynamics of contact, the scene intimates 'the active and passive affects of which the animal is capable in the individuated assemblage of which it is a part'.[95] Here, in contrast to the distant framing of the chimps in the scene that follows, a close-up, tactile engagement with the chimps' bodies works to overlap with the viewer's own perceptual, affective field, in a 'collective assemblage', a mode of 'mutual becoming'.[96] In its attention to tactility, and to animals engaging with one another rather than simulating attention to us (in the looks to camera discussed above), the scene moves beyond a hypnotic, ocularcentric staging of animal presence.

In lingering on a moment of intraspecies exchange, the scene intimates ways in which the richness of animal worlds exceeds the 'poverty' of world imposed by the zoo.[97] This is underlined in formal terms too: the bars of the cage are so blurred (by the close-up framing of the shot) as to be almost, but not quite, imperceptible: the image splits into the actual and the virtual, evoking lines of flight, ways of being otherwise, that coexist with the strata of imprisonment (rather than disavowing that strata, as in the earlier unobstructed looks to camera). This is close to what Deleuze and Guattari describe, in their reflections on animals in Kafka, as 'the line of escape, even if it takes place in place, or in a cage. *A line of escape, and not freedom.*'[98] Here in *Bestiaire*,

Figure 2.5 Biopolitical governing (*Bestiaire*).

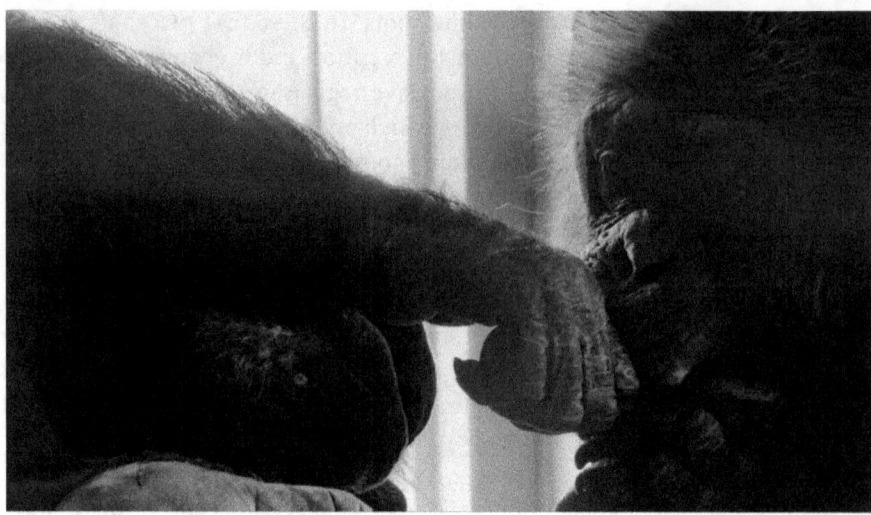

Figure 2.6 Intraspecies care and lines of flight (*Bestiaire*).

the splitting of the image into the actual and the virtual works as a mode of deterritorialisation that gestures both to and beyond the biopolitical grid of 'bare life' within which these bodies are imprisoned. For we witness a moment of intraspecies care that falls outside the terms of the biopolitical governing of animal life viewed in the scene of feeding. Prompted by the juxtaposition of these scenes and also by the blurring of the cage bars, we are asked to imagine animal lives beyond captivity, lives in which such moments of care and exchange might unfold freely. Thus, while the scene evokes the tactile and the embodied, there is also a sense in which it reaches beyond the phenomenologically lived bodies that it frames,[99] ushering in virtual worlds and planes of becoming.

As Burt suggests, we can make no assumption about subjectivity or interiority from images of animals in film.[100] Rather, here in *Bestiaire*, these images occupy a documentary 'realm of *witnessing*' – they register as meaningful even if we cannot confirm their signification. Opacity remains: as Bailly puts it, 'the abyss cannot be crossed'.[101] But to Descartes's dismissal of the animal ('the human mind cannot penetrate their hearts'), we find Bailly's rejoinder: '*But there are those hearts*, those existences; there is the whirlwind of all those lives and the beating of each and every heart . . .'.[102] *Bestiaire* bears witness to such existences, to the whirlwind and worlds of 'pensivity' of which Bailly writes.

Significantly, during his discussion of animal pensivity, Bailly evokes an imaginary bestiary. Citing Plotinus ('Every life is some form of thought, but of a dwindling clearness like the degrees of life itself'), Bailly suggests that the word 'Thoughts' might be taken as:

the title or subtitle of a bestiary that would deal only with appearance, only with animals' power of impregnation and with what can appropriately be called their styles – that is, the way in which each adheres to its being and slips that adhesion into the world like a thought [. . .] Thoughts, not as signs whose meaning would be reduced to us, for us [. . .] but in an entirely different contemplation, an entirely different dispatch, that of signs gone away [. . .].[103]

Focusing on gestures, percepts and affects, *Bestiaire* traces the singular and multiple styles of its animals – the repetitive pacing of a llama, the hindered gestures of a bird with one wing, the hyena trapped in ever-decreasing space. Conventional animal signs slip away, replaced by the 'power of impregnation', as the film refuses to reduce these animal existences and thoughts to a particular set of meanings for the viewer.[104] Here we might invoke Bailly's description, in the opening pages of *The Animal Side*, of his momentary encounter with a deer, glimpsed from the window of his car at night: 'that instant opening onto another world'[105] – while fleeting for Bailly, such an encounter is sustained, extended, deepened in *Bestiaire*. In *Bestiaire*, of course, the very possibility of this extension, this deepening, is predicated on the animal's captivity: unlike Bailly's deer, these animals cannot flee. Yet the opening onto other worlds that Bailly describes arguably applies to *Bestiaire* too.

And it is in this sense that we might wish to reconsider the reading of 'telepathic' animal looks that I proposed above. *Bestiaire* can certainly be seen to instrumentalise the animal look as a prop for cinematic self-reflexivity. Yet the extended long takes that bear witness to animal looks also register something in excess of this instrumentalising logic. Bailly frames the animal look in ways that have the potential to move beyond fetishisation:

The world of gazes is the world of *signifiance*, that is, of a possible, open, still indeterminate meaning. For the percussive impact of difference that is produced by discourse, the gaze substitutes a sort of dispersal: the unformulated is its element, its watery origin. The gaze gazes, and the unformulated is, in it, the pathway of thought, or at least of a thinking that is not uttered, not articulated, but that takes place and sees itself, holds itself in this purely strange and strangely limitless place which is the surface of the eye.[106]

In its images of direct looks to camera – by the wildebeest, the bull, the antelope – *Bestiaire* allows us to feel ourselves 'in the presence of an unknown force, at once supplicating and calm, that in effect traverses us' – a presence that marks, as Bailly puts it, 'a different form of thought'.[107] As Bailly goes on to suggest, the 'pensivity' of animals manifests itself in multiple different ways, depending on species, individual and situation. But the animal, Bailly argues, 'is the only form with which we share the power to look'.[108] *Bestiaire* captures something of the 'surprise' that Bailly describes in encountering the gaze of an animal:

> the infinite surprise that there is a being here and that it has this particular form, so small or so large, this form that is also a tension and a warmth, a rhythm and a grasping: some life has been caught and condensed, has ended up finding a place in a corner of space-time; the reservoir of existence that connects us to creatures also passes through this universal condition of breathing and fever.[109]

For the animal look is never just a look – as *Bestiaire*'s durational aesthetic makes so forcibly felt, the animal look is embodied, bringing with it breath, tension, warmth, rhythm, grasping. We sense the life that has been 'caught and condensed', that occupies this 'corner of space-time'. When in *Bestiaire* the white bull stares at the camera, the extended close-up allows for a textured focus on the surfaces of the face, on the drooling mouth, glistening nose and alert gaze, marking 'the reservoir of existence that connects us to creatures'. For Bailly, the animal look announces a presence that dislodges any exclusively human claim to thought, being and 'world'. In the animal look, 'what is established is that the world in which we live is gazed upon by other beings, that the visible is shared among creatures, and that a politics could be invented on this basis, if it is not too late'.[110] In this sense, a cinematic registering of the animal look – as an unformulated 'pathway of thought' – opens to the political, to questions of commonality and coexistence that, posed in the context of the zoo, become particularly unsettling for the human.[111] Just as the scene with the chimps gestures beyond the phenomenologically lived body to virtual worlds of becoming, so the yet-to-be-formulated 'pathway to thought' proposed by *Bestiaire* more broadly asks us to imagine different political futures for animals beyond the biopolitical regimes of zoo captivity.

Bestiaire explores a fascination with cinematic 'animality', mobilised via the metaphors of cinema as zoo and cinema as taxidermy, and interrogated through the display of animals living and dead, still and moving. In this sense, Côté's film positions animal presence onscreen – morbidly, fetishistically, hypnotically – as revealing something of the essence of cinema. Yet the film also moves beyond this problematic equation of animal and cinema to weave an implicit critique of the biopolitical appropriation of animal life within the realm of the zoo. Animal life is reconfigured as something more than the 'bare life' of zoopolitics as, through the wandering rhythms of its time-images, *Bestiaire* works to suggest the perceptual and affective worlds of animals, as well as lines of flight and virtual modes of becoming. By documenting such scenes in durational terms, the film suggests to us the possibility, from within this space of captivity, of worlds of 'pensivity' that coexist with, and extend beyond, the human. With Bailly, we can reconfigure our understanding of the instant jolt of the telepathically charged animal look as forming part of a broader 'reservoir of existence' or 'world of *signifiance*'. In excess of any attempt to electrify the human and confirm for us cinematic specificity, *Bestiaire*'s attentiveness to the looks, gestures and responses of animals allows for other worlds to flicker suggestively into view.

NOTES

1. On the DVD of *Bestiaire* (KimStim Collection, 2012), the chapter divisions are as follows: Art, Snow, Indoors, Feeding, Caged, Stuffed, Grazing, Zoo, Entertainment.
2. Deleuze, *Cinema 2*, p. 261.
3. 'Animal films reveal the cinema to us.' Bazin, 'Les Films d'animaux nous révèlent le cinéma'.
4. Côté, 'The Animal Equation', *Cinema Scope*, 14 (2012), 10–12 (p. 12). Jean-Claude Raspiengeas describes *Bestiaire* as 'a film about the place of the film spectator'. Raspiengeas, 'En cage, au zoo', *La Croix*, 27 February 2013.
5. In interview, Côté explains that the idea to make *Bestiaire* was prompted by an invitation by the Parc Safari itself: Côté had filmed images of a caged tiger there for an earlier film, *Curling* (2010), and the zoo invited him to return. Côté, 'Interview with the Filmmaker Denis Côté', 12 October 2012, *Bestiaire* DVD, The KimStim Collection.
6. Ibid.
7. Sabine Nessel, 'The Media Animal: On the Mise-en-scène of Animals in the Zoo and Cinema', in Nessel et al. (eds), *Animals and the Cinema: Classifications, Cinephilias, Philosophies* (Berlin: Bertz and Fischer, 2012), pp. 33–48.
8. Pick, *Creaturely Poetics*, p. 105.
9. Berger, 'Why Look at Animals?', p. 26.
10. Burt, *Animals in Film*, pp. 35–8.
11. Pick, *Creaturely Poetics*, p. 105.
12. Côté, 'Interview with the Filmmaker Denis Côté'.
13. On animal 'mediality', see Nessel, 'The Media Animal'.
14. Côté, 'The Animal Equation', p. 11.
15. Ibid., p. 11.
16. One thinks in particular of the enigmatic scene in *Au hasard Balthazar*, in which the donkey Balthazar exchanges looks with a group of caged animals at the circus.
17. Of Frammartino's *Le Quattro Volte*, Côté writes: 'Doesn't its unanimous success have something to do with its refusal to give a conscience other than a utilitarian one to its animal-protagonists?'; of *Sweetgrass*: 'The negation of narrative, a resistance to spectacle, and a willful abandon toward purely visual and sonic itineraries'; of *Bovines*: 'At times too in search of beautiful images, France's Emmanuel Gras reveals the nobility of cows in *Bovines* (2011). Just cows! And do not expect to see or find signs attempting to clarify the intentions around this quiet visual adventure, which borders on reverence.' Côté explicitly aligns his work with that of Gras: 'My most recent film, *Bestiaire*, grazes in the latter pastures' ('The Animal Equation', p. 12).

18. Ibid., p. 11.
19. Referencing Berger, one review compares the two films, suggesting that, like *Nénette*, '*Bestiaire* exposes the mechanics of a strange, multi-layered voyeurism: watching animals watch – or, more accurately, look past – those who gape at them. As Berger writes: "At the most, the animal's gaze flickers and passes on [. . .]".' Melissa Anderson, '*Bestiaire* ponders what transpires when we look at animals', *The Village Voice*, 17 October 2012. Available at http://www.villagevoice.com/2012-10-17/film/bestiaire-ponders-what-transpires-when-we-look-at-animals/ (last accessed 14 September 2018).
20. Côté, 'Interview with the Filmmaker Denis Côté'. Critical commentary has also pointed to the intermedial dimensions of the film, comparing *Bestiaire* to photography and video installation art; see Stéphane Delorme and Céline Gailleurd, '"Mes films de vengeance": Entretien avec Denis Côté', *Cahiers du cinéma*, 687 (March 2013), 49–51, p. 50.
21. Côté, 'Interview with the Filmmaker Denis Côté'.
22. Delorme and Gailleurd, '"Mes films de vengeance"', p. 50.
23. Côté, 'Interview with the Filmmaker Denis Côté'.
24. Delorme and Gailleurd, '"Mes films de vengeance"', p. 50.
25. Côté, 'Interview with the Filmmaker Denis Côté'.
26. *Bestiaire*'s opening – its delayed reveal of the animal – is possibly influenced by *Bovines*, which introduces the territory of the cows before the cows themselves; see Chapter 5.
27. In her review of *Bestiaire*, Gailleurd refers to the film's desaturated 'crepuscular colours'. Gailleurd, 'Mécanique de l'absurde', *Cahiers du cinéma*, 687 (March 2013), p. 48.
28. See Delorme and Gailleurd, '"Mes films de vengeance"'. Côté discusses the plasticity of the film at several points during the interview.
29. Gérard Grugeau critiques the film along these lines. Grugeau, 'L'enfermement', *24 images*, 157 (2012), 43.
30. Bruno Dequen, 'Mécanique animale', *24 images*, 157 (2012), 42.
31. Margulies, *Nothing Happens*, p. 46; p. 186. Reading the ZooCam in the context of experimental cinema's investments in uneventfulness, Burke observes, in a fascinating aside, that *Jeanne Dielman*, 'in its static extended gaze on a protagonist confined to an enclosed space, seems almost zoological in its observations'. Burke, 'ZooTube', p. 81n7.
32. Margulies, *Nothing Happens*, p. 120; p. 46.
33. Ibid., p. 10.
34. Gailleurd, 'Mécanique de l'absurde', p. 48.
35. Julien Gester writes: 'With extreme formalist rigour, the gridded shots are composed of all the lines traced by the human hand – bars, enclosures, electric lines – all the better to contemplate the magnetism of caged life and the enamoured fascination, and the well-meaning cruelty that subtends this.' Gester, 'Ovni documentaire sans parole entre élégie zoologique et fantastique clinique', *Libération*, 27 February 2013.
36. Yi Fu Tuan, *Dominance and Affection: The Making of Pets* (New Haven: Yale University Press, 1984), pp. 75–6.
37. Randy Malamud, *An Introduction to Animals and Visual Culture* (Basingstoke: Palgrave Macmillan, 2012), p. 117.
38. Nichols, *Representing Reality*, p. 31.
39. Malamud, *An Introduction to Animals and Visual Culture*, p. 123.
40. Yet Michal Oleszczyk notes that in contrast to *Zoo*, which 'examined the practical ways the eponymous facility was run', 'Côté is so disinterested in the mundane aspects of the institution he portrays as to make it look positively abstract.' Oleszczyk, 'Sundance Film Festival 2012: *Bestiaire*', *The House Next Door*, 24 January 2012.

Available at http://www.slantmagazine.com/house/2012/01/sundance-film-festival-2012-bestiaire/ (last accessed 14 September 2018). Certainly Wiseman's film gives more mundane information verbally (for example, via conversations between zookeepers), yet the claim that *Bestiaire* is disinterested in the mundane aspects seems questionable, given the visual attentiveness to the zoo's environment that I have described above, as well as long takes that feature, among other things, the cleaning of indoor spaces.
41. Pick, *Creaturely Poetics*, p. 143; original emphasis.
42. Ibid., p. 145.
43. Foucault, *Society Must Be Defended: Lectures at the Collège de France, 1975–76*, translated by D. Macey and edited by M. Bertani and A. Fontana (New York: Picador, 2003). On connections between Foucault's thought and critical animal studies, see Matthew Chrulew and Dinesh Joseph Wadiwel (eds), *Foucault and Animals* (Leiden and Boston: Brill, 2017).
44. Shukin, *Animal Capital*, p. 156.
45. Ibid., p. 155.
46. Ibid., p. 155.
47. On the 'docile bodies' of human prisoners, see Foucault, *Discipline and Punish: The Birth of the Prison*, translated by Alan Sheridan (New York: Vintage, 1995).
48. Shukin, *Animal Capital*, p. 155. As *Bestiaire* suggests, humans also occupy this role of 'docile, willing performers of capitalist spectacles', emphasised in scenes such as the one in which a woman dresses as a giant cartoon animal. And, of course, the surveillant gaze – of the zoo and of the film – extends also to the humans. In this sense, as Gailleurd contends, the film is not just about animals: 'we end up seeing the zoo as a strange invention, finding points of correspondence with society where entertainment resembles organised surveillance' (Gailleurd, 'Mécanique de l'absurde', p. 48). Yet any such correspondence is also shot through with asymmetry: animals remain particularly stripped of agency within these structures.
49. Bailly, *Le Parti pris des animaux*, p. 8. This connection is also made by Béghin: '*Bestiaire* is a sort of cinematographic equivalent of the oeuvre of the painter Gilles Aillaud, essentially dedicated to caged animals, and of which Bailly wrote that they showed animals "exiled in visibility".' Béghin, 'L'animal sans image', p. 75.
50. Available at https://www.parcsafari.com/en/animaux/lions-tunnel/ (last accessed 14 September 2018).
51. Berger, 'Why Look at Animals?', p. 24; original emphasis.
52. Malamud, *An Introduction to Animals and Visual Culture*, p. 115.
53. Ibid., p. 55.
54. Foucault, *Society Must Be Defended*, p. 241; original emphasis.
55. Agamben, *Homo Sacer*, p. 13. See the discussion of Agamben's work in the Introduction.
56. One survey cited by Malamud reveals that zoo visitors typically spend an average of forty- four seconds in front of each cage; see Garry Marvin and Bob Mullan, *Zoo Culture* (London: Weidenfeld & Nicolson, 1987), cited in Malamud, *An Introduction to Animals and Visual Culture*, p. 122.
57. Bousé has argued that conventional wildlife film and television contribute to a 'pervasive media image of nature as a site of action and excitement', despite the 'torpor' that generally characterises animal being. Bousé, *Wildlife Films*, p. 6.
58. Confronted by the general inactivity of its animals, *Bestiaire*'s viewer, like Berger's zoo visitor, might be tempted to ask: 'Why are these animals less than I believed?'. Berger, 'Why Look at Animals?', p. 23.
59. Shukin, *Animal Capital*, p. 39. Here Shukin is drawing on Derrida's reflections on the 'interminable survival' of animals in an era of unprecedented instrumentalisation of, and intervention in, animal life. Derrida, *The Animal That Therefore I Am*, p. 26.

60. Deleuze, *Cinema 2*, p. 17.
61. Ibid., p. 39.
62. Doane, *The Emergence of Cinematic Time*.
63. Deleuze, *Cinema 2*, p. 39.
64. Burke, 'ZooTube', p. 80n6.
65. Ibid., p. 74.
66. There are other distinctions to be made here too, not least because while ZooCams offer 'a feed that is both uninterrupted and unedited' (Burke, 'ZooTube', p. 66), *Bestiaire* is of course not live and, despite its investment in long takes, it is profoundly shaped by editing. Nor does *Bestiaire* offer the surveillant fantasy of unmediated access to animal life promised by the ZooCam – indeed, as seen above, through strategies of visual fragmentation, it actively seeks to interrupt that fantasy.
67. Rancière, *The Future of the Image*, translated by Gregory Elliott (London: Verso, 2007), p. 124. A reading in terms of Rancière's 'pensive image' seems particularly apt given *Bestiaire*'s intermedial affiliations with photography and video installation art as well.
68. On boredom and duration in cinema, see, for example, Misek, 'Dead Time'.
69. Or as Béghin puts it: 'The animals in the cage seem to be waiting to be stuffed, seen and drawn.' Béghin, 'L'animal sans image', p. 75.
70. Rachel Poliquin, *The Breathless Zoo: Taxidermy and the Cultures of Longing* (University Park: Pennsylvania State University Press, 2012), p. 115.
71. Haraway, *Primate Visions: Gender, Race and Nature in the World of Modern Science* (New York: Routledge, 1989), p. 41.
72. Baker, *The Postmodern Animal*, p. 62. In his discussion of the use of dead animals in art, Baker coins the term 'botched taxidermy' to denote moments in which taxidermy's realism fails, and the art object reveals itself as fractured: 'if tattiness, imperfection and botched form count for anything, it is that they render the animal *abrasively visible*' (p. 62; original emphasis). Though Baker stresses the looseness of the concept of 'botched taxidermy' – it can apply to artworks including living animals, or even works that do not directly represent the animal – I follow the literalness of the term here.
73. On cinema's evocations of corporeal vulnerability across species lines, see Pick, *Creaturely Poetics*.
74. Sarah Cooper, *Chris Marker* (Manchester: Manchester University Press, 2008), pp. 54–5.
75. Maria Braun, *Eadweard Muybridge* (London: Reaktion Books, 2010).
76. Bellour, *Le Corps du cinéma*, p. 504.
77. A certain fetishisation of the animal look underpins some of Côté's comments: 'a giraffe doesn't make a sound. You're there, you film your giraffe for two minutes and she watches you: no sound. When you look into the eyes of an animal for two minutes, something happens which exceeds words, it's unbelievable . . .' (Delorme and Gailleurd, '"Mes films de vengeance"', p. 51). This echoes, quite strikingly, Parc Safari's publicity on its website: 'You can stand nose-to-nose with a white lion from Timbavati and look right into its eyes. It's magical!'. Available at https://www.parcsafari.com/en/animaux/lions-tunnel/ (last accessed 14 September 2018).
78. Lippit, *Electric Animal*, p. 197.
79. Shukin, *Animal Capital*, p. 141.
80. Ibid., p. 141.
81. Lippit, *Electric Animal*, p. 196.
82. Libby Saxton, *Haunted Images: Film, Ethics and the Holocaust* (London: Wallflower Press, 2008), p. 108.
83. Burt, *Animals in Film*, p. 64.

84. These material conditions include the 'capturing' of the animal not only by the zoo but by the film itself: what prompts these animals to look directly at the camera? One wonders about the material conditions – of animal attention, distraction and performance in response to human activity offscreen – shaping these particular images. At the same time, *Bestiaire*'s end credits remind us of the institutional conditions that enable the film's own capturing of life: 'The production of this film was made possible by the permission and generosity of the team of employees at the Parc Safari (Hemmingford, Quebec).'
85. Haraway, *Primate Visions*, p. 30.
86. Lippit, *Electric Animal*, p. 197.
87. In this sense *Bestiaire* echoes the productively conflicted relation between aestheticisation and politics at stake in Geyrhalter's *Our Daily Bread* (cited by Côté as an influence above); on the 'dynamic ambiguity or ambivalence' of this relation in Geyrhalter's film, see Helen Hughes, 'Arguments without words in *Unser täglich Brot* (Geyrhalter 2005)', *Continuum: Journal of Media & Cultural Studies*, 27:3 (2013), 347–64.
88. Colebrook, *Gilles Deleuze*, p. 42.
89. Deleuze, *Cinema 2*, p. 1.
90. Shukin, *Animal Capital*, p. 155. In interview, Côté's position seems broadly welfarist; he does not explicitly address modes of biopolitical control or less overt forms of violence in the zoo, but his comments gesture to a critique of certain aspects of animal captivity. Asked about the scene with the hyena, he says: 'There is unconditional love on one side, and restraint on the other. The animal obeys. The system of restraint is necessary. The machine functions. It's horrible, but it's for the good of the animal. It's above all the ritual that interests me [. . .] I don't perceive any real violence: the hyena was given an injection for its own good. At no moment did I see any act of cruelty against the animals. However, it's up to each viewer to decide if it's horrible to keep the two zebras in a *douze par douze* [i.e. confined space] for four or five months during the winter; it's horrible. I can't decide' (Delorme and Gailleurd, '"Mes films de vengeance"', p. 51).
91. Burt, 'Morbidity and Vitalism', p. 169; p. 174.
92. Colebrook, *Gilles Deleuze*, p. 42.
93. Deleuze and Guattari, *Kafka*, p. 22.
94. This resonates with Pick's reading of Wiseman's *Primate*: 'An expanded notion of life – around the shared creatureliness of vulnerable bodies – is apparent in the film's glimpses of the so-called extracurricular activities of animals as they play together in their cages, care for their infants, sit pensively in their cells, cling to, show affection for, or actively resist their human captors. *Primate* flatly refuses to cast such gestures as anthropomorphic.' Pick, *Creaturely Poetics*, p. 145.
95. Deleuze and Guattari, *A Thousand Plateaus*, p. 257.
96. One might argue that the scene with the chimps is particularly open to anthropomorphisation, given that they so readily inhabit the border zone between the human and the animal. Yet if there is anthropomorphisation here, it arguably works evocatively to draw attention to the overlapping of animal and human worlds. On the strategic value of anthropomorphisation, see Jane Bennett, *Vibrant Matter: A Political Ecology of Things* (Durham, NC and London: Duke University Press, 2010), p. 99.
97. On Heidegger's suggestion that the animal is 'poor in world', see Chapter 1.
98. Deleuze and Guattari, *Kafka*, p. 35; original emphasis. They continue: 'the metamorphosis is a sort of conjunction of two deterritorialisations, that which the human imposes on the animal by forcing it to flee or to serve the human, but also that which the

animal proposes to the human by indicating ways out or means of escape that the human would never have thought of by himself [. . .]' (Ibid., p. 35).
99. This recalls Deleuze's observation: 'The phenomenological hypothesis is perhaps insufficient because it merely invokes the lived body. But the lived body is still a paltry thing in comparison with a more profound and almost unlivable power [*puissance*].' (Deleuze, *Francis Bacon*, p. 44).
100. Burt, *Animals in Film*, p. 31.
101. Bailly, *The Animal Side*, p. 5. As Gester writes: 'The hypnotic procession of animal sights embraces the behaviour of the animals in all their opacity.' Gester, 'Ovni documentaire'.
102. Bailly, *The Animal Side*, p. 5; original emphasis.
103. Ibid., p. 57.
104. As Delorme and Gailleurd suggest, the film 'gives back to animals their *puissance* of appearance [. . .]' (Delorme and Gailleurd, '"Mes films de vengeance", p. 50). Sensitive to this *puissance* in *Bestiaire*, and to the singularities and opacities at stake, Béghin writes: 'Off-centre framing in long takes reveals the singularity of paws, horns and furs, focusing on the spasms and breathing, capturing in detail the mute and inaccessible panics' ('L'animal sans image', p. 75).
105. Bailly, *The Animal Side*, p. 3.
106. Ibid., p. 14.
107. Ibid., p. 15.
108. Ibid., p. 31.
109. Ibid., p. 42.
110. Ibid., p. 15.
111. Indeed, *Bestiaire* does not allow the place of the human to remain secure amid all of this. Visual fragmentation extends to humans as well as animals (for example, in the close-ups in the art scene), and rhythms of editing gradually train us to watch humans as we have been watching animals (such as in the scene in which a zookeeper eats an apple, following scenes of animals feeding). In *Bestiaire*, species indeterminacy is forged above all through that which Bazin seeks to expel from his account of cinematic realism and cross-species interaction: montage. See Bazin, 'The Virtues and Limitations of Montage', in *What is Cinema?*, Vol. 1, edited and translated by Hugh Gray (Berkeley: University of California Press, 1967), pp. 41–52. *Bestiaire*'s editing and construction of visual patterns between and across shots function zoomorphically, encouraging a mode of species indeterminacy that dovetails with the film's exploration of pensivity, perception and worldhood across species lines.

CHAPTER 3

The Turin Horse: Animal Labour and Lines of Flight

Béla Tarr and Ágnes Hranitzky's *The Turin Horse* (*A torinói ló*, 2011) resonates with *Bestiaire*'s focus on lives suspended and time being endured. But it explores these questions through fiction rather than documentary, and through a specific set of connections between suffering, exhaustion, labour and precarity that cross species boundaries while foregrounding ways in which human and animal lives are differentially exposed. *The Turin Horse* traces the implications of this differential exposure via extreme modes of temporal dilation that render all the more potent its investigations into endurance, suffering and the seemingly inexorable movements towards death envisaged by the film. In this chapter, I privilege above all the question of animal labour (a question often overlooked by contemporary philosophies of animal life, as I suggested in the Introduction) and its connection to the 'worlding' of the film, especially the affective assemblages to which the film so gradually and painstakingly attends.

But I want to turn first to Jacques Rancière's reflections in *Béla Tarr, The Time After*, since they help us to make an initial sketch of issues of time in Tarr's work:

> The events that comprise a film are sensible moments, slices of duration: moments of solitude in which [. . .] the affections of the external world are converted into repetitive accordion tunes, feelings expressed by songs, footsteps on the ground [. . .] This global affect does not allow itself to be translated into feelings experienced by the characters. It is a matter of circulation between several partial points of condensation. The matter proper to this circulation is time. The slow camera movements, which depart from a stack of glasses, from a table, or from a person [. . .] these make up the events of the film: a minute of the world, as Proust would have said, a singular moment of coexistence between the assembled

bodies, in which the affects – born of 'cosmological' pressure, the pressure of rain, of fog, and of mud, and converted into conversations, tunes, shards of voice, or gazes lost in the void – circulate.¹

As Rancière suggests, this is a form of cinema in which 'slices of duration' replace a focus on narrative events, lingering camera movements map an intimate coexistence between bodies, objects and the 'cosmological', and a global circulation of affect resists any direct translation into character psychology. While the Deleuzian dimensions of Rancière's reading are already implicit in the temporal and affective contours of this outline, Rancière goes on to render them explicit in what follows, through a vocabulary of assemblage, crystals of time and the time-image:

> a Béla Tarr film will be an assemblage of these crystals of time, in which the 'cosmic' pressure is concentrated. More than all others, his images deserve to be called time-images, images from which duration is made manifest – the very stuff of which those individualities, which we call situations or characters, are woven [. . .]²

Intriguingly, from the early stages of this text, Rancière links these issues of time – and in particular a Deleuzian framework of nonlinear cinematic time – to the question of the border between the human and the animal. In Tarr's work, Rancière suggests, 'lived time is connected with pure repetition, there, where human speech and gestures tend toward those of animals'.³ While Rancière detects here a repetitive paring away of what he sees as certain indices of human agency (speech, gesture), he also points to a more direct figuration of the borderline between the human and the animal – and its unravelling – that recurs across Tarr's work. Referring to Tarr's 1988 film, *Damnation*, Rancière writes: '*Damnation* left Karrer barking in the face of a dog, like a final image of the human condition.'⁴ Citing further examples such as the dead whale in *Werckmeister Harmonies* (2000) and the cat tortured by the young girl, Estike, in *Sátántangó* (1994), Rancière suggests that 'the animal inhabits Béla Tarr's universe as the figure in which the human experiences its limit'.⁵ Indeed, as he has argued elsewhere: 'The threat of animality, the threat of the non-human and possibly the inhuman is present almost everywhere in Tarr's films, running alongside these stories of swindle and betrayal.'⁶

While these comments are richly suggestive, they tend to limit a reading of animals in Tarr's work to their metaphorical meanings, to the ways in which the animals stand in for, and are seen to reflect, 'the human condition'.⁷ This logic of metaphoricity is underlined by Rancière's slippage between 'animality' (a concept already abstracted from actual animals, as I suggested in the Introduction), the nonhuman and the inhuman.⁸ Here in Rancière's brief reflections on animals one detects an unfortunate echo of the tendency in Agamben's work critiqued by LaCapra: 'animals in their diversity are not figured as complex, differentiated living beings but instead function as an abstracted philosophical topos [. . .]'.[9] Countering this tendency towards abstraction, and following Tarr's own insistence that his work is embedded primarily in the material rather than the allegorical,[10] my reading of *The Turin Horse* is interested in what the film suggests about the actual animal (rather than the 'animality') at its centre – that is, the 'complex, differentiated living being' of the horse. At the same time, the links that Rancière draws between duration, the circulation of affect and the troubling of species borderlines remain highly pertinent, as we shall see, to the reading of time, labour and 'enduring' that I seek to develop in what follows.

ENDURING

Reputedly Tarr's final film, *The Turin Horse* intensifies and crystallises an interest in animals that is present, as we have seen, in his earlier work. The film opens with an account of Nietzsche's apocryphal encounter with a horse in the street in Turin on 3 January 1889. Over a black screen, the voiceover describes how Nietzsche witnesses the horse refusing to move and being whipped.[11] As the voiceover recounts, Nietzsche

> suddenly jumps up to the cab and throws his arms around the horse's neck, sobbing. His neighbour takes him home, where he lies still and silent for two days on a divan until he mutters the obligatory last words, 'Mutter, ich bin dumm,' and lives for another ten years, gentle and demented, in the care of his mother and sisters. Of the horse, we know nothing.

As readings of this episode often have it, the suffering of the horse seems to prompt an act of compassion that cataclysmically overturns Nietzsche's life-long condemnation of pity in his writings.[12] But, as the film suggests, the horse only ever figures fleetingly in this apocryphal account of the philosopher's descent into madness.[13]

The Turin Horse does not attempt to reimagine directly the horse witnessed by Nietzsche. Rather, it approaches this history obliquely, through the fictional story of another horse, a horse kept by a man, Ohlsdorfer (János Derszi), and his daughter (played by Erika Bók) in a desolate, inhospitable place, in an unidentified part of Hungary, in an unidentified time. Following the opening voiceover and black screen, the first image is that of the horse pulling a cart driven by Ohlsdorfer in the midst of a vicious gale. The scenes that follow show the horse seeming to fall ill and refusing to move any further. Over the course of six days, indicated in the form of chapter divisions, the film documents the daily routines of Ohlsdorfer and his daughter (waking, dressing, washing, cooking, eating), alongside the deteriorating condition of the horse as she resists eating or moving – human lives of routine pitted against a nonhuman life refusing to submit to routine any longer.

Yet the film emphasises how deeply entangled these lives are: the apparent illness and withdrawal of the horse upsets the routines of the father and daughter since they are forced to keep the horse in the stable rather than using her for transport and labour. And this upset coincides with a series of other disruptions: by the fourth day, the water well that they depend on has run dry; by the fifth day, the lamps in the house will no longer light; on the sixth day, Ohlsdorfer and his daughter sit at the table in near darkness, now with only raw potatoes on their plates; while the father tries in vain to eat, the daughter sits motionless, resigned. The film stages what one critic describes as 'a kind of Genesis story in reverse, an account not of the world's apocalyptic destruction but rather of its step-by-step de-creation'.[14]

This 'step-by-step de-creation' is documented in the deliberately slow and patient terms that are characteristic of Tarr's style. Developing his reflections on duration in Tarr's work, Rancière suggests that Tarr's cinema is interested in a form of realism that 'opposes situations that endure to stories that link together and pass from one to the next'.[15] I am interested in this notion of the situation that *endures* – and the ways in which this is explored by *The Turin Horse* as a question that is both formal and existential, with particular implications for how we read the horse in the film. Discussing *The Turin Horse* alongside other examples of slow cinema, Gorfinkel refers to 'cinema's capacity to make perceptible otherwise imperceptible experiences of the ordinary endurance of bodies on the margins'.[16] Here 'endurance', as Gorfinkel suggests, denotes a conjoining of endurance and duration. Enduring is about cinema's use of delayed temporality, and about the refusal of the kind of action-orientated narrative that Rancière identifies. But as Gorfinkel indicates, enduring is also about questions of marginality, suffering and survival – the question of the persistence of life itself.[17]

Critical commentary on *The Turin Horse* has tended to emphasise an existentialist, Beckettian focus on the inescapability of death and an apocalyptic 'end time'.[18] These readings have been prompted in part by Tarr's own comments. Speaking of *The Turin Horse*, he has remarked: 'Everything in the world passes away. Perhaps the world itself will pass away.'[19] Yet while in dialogue with this ostensibly existentialist focus, I seek to read *The Turin Horse* in political terms as a film about labour, and about animal labour in particular – issues that have been almost entirely absent from discussions of the film thus far (including Rancière's study).[20] In this chapter, I thus attend to the dynamics of cinematic duration through an emphasis on the question of labour in particular and its links to the issues of 'endurance', exhaustion and suffering signalled above. Connecting this to broader contexts hovering at the edges of Tarr and Hranitzky's film – postcommunism, environmental crisis and other contemporary forms of precarity – I seek to move beyond the ahistorical conception of existentialist struggle through which *The Turin Horse* has often been understood. In this sense, I read *The Turin Horse* both literally – as a non-metaphorical, material account of equine labour and resistance – and allegorically – as gesturing beyond the preindustrial agricultural context of the diegesis to engage implicitly with contemporary biopolitical contexts of work, precarity and survival. Yet through all of this the horse remains central, as I seek to emphasise through close readings of the film's formal engagement with equine embodiment and gesture. In its final stages, the chapter turns to develop a reading of animal worlds and lines of flight in Tarr and Hranitzky's film, and of the horse's resistance not only to work but also to visibility.

THE LONG TAKE

Following the opening voiceover, the film cuts to the scene of the horse pulling the cart, setting up an enigmatic relation between Nietzsche's horse and *this* horse, between the apocryphal 'story' offscreen and the lived situation onscreen. As the long take patiently traces the horse's lurching movement against the unrelenting gale, her gestures suggest weight, force, pressure, burden, her blinkered eyes widening in a way that signals stress, exertion. As the road inclines, we note further signs of physical exertion – her head pulling to the side, her mouth opening. As Zsuzsa Selyem observes, the horse pulls a cart built for two horses – 'it is hooked in on the left side while its partner on the right side is absent'[21] – thus making the journey even more of a struggle. The camera is not static: it moves with the animal, varying the angle of approach, inhabiting the space with her. At times the camera moves to focus on Ohlsdorfer in the cart. But the shot tracks the animal's motion above all, the camera's movement hovering ambiguously between a surveillant gaze and a mode of embodied attentiveness or being-with.

In her description of this scene, Stella Hockenhull writes:

> with her ears set back and her eyes showing white, the animal's demeanour signals unease and discomfort. [. . .] At one point she lowers her head and gathers her strength to pull harder against the wind and, surrounded by dust, she opens and closes her mouth, quickening her pace in the process.[22]

As Hockenhull suggests, there are various signs that indicate the stress that the horse is under – indexical traces that exceed and puncture the film's diegetic frame. But we cannot simply ascribe to these images the pure, unmediated charge of the real. The scene stages its own artifice, silencing the horse's movement in favour of repetitive string sounds, offering up – in consonance with its black-and-white images – a disturbing kind of hypnotic beauty. At the same time, the gestures of the horse carry an extradiegetic charge – they bear witness to a referential force of pressure, burden and struggle that shapes these images, troubling the boundary between the diegetic and the nondiegetic.[23]

Though not theorised by Hockenhull in her reading (her focus is more on the dynamics of performance), the question of cinematic duration is crucial here. Rancière writes that Tarr's cinema seeks 'to give each sensation the time of its development'.[24] The long take allows for a documenting of what Rancière sees as 'lived time',[25] a situation that *endures*.[26] Rancière's configuring of duration resonates with Bazin's phenomenology of lived time, but it points perhaps still more persuasively to Deleuze's conceptualisation of cinematic time. Suggesting that '[a] sequence of gestures is also the constitution of a certain sensible world',[27] Rancière refers to Tarr's use of the long take in particular: 'Each sequence shot has a duty to the time of the world, to the time in which the world is reflected in intensities felt by bodies.'[28] In the movement beyond lived time as such, towards the 'time of the world', and beyond an intentional subject grounded in a *corps propre* (or corporeal propriety), towards a set of 'intensities felt by bodies', one senses the post-phenomenological orientation of Rancière's reading. Thus at this stage Rancière seems implicitly in dialogue with Deleuze, and with the ways in which Deleuze's understanding of cinematic time both evokes and reaches beyond the experiential. In Deleuze's thinking, the long take does not only give us 'lived time': 'it makes thought immanent to the image'; it has a 'theorematic' dimension.[29] For Deleuze, as Matilda Mroz notes: 'the long-take is not just experiential, but also makes immanent a conceptualisation of passing time [. . .] the camera probes a space to become questioning, provoking, theorematising, and experimenting, a process that can happen within the duration of a long-take'.[30] The long take does not simply record and show: it asks a question, generates an uncertainty. As Mroz suggests in her reading of Antonioni: 'The longer the shot is held, the more intense the uncertain affect of its movement grows.'[31]

In the opening images of *The Turin Horse*, the long take engenders an unfolding of intensities, as the moving camera traces 'a sequence of gestures' intimating sensible worlds – both human and animal, though the focus is predominantly on the latter. Yet while this may suggest a form of embodied spectatorship[32] – a spectatorial inhabiting of the scene, a phenomenological sharing of 'lived time' – at play here too are the potentially estranging effects of the long take. The protracted shot allows for an image familiar to us from the history of cinema – a horse pulling a cart – to become defamiliarised, uncertain, 'questioning, provoking'. The long take gives us time to notice the ways in which the animal's muddied body, rendered in all its tactility by the image, is bound by harness, straps, saddle, blinder, chains, bit – the various accoutrements of domination. And it gives us time, perhaps, to imagine such a burden, to feel our way into its intensities. This does not necessarily entail an act of identification reducing nonhuman difference to human sameness. Rather it might involve a mode of ethical attentiveness to what Pick sees as 'the vulnerability of bodies in their affliction and exposure',[33] to a 'creaturely vulnerability' that crosses species lines.

At the same time, interrupting that potential gesture of mutual exposure, the whip remains in view – an ever-present threat, a visual signifier of a certain power casually wielded over the animal. Prefacing these images, the voiceover has recounted of the horse witnessed by Nietzsche: 'the horse refuses to move, whereupon the cabman [. . .] loses his patience and takes a whip to it'. We sense the ease of this conjunction 'and' – the sleight of hand it enacts, quickly sliding from frustration to violence. As Pick observes, 'when it comes to animals, power operates with the fewest of obstacles'.[34] That power is made felt through everything we see here, shaping these images, haunting them, deepening the enigmatic relation between *that* horse (encountered by Nietzsche) and *this* horse (here onscreen). And of the struggling, exhausted horse onscreen we understand that power operates both diegetically (the horse is subjected to Ohlsdorfer's force) and extradiegetically (the horse is subjected to the will of the filmmaker).

While every film slips between 'document and diegesis',[35] there are particular questions here that are specific to animal images. The images of the horse – perpetually pointing to the extradiegetic – exemplify Burt's theory that the animal onscreen introduces a 'rupturing effect', a radical instability in cinema's own acts of framing. As noted in Chapter 1, Burt argues that the semiotic instability of animal images is linked to the material vulnerability of animal bodies, their exposure to human domination:

> the power of the animal film image stems from the fact that, because it is more prone to collapse the boundary of representation and reality than other forms of imagery, it threatens to reveal not just the isolated fact of coercion or cruelty but the whole system by which such coercion and cruelty are reproduced.[36]

Burt's emphasis on coercion and cruelty further reshapes how we read the horse in this opening scene. For the stress on the horse that takes place both diegetically and extradiegetically is exacerbated of course by the demands of Tarr's signature long take: the four-minute shot begins mid-action, suggesting that the horse has already been running, and towards the end of the shot she looks noticeably more tired and strained. We might wonder too about the takes we have not seen: no doubt there is a certain amount of repetition involved in getting the 'right' shot here (a challenge often exacerbated by the technical difficulties of the long take). In *The Turin Horse*, the potentially 'ethical' gesture of the long take – its attentiveness to creaturely vulnerability – thus becomes disturbingly compromised. For in its gesture of durational attentiveness, the film not only exploits but actively produces the vulnerability that it documents.[37]

Reminiscent of the critique that slow cinema instrumentalises the often marginalised human lives that it frames,[38] this is long-take cinema reliant upon animal labour, struggle, suffering. Reading the technique of the long take (in general) in ecological terms, Nadia Bozak sees it as a form of 'conspicuous consumption': 'cinema itself might be viewed as a glorious expenditure of energy, and the long take an aesthetic marker of the same – one way in which to burn off surplus wealth and resources'.[39] While Bozak's emphasis is on environmental resources, *The Turin Horse* provides a different lens through which to view Bozak's insights: the surplus gloriously expended here is not a 'natural resource' but animal labour.[40] There is an uneasy relation between beauty and cruelty here, as well as a troubling fusion of the energies of horse and cinema, recalling not only a history of 'the use of horses to provide dramatic spectacle' and cinema's attendant instrumentalisation of horse power (an instrumentalisation that begins with Muybridge),[41] but also, beyond cinema, a centuries-long tradition of breeding and domestication that has positioned horses, as Ann Norton Greene has argued, as a 'biotechnology', as 'living machines'.[42] At the same time, *The Turin Horse*'s attentiveness to the struggle of the animal interrupts any smooth logic of energy extraction. In the lurching gait of the horse onscreen, *The Turin Horse* summons forth – and simultaneously troubles – histories of horse power aggressively harnessed both onscreen and off.

ANIMAL WORK

As Jean-Louis Comolli has observed: 'The cinema, in documentary and other forms, has rarely filmed work.'[43] Indeed, from Louis Lumière's *Workers Leaving the Factory* (1895) onwards, 'work and its figuration are *ambiguously central* to the history of cinema', as Gorfinkel suggests.[44] In Lumière's film, 'we never see the actual labor inside the factory walls. The actors, Lumière's own employees, are put to work by the new invention of the cinema precisely at the fulcrum point of the day which signals their escape from the rationalized, measured time of the industrial workplace.'[45] Cinema has often relegated labour to off-screen time and space, turning a blind eye to the exertions of work. As Martin O'Shaughnessy observes: 'Ever since the Lumière brothers famously filmed their workers exiting rather than entering the factory, cinema has associated itself more with leisure, with the escape from toil, than with what happens in the factory, the office, or other place of labor.'[46] In this sense, as Gorfinkel puts it, 'all of cinema is in some sense a spectacularized product of a labor that remains consistently off-scene – be it the labor behind the camera, in the bodies placed before it, or in those exertions that evade its view, transpiring offscreen, out of frame, before, after, and beyond it.'[47] Underlining the 'paradox of labor's simultaneous visibility and invisibility' in the cinema, Gorfinkel notes that there is '[o]n the one hand, a materialization of labor, its traces, and effects, and on the other, a dissipation into abstraction so central to the constitution of capital's circulations, exchanges, flows, and substitutions. Films screen and also screen out the labor that subtends them as aesthetic "works," as works of art.'[48]

This dynamic of labour's cinematic (in)visibility – and its intricate links to questions of the (extra)diegetic, on/offscreen and the (im)material – is thus not limited to animal images but is rather central to the exertions and flows of cinema in general and the various labouring bodies that shape it.[49] But while Gorfinkel notes that 'human labor often remains the repressed of filmic representation',[50] we might add that animal labour has been especially repressed: animal work – and the suffering of labouring animals in particular – has been

Figure 3.1 Equine labour (*The Turin Horse*).

rendered difficult to see, both in the cinema and beyond.[51] Indeed, it is less often noted that in *Workers Leaving the Factory* we see not only humans leaving the factory but also horses. The horses are pulling carriages, providing transport. For the horses, then, this is not the end of a day's work but its continuation[52] – a crucial detail that upsets the neat opposition between invisible labour and visible leisure posed by both Gorfinkel and O'Shaughnessy above. And again, coercion is never far away: in one version of the film, as two horses pulling a carriage emerge from the factory, we see the driver crack his whip. In a form of chiasmus, Lumière's employees are put to work by cinema in the very moment that signals their 'escape from the rationalized, measured time of the industrial workplace', as Gorfinkel suggests. But the film figures no such escape for the horses, and no such chiastic reprieve – remaining harnessed to 'the rationalized, measured time of the industrial workplace', they continue to labour both in and for the images.[53]

In a critique of Marx's understanding of labour as 'an exclusively human characteristic',[54] Hribal has argued that animal labour 'played an indispensable role in the development of capitalism',[55] and that animals should be seen as part of the working class. That the labour of animals has been unwaged is just one indication of the ways in which it has been rendered invisible.[56] Tracing histories of animal work across the agricultural and industrial revolutions, Hribal notes in particular that: 'Horses, mules, donkeys, and oxen had been the primary suppliers of power for a millennium' – they were essential to agriculture, transportation and milling.[57] Horses worked hard, for incredibly long hours, and suffered intensely, as suggested by their drastically shortened working-life spans. Elaine Walker observes that, from the eighteenth century onwards, '[a]s the great range of horse-drawn vehicles struggled to keep up with the demands of burgeoning human development', it was common to see 'horses collapsing under impossible loads, quite literally worked to death on the streets in full view of the public'.[58] As Hribal notes:

> During the 1800s, the average working life of a horse was only about four years on a fast coach and seven on a slow. On the mail-coaches, they could only handle about three years before their bodies gave out. Even more unfortunate, there was no retirement for these employees. They would either be sold to farmers or, worse yet, livery stables. These stables would then lease out their services on a part-time or full-time basis for commercial transport, personal carriages, cab service, or public buses. So once again, these same horses would be sent out to work in the already crowded streets.[59]

Both Walker and Hribal give historical accounts of the strain placed on horses, of the labour extracted from them until their bodies gave up.[60] Such histories ask us to see the horse witnessed by Nietzsche, a horse pulling a cab in a crowded urban street, otherwise – that is, as a labourer, not just a victim. It is this history of labour that surfaces in *The Turin Horse*. It is made manifest by the scenes discussed above, but also by the transition staged by the film's opening scene: the move from the streets of Turin (in the voiceover) to a field in Hungary (in the image) uncannily re-enacts the typical trajectory of a working horse's life of labour – from urban cab to farm cart – in the nineteenth century, as described by Hribal here.[61] Though tempting to read the horse in Tarr and Hranitzky's film as an imagining of the 'afterlife' of Nietzsche's horse, the connection remains ambiguous. But the historical contexts cited by Hribal further an understanding of the film's articulation of equine labour. In the context of the broader dynamics of (in)visibility that shape cinema's relation to work, Gorfinkel notes 'the straining necessary to see and read labor in cinema and in aesthetic objects more broadly'.[62] The straining of the horse in the long take inadvertently reflects back to us the labour of reading labour, particular the unrecognised labour of animals.[63]

When Rancière turns to reflect on the place of the horse in Tarr and Hranitzky's film, he writes:

> it is the tool for work, the means of survival for old Ohlsdorfer and his daughter. It is also the beaten horse, the animal martyred by humans that Nietzsche embraced in the streets of Turin before entering the night of madness. But it is also the symbol of the existence of the disabled coachman and his daughter, kin to the Nietzschean camel, the being made to be loaded with all possible burdens.[64]

Here the horse is figured as a 'means' both within the film (for survival) and for the film (as symbol). Rancière's reading demonstrates an awareness of the various kinds of 'burdens' this entails. But implicitly, according to his reading, the animal does not work: she can only be a 'tool for work'. Despite the sustained attention that Rancière gives to labour elsewhere in his writings,[65] here, as for Marx, the animal does not labour. Thus, while we find a certain awareness of the place of the animal in Rancière's reading of *The Turin Horse*, we also note the limitations of that awareness. As I suggested in the Introduction, animal labour figures as a recurrent blindspot in contemporary philosophy's engagements with animal life, including in the work of Derrida and Bailly. One of the many aspects that a critical animal studies perspective might contribute to, and demand of, philosophy and film theory is the labour of close reading lives (and labours) that are other-than-human – a labour neglected here by Rancière but one that is necessary if we are to attend to what he himself describes as 'situations that endure'.[66]

CRUELTY

As *The Turin Horse* progresses, the threat of the whip's violence is realised. On the second day, Ohlsdorfer leads the horse out of stable; she walks slowly, seemingly resisting. She moves towards the camera, head thrust towards us as she enters the bridle, muzzle very close to the camera. As the bit is adjusted, the horse's mouth makes movements similar to the ones in the opening scene, suggesting discomfort. As Hockenhull notes (referring to the horse's real name, Ricsi): 'She champs at her bit and shifts uneasily from side to side, clearly affected by the relentless winds that continue to rage. Ears laid back – which is a sign of unease in horses – Ricsi seems apprehensive yet accepting of her situation.'[67] Ohlsdorfer mounts the cart and pulls on the reins, shouting. On the first shout, the horse's head pulls to the side, mouth open, neck straining – we see the bit pulling at her mouth. But the horse stands her ground, refusing to move. Ohlsdorfer then starts to whip the horse with the reins. She whimpers.[68] We see her body shuddering with each whip. There is a cruelty at work that cannot be contained by the diegetic frame that ostensibly motivates it.

I am reminded here of Pick's reading of moments of violence that cross the threshold between the diegetic and the nondiegetic in Bresson's *Au hasard Balthazar* (such as when the donkey is kicked or his tail set on fire) – moments that she describes in terms of the film's 'cost on living bodies'.[69]

Figure 3.2 Vulnerability and domination (*The Turin Horse*).

This is a cost – and a cruelty – about which *The Turin Horse* seems highly self-reflexive. The presence of Erika Bok, playing Ohlsdorfer's daughter, embeds this scene in a longer history of animal cruelty enacted in and for Tarr's films. In *Sátántangó* (1994), Bok plays Estike, a little girl who tortures her cat, in a long and painfully protracted scene that similarly seems to breach the boundary between the diegetic and the extradiegetic.[70]

In *The Turin Horse*, this 'cost on living bodies' is complicated further by the history of Ricsi, the horse filmed by Tarr and Hranitzky. As Tarr reveals in interview:

We found her in a market in a small village in the Hungarian lowland. I said immediately, 'This is the horse we need.' You could see this horse was humiliated. She's not that old, just around seven. She was a very sad horse. But I have to tell you, all horses are sad who are around people. The owner wanted to make her work, and she refused. And it happened like with Nietzsche, in real life – I stopped him immediately. I was screaming at him, and then he sold us this horse, and she's our horse now. Now she's OK – we found a nice place for her.[71]

Tarr doubles as Nietzsche here, just as the horse in Hungary will double as the horse in Turin. But if Nietzsche went 'mad for Pity's sake', as Barthes puts it,[72] Tarr has in mind something more political than pity (recalling Julian Murphet's argument for politics rather than pity in our consideration of animals).[73] Tarr demonstrates an intense awareness of a history of labour and cruelty that has shaped this particular horse's life.[74] He is sensitive to what he sees as her humiliation – a denial of her dignity – but also her agency, her stubborn refusal to work.[75]

The history revealed here further complicates the ethical and political dimensions of *The Turin Horse*. For while the film requires Ricsi to labour in and for the images it seeks,[76] the film has rescued her from a longer history of labour and cruelty. Yet, in a further twist, images in the film of Ricsi's unease – for example, her agitated movement as she resists the harness – register a sensitivity in the horse shaped by previous situations of suffering and duress. As Hockenhull suggests, 'she is sensitised to ill treatment, particularly when in harness'; 'knowing something about the mare's background, one must assume that Ohlsdorfer's behaviour clearly disturbs Ricsi'.[77] Traces of a history of domination surface in the film's framing of Ricsi's discomfort. The film's awakening of this history deepens the complexities of its relation to the horse and of its conflicted investments.[78] I return to this question of the film's animal politics below. In what follows, I want to connect these issues of labour and suffering with the broader political contexts of the film before coming back to the specific question of animal labour and resistance.

END TIME

For Rancière, Tarr's films, indelibly shaped by the contemporaneous context of postcommunist Hungary, 'deal with the end of the faith in the historical advent of a new world of freedom and equality and with the disenchantment regarding the capitalist promise following the collapse of the socialist one'.[79] This context is signalled in *The Turin Horse* in particular through the arrival of a visitor at the house on the second day, who announces that the world has gone to ruin. In a repetitive, circular speech, he speaks of judgement, God ('whatever he takes part in is the most ghastly creation that you can imagine'), and how 'the world has been debased': 'everything has been debased that they've acquired, and since they've acquired everything in a sneaky, underhand fight, they've debased everything.' He continues:

> Because whatever they touch – and they touch everything – they've debased. This was the way it was until the final victory. Until the triumphant end. Acquire, debase, debase, acquire. Or I can put it differently if you like: to touch, debase and thereby acquire, or touch, acquire and thereby debase. It's been going on like this for centuries. On, on and on.

While the references to 'they' are obscure and non-specific, these comments register an unrelenting drive for acquisition that – while reaching back across the centuries, as the visitor suggests – speaks in particular to the postcommunist context signalled by Rancière and to an ecological context made forcibly present by the film as well, as we witness the gradual disappearance of the family's meagre resources. For while Ohlsdorfer and his daughter already lead an impoverished existence, getting by on boiled potatoes, water from the well, and a few logs on the fire each day, by the end of the film their environment has been depleted still further: the well is dry, and they can find no way to light the lamps in the house. Water, light, heat – the very elements that form the basis of survival – are now absent. By the end of the fifth day, even the raging wind has stopped. As the voiceover states: 'Dead silence outside, the storm is over. Dead silence falls on the house too.'

For Franklin Ginn, Tarr and Hranitzky's film 'distills into an intense form many anxieties of Anthropocene apocalypse [. . .]'[80] – not least through its reflections on the dwindling of fuel reserves and implicit links to 'fears shaped by the geopolitics of oil' and the 'end of carbon modernity'.[81] Ginn suggests:

> The sixth day's separation of life from the sun (as the great darkness descends to block the ultimate source of fossil fuels) refers to the inevitability of the end of carbon humans not just in this film, but in our own world. The characters' inability to respond to this crisis evokes the

Figure 3.3 Refusing to work (*The Turin Horse*).

way in which imaginations of the Anthropocene have been colonized by fossil fuels.[82]

Mysteriously, the daughter finds it impossible to relight the lamp, though she assures her father that she has filled it with paraffin. As Ginn notes, 'rather than seek an explanation or another fuel source, the pair grope their way to bed in the dark',[83] their relinquishing of action and understanding gesturing to a certain resignation in the face of 'a disaster that has already occurred',[84] and outwards, beyond the diegesis, towards the irreversibility and radical opacity of environmental crisis (thereby lending ecological contours to Tarr's own statement on the film: 'Everything in the world passes away. Perhaps the world itself will pass away').[85]

The Turin Horse traces a relentless movement of disappearance, of extinction, through other indices too. At the end of the first day, Ohlsdorfer, lying in bed, tells his daughter that he can no longer hear the woodworm, despite having heard them 'for fifty-eight years'. The 'lone tree, stripped bare, looming on the horizon of wind-swept hills'[86] also becomes a figure of life reduced to a bare minimum. The film signals that a cataclysmic change in the environment has taken place – one that coincides in an enigmatic manner with the interruption to routine brought about by the withdrawal of the horse. The threat to survival on which the film ends – and to which Ohlsdorfer and his daughter now seem resigned – assumes particularly urgent dimensions, beyond the diegetic frame of the film, in the current era of ecological crisis by which it is haunted. There is an intense kind of 'resource consciousness'[87] staged here, both thematically and formally, as in these final scenes, cinema too is pared down to its barest elements – remnants of light and sound that then fade into darkness and silence.

The extradiegetic context from which the film speaks – that of current biopolitical regimes – implicitly informs its critical engagement with questions of life, suffering, extinction. Citing 'global-scale events such as climate change and loss of biodiversity', Shukin suggests that '"the survival of biological life" itself is reemerging as an object and project of biopower'[88] – a biopolitical context by which *The Turin Horse*'s focus on survival and power seems haunted. Yet the 'resource consciousness' articulated here – and undergirded by the critique of relentless acquisition voiced by the film – also intersects with questions of 'animal capital', as staged by Ohlsdorfer's extraction of labour from the horse.[89] While survival is at stake here for both the human and the animal, in the shudder of the horse under the whip, we sense a particular kind of violence reserved for the animal, and the ways in which bodies are unequally exposed.[90] As we will see, this differential exposure of human and animal bodies is made particularly manifest by the film's reflections on exhaustion and suffering.

EXHAUSTION

Though *The Turin Horse* traces a seemingly inexorable movement towards death,[91] we do not actually see any of the characters die: the horse is absent from the final scenes, and the closing image shows Ohlsdorfer and his daughter at the table, listless and immobile. Lives here, both human and animal, seem locked in a state of 'interminable survival'[92] – suspended, left in limbo, in a mode of 'death-in-life'.[93] This state of suspension orientates our attention towards the gestures of bodies struggling to persist. This struggle is often read by critical commentary in existentialist terms, as noted above, but such readings tend to impute a form of ahistoricity to the concerns of the film. Such ahistoricity seems prompted in part by the film's indeterminate historical setting. But I want to suggest here that by moving beyond a timeless conception of existentialist struggle, we might read *The Turin Horse* as an interrogation of contemporary contexts of labour, precarity and survival.

Through its own depleted pace, *The Turin Horse* attends to the efforts of tired and weary bodies, detailing the repetition with difference of certain routines – of dressing, cooking, eating, fetching water – across the six days. The girl's repeated trips to the well, straining against the relentless gale, furnish a particular archive of struggle. Her tramping across the field recalls the same actress, Bok as Estike, determinedly trudging on in *Sátántangó*. In *The Turin Horse*, on the third day, the girl struggles to pull up the bucket from the well,

Figure 3.4 Exhaustion (*The Turin Horse*).

her contorted expression registering the immense effort that it costs her. She stumbles and struggles with the well cover. And as she walks back to the house with the pail of water, we see her body straining under the weight, recalling the lurching of the burdened body in the opening images of the horse's movement. As Gorfinkel suggests, 'tiredness is a problem of work expended and strain made manifest, a bending under weight, a bulging distension, a flexing shape'.[94] As *The Turin Horse* traces such strain and distension, exhaustion becomes the place at which the human and the animal converge. The 'resource consciousness' of the film – its reflection on scarcity and disappearance – extends to the resources of the body itself: echoing Gorfinkel's reflections on exhaustion in other films, here in *The Turin Horse*, for both the human and the animal, '[i]t is a question of endurance, how much a body can endure as a condition of its continuous survival, set against the entropic and deteriorating force of gravity, decomposition, decay.'[95]

The Turin Horse's registering of exhausted perseverance makes manifest an allegorical dimension that resonates both with and beyond the period in which the film is set. For although on the surface the film documents the hard labour of survival in a time loosely framed as belonging to a preindustrial agricultural context, it also gestures – implicitly, allegorically – to relations between work and survival in a neoliberal capitalist context. As Gorfinkel suggests, in an era of post-Fordist, 'immaterial' labour, characterised by flexibilisation, casualisation and insecurity, '[b]eing in a state of constant exhaustion and wearing out, of "energy departing," is what many theorists of our economic and affective present describe as the basic condition of the postindustrial, information driven, neoliberal global economy.'[96] And thus:

> In a perverse reversal of effects (tiredness) and causes (labor), fatigue is thus no longer a consequence of work but instead is a precondition for survival, a product of [. . .] [an] indistinction between work and leisure, of work's flexibilization. Thus, fatigue seems to become a necessity for the seeking and securing of a livelihood of any sort.[97]

In an allegorical mode, *The Turin Horse* arguably reflects on this state of perpetual labour, precarity and fatigue-as-survival that increasingly defines our current era. And in this sense, the film also binds itself to the context of (Hungarian) postcommunism in particular. As Eva Mazierska notes:

> Some of the main changes brought about by the collapse of communism were related to work. Capitalism replaced communism and, with that, free market replaced a regulated, centrally planned economy, post-Fordism replaced Fordism, and flexible employment and unemployment replaced jobs for life.[98]

The mapping of a post-Fordist context back onto the depiction of rural labour in *The Turin Horse* that I propose here may seem anachronistic. But though ostensibly set in an earlier time, Tarr and Hranitzky's film speaks from and to a postcommunist, post-Fordist present. And the conceptual overlapping of material and immaterial labour, underlined by Maurizio Lazzarato among others,[99] suggests still further the potential slippages and mobility of the figuration of work in *The Turin Horse*: the film might be read as gesturing to ways in which 'material terms of exploitation, displacement, and expropriation' persist in an age of so-called 'immaterial' labour.[100] At the same time, the film is inflected by contemporary contexts of 'labor's de-securitization and precarization'[101] as it traces the ease with which work, energy and resources can slip away.[102] (Hovering in the background here too is the political precarity of postcommunist Hungary, and of central Europe more broadly, in the aftermath of Soviet rule – perpetually positioned to some extent 'on the edge of extinction or absorption by larger powers', as Jaffe suggests.)[103]

While Tarr's earlier films explore the shifting ground of promises, betrayals and lies, such narrative dynamics and character intrigues have been stripped away in *The Turin Horse* in order to focus more unflinchingly on the question of brute survival. This is, as Rancière writes:

> A mundane time, which no promise interrupts, confronted by a lone possibility: the risk of no longer being able even to repeat. No longer any

cafés, in which expectations intersect and deals are proposed. Only a lost house in a wind-swept countryside. No longer any illusions, deals, or lies: a simple question of survival, the only possibility of carrying on the next day being that of eating a meal consisting of a single boiled potato with one's hands.[104]

Gone are the deals and failed promises of *Damnation* and *Sátántangó*. In *The Turin Horse*, the future has fallen away. All that remains is 'the risk of no longer being able to repeat' (as the film gestures allegorically once more, perhaps, to the contemporary context of 'labor's de-securitization and precarization'). Within these contexts of precarity and fatigue-as-survival, *The Turin Horse* registers, in a mode of durational attentiveness, the unremitting rituals of perseverance, the stubborn gestures of enduring.

In the final image of Ohlsdorfer and his daughter, listless and immobile, one senses that the film has moved from tiredness to exhaustion, from 'exhausted realization' to that which 'exhausts all of the possible', as Deleuze puts it in his reading of Beckett.[105] In exhaustion, 'you press on, but toward nothing'.[106] Indeed, Rancière's reading of the final scenes suggests both 'pressing on' and resignation, as the film's move towards nothingness remains marked by a memory of resistant gestures:

> [their] relentless and patient gestures have ceaselessly sketched the image of a refusal to be abandoned to the sole fatality of wind and misery for the entire length of the film. The resigned bodies that are effaced in the night are also marked by the memory of the gestures with which they steadfastly applied themselves, each morning, to prepare for the morning to come. In the night that descends upon the final silence of the characters, the filmmaker's rage remains intact against those who debase the lives of men and horses, those 'victors' who, like the Nietzschean prophet of the second day says, have degraded all they have touched by making it into an object of possession [. . .][107]

The final image, in which the possible has been exhausted, remains shaped, Rancière suggests, by our memory of the persistence with which survival has been so determinedly, desperately, pursued throughout. Rancière focuses here on human gestures of refusal. But he also extends his argument across species lines, registering the film's interrogation of a totalising system that debases all lives, human and nonhuman. While Tarr and Hranitzky's film resists any precise description of this system, leaving it open, anonymous, and perhaps all the more monstrous, a reading of the film in contemporary contexts prompts certain names that we might give this system – names such as capital, biopower, globalisation.

And under this system, the dividing lines between humans and animals become less clear, particularly when both are reduced to forms of drastically impoverished existence or 'bare life'.[108] If, as Rancière suggests, in Tarr's cinema 'lived time is connected with pure repetition, there, where human speech and gestures tend toward those of animals',[109] then in *The Turin Horse*, the registering of exhausted bodies on the margins of survival – coupled with the resistance to character interiority staged by the film's formal approach – threatens to reduce the gap between the human and the animal.[110] This gap seems particularly narrowed by the film's tracing of affinities between the daughter and the horse. There are surface affinities, signalled visually, for example through the echoes between the daughter's tangled hair in the wind and that of the horse. But these affinities run deeper too, coursing through the film's observation of female bodies – human and animal – made to labour strenuously at Ohlsdorfer's command.[111] Apparently able to use only one arm, he relies on his daughter to fetch water, cook for him and help him dress, barking orders at her, extracting labour.[112] The daughter voices her affinity with the horse at certain points: it is she who says to Ohlsdorfer when he is whipping the horse: 'Can't you see she won't move?'. This question, uttered offscreen, marks the film's first reference to the horse's gender and implies a particular connection between the girl and the horse.[113] This convergence between female bodies – human and animal – will be literalised when, on the fourth day, Ohlsdorfer decides that they must leave, and they pack their belongings into a handcart. As they set off, the daughter pulls the handcart, having now replaced the horse (who follows on behind). Like a cruel joke, the scene hovers uncertainly between the 'comedy and miserabilism' that inhabits Tarr's work more broadly[114] – a tension that surfaces at other moments in *The Turin Horse*, such as in the potato-eating scenes. Yet, puncturing any possible comic dimension, we see the girl's body battling once more against the forces of wind and weight. Charting endurance through distended cinematic time, this is a cinema of 'endurance' that unravels clear distinctions between the human and the animal, while emphasising ways in which – in relation to questions of power and domination – beings are always differentially exposed (here in relation not only to species but gender too).

LINES OF FLIGHT

Of the many connections and divergences between the human and the animal staged by the film, their differing relations to repetition seem particularly decisive. Rancière identifies three kinds of time at work in *The Turin Horse*: the 'time of decline', the 'time of change' and the time of repetition.[115] He locates the 'time of change' in the attempted departure of the Ohlsdorfers when they set off with the handcart. But in one protracted long take, the film shows them disappearing on the horizon, only to return. It thus seems more pertinent to align Rancière's notion of the 'time of change' with the resistance of the horse. For while Ohlsdorfer and the daughter pursue a form of survival-as-repetition, the horse seeks to break out of this cycle of repetition. Giving up on survival, she effectively decides to die.

The interruptive place of the horse recalls Rancière's discussion of 'the victims of manipulations' in Tarr's work. He focuses on Estike in *Sátántangó* and János in *Werckmeister Harmonies*, describing these characters as 'idiots' – a term that implicitly harks back to figures such as Dostoyevsky's Prince Myshkin, in *The Idiot* (1874), and the reworking of such figures by Deleuze.[116] Rancière reads the 'idiot' in Tarr's work as a marginalised, peripheral yet circuit-breaking figure, in terms that consciously recall a Nietszchean escape from eternal return.[117] From within the repetitive cycles of manipulation and betrayal in Tarr's films, such figures pursue 'a plot of deviation'.[118] As Rancière puts it: 'The idiots then witness the capacity of the most destitute persons to split up the time of repetition and to break the round-and-round movement which it engenders in order to draw straight lines or harmonious circles.'[119] Though Rancière does not pursue this idea in relation to *The Turin Horse*, it is clear that the horse follows a similar trajectory: marginal, destitute, equipped only with refusal, the horse interrupts the cycle of labour and cruelty to which she is subjected (a cycle metonymically captured by the repetitive movement of the film's opening images). Thus in *The Turin Horse*, while the human persists through repetition, the horse resists by breaking out of repetition. This reading is risky, not least because of its utopianism. But it connects in significant ways with the 'frame story' of Tarr and Hranitzky's film. For an 'idiotic' breaking of the 'round-and-round movement' is staged by the episode with Nietzsche: he interrupts the beating of the horse only to fall – the apocryphal narrative suggests – into madness ('gentle and demented', as the opening voiceover tells us). In Tarr and Hranitzky's film, Nietzsche's circuit-breaking 'idiocy' is transferred to the horse.

As noted above, the horse's refusal is then enigmatically linked by the film to a set of other disruptions: the drying up of the well, the disappearance of fuel. These dissipations of energy and resource register a general movement in the film towards entropy. But from within this dynamic of depletion, the horse's refusal can also be read otherwise – as a mode of flight rather than dissipation, recalling Rancière's description of Tarr's work in general as committed to:

> a visual scenario which extracts the power of situations that endure from the narrative that binds them together, but which also breaks the circularity of the narrative by giving all the force of these situations to straight lines, to positive lines of flight, forward in the pursuit of a shadow – to

the straight lines around which the circular narrative closes its nihilistic logic.[120]

Again, Rancière's approach is inflected by the thought of Deleuze; as we saw in Chapter 2, Deleuze and Guattari reflect on lines of flight in their consideration of animals in Kafka, writing of '*A line of escape, and not freedom.*'[121] This seems to be what is traced by the horse's refusal in Tarr and Hranitzky's film: not freedom, but a line of flight, a mode of escape[122] – that is, something other than the general dynamic of entropy against which it is registered. The place of the horse in the film cannot be collapsed into a more general category of the nonhuman, or a more general wasting away of nonhuman resources (not least because of the intentional withdrawal of labour that the film suggests). Writing of 'the lone tree, stripped bare, looming on the horizon of wind-swept hills, and the man, prostrate upon his stool, who no longer expects anything from this desolate landscape, nor from the worn-out horse, shut away by the stable doors as if by a tombstone',[123] Rancière reveals a horizontalising gesture that implicitly flattens the differences between the animal and the environment, subsuming the horse – alongside the tree and the landscape – within a more general logic of resource scarcity. Enveloping the place of the horse within a broader thematics of dissipation and decomposition, Rancière is not willing to see the horse's line of flight – or to see something like animal agency, refusal, resistance. But it is something that the film asks us to see.

Problematising notions of the animal as 'voiceless victim', Hribal has documented histories of animal resistance, made manifest in particular through refusals to work.[124] Hribal cites, for example, a passenger's account of 'a worn-out horse' refusing to turn the paddles of a ferry crossing the Hudson River in 1827 (only to be whipped and punched by the ferryman). Such historical accounts question the idea of animal passivity, asking us to see animals not only as victims but also as agents.[125] In a scene in Tarr's *Sátántangó*, a group of horses run into a town square. A boy watching remarks: 'The horses got away from the slaughterhouse again.' Though only a fleeting moment in the film, seemingly disconnected from the central narrative, it is suggestive of Tarr's sustained interest in the agency of horses, in their disruptions and refusals.

In *The Turin Horse*, while the horse's resistance to work on the second day is initially registered in emphatically physical terms (as she twists about and refuses to move while being whipped), what follows this reveals a quieter, less spectacular form of animal resistance, one that is patiently traced by the film as a series of gradual steps. On the fourth day, the camera accompanies the girl as she enters the stable. Framed centrally, the horse faces the camera; as the girl moves into the background (and slightly out of focus), the scene visually foregrounds the horse, announcing the animal as the focus of the scene. The girl asks: 'Why haven't you eaten?'. As she walks around to stand in front of

Figure 3.5 Animal resistance (*The Turin Horse*).

the horse, the camera changes places with her, rotating ninety degrees to the left. The horse and the girl now stand in profile (recalling similar images in *Au hasard Balthazar*). The horse bows her head and looks down. As the girl touches the horse's muzzle, the animal moves her head to the side and away from her. The girl says: 'You're not going anywhere.' The horse keeps moving her head away as though she doesn't want to be touched. The girl brings a bucket of water to her, imploring her to drink ('Drink! For my sake'). She puts her hand in the water and touches the horse's mouth. The horse pulls her head up and away in a further gesture of refusal.

On the fifth day, when the Ohlsdorfers open the stable door, the horse stands immobile, head down. Unlike the previous day, she does not seem to respond to the door opening or to their arrival. She seems impassive, almost lifeless. The camera tracks in so that the horse's head is centrally framed in close-up. There is a thick rope across her nose. She blinks. Ohlsdorfer simply pulls the rope off the horse's head and walks out. The camera moves out of the stable too. The girl stands looking at the horse and then slowly walks out and closes the door. On the sixth day, the camera remains inside the house. We do not see the horse.

Thus in the final images of the horse given to us by the film, she is immobile, lifeless, as though passive. This might be read, as some critical commentaries have tended to do, in purely physical, biological terms – that is, as a narrative of illness. But the film does not articulate the horse's withdrawal explicitly in those terms, and such a narrative justification denies the possibility that there is any sort of decision or agency shaping the events here. For the various gestures of refusal traced by the film tell another story – a story of resistance. This resistance is complicated of course: it leads to death. The horse's insurrection, if we read it as such, is suicidal.[126] But it is also a mode of escape, a breaking out of the cycle of repetition, a line of flight. In this sense, the film is quietly revolutionary about the place of the animal.[127] It reminds us that this is an animal who has laboured and who has now withdrawn her labour. In opening attention to the possibility of animal agency and resistance, *The Turin Horse* refuses the general dissipation of the will that we find in such frameworks as Actor-Network-Theory (and the 'new materialist' thought in dialogue with this).[128] And it unsettles the image of the animal as pure victim and object of pity as she appears in the apocryphal scene with Nietzsche.[129] Indeed, if Nietzsche's work is concerned with the potential 'for life to burst through power's systematic operation in ways that are more and more difficult to anticipate',[130] as Wolfe suggests, then *The Turin Horse* seems particularly faithful to this strand of Nietzsche's thought, extracting the horse from an all-encompassing narrative of passivity and pity to bear witness also to her repetition-escaping potential, and to the resistance of life to the 'systematic operation' of power. As Deleuze puts it in his reflections on Foucault, power 'passes through the hands of the mastered no less than through the hands of the masters (since it passes through every related force). A profound Nietzscheanism.'[131]

IN/VISIBILITY

This idea of animal recalcitrance is also articulated formally by the film in terms of an increasing resistance to the visible. Following the camera's proximity to the horse in the initial stages of the film – epitomised by the patient registering of her movement in the opening images – the film gradually decouples itself from the animal. On the fourth day, when the girl exits the stable and closes the door, the camera remains inside with the horse. But the animal is left in the dark, our vision of her now impaired. From what we can make out from the darkened image, she stays in the same position (we see an ear twitching; we hear one hoof shifting slightly); the camera has remained with her, but our visual access to the animal is now being problematised. On the fifth day, the horse's head is framed in close-up, as noted above. But after Ohlsdorfer walks out of the stable, the camera moves outside too, while the daughter remains in the stable, looking at the horse. The girl then slowly walks out and closes the door. The long take culminates in a static close-up of the stable door, while leaves skitter across the frame. Placed outside the stable, the camera is no longer with the horse: the closed door signals the way in which our view is now blocked, refused. On the sixth day, the camera does not enter the stable at all. By this point, the horse has disappeared from the film's vision.

The Turin Horse thus visually weds itself to the animal and then gradually leaves her behind, relinquishing her. This might be read as a forgetting of the animal, thus confirming a sense that Tarr and Hranitzky's film is really about the human characters. But this move towards disappearance might also be read otherwise, that is, beyond a logic that assumes an alignment of rights and visibility. In a different context, Debarati Sanyal has discussed 'the right to disappear' – an escape from an order that equates visibility with rights and representation.[132] And in relation to animal images in particular, Pick writes of the enabling possibilities of animal invisibility, particularly within regimes of animal tracking and surveillance. Reversing Berger's well-known question, 'Why look at animals?', Pick asks 'Why not look at animals?', suggesting that: 'When confronting advanced optical and tracking technologies that render animals permanently visible, the possibility of *not-seeing* emerges as a more progressive modality of relation to animals.'[133] She continues:

> By not-seeing I do not mean to endorse the censorious attitude to images promoted by Berger, harking back to some bygone (if still violent) interspecies relation; nor does not-seeing bolster ideas about animal mystery that mythologise animals in the human imaginary. Not-seeing in the sense I am using it here connotes the mundane, civic notion of animal privacy that denies human eyes and their technological proxies unlimited access.[134]

In divergence from the perpetual surveillance of its human subjects, Tarr and Hranitzky's film limits our access to the animal; the film gradually leaves the horse behind. While the human characters are submitted to constant observation, the film seems to grant the horse privacy in dying.[135] While the film initially addresses the invisibility of Nietzsche's horse ('Of the horse we know nothing') by making visible Ohlsdorfer's horse, by the end of the film, this right to visibility has been replaced by a 'right to disappear', as the animal slips away from sight. While Rancière sees this as a form of entombment ('the worn-out horse, shut away by the stable doors as if by a tombstone'),[136] the animal's disappearance from the visible arguably gestures still further to a line of flight traced by the film. The horse no longer has to labour for Ohlsdorfer or for the film. She escapes work and escapes the frame. Thus while the film makes animal labour visible, it grants a certain invisibility to the animal herself.[137]

Baker discusses a slipping away from visibility in terms of a Deleuzian line of flight in his analysis of Jaschinski's photographic series, *Animal* (1996). The (often caged) animal body is present in Jaschinski's images only as an indistinct, shadowy shape, 'an obscure dark presence', a 'hazy silhouette';[138]

for Baker, following Deleuze's reflections on Francis Bacon's paintings, the body 'waits to escape from itself'.[139] And here, Baker suggests, 'power resides in darkness'; 'the aesthetic experience is of the creatures drawing that power into their own dense black centres, internalizing it, incorporating it, keeping knowledge of their bodies to themselves, and refusing to be drawn on what it is that they are.'[140] (Significantly, Baker also indicates a mode of refusal here.) We recall the use of darkness in *The Turin Horse* as well, on the fourth day, when the girl closes the stable door and the camera remains with the horse left in the dark. The film allows us to sense here, in its own 'dense black centre', a 'power [that] resides in darkness', the sound of the horse's hoof still shifting acting as a persistent utterance of life and, with it, the possibility of refusal.

ANIMAL WORLDS

What kinds of worlding are at stake in *The Turin Horse*? As we saw in Chapter 1, Deleuze and Guattari engage with von Uexküll's thinking of animal worlds but shift away from his emphasis on the subjective, moving towards a processual model of 'the active and passive affects of which the animal is capable in the individuated assemblage of which it is a part'.[141] Following this passage in *A Thousand Plateaus*, Deleuze and Guattari turn to equine assemblages and affects in particular, in their discussion of Freud's study of Little Hans, a young boy with a fear of horses.[142] Hans's family lived opposite a coaching inn, and Hans witnessed horses drawing heavy carts in the street; on one occasion, he saw an overburdened horse collapse and die. Prompted by Hans's apparent obsession with the 'widdlers' of horses and various animals, Freud elaborates an Oedipal reading of the horse as father. Countering this, Deleuze and Guattari suggest:

> Little Hans' horse is not representative but affective. It is not a member of a species but an element or individual in a machinic assemblage: draft horse–omnibus–street. It is defined by a list of active and passive affects in the context of the individuated assemblage it is part of: having eyes blocked by blinders, having a bit and a bridle, being proud, having a big peepee-maker, pulling heavy loads, being whipped, falling, making a din with its legs, biting, etc. These affects circulate and are transformed within the assemblage: what a horse 'can do'. They indeed have an optimal limit at the summit of horse-power, but also a pessimal threshold: A horse falls down in the street! It can't get back on its feet with that heavy load on its back, and the excessive whipping; a horse is going to die! – this was an ordinary sight in those days (Nietzsche, Dostoyevsky, Nijinsky lamented it).[143]

Here psychoanalytic symbolism, and its abstraction of the animal as Oedipalised sign, is replaced by a system of situated affects and connections, shaping where the horse is and what the horse can do. By invoking the figure of the 'machinic assemblage', Deleuze and Guattari are not returning to a Cartesian notion of the animal as machine – they use 'machinic' in a particular sense to denote an affective assemblage that reaches beyond organicist or mechanistic models.[144] In its invocation of Nietzsche, and in its attentiveness to blindness, discomfort, labour, burden, 'excessive whipping', pain and dying, the passage speaks to the affective presence of the horse in Tarr and Hranitzky's film, while working to trouble the general assumption, by Shukin, Haraway and others, that Deleuze and Guattari are not interested in the material conditions of actual animals.[145] Their comments here, combined with a remark that follows on the same page – 'A racehorse is more different from a workhorse than a workhorse is from an ox'[146] – mark a recognition of the varied material conditions of labour that shape the lives of different animals, and of the workhorse in particular.[147] But as Deleuze and Guattari suggest here, this may need to be understood in terms of a logic of assemblage rather than one of subjecthood. As the reference to von Uexküll suggests, Deleuze and Guattari interpret this as a form of worlding, but one that designates what they describe elsewhere in *A Thousand Plateaus* as 'an enterprise of desubjectification'.[148]

The Turin Horse stages this desubjectifying move by attending to the lifeworlds of its characters – registering affects of labour, survival, exhaustion – in a mode of impersonalisation or, we might say, deterritorialisation. While the minimal dialogue and lack of other legible psychologising gestures trouble spectatorial interpretations of character interiority, the film refuses to harness itself visually to the subjective point of view of any character – human or animal. At times the camera moves with its characters, tracking the gestures of Ohlsdorfer, his daughter and the horse. But at other times, as Jaffe points out, 'both the camera's trajectory and the length of the shot often seem relatively independent of the doings of persons, animals and things'.[149] Jaffe cites examples such as the framing of Ohlsdorfer's empty bed, and we might add to this the framing of the closed door of the stable (one of a number of examples cited by Peter Szendy, in which the point of view appears 'not to belong to any human gaze').[150] *The Turin Horse* is full of moments in which the camera lingers in a space seemingly emptied of human or animal presence or perspective, suggesting ways in which its mode of worlding is unharnessed from any one subject position. As Jaffe suggests: 'At such moments the camera appears both disengaged from *The Turin Horse*'s characters and possibly in greater command of their world than they are.'[151] He continues: 'Hardly subservient to Tarr's characters, the camera in *The Turin Horse* often seems in step with impersonal, perhaps ominous forces such as the darkness, the silence, the windstorm and the dessication [. . .].'[152] Jaffe cites Tony McKibbin's suggestion that in the 'complicatedly blocked sequence shots in Tarr', '[t]he characters don't act in the world so much as seem to be acted upon by the world; a decision made is secondary to the forces compelling them.'[153] Jaffe sees this sense of being acted upon by the world as reinforced by the long take:

> the tendency of the long-take style to forgo or limit point-of-view shots and shot/reverse shots perhaps reduces the sense that characters possess narrative agency – or distinctive visions and perspectives conducive to effective action.[154]

Here, as Jaffe suggests, Tarr and Hranitzky's particular use of the long take, and concomitant eschewal of point-of-view shots, works further to indicate a dwindling of character agency. And as Jaffe goes on to argue, this sense of being acted upon by the world also relates to Tarr's interest in the 'cosmic', an interest that becomes more emphatic in his later works. As Tarr stated after finishing *Werckmeister Harmonies*: 'Everything is much bigger than us. I think the human is just a little part of the cosmos.'[155] This emphasis on the cosmos and a dislodging of a human point of view is also identified by Rancière in his reading of Tarr's work: we see this in his focus on the circulation of affects 'born of '"cosmological" pressure' (in the comments I cited at the beginning of the chapter). And as Rancière suggests later in the text: 'the situation is given in its entirety, without subjective filter'; 'there is no perceptive center';'[t]here is no consciousness in which the universe is visibly condensed'[156] – what Rancière describes here is effectively a form of deterritorialisation.

The long take, the reduction of point-of-view shots – and the dispossession of narrative agency to which this points – thus intimate a decentring of human agency. Yet this also complicates the reading of equine agency that I have suggested above. For there is a fundamental indeterminacy of subject position articulated by the film in formal terms that reorientates our attention to the world acting upon the subject, rather than the subject acting in the world, thereby resisting any definitive ascription of decision, agency, action. This is, of course, the realm of the Deleuzian time-image, in which (as discussed in Chapter 1) the emphasis is often on 'world' rather than 'subject'. In shots in which Ohlsdorfer, the daughter or the horse appear immobile while the camera continues to move through space, we sense the ways in which, as Deleuze puts it, 'The world takes responsibility for the movement that the subject can no longer or cannot make.'[157]

And as Deleuze continues: 'This is a virtual movement, but it becomes actual at the price of an expansion of the totality of space and of a stretching of time.'[158] In the stretching of time at work in *The Turin Horse*, we witness gestures of labour, survival and exhaustion that speak to contemporary contexts of precarity, capital and biopolitical regimes. We sense the ways in which the world acts upon these beings – human and animal. To Deleuze's remarks about the world taking 'responsibility for the movement that the subject can no longer or cannot make', *The Turin Horse* lends a new urgency in its tracing of resignation and helplessness against the implicit backdrop of ecological crisis. At the same time, however, the film's interest in animal resistance indicates ways in which physical inaction does not necessarily correspond with a lack of agency. As I have suggested, in the context of animal politics, the images of the horse's withdrawal of labour assume a quietly revolutionary dimension. If there is a virtual movement to be traced here, it is above all in the horse's line of flight – in her slipping away from work, and from visibility.

NOTES

1. Jacques Rancière, *Béla Tarr, The Time After*, translated by Erik Beranek (Minneapolis: Univocal 2013), pp. 34–5.
2. Ibid., pp. 35–6.
3. Ibid., p. 9.
4. Ibid., p. 37.
5. Ibid., p. 77.
6. Rancière, 'Béla Tarr: The Poetics and Politics of Fiction', in De Luca and Jorge (eds), *Slow Cinema*, pp. 245–60 (p. 247). One might also read the political symbolism of the figure of the animal in Tarr in relation to the terms suggested by Pick's reading of the work of the Ukrainian filmmaker Kira Muratova: 'Animals and animality communicate the exhaustion of both the Soviet and the neoliberal project and return the human to the zoological fold.' Pick, *Creaturely Poetics*, p. 120.
7. In his reflections on *The Turin Horse*, Peter Szendy criticises Rancière's reading for imposing homogeneity upon a heterogeneity of animal presences in Tarr's work (as we see above, for Rancière 'the animal' is reduced to 'the figure in which the human experiences its limit'). See Szendy, 'Animal Filmicum', in Corinne Maury and Sylvie Rollet (eds), *Béla Tarr: de la colère au tourment* (Crisnée: Yellow Now, 2016), pp. 97–109 (p. 98). Yet there appears to be a similarly homogenising move at stake in Szendy's own reading, as he seeks to position the various animal presences in Tarr's films as a figure for cinema itself. His term *animal filmicum* designates 'the animality constitutive of film, that is, the animal *as* film' (p. 102; original emphasis), in line with what he posits as a machinic animality ('machinanimal' (p. 100)) – a potentially reductive logic that I critique in Chapters 1 and 2.
8. Even when Rancière suggests that the herd of cattle in the opening scene of *Sátántangó* has 'weak symbolic power' and should therefore be read as 'an actual herd, and not as an image of herd mentality', he still limits his reading of the animals to their narrative function: they are 'the last stock of a collective farm [. . .] being liquidated'; 'it is the money from this sale that will be the centre of the intrigue' (Rancière, *Béla Tarr, The Time After*, p. 37).
9. LaCapra, *History and Its Limits*, p. 166. In Rancière's defence, it should be noted that the question of the animal is not the main focus of his text (whereas it is the ostensible focus of Agamben's *The Open*, the text examined by LaCapra here).
10. See Rancière, *Béla Tarr, The Time After*, p. 50. Peter Hames notes: 'Tarr denies that his films convey any symbolic or allegorical meaning – "film is always something definite – it

can only record real things".' Hames, 'The Melancholy of Resistance', *Kinoeye*, 1:1, 3 September 2001. Available at http://www.kinoeye.org/01/01/hames01.php (last accessed 14 September 2018). However, one needs to read such statements critically: despite Tarr's assertions, allegorical meanings clearly persist in his work.
11. *The Turin Horse*, including the opening voiceover, draws on a text written by László Krasznahorkai for Tarr's film – a text which is in turn based on material from an essay by Krasznahorkai, 'At the Latest, in Turin', in *The World Goes On*, translated by John Batki, Ottilie Mulzet and George Szirtes (London: Tuskar Rock Press, 2017), pp. 21–3. On the writing process for *The Turin Horse*, see Vladan Petkovic, 'Simple and Pure' [interview with Tarr], *Cineuropa*, 4 March 2011. Available at: http://www.cineuropa.org/en/interview/198131/ (last accessed 14 September 2018). Tarr has frequently collaborated with, and drawn on the works of, Krasznahorkai, including for the film *Sátántangó*, based on a novel (by the same name) by Krasznahorkai. Significantly, Krasznahorkai repeatedly returns to the question of the animal in his works: see, for example, Krasznahorkai, *Animalinside*, translated by Ottilie Mulzet, illustrated by Max Neumann (London: Sylph Editions, 2012), and Krasznahorkai, *The Last Wolf & Herman*, translated by George Szirtes and John Batki (New York: New Directions, 2016).
12. For a useful account drawing on various sources, see Michael John Di Santo, '"Dramas of Fallen Horses": Conrad, Dostoevsky and Nietzsche', *Conradiana*, 42:3 (2010), 45–68. On animals in Nietzsche's thought, see Christa Davis Acampora and Ralph R. Acampora (eds), *A Nietzschean Bestiary: Becoming Animal Beyond Docile and Brutal* (Lanham, MD: Rowman & Littlefield, 2004).
13. This might be seen as indicative of the ways in which animals have often been written out of history by an anthropocentric perspective; on this, see Fudge, 'A Left-Handed Blow'. We might contrast Fudge's valuable consideration of the fault lines in human accounts of animal histories with the distinction drawn by Nietzsche between animal ahistoricity and human historicity, based on what he sees as the animal's ignorance of his/her own past. See Nietzsche, 'On the Uses and Disadvantages of History for Life', in *Untimely Meditations*, translated by R. J. Hollingdale, edited by Daniel Breazeale (Cambridge: Cambridge University Press, 1997), pp. 57–124. Nietzsche's distinction relies on a problematic idealisation of the animal as living in blissful forgetfulness – an idea that might be immediately countered, for example, by contemporary studies of animal memory, trauma and mourning; on this, see Barbara J. King, *How Animals Grieve* (Chicago: University of Chicago Press, 2014).
14. A. O. Scott, 'Facing the Abyss with Boiled Potatoes and Plum Brandy: Béla Tarr's Final Film, "The Turin Horse"', *The New York Times*, 9 February 2012. Available at http://www.nytimes.com/2012/02/10/movies/the-turin-horse-from-bela-tarr.html (last accessed 14 September 2018).
15. Rancière, *Béla Tarr, The Time After*, p. 7.
16. Gorfinkel, 'Weariness, Waiting', p. 313.
17. Fred Kelemen, the Director of Photography on *The Turin Horse*, underlines the centrality of this notion of 'enduring': 'Unlike in Andrei Tarkovsky's movies, time in Béla's movies is not metaphysical; time in Béla's films is existential. It has to be endured.' Kelemen, 'The Last Dance', *Sight and Sound*, June 2012, p. 39.
18. See, for example, Ira Jaffe, *Slow Movies: Countering the Cinema of Action* (New York: Columbia University Press, 2014), pp. 155–6.
19. Tarr cited in Jaffe, *Slow Movies*, p. 156.
20. An important exception is Christina Stojanova's reading of labour in Tarr's films, including *The Turin Horse*; see Stojanova, 'The Damnation of Labor in the Films of

Béla Tarr', in Ewa Mazierska (ed.), *Work in Cinema: Labor and the Human Condition* (New York: Palgrave Macmillan, 2013), pp. 169–87. Citing the opening voiceover ('Of the horse we know nothing'), Stojanova writes: 'there is not much to be learned about the horse that is not already known from general parlance, always already equating the "work horse" with excruciatingly demeaning physical labor, patience, and loyal endurance' (p. 183). There is a valuable recognition of animal labour here, though the chapter does not sustain any further critical engagement with the horse.
21. Zsuzsa Selyem, 'How Long and When: Open Time Interval and Dignified Living Creatures in *The Turin Horse*', *Acta Universitatis Sapientiae: Film and Media Studies*, 10 (2015), 105–20 (p. 115).
22. Stella Hockenhull, 'Horseplay: Equine Performance and Creaturely Acts in Cinema', *NECSUS: European Journal of Media Studies*, Spring 2015. Available at http://www.necsus-ejms.org/horseplay-equine-performance-and-creaturely-acts-in-cinema/ (last accessed 14 September 2018).
23. The question of the relation between the diegetic and the extradiegetic is central to the ways in which animal film images have been theorised by Sobchack, Lippit and Burt among others; on this, see Chapter 1.
24. Rancière, *Béla Tarr, The Time After*, p. 9.
25. Ibid., p. 8.
26. In his discussion of slow cinema, realism and the long take, De Luca draws on Bazin to argue that 'non-human creatures – and in a more radical form, their death – have come to embody one of the strongest markers of contingency in the filmic image'. De Luca, 'Natural Views', p. 220. In relation to *The Turin Horse*'s opening scene, one could certainly follow De Luca in reading the relation between the long take and the animal in terms of an opening to contingency or the real. However, I seek to avoid essentialising the role of the animal onscreen in this manner, as discussed in Chapter 1.
27. Rancière, *Béla Tarr, The Time After*, p. 59.
28. Ibid., p. 35.
29. Deleuze, *Cinema 2*, p. 168. Strictly speaking, Deleuze is writing here of depth-of-field shots in Renoir and Welles, but he sees these as necessarily also shots of extended duration. In relation to Welles in particular, he associates depth of field with the long take, describing the former as opening to 'a continuity of duration' (pp. 103–5). And thus: depth of field 'makes the unrolling of the film a theorem rather than an association of images [. . .]' (p. 168).
30. Matilda Mroz, *Temporality and Film Analysis* (Edinburgh: Edinburgh University Press, 2012), p. 94.
31. Ibid., p. 69.
32. On embodied spectatorship, see, for example, Sobchack, *The Address of the Eye: A Phenomenology of Film Experience* (Princeton and Oxford: Princeton University Press, 1992).
33. Pick, *Creaturely Poetics*, p. 186.
34. Ibid., p. 15.
35. Gorfinkel, 'The Body's Failed Labor: Performance Work in Sexploitation Cinema', in Gorfinkel (ed.), 'The Work of the Image: Cinema, Labor, Aesthetic', *Framework: The Journal of Cinema and Media*, 53:1 (Spring 2012), 79–98 (p. 83). Gorfinkel is drawing here on Rosen's *Change Mummified*, pp. 147–200.
36. Burt, *Animals in Film*, pp. 140–1.
37. On work, realism and documentary images, see Silke Panse, 'The Work of the Documentary Protagonist: The Material Labor of Aesthetics', in Alexandra Juhasz and

Alice Lebow (eds), *A Companion to Contemporary Documentary Film* (Chichester: Wiley Blackwell, 2015), pp. 155–75, especially her apt description of (documentary) film images as 'parasitical upon the materialities they index' (p. 171).
38. See, for example, De Luca and Jorge, 'Introduction: From Slow Cinema to Slow Cinemas', p. 13.
39. Nadia Bozak, *The Cinematic Footprint: Lights, Camera, Natural Resources* (New Brunswick: Rutgers University Press, 2012), p. 126.
40. Bozak explores films featuring animals, for example in her analysis of *Nanook of the North*, but her focus is on the animal as resource rather than animal labour.
41. Lawrence, 'Muybridgean Motion/Materialist Film: Malcolm Le Grice's *Berlin Horse*', in Lawrence and McMahon (eds), *Animal Life and the Moving Image*, pp. 72–91 (p. 84). For a useful overview of the role of horses in cinema, see Elaine Walker's *Horse* (London: Reaktion, 2008), pp. 172–82.
42. Ann Norton Greene, *Horses at Work: Harnessing Power in Industrial America* (Cambridge, MA and London: Harvard University Press, 2008), p. 4; cited in Lawrence, p. 75. This set of interrelated histories between horse–human relations, industrial capitalism and cinema is traced by Lawrence's 'Muybridgean Motion/Materialist Film'. It is worth noting Hribal's critique of Greene's work, particularly her positioning of horses in 'machinic' terms and her argument that only humans have agency, intentionality and thus the capacity to labour. See Hribal, 'Animals Are Part of the Working Class Reviewed', p. 9.
43. Jean-Louis Comolli, 'Mechanical Bodies, Ever More Heavenly', translated by Annette Michelson, *October*, 83 (Winter 1998), 19–24 (p. 19).
44. Gorfinkel, 'Introduction', in Gorfinkel (ed.), 'The Work of the Image', 43–6 (p. 43); original emphasis.
45. Ibid., p. 43.
46. Martin O'Shaughnessy, 'French Film and Work: The Work Done by Work-Centered Films', in Eva Mazierska (ed.), 'Working Life Now and Then', *Framework*, 53:1 (Spring 2012), 155–71 (p. 156). O'Shaughnessy is drawing on Comolli's *Voir et pouvoir. L'innocence perdue: cinéma, télévision, fiction, documentaire* (Lagrasse: Verdier, 2004).
47. Gorfinkel, 'Introduction', p. 43.
48. Ibid., p. 44.
49. For an apt example, see Gorfinkel's discussion of Dequenne's performance in *Rosetta*: 'the despair of Rosetta and the endurance of Dequenne congeal in this cinematic moment as the two forms of labor – acting labor and the physical labor of carrying the tank – are laminated onto one surface'. Gorfinkel, 'Weariness, Waiting', p. 332.
50. Gorfinkel, 'Introduction', p. 43.
51. While labouring animals have often appeared onscreen throughout the history of cinema, particularly in films about agriculture, reflections on animal suffering in such contexts have been frequently absent (despite exceptions such as Robert Bresson's *Au hasard Balthazar* (1966)). For example, in *The Farmer's Horse* (1951), we see multiple scenes of equine labour without any acknowledgement of the suffering experienced by the horses involved (this is unsurprising, given that the film was partly sponsored by the UK's Ministry of Agriculture); the film positions the horse as a form of technology, promoting equine labour as more useful than tractors for hauling small loads ('a horse is just the right unit of power').
52. Note also how the situation of the horses contrasts with that of the dogs in these images: one dog sits outside the factory, waiting for the workers to leave; another skips along with

a worker on his bicycle. Dogs here, in their privileged role as pets, are associated with idleness, leisure and play rather than work.
53. There is a broader history of animals working in film to be traced here, though this is beyond the scope of the present argument. On animals, and horses in particular, working in theatre, see Nicholas Ridout, 'Animal Labour in the Theatrical Economy', *Theatre Research International*, 29:1 (2004), 57–65.
54. Karl Marx, *Capital: A Critique of Political Economy*, Vol. 1, translated by Ben Fowkes (New York: Penguin, 1990), pp. 283–4; cited in Hribal, 'Animals Are Part of the Working Class Reviewed', p. 3.
55. Hribal, 'Animals Are Part of the Working Class Reviewed', p. 2.
56. As Hribal points out, there is a clear divergence between Haraway and himself on the question of animal labour ('Animals Are Part of the Working Class Reviewed', p. 6). While Hribal points to the injustice of unwaged animal labour, Haraway asserts that dogs 'are not human slaves or wage laborers, and it would be a serious mistake to theorize their labor within those frameworks'; 'They are paws, not hands' (*When Species Meet*, pp. 55–6). Instead, Haraway theorises animal work via science and technology studies, with particular recourse to the work of Edmund Russell. Hribal critiques Haraway's subsequent positioning of animals as living forms of technology, or 'biotechnology' ('Animals Are Part of the Working Class Reviewed', p. 6). For a further useful critique of Haraway's reflections on animal labour, see Ryan, *Animal Theory*, pp. 95–9.
57. Hribal, '"Animals Are Part of the Working Class": A Challenge to Labor History', *Labor History*, 44:4 (2003), 435–53 (p. 443).
58. Walker, *Horse*, pp. 151–2.
59. Hribal, '"Animals Are Part of the Working Class"', pp. 446–7.
60. At which point the horse would be passed on for further work, as Hribal suggests here, or sent to the slaughterhouse. See also Hribal, '32 Million Reasons: NYC Horse Carriages vs. Carriage Horses', *Counterpunch*, 24 June 2014. For a further useful historical account of horse labour, see Walker, *Horse*, especially Chapter 6, 'From Breadwinner to Performer', pp. 143–67.
61. Within the diegesis, the film draws an implicit contrast between the Ohlsdorfers' horse and the much healthier white horses arriving on the third day with the gypsies seeking water from the well – still labouring (pulling a cart), they signal none of the exhaustion indicated by the weary body of the Ohlsdorfers' horse.
62. Gorfinkel, 'Introduction', p. 45.
63. There has been a tendency in recent critical animal studies to read animal work as a form of collaboration, as exemplified by Haraway's *When Species Meet*. One finds a similar emphasis on collaboration in readings of animal work in film; see, for example, Smaill, *Regarding Life*, especially Chapter 2, 'Labor, Agriculture, and Long Take Cinema: Working on the Surface of the Earth' (pp. 21–44); and Ladino, 'Working With Animals'. On documentaries including *Sweetgrass*, and drawing on Haraway, Ladino writes: 'these animals are co-evolving agents in shared environments and collaborative projects' (p. 131). What this emphasis on collaboration underplays at times, though, is the exploitative dimension of animals working for humans. As *The Turin Horse* so starkly lays bare, what Haraway would call the 'contact zone' between human and horse is shaped by the crack of the whip.
64. Rancière, *Béla Tarr, The Time After*, p. 78.
65. Rancière, *The Nights of Labor: The Workers' Dream in Nineteenth Century France*, translated by John Drury (Philadelphia: Temple University Press, 1989).

66. The question of the nonhuman has often been overlooked by Rancière's philosophy, despite his emphasis on equality. As Shukin and Sarah O'Brien suggest, Rancière 'routinely presupposes that the subject of politics is the "human animal" who possesses a capacity for speech'; Shukin and O'Brien, 'Being Struck: On the Force of Slaughter and Cinematic Affect', in Lawrence and McMahon (eds), *Animal Life and the Moving Image*, pp. 187–202 (p. 189). See also Bennett, *Vibrant Matter*, p. 106.
67. Stella Hockenhull, 'Horseplay'.
68. Though postsynch, the sound emphasises the unease of the horse clearly evident in the images.
69. Pick, *Creaturely Poetics*, p. 192.
70. As one review puts it, 'Tarr insists that the cat was treated humanely and not truly harmed, but it's still discomfiting to see the girl flail around, swinging the cat around with her, then trapping it in a net and shoving its head into a bowl of milk.' Ed Howard, *Only the Cinema* [blog], 13 February 2012. Available at http://seul-le-cinema.blogspot.co.uk/2012/02/s.html (last accessed 14 September 2018). Rancière mentions this scene at several points in his text, though he treats it in a purely diegetic dimension (see *Béla Tarr, The Time After*, pp. 40–3).
71. Jonathan Romney, 'Gone with the Wind', *Sight and Sound*, June 2012, 34–6 (p. 36).
72. Roland Barthes, *Camera Lucida: Reflections on Photography*, translated by Richard Howard (London: Vintage, 1993), p. 117.
73. Referring to Derrida's reflections on animal suffering, and to Barthes's description of Nietzsche 'gone mad for Pity's sake', Julian Murphet suggests attending also to the 'political will of the overhuman' (Alain Badiou, *The Century*, translated by Alberto Toscano (Cambridge: Polity, 2007), p. 177), which, as Murphet puts it, 'begins precisely where that suffering and that Pity leave off'; Murphet, 'Pitiable or Political Animals?', *SubStance*, 37:3, Issue 117: 'The Political Animal' (2008), 97–116 (p. 114). Murphet argues: 'it will be worth risking an axiomatic proposition right away, to the effect that pity is categorically incompatible with politics, and triggers amoralistic derailment of the "political animal's" necessarily collective and social endeavors' (p. 98). See also Deleuze and Guattari: 'it is not a question of imitating a horse, "playing" horse, identifying with one, or even experiencing feelings of pity or sympathy'; Deleuze and Guattari, *A Thousand Plateaus*, p. 257. Is there not also, though, a place for pity in considering the political positions of animals? Derrida's reflections on compassion in relation to animals would suggest so. He writes of the need to reconsider 'the immense question of pathos and the pathological, precisely, that is, of suffering, pity, and compassion; and the place that has to be accorded to the interpretation of this compassion, to the sharing of this suffering among the living, to the law, ethics, and politics that must be brought to bear upon this experience of compassion' (*The Animal That Therefore I Am*, p. 26). Turning to Nietzsche and the horse in particular, Derrida reiterates the question of compassion: 'Sometimes I think I see him call that horse as a witness, and primarily in order to call it as a witness to his compassion, I think I see him take its head in his hands' (p. 35).
74. When Romney asks whether 'the Nietzsche story is just a parable to begin the film', Tarr replies: 'No, it's not a parable. This is a horse who has history, who has background, who is definitely somebody. In Hungarian if you say *torinoi* with a small 't', it just means "from somewhere" ["from Turin"]. But if you write it with a big 'T', it looks like a name ["The Turin Horse"]. She has a *name*. "She" – because we have a female horse' (Romney, 'Gone with the Wind', p. 36; original emphasis). Tarr's film is motivated by this question of a horse with a material history rather than a horse as a symbol in a parable.

75. This might be compared to what LaCapra, in his reflections on animals, describes as an ethics that would not rely on passivity but rather 'a form of acknowledged or even affirmed vulnerability that does not exclude agency [...]' (*History and Its Limits*, p. 186n49). On the dignity of animals, see Lori Gruen, 'Dignity, Captivity, and an Ethics of Sight', in *The Ethics of Captivity* (New York: Oxford University Press, 2014), pp. 231–48.
76. Often selecting nonprofessionals, Tarr sees his characters as 'personalities' rather than performers. As Rancière notes, these 'actors who are not actors' are called upon 'not to perform these situations, but to live them' (*Béla Tarr, The Time After*, p. 8). The nonprofessional horse arguably functions as a radical extension of this logic.
77. In a footnote, citing Stephen Budiansky's work on horse behaviour (Budiansky, *The Nature of Horses: Their Evolution, Intelligence and Behaviour* (London: Phoenix, 1997)), Hockenhull suggests that 'Ricsi, in part, conforms to signs of equine fear'. Hockenhull, 'Horseplay'.
78. If the long take might be read as 'a "macho" style' (Christine Vachon, cited in David Bordwell, 'Intensified Continuity: Visual Style in Contemporary American Film', *Film Quarterly*, 55:3 (2002), 16–28 (p. 23)), one cannot help reflecting on the particular power dynamic here too of a male director extracting labour from a female animal.
79. Rancière, 'Béla Tarr: The Poetics and Politics of Fiction', p. 246.
80. Franklin Ginn, 'When Horses Won't Eat: Apocalypse and the Anthropocene', *Annals of the Association of American Geographers*, 105:2 (2015), 351–9 (p. 352).
81. Ibid., p. 355; p. 357.
82. Ibid., p. 355.
83. Ibid., p. 355.
84. Ibid., p. 356. On the temporality of environmental disaster as that which has already happened, see Timothy Morton, *Hyperobjects: Philosophy and Ecology After the End of the World* (Minneapolis: University of Minnesota Press, 2013); cited by Ginn, 'When Horses Won't Eat', p. 356.
85. Tarr, cited in Jaffe, *Slow Movies*, p. 156.
86. Rancière, *Béla Tarr, The Time After*, p. 26.
87. I borrow this term from Bozak's *The Cinematic Footprint*, p. 65.
88. Shukin, *Animal Capital*, p. 182.
89. This association is invited further by Krasznahorkai's text for the film, in which the visitor is a horse dealer, though this detail is not made explicit by the film; on this, see Selyem, 'How Long and When'.
90. However, in the context of Tarr's work we might also recall scenes in *Werckmeister Harmonies*, in which patients in the town hospital are violently beaten. And the role of the whip in the history of human slavery also problematises any distinct separation between the human and the animal along these lines.
91. Jaffe, *Slow Movies*, p. 155.
92. Derrida, *The Animal That Therefore I Am*, p. 26.
93. Jaffe, *Slow Movies*, p. 156.
94. Gorfinkel, 'Weariness, Waiting', p. 314.
95. Ibid., p. 314.
96. Ibid., p. 319.
97. Ibid., p. 320.
98. Mazierska, 'What Happened to the Polish Multitude? Representation of Working People in Polish Postcommunist Cinema', in Mazierska (ed.), 'Working Life Now and Then', 207–27 (p. 207).

99. As Lazzarato suggests: 'Manual labor is increasingly coming to involve procedures that could be defined as "intellectual" [. . .] The old dichotomy between "mental and manual labor," or between "material labor and immaterial labor," risks failing to grasp the new nature of productive activity, which takes this separation on board and transforms it.' Lazzarato, 'Immaterial Labor', translated by Paul Colilli and Ed Emory, in Paolo Virno and Michael Hardt (eds), *Radical Thought in Italy: A Potential Politics* (Minneapolis: University of Minnesota Press, 1996), pp. 132–47 (p. 133).
100. As Gorfinkel notes, work described as 'immaterial', such as in 'cognitive information-based labor models', 'all conceal very persistently material terms of exploitation, displacement, and expropriation that are continuous with the forms and forces of earlier stages of capitalist organization'. Gorfinkel, 'Weariness, Waiting', p. 345n26.
101. Ibid., p. 345n26.
102. As Stojanova suggests, Tarr's films are critical about conditions of labour (and leisure) under communism as well. Treating Tarr's work chronologically, and aligning Tarr's approach with Nietzsche's critique of work as that 'which keeps everybody in harness' (Nietzsche, 'The Dawn', in Walter Kaufmann (ed.), *The Portable Nietzsche*, translated by Kaufmann (New York: Penguin, 1977), pp. 76–92 (p. 82)), Stojanova sees the films tracing a 'gradual devolution of labor as a meaningful human activity for social and self-expression' in both communist and postcommunist contexts (Stojanova, 'The Damnation of Labor in the Films of Béla Tarr', p. 169). Yet Stojanova reads *The Turin Horse* as an overturning, to a certain extent, of this 'gradual devolution', suggesting that the film might be read as 'in favor of labor as a purely heroic expression of existence – human as well as animal [. . .]' (p. 185). However, this seems overly redemptive, and it also overlooks the asymmetries of power (along species and gender lines) at work in the film. Nevertheless, Stojanova's detailed focus on Tarr's interest in labour remains important.
103. Jaffe, *Slow Movies*, p. 170. Here Jaffe is drawing on Milan Kundera's essay, 'The Tragedy of Central Europe', translated by Edmund White, *New York Review of Books*, 31:7 (26 April 1984).
104. Rancière, *Béla Tarr, The Time After*, p. 77.
105. This distinction between tiredness and exhaustion is drawn in Deleuze, 'The Exhausted', translated by Anthony Ullman, *SubStance*, 24:3, 78 (1995), 3–28 (p. 3); cited in Gorfinkel, 'Weariness, Waiting'.
106. Deleuze, 'The Exhausted', p. 4.
107. Rancière, *Béla Tarr, The Time After*, p. 80.
108. On 'bare life' extending across species lines, see Wolfe, *Before the Law*.
109. Rancière, *Béla Tarr, The Time After*, p. 9.
110. Dennis Rothermel reads *The Turin Horse* in terms of 'becoming-animal': 'Together, the man, his daughter and the horse compose a herd, a multiplicity.' Rothermel, 'Becoming-Animal Cinema Narrative', in Gardner and MacCormack (eds), *Deleuze and the Animal*, pp. 266–74 (p. 271).
111. *The Turin Horse* is particularly attentive to female labour, recalling the struggling female bodies of *Rosetta* (Jean-Pierre and Luc Dardenne, 1999) and *Wendy and Lucy* (Kelly Reichardt, 2008) traced by Gorfinkel ('Weariness, Waiting'), and also Bresson's *Mouchette* (1967), a film to which *Rosetta* is indebted. It also calls to mind the stultifying routines of female domestic labour in *Jeanne Dielman* (the cooking of potatoes in *The Turin Horse* particularly recalls Akerman's film).
112. One might also trace here an intersection between disability studies and animal studies, given the film's interest in connections between various 'non-normative' bodies (human and animal). On such intersections, see Wolfe, 'Learning from Temple Grandin,

or, Animal Studies, Disability Studies, and Who Comes After the Subject', *New Formations*, 64 (2008), 110–23. Interestingly, Wolfe's article ends with an invocation of Derrida's reflection, in *Memoirs of the Blind*, on Nietzsche and the horse, highlighting an unravelling of humanist tropes of vision in Derrida's reference to 'the gaze veiled by tears' (Derrida, *Memoirs of the Blind: The Self Portrait and Other Ruins*, translated by Pascale-Anne Brault and Michael Naas (Chicago: University of Chicago Press, 1993), p. 127), cited in Wolfe, 'Learning from Temple Grandin', p. 123).

113. This mirrors to a certain extent the relationship between Marie and the donkey in Bresson's *Au hasard Balthazar*, a film that also explores animal labour, resistance and suffering.
114. On comedy and miserabilism in Tarr, see Hames, 'The Melancholy of Resistance'.
115. Rancière, *Béla Tarr, The Time After*, pp. 78–9.
116. Philippe Mengue aligns Deleuze's interest in such idiot figures as Prince Myshkin and Melville's Bartleby with the focus, in Deleuze's later writings, on control societies, with 'circuit breakers' that 'escape from control'. Deleuze, *Negotiations 1972–1990*, translated by Martin Joughin (New York: Columbia University Press, 1995), p. 175; cited in Mengue, 'The Idiot in Societies of Control', *Theory & Event*, 16:3 (2013). If *Au hasard Balthazar* is a loose adaptation of Dostoevsky's *The Idiot*, reimagining the donkey as the saintly 'idiot', then Tarr's film might be read, on one level, as a continuation of this reimagining, which also implicitly draws upon Raskolnikov's dream of a horse being beaten to death in *Crime and Punishment* [1866] (London: Penguin, 2014), inspired by Dostoyevsky having witnessed a similar scene in 1837 (on this, see Di Santo, '"Dramas of Fallen Horses"').
117. On this connection to the question of repetition in Nietzsche, traced with reference to Rancière's reading, see Ginn, 'When Horses Won't Eat', p. 355.
118. Rancière, 'Béla Tarr: The Poetics and Politics of Fiction', p. 251.
119. Ibid., p. 251.
120. Rancière, *Béla Tarr, The Time After*, p. 44.
121. Deleuze and Guattari, *Kafka*, p. 35; original emphasis.
122. Ginn also suggests a reading of the horse's escape, though with an emphasis on human desire rather than animal resistance: 'An animal offers a line of escape from the encroaching gloom [. . .] The horse shows the need for a desire that overflows the self and seeks connections, ways to feel more deeply our debts and obligations to nonhuman others' (Ginn, 'When Horses Won't Eat', p. 357). But these reflections are not accompanied by an analysis of animal labour that would illuminate in more precise ways such 'debts and obligations'. And when Ginn addresses the place of the horse elsewhere in his article, it is via the lens of work by Bennett and Haraway, and with what might be critiqued as a depoliticised emphasis on multispecies 'entanglement' (pp. 355–6) that fails to engage explicitly with the asymmetries of labour, violence and power that I seek to address here. While Ginn's analysis of animal life seems limited in these respects, his reading of the ecological aspects of *The Turin Horse* remains useful, as signalled above. Towards the end of his article, he suggests that the film proposes not so much a mode of 'enduring' or maintaining life as it is but rather demands 'possibilities for other ways of being human, for a people to come after carbon humans' (p. 357).
123. Rancière, *Béla Tarr, The Time After*, p. 26.
124. Hribal, 'Animals, Agency, and Class: Writing the History of Animals from Below', *Human Ecology Review*, 14:1 (2007), 101–12 (p. 104). See also Hribal, '"Animals Are Part of the Working Class"'. Writings on animal work and resistance by Porcher and Despret are also relevant here, though their emphasis tends to be on 'cooperation'

rather than exploitation; see Porcher, 'The Work of Animals', and Despret, 'Do Animals Work? Creating Pragmatic Narratives', in Senior, Clark and Freccero (eds), '*Animots*: Postanimality in French Thought', *Yale French Studies*, 127 (2015), 124–42.
125. For an important reflection on manifestations of animal agency and resistance, see Robert McKay, 'James Agee's "A Mother's Tale" and the Biopolitics of Animal Life and Death in Postwar America', in Alastair Hunt and Stephanie Youngblood (eds), *Against Life* (Evanston, IL: Northwestern University Press, 2016), pp. 143–60.
126. And in this sense we are reminded of the suicide of Estike, played by Bok, in *Sátántangó* – and of that act's own entanglements with passivity and cruelty, this intertextual connection lending a particular potency to scenes between the horse and Bok as the daughter here.
127. Jaffe describes the horse's actions as a 'rebellion of a sort' (*Slow Movies*, p. 153).
128. As Hribal suggests: 'Actor-Network-Theory has long engaged "nonhumans". But it defines their agency in terms of social associations, not in their own active ability to create social and historical change. Nonhumans are but 'participants in the course of action waiting to be given a figuration'. Indeed, "any thing that does modify a state of affairs by making a difference is an actor" (Latour 2005, p. 71). This could include a basket, a hammer, a cat. Thereby, a horse works because of the difference that it makes in the course of some other agent's actions. Horses do not "determine" their own actions. They cannot be "intentional" or "meaningful" (2005, p. 71). Horses work only in the sense that they are worked by humans.' Hribal, 'Animals Are Part of the Working Class Reviewed', p. 9. Hribal is citing Bruno Latour's *Reassembling the Social: An Introduction to Actor-Network-Theory* (Oxford: Oxford University Press, 2005).
129. Yet, as Jaffe suggests, the film also questions the possibility of revolution, tracing the limits of rebellion in ways that recall the satirical reflections on revolution in *Werckmeister Harmonies* (Jaffe, *Slow Movies*, pp. 152–3).
130. Wolfe, *Before the Law*, pp. 32–3.
131. Deleuze, *Foucault*, p. 60.
132. Debarati Sanyal, 'Calais's "Jungle": Refugees, Biopolitics, and the Arts of Resistance', *Representations*, October 2016. Available at http://www.representations.org/advance-publications/#_edn30. The 'right to disappear' is a formulation that Sanyal borrows from Blanchot.
133. Pick, 'Why Not Look at Animals'; original emphasis.
134. Ibid. On the privacy of animals, specifically in the context of wildlife documentary, see Brett Mills, 'Television Wildlife Documentaries and Animals' Right to Privacy', *Continuum: Journal of Media & Cultural Studies*, 24:2 (2010), 193–202 (cited by Pick). Hockenhull also discusses questions of animal privacy and subjective worlds in relation to the horse's performance (Hockenhull, 'Horseplay').
135. For Deleuze, 'it's not men who know how to die, but animals [. . .] an animal seeks a corner to die in. There is a territory for death as well, a search for a territory of death, where one can die.' Deleuze, 'A is for Animal', *Gilles Deleuze from A to Z* [television documentary], with Claire Parnet (directed by Pierre-André Boutang, 1988–9). Available at https://vimeo.com/108004617 (last accessed 14 September 2018).
136. Rancière, *Béla Tarr, The Time After*, p. 26.
137. And if *The Turin Horse* is indeed to be Tarr's last film, it also marks an end to his labour (of filmmaking), a further line of flight.
138. Baker, *The Postmodern Animal*, pp. 145–8 (p. 145).
139. Deleuze, *Francis Bacon*, p. 15. The exact sentence quoted by Baker is: '[t]he body endeavours precisely [. . .] to escape' (a different version of the quotation cited here).

140. Baker, *The Postmodern Animal*, p. 146.
141. Deleuze and Guattari, *A Thousand Plateaus*, p. 257.
142. Sigmund Freud, 'Analysis of a Phobia of a Five Year Old Boy' [1909], in *The Pelican Freud Library* (Harmondsworth: Penguin, 1977), Vol. 8, Case Histories 1, pp. 169–306.
143. Deleuze and Guattari, *A Thousand Plateaus*, p. 257.
144. While '[a]n *organism* is a bounded whole with an identity and end', and '[a] *mechanism* is a closed machine with a specific function', '[a] *machine* [. . .] is nothing more than its connections; it [. . .] has no closed identity'. Colebrook, *Gilles Deleuze*, p. 56; original emphasis.
145. My reading here thus diverges not only from the critiques of Deleuze and Guattari offered by Shukin and Haraway (outlined in the Introduction and Chapter 1 respectively) but also Mullarkey's critique of their representations of horses (in relation to politics and becoming); see Mullarkey, 'Animal Spirits', p. 16.
146. Deleuze and Guattari, *A Thousand Plateaus*, p. 257.
147. However, I do not want to exaggerate Deleuze and Guattari's attention to the lived conditions of animal life – though it surfaces at certain points, it is not sustained. But while Buchanan suggests that 'Deleuze and Guattari show little interest in the environmental world of animals' (p. 177), the example above, as well as the discussions of animal territories in *A Thousand Plateaus* and especially *What is Philosophy?* suggest otherwise. Similarly, Deleuze's discussion of worlds in works such as *A Thousand Plateaus* and the cinema books is potentially in tension with Buchanan's claim that 'Deleuze fails to adequately conceptualize "world"' (p. 156), although it is possible that Buchanan intends to refer, more precisely, to a failure to conceptualise the *Umwelt* (as later discussed in *Onto-Ethologies*, p. 177).
148. Deleuze and Guattari, *A Thousand Plateaus*, p. 270.
149. Jaffe, *Slow Movies*, p. 163.
150. Szendy, 'Animal filmicum', p. 103.
151. Jaffe, *Slow Movies*, p. 163.
152. Ibid., p. 163.
153. Tony McKibbin cited in Jaffe, *Slow Movies*, pp. 163–4.
154. Jaffe, *Slow Movies*, p. 164.
155. Tarr, cited in Jaffe, *Slow Movies*, p. 165.
156. Rancière, *Béla Tarr, The Time After*, p. 52; p. 66; p. 65.
157. Deleuze, *Cinema 2*, p. 57.
158. Ibid., p. 57.

CHAPTER 4

Leviathan, Meat and the Annihilation of Worlds

Perhaps more than any other beings, animals have borne the material burden of cinema's explorations of movement and stillness, life and death. While frequently embodying liveliness, animation and motion onscreen, animals have often been treated throughout the history of film production as 'disposable subjects',[1] as lives to be expended in the service of cinema's investigations of contingency, vulnerability and death. As noted in Chapter 1, in the hunting sequence of Renoir's *The Rules of the Game* (1939), we witness the actual deaths of a number of rabbits onscreen, which function proleptically to signal a fictional death to come in the narrative: that of the pilot André Jurieu. As Sobchack observes, 'it is a real rabbit that we see die in the service of the narrative and *for* the fiction'.[2] The deaths of Renoir's rabbits undertake a particular kind of narrative, metaphorical and aesthetic labour. Here cinema exemplifies the broader contradictory relationships that shape what Shukin describes as the 'fetishistic potency' of animals in their capacity 'to be taken both literally and figuratively, as a material and symbolic resource'.[3]

Probing cinema's entanglements of the material and the symbolic in relation to the 'fetishistic potency' of animals, and building on the previous chapter's focus on animal labour, this chapter explores the aesthetic and affective labour extracted from animal death in Lucien Castaing-Taylor and Véréna Paravel's experimental documentary *Leviathan* (2012). Filmed off the coast of New Bedford, Massachusetts – a major fishing (and formerly whaling) port and Herman Melville's inspiration for *Moby-Dick* (1851) – *Leviathan* charts the daily activities of a commercial fishing boat, captured on multiple GoPro cameras often attached to the bodies of the filmmakers and fishermen.[4] This method of filming, combined with the lack of any expository voiceover or discernible dialogue, produces a destabilised, often close-up, intimate yet dispersed perspective, which – together with the stylised, digitally edited colours and Ernst Karel's tumultuous sound design – works to create the film's experimental, hallucinatory effects. As noted in the Introduction, *Leviathan* is very different from the rest of the films in this study: despite its eschewal of narration and use of long, unedited takes, it cannot be said to constitute a 'slow' film (as De Luca and Jorge note, long-take films that deploy 'kinetic camerawork' seem at odds with the characteristics of slow cinema).[5] Though it invests in stretches of unedited time, *Leviathan* privileges above all not static shots but restless, agitated movement – of the camera, of the trawler and of the bodies that tip in and out of its flitting, unstable frames.

Within this aesthetic framework, the film documents the slaughter of fish vividly in close-up, in multiple scenes. While animal death in *The Rules of the Game* 'violently, abruptly, punctuates fictional space with documentary space',[6] destabilising the fictional frame, here in *Leviathan*, conversely, animal death works to confirm the documentary frame, functioning as a particularly powerful index of the real. Thus, while animals in *Leviathan* are killed primarily for extradiegetic rather than diegetic purposes – for food, rather than '*for* the fiction' – animal death still enacts a particular kind of aesthetic labour *for* the film by implicitly reinforcing its documentary claims.[7]

Leviathan's proximal, visceral, embodied engagement with slaughter is striking.[8] The film refuses the general invisibility of the slaughterhouse in both life and art, appearing to bear witness to the material realities of industrialised killing.[9] As Siegfried Kracauer writes of Georges Franju's *Blood of the Beasts* (1949), a surrealist documentary about a slaughterhouse in Paris, such images ask us to encounter 'the real face of things too dreadful to be beheld in reality'; 'we redeem horror from its invisibility behind the veils of panic and imagination'.[10] Yet to read *Leviathan* straightforwardly as a testimonial act of unveiling that 'redeems' slaughter from invisibility would be to miss the profound contradictions that structure this film.[11] For while making slaughter visible, *Leviathan* articulates a particular set of tensions around the 'fetishistic potency' of animal life and death. Its aesthetic approach – self-consciously and performatively embedded in the material, the visceral, the fleshed – threatens to convert the animal into an 'overly free-floating signifier'[12] for the film's apocalyptic vision of the real. In contrast to *The Turin Horse*, which makes visible the dynamics of animal labour, *Leviathan* disavows the affective labour extracted from its dying animals. In place of the durational attentiveness to animal lives that I trace elsewhere in the book, *Leviathan*'s flitting, indiscriminate vision reduces the fish to undifferentiated matter, closing down the possibility of singularity and the emergence of animal worlds.

In this chapter, I am interested in how these processes of conversion and extraction – or what Shukin calls 'rendering'[13] – are in tension with dimensions of *Leviathan*'s self-positioning and critical reception as non-anthropocentric or posthumanist.[14] It is worth noting, given the theoretical framework of my own study, that the work of Deleuze (and Guattari) has been invoked in some of the more celebratory responses to the film. Selmin Kara and Alanna Thain, for example, draw on the work of Deleuze, and on Deleuzian theorists such as Brian Massumi, in their affirmative commentary on *Leviathan*.[15] But these particular uses of Deleuze problematically overlook the workings of biopower and the hierarchies of power that subtend the acts of slaughter recorded by the film. This inattention to the specific vulnerabilities of animal lives within biopolitical frames is particularly ironic given the celebratory 'posthumanist' framing of the film by critical commentary and by the filmmakers themselves. Deploying various forms of sublimation and displacement, commentary on *Leviathan* often turns a blind eye to the realities of industrialised slaughter, turning instead to devote attention to its sensory, immersive forms,[16] thereby converting animal death onscreen into a form of theoretical capital.

In what follows, I argue that this inadvertently replicates a move made by *Leviathan* itself, which is to sublimate animal death as part of the film's own extravagant, highly self-conscious performance as embodied and immersive in aesthetic terms and 'posthumanist' in theoretical terms.[17] In developing this argument, I also explore the ways in which *Leviathan*'s indiscriminate mode of vision effects an erasure of singularities and of distinctions between life and death, working against an attentiveness to animal worlds of perception and meaning-making. At the same time, the film positions the human within a domain of animalised anonymity that mirrors, to a certain extent, that of the nonhuman animals in the film. But I turn first to consider the contradictions that structure the film's self-positioning and critical reception.

THEORETICO-AESTHETIC CAPITAL

In their 'Introduction' to a special issue on *Leviathan* in the *Visual Anthropology Review*, Mark R. Westmoreland and Brent Luvaas describe the film as an exercise in 'posthumanist ethnography'.[18] In an essay in the same issue, Lisa Stevenson and Eduardo Kohn suggest that *Leviathan* 'allows the viewer to be made over by a world beyond the human', initiating 'a modality of attention that can open us to the beings with whom we share this fragile planet. As such, *Leviathan* gestures to a sort of ontological poetics and politics for the so-called Anthropocene.'[19] This critical emphasis on the film's non-anthropocentrism is prompted by the positioning of the work by the filmmakers themselves, and by the approach of Harvard University's Sensory Ethnography Lab, which Castaing-Taylor directs and where *Leviathan* was produced.[20] The Lab states on its website: 'Most works produced in the SEL take as their subject the bodily praxis and affective fabric of human and animal existence.'[21] Indeed, Castaing-Taylor and Paravel's previous works – *Sweetgrass* (Barbash and Castaing-Taylor, 2009) and *Foreign Parts* (Paravel and J. P. Sniadecki, 2010) – indicate 'an enduring interest in human relations to the nonhuman',[22] anticipating *Leviathan*'s concerns. Paravel has suggested in interview that *Leviathan* is orientated towards the 'question of reducing the human, to relativize the human in a wider spectrum, a global environment [. . .]'.[23]

However, within the posthumanist or non-anthropocentric frameworks through which *Leviathan* is both positioned and received, questions of politics, power and capital are often elided. In their appreciative response to the film, drawing on models of Deleuzian folds and assemblages, Kara and Thain seek to point to the biopolitical dimensions of the film:

> An intensive folding of subjectivities and materialities is precisely the political feeling conveyed by Castaing-Taylor and Paravel in *Leviathan*, which enacts practice-based research grounded in an emergent critique of biopolitics. Here, the film's biopolitical intervention lies in its blurring of the boundaries between human, animal, and machinic bodies, making them a part of a mutant and monstrous assemblage of audiovisual materialities, micro-rhythms, and micro-affects. The sensationally rich document of the social, mental and environmental ecologies held together on the ship activates a strong sense of the 'ethico-political' through aesthetic practice, which places it with a new materialist framework.[24]

While there is much of interest in this theoretical approach – in its affinity with assemblages, taxonomical uncertainties, and in the idea of an ethical-political framework that reaches across species lines – such readings of *Leviathan* lack any sustained engagement with the industrial and aesthetic organisation of killing that lies at the heart of the film, and the particular biopolitical regimes and vectors of power that govern this. The notion of the biopolitical that Kara and Thain invoke has little ethico-political traction unless we understand it in relation to Foucault's conception of biopower – that is, as a governing via what Foucault calls '*the right to make live and let die*',[25] a form of power that not only controls but produces life, shaping it across a network of political, economic and technological domains. Despite citing Deleuze's book on Foucault in their essay, Kara and Thain seem to overlook this fundamental aspect of the biopolitical. If 'the film's biopolitical intervention lies in its blurring of the boundaries between human, animal, and machinic bodies', in tension with this are the scenes of killing that – while inevitably setting in play commonalities and indeterminacies between the human and nonhuman[26] – also reinstate very clearly particular limits, species divisions and hierarchies of power.

The blindspots that structure Kara and Thain's reading seem symptomatic of a recurrent problem within the new materialist frameworks that they invoke here. As Pick has argued, 'some "new materialist" relational ontologies [. . .]

treat all bodies and objects as networked together in more or less horizontal arrangements of commingling matter'.[27] And as Pick writes elsewhere:

> New materialist ontologies that highlight the enmeshment of human and nonhuman agents are an important corrective to transcendent conceptions of nature, but they risk political and ethical vacuity by downplaying the overdetermined relations rooted in violence against animals. By distributing agency flatly across the network, issue[s of] hierarchy and power can be subsumed under the vital flow of 'relations' and 'contact'.[28]

Pick's critique is directly relevant here. For despite Kara and Thain's rather vague assertion about 'political feeling', there appears to be a 'political and ethical vacuity' at stake in readings of *Leviathan* by Kara and Thain and others that emphasise 'more or less horizontal arrangements of commingling matter', and the 'enmeshment of human and nonhuman agents' without remaining attentive to the fact of killing and the hierarchies of power that subtend this. While for Carol J. Adams the animal is the 'absent referent' often disavowed in the consumption of meat,[29] here in Kara and Thain's new materialist reading it is the meat itself – and the fact of killing that produces it – that becomes the 'absent referent'.

Indeed, as Rosemary Deller has argued, the power structures of meat production are often overlooked by new materialist frameworks. Deller points to Jane Bennett's discussion of 'edible matter' as a form of dynamic 'assemblage', and specifically to Bennett's reluctance 'to attribute particular qualities to meat over and above other food such as vegetables' because all edible matter, as Bennett puts it, is 'vulnerable to decay'.[30] Reflecting on Henry David Thoreau's objection to eating 'fish-flesh', Bennett reads his 'disgust for meat' as 'a certain Platonic revulsion at that which is subject to change, a certain preference for eternal forms over transient matter [. . .]'.[31] Yet, as Deller suggests, Bennett's position here – and the horizontalising gesture that aligns meat with any other edible or 'transient' matter – is symptomatic of a tendency in new materialist frameworks to view change, becoming and dynamism as 'a *prima facie* good'.[32] In Bennett's view, meat is just another kind of 'vibrant matter'. Yet as Deller argues, Bennett's approach:

> elides how animals killed by the meat industry are not showing a 'propensity to change', but are deliberately transformed into meat through animal slaughter. Meat is not a state that is evidence of the vitality of matter [. . .], but is rather a potent example of the destructive relations between humans and animals that Bennett otherwise seeks to challenge.[33]

Indeed, 'new materialist approaches to meat often elide what might be thought of as the "negativity" of becoming and the ethical issues therein'.[34] What such new materialist positions reveal, as Deller contends, is 'the difficulty posed to ethics when the mutability of bodily boundaries becomes inherently valorised'[35] – in other words, when the transgression of bodily boundaries is universally understood, as Pick puts it, as part of 'the vital flow of "relations" and "contact"'.

This valorisation of mutability within new materialist frameworks is often elaborated in theoretical terms via reference to Deleuzian notions of becoming (indeed, Bennett draws on Deleuzian concepts of affect and assemblage). We see these conceptual associations at work in Kara and Thain's affirmation of the 'intensive folding' and 'blurring of the boundaries between human, animal, and machinic bodies' in *Leviathan* above. But it is important to note that Deleuze himself draws attention to the particularities of meat and its links to suffering. Reflecting on Francis Bacon's fascination with butcher shops, Deleuze writes:

> Pity the meat! Meat is undoubtedly the chief object of Bacon's pity, his only object of pity, his Anglo-Irish pity. [. . .] Meat is not dead flesh; it retains all the sufferings and assumes all the colors of living flesh. It manifests such convulsive pain and vulnerability, but also such delightful invention, color, and acrobatics. Bacon does not say, 'Pity the beasts', but rather that every man who suffers is a piece of meat. Meat is the common zone of man and the beast, their zone of indiscernibility; it is a 'fact', a state where the painter identifies with the objects of his horror and his compassion.[36]

While acknowledging the vivid visual power of meat in Bacon's work, Deleuze remains attentive to the suffering, horror, 'convulsive pain and vulnerability' to which meat attests. What he invokes here is a vulnerability that crosses species lines (thus resonating with Derrida's position in *The Animal That Therefore I Am*) – 'the common zone of man and the beast, their zone of indiscernibility'. Yet this is not, Deleuze specifies, a straightforward question of pity for the animal[37] nor a simple relation of 'resemblance': 'it is a deep identity, a zone of indiscernibility more profound than any sentimental identification: the man who suffers is a beast, the beast that suffers is a man. This is the reality of becoming.'[38] Deleuze's crossing of species divisions here is akin to the 'blurring of boundaries' invoked by Kara and Thain. But in the specific context of meat, he links this form of 'becoming' to horror, suffering and compassion, retaining the ethical and political dimension that seems missing from Kara and Thain's analysis. Interestingly, this focus on suffering also surfaces in Deleuze's reading of the scenes of tuna fishing in Rossellini's *Stromboli*

(1950) – documentary scenes of fish death that are recalled by the slaughter sequences in *Leviathan*. Deleuze writes that Karin (Ingrid Bergman), who witnesses these scenes, 'cannot react in a way that softens or compensates for the violence of what she sees, the intensity and the enormity of the tunny-fishing [. . .]'.[39] Deleuze associates meat with violence and 'convulsive pain', and the 'becoming' of meat with vulnerability and suffering in ways that are often overlooked by certain theoretical positions that cite his work, including new materialist approaches such as Bennett's and (new materialist) readings of *Leviathan*.

Yet while returning to Deleuze offers an important corrective to such blindspots, his reflections on meat are rather fleeting and not developed in any sustained form. By contrast, Shukin's work remains rooted in a close analysis of the politics of meat and the workings of biopower upon animal life. Examining 'the ways that animal life gets culturally and carnally rendered as capital', she seeks to track the 'semiotic currency of animal signs *and* the carnal traffic in animal substances'.[40] Drawing on Shukin, I am interested in how the 'carnal traffic' of *Leviathan* is simultaneously exploited and disavowed – by the film and its reception – as a form of 'semiotic currency', or theoretico-aesthetic capital, that frames the film's immersive, visceral vision as a posthumanist return to materiality and to the real. Paravel describes *Leviathan* as 'a film that restores us, in a way, to the fabric of the world'.[41] Similarly, Castaing-Taylor states: 'I think we want to get to a much more embodied, a much more corporeal representation of reality that's almost a presentation of reality.'[42] How do such investments in 'affective, immediate communication' take place under what Shukin describes as 'the charismatic sign of animal life'?[43] What unacknowledged labour is undertaken by animal death in *Leviathan* in order to produce a film that claims to offer 'a much more corporeal representation of reality', a film that 'restores us [. . .] to the fabric of the world'?

MONSTRATION

Following the dark, disorientating opening scenes of the film – a blur of indiscernible activity and metallic noise – we witness the first arrival of a net, heaving with the weight of its catch. The net opens to dump fish on the deck. Framed at ground level, and in extreme close-up, fish lie in wet, gelatinous piles. Thrust into this fleshy, viscous scene, the GoPro camera tracks the fish as they are shunted back and forth by the tipping movement of the trawler. The scene then cuts to images of fish being hacked apart. The framing ensures that the fishermen are faceless, towering, shadowy figures. Blood and viscera cover every surface as we see animal bodies wrenched open. Such images of bodily deformation recall the scientific surrealism of *Blood of the Beasts*, and what Pick describes as Franju's invocation of 'modern technoscience's cool monotony of violence'.[44] But while *Blood of the Beasts* deploys a voiceover commentary, *Leviathan* refuses any such verbal exposition. As a work of 'sensory ethnography', this is a filmmaking practice that, as the SE Lab Manager Karel puts it, privileges 'the ways in which our sensory experience is pre- or non-linguistic, and part of our bodily being in the world'.[45] The 'pre- or non-linguistic' dimensions of *Leviathan*'s sensory ethnography surely find their apotheosis in these visceral, deforming scenes of slaughter, but in ways that significantly question Kara and Thain's framing of sensory ethnography's focus on 'the machinic, natural, animal, and human actors as equally powerful agents'.[46]

In *Electric Animal*, Lippit charts the ways in which animals have been denied a relation to language in Western philosophical thought.[47] Expelled from the realm of the discursive, animals have been traditionally conceived, as Shukin notes in her critical engagement with Lippit, as 'eloquent in their mute acts of physical signing and their sympathetic powers of affect (in "showing")'.[48] Cinema invests in the animal as a particular site of 'showing', or what Shukin calls (drawing on the film theory of André Gaudreault) 'monstration' – a form of narrativity embedded iconically, mimetically, at the level of the image.[49] In the scenes described above, the fish – writhing, gasping, dying – might be seen as 'eloquent in their mute acts of physical signing', generating a series of affects extracted, and put into circulation, by the film. What work is being done here by the fish in the elaboration of the film's own register of 'pre-linguistic' affect, of monstration, or of what Shukin terms 'prediscursive mimesis'?[50] The question could extend to the fishermen, also 'eloquent in their mute acts of physical signing' (human speech in *Leviathan* is rare and often distorted), or to the many subjects and/or objects set in motion by the film. But the monstration, or 'showing', of violence and death highlights the particular place of the fish within the film's assemblage of affects.

For Lippit, the monstrative function of the animal connects it to the realm of the technological. From Muybridge's photographic studies of horse motion onwards, animals become a privileged figure for what Lippit identifies as an affective, transferential relation between biological life and visual technologies.[51] As Shukin suggests, 'Lippit is compelled by the vitalistic notion that the electric, or affective, act of technological communication is paradigmatically animal.'[52] Shukin goes on to critique this logic – and the violence to animals that it often entails – as she turns to analyse Edison's *Electrocuting an Elephant* (1903). Edison's film exemplifies what Shukin theorises more broadly as 'a transfer of life from animal body to technological media'.[53] Captured during the early days of cinema, the animal body is instrumentalised in a sensory staging of the power not only of electricity but also cinema itself. As with Renoir's rabbits, animal life is 'rendered' by film technology – affectively, transferentially – as both 'material and symbolic resource'.[54]

In *Leviathan*, the GoPro cameras become a particular conductor for what the film presents as the communicative power of 'pre- or non-linguistic' animal affect – the close-ups of fish writhing, dying, are rendered with a particular immediacy, tactility and viscerality. But, we might also ask, conversely, how – like Edison's elephant mediating the power of electricity and of cinema – the fish in *Leviathan* become a particular kind of conductor for the communicative power of the GoPro camera, a recent technological innovation. If for Lippit, '[t]ransference is the means by which nonverbal energy circulates within the world',[55] then the presence of bodies twisting in nets, on the verge of death, or of lives expired, their remains scattered across the deck, transfer a particular affective charge to this new kind of cinematic vision. The GoPro cameras extract from the killing scene, and from the place of the animal within that scene, a particular kind of nonverbal energy that functions with 'fetishistic potency' to create a circuit of sensory communication. *Leviathan* finds within what Shukin describes as 'the carnal medium of animal flesh'[56] an especially vivid conductor for the force of its 'prediscursive' vision.

Such a prediscursive vision had already been conceived by Castaing-Taylor in 1996, in an essay entitled 'Iconophobia' (1996). Critiquing what he sees as ethnography's anxiety about images, while emphasising the importance of the 'iconic and affective properties of film', Castaing-Taylor advocates a shift from '"anthropological knowledge" on film – the attempt to *linguify* film – to the idea that ethnography can itself be conducted "filmically"'.[57] Though not mentioned in the 'Iconophobia' essay, the animal – deprived of language, according to the philosophical tradition outlined by Lippit – might be seen as perfectly positioned to embody a resistance to what Castaing-Taylor sees as the 'linguification' of filmic ethnography. His essay is often approvingly cited in critical commentary on *Leviathan*, though without any examination of the unacknowledged role of the animal within this mapping of Castaing-Taylor's theory onto his filmmaking practice. Shukin's analysis of 'prediscursive' animal mimesis prompts us to reconsider *Leviathan*'s relation to the 'Iconophobia' essay (and to the 'pre-linguistic' dimensions of 'sensory ethnography'). It allows us to identify the particular labour of iconicity and affectivity undertaken by the fish, and by their deaths in particular: the animal's general resistance to 'linguification' is redoubled by the challenge to symbolisation posed by real death onscreen. In 'Iconophobia', Castaing-Taylor writes: 'But what if film doesn't speak at all? What if film not only constitutes *discourse about* the world but also (re)presents *experience of* it? What if film does not *say* but *show*? What if a film does not just *describe* but *depict*?'[58] The 'monstration' of the mute, dying animal in *Leviathan* fulfils Castaing-Taylor's theoretical fantasy of showing rather than saying, of depicting rather than describing.

Presented as an inexhaustible resource for this affective 'showing', 'the animal' in *Leviathan* is seen to be killed over and over again; in sensory ethnography's resistance to 'linguification', one animal death is simply replaced by another. In one scene, a series of skates have their wings cut off and kept, their torsos thrown away, in an efficient conversion of animal into capital.⁵⁹ Parts of bodies, leftovers, waste, are kicked over the side, through gaps at the edge of the deck. In the images that follow, shot from the side of the trawler, viscera streams into water, just as blood flows elsewhere in the film, signalling an incalculable excess generated by unlimited forms of production and consumption, by the infernal cycle of capital. The seriality of the production line – one skate after another – conjures forth the problematic figure of the undying animal, a figure that haunts Lippit's thesis: 'Undying, animals simply expire, transpire, shift their animus to other animal bodies.'⁶⁰ Lippit is referring here to a particular lineage of philosophical thought, that finds its apotheosis in Heidegger, in which animals have been traditionally denied an 'authentic' relation to death (as noted in Chapter 1). Shukin pulls this thesis away from the undying animal towards the 'material politics of animal capital':⁶¹ animals *do* die – rendered by industrialised slaughter as 'undying' capital, and here by *Leviathan* as infinite monstration.

The film offers up a series of images and sounds in which animal death is not only rendered as 'affective, immediate communication' but also converted into apocalyptic, immersive, hypnotic aesthetics. Following the scene with the skates, a hallucinatory view from underwater shows viscera and fragments of fish carcasses; the camera is on a stick here, diving in and out; when it surfaces, we catch glimpses of seagulls above. The sound is loud, aqueous. The images and sounds work through an assemblage of forces – bird, fish, wind, water,

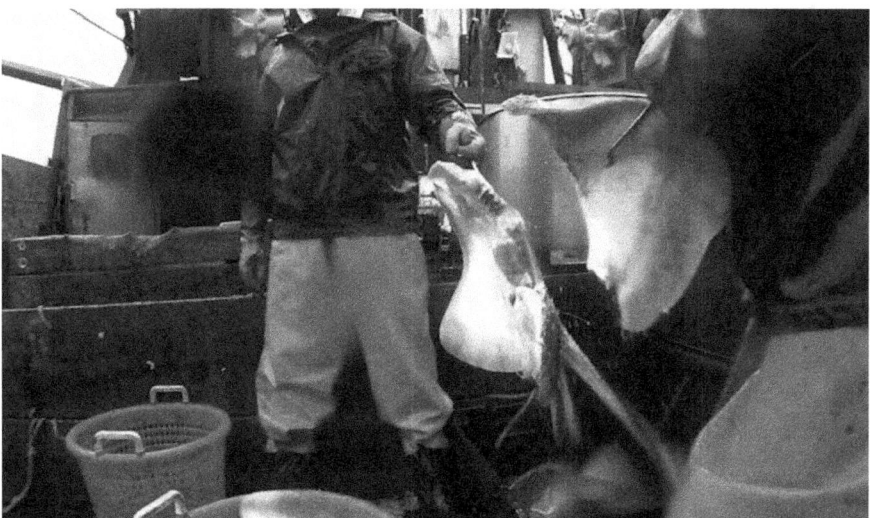

Figure 4.1 The seriality of slaughter (*Leviathan*).

camera – an affective composition in line with the posthumanist framing of the film: the position of the GoPro camera performs a transcendence of human situatedness, a de-hierarchising of vision and matter, or what Kara and Thain call 'distributed embodiment'.[62] Yet this posthumanist approach is simultaneously undercut by *Leviathan*'s instrumentalisation of the 'semiotic currency' of animal death, by an aesthetic of 'distributed embodiment' carnally commuted through viscera in water and electrified by the scene of killing that precedes it. If categories of blood and water, and of inside and outside, no longer hold in the film, that is in part an effect of slaughter and the violent literalisation of the 'blurring of boundaries' for which the film has been celebrated.

Describing such scenes, Kara and Thain refer to 'a bestial immersion by voracious sensory stimuli',[63] while Cyril Neyrat writes:

> The montage of sound and image produces a fluid and continuous matter, converting the fishing expedition at the ocean's surface into a blind plunge into the beast [. . .] one travels through this film as through the guts of a monster, bright wet flesh of innards and the rumbling of digestive noises.[64]

As we have seen, the film draws on animal death in order to generate this idea of 'fluid and continuous matter' and 'the bright wet flesh of innards'; the animal captured by *Leviathan* is converted into mesmeric aesthetic value, making possible, fleshing out, a set of metaphors that work to communicate the 'animality' of the film itself, according to the transferential logic between

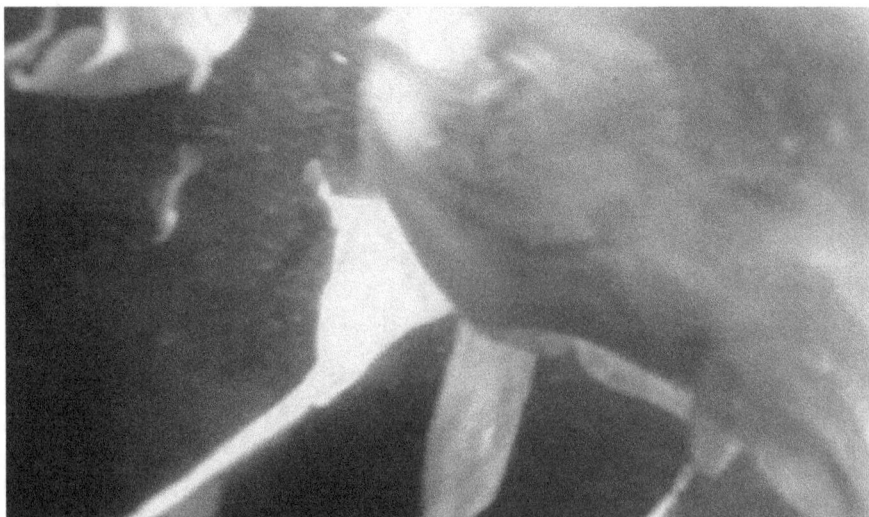

Figure 4.2 Fragments underwater (*Leviathan*).

animal and technological media that Shukin critiques. Animal death generates a non-'linguifying' excess converted back into the communicative power of the film's sensory ethnography.

MASSIFICATION

Neyrat's description of 'fluid and continuous matter' inadvertently draws attention to the ways in which *Leviathan*'s presentation of the fish rehearses a representational trope of animal life as an anonymous mass – a trope productively pursued by Lippit in his discussion of animal death in film. Reflecting on the disclaimer that usually accompanies the presence of animals within live action films – 'No animal was harmed in the making of this film' – Lippit notes that there is no direct equivalent for human actors. Rather: 'The human counterpart to this disclaimer assumes a different form: "All resemblances to persons living or deceased is purely coincidental."'[65] Though Lippit doesn't directly approach the biopolitical stakes of this question, the difference between these disclaimers is clearly shaped by a speciesist logic whereby animal life is disposable: animals are so often and readily harmed offscreen that – perversely, paradoxically – film audiences need to be reassured that they are not being harmed onscreen.[66] Thus, as Lippit summarises, '[d]ifferent taboos seem to restrict animal and human representation: animals cannot be harmed, individual human beings resembled'. But, Lippit argues, these taboos are also profoundly linked:

> Copying the human figure amounts to a form of killing if it is seen as eliminating the singularity thought to establish human identity. Killing a particular animal suggests that animal's individuality, disturbing the frequent representation of animals as constituting packs or hordes. The two modes of violation are linked by the singularity ascribed to humanity and the multiplicity that is said to determine animality. Taking this logic one step further, to imitate another human being is to assail that individual's singularity and force it to become, like an animal, multiple; to kill an individual animal is to grant it singularity, allowing it to become unique, to become human.[67]

While the possibility of this inversion (the human becoming multiple; the animal becoming individual) is fascinating and productive, there are difficulties here too. Lippit's argument depends on a strained logic that aligns copying with killing, flattening out the very different implications of those acts. And there is a troubling suggestion that the animal can only be recognised as singular by being killed. The workings of the meat industry suggest how this claim is systematically undermined – there the act of killing contributes further to the de-individualisation of the animal as part of its conversion into anonymous meat.

In *Leviathan* we tend to see hordes of fish being killed rather than individual fish dying. And when we witness a particular fish being killed, it is within a scene in which other fish are killed in precisely the same manner, suggesting a sense of interchangeability through repetition, working against the granting of singularity that Lippit identifies here. Asked in interview about how '[t]he film doesn't necessarily seem so sympathetic to the fish's plight', Paravel comments, 'the way they are killed, it's disturbing and grotesque'.[68] She then goes on to say (in a remark partially cited above): 'It's also more of a question of reducing the human, to relativize the human in a wider spectrum, a global environment, rather than trying from the beginning to show how the fish are suffering. It's like trying to spread the perspective.'[69] Paravel's comments work to support the sense that the question of individual animal death and suffering is not the film's primary concern.[70] Seemingly reluctant to foreground what Derrida describes as the 'unsubstitutable singularity' of each animal,[71] *Leviathan* portrays an ongoing scene of general perishing rather than individual deaths.

This representation of the animal as monstrous horde locks the film back into an anthropocentric logic consigning the animal to anonymous multiplicity.[72] The lack of narrative framework, the GoPro camera's indiscriminate attention, and the film's visual interest in abstraction all work to further this

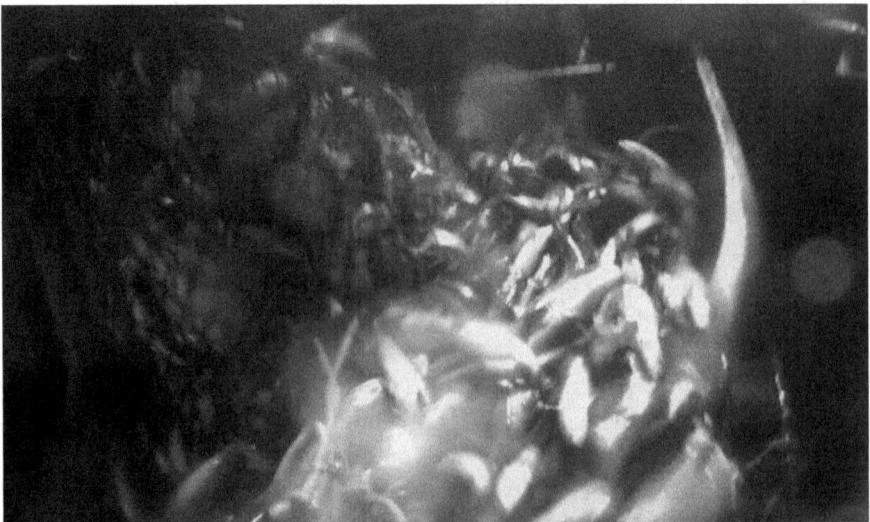

Figure 4.3 Massification (*Leviathan*).

anonymity. As Adam O'Brien suggests, the fish seem 'infinitely replicated', 'almost abstract' in their sheer abundance.[73] One might be tempted to read this, with Deleuze and Guattari, as a figure of 'becoming-animal', in all its liberating affirmation of multiplicity and impersonality ('a pack, a gang, a population').[74] Yet, as *Leviathan* demonstrates, this logic of impersonality is capitalised on by organised killing, suggesting ways in which strategies of industrialised slaughter – and of agricapital more broadly – figure as material points of resistance to theories of becoming-animal.[75] There is a recursivity at work in *Leviathan*, whereby the film's aesthetic approach mimes the massifying logic of the practice of industrial fishing itself. As Sajay Samuel and Dean Bavington note, the introduction of industrial fishing technologies, such as the jigger and the seine in the second half of the nineteenth century, 'aimed at increasing catch size' and 'transformed codfish into biomass'.[76] Through its indiscriminate attention, *Leviathan* replicates these biopolitical processes of massification, presenting the fish as a monstrous horde of anonymous animality to be tamed as 'harvestable' biomass.

This turn away from questions of animal singularity and suffering is redoubled by *Leviathan*'s uncertainty around the event of dying itself. The moment at which each fish dies is often not clear. While death may be considered to be ontologically inaccessible in any situation for any being,[77] in *Leviathan* death figures emphatically as a blindspot, often obscured by the fish being thrown offscreen or back into the 'horde' after having been cut by the fishermen. In any image of a mass of fish – caught up in a net or strewn across the deck – a number of fish may die during the duration of that shot, but it is often impossible to identify which ones, particularly given the constant motion of the trawler shuttling bodies to and fro, conflating corporeal signs of life and death. Malin Wahlberg's reading of *Leviathan* marks this ontological hesitation, referring to cameras 'poked into the chaos of not-yet-dead creatures'.[78] The multiplicity of bodies filling and exceeding the cinematic frame is such that the singularity of each death is made radically difficult to locate in both space and time. This indeterminacy around death also relates to an indeterminacy around killing, because the act of killing is initiated far before the fish meet the knife: it begins as soon as the fish leave the water, caught by the net and pulled up onto the trawler. My intention here is not to make an abstract claim about the impossible or indeterminate deaths of the Animal (that monolithic category that Derrida critiques).[79] Rather, it is to note that the uncertain eventhood of death and killing in the film is profoundly shaped by the species-specific relations between fish and their natural habitat.[80] The multiple deaths taking place throughout the film often inhabit an indistinct realm between the visible and the invisible.

In *Leviathan*, the particular ontological instabilities around the event of death deny any easy fulfilment of what Bazin sees as the capacity for cinema, as a durational medium, to present the transition from life to death – 'the elusive passage from one state to the other'.[81] Bazin elaborates this view of cinema in his discussion of Braunberger's documentary *Bullfight* (1951), in the essay 'Death Every Afternoon'. *Leviathan* problematises Bazin's theory about cinema's ability to register death, while corresponding with the elusiveness that Bazin identifies – an elusiveness compounded by the species characteristics of fish, whose deaths are less 'charismatic', less visible, less *cinematic* than that of the bull to which Bazin gestures. Fish morphology renders impossible the dramatic death fall of large mammals – of the elephant in Edison's film or of the white horse in *Blood of the Beasts*. The bodily signs of fish are generally more difficult to read: without eyelids, their eyes remain open and unblinking in both life and death.[82] In *Leviathan*, the fish contained within the visible frame undergo the passage from life to death that foregrounds '*cinematic specificity*' for Bazin.[83] But the precise moment of death remains unseen, invisible – in ways that are specific to the cinematic medium,[84] to species characteristics and to the massifying scale of slaughter discussed above. Here, then, the animal becomes less transparently 'monstrative', less mutely 'eloquent', than Lippit appears to suggest, and the questions of 'showing' and 'depicting' celebrated by Castaing-Taylor's 'Iconophobia' essay become similarly problematised. *Leviathan* suggests ways in which such scenes of industrialised slaughter mark a particular blindspot within – and limit point for – these various theories of cinematic representation (Bazin, Lippit, Castaing-Taylor): none of them have the theoretical resources to respond to the ungraspability of multiple lives extinguished at indistinct moments within each frame.

Contributing to this confusion of the living and the dead, *Leviathan* flirts with – without strictly inhabiting – the embodied perspectives of the fish, as GoPro cameras positioned at the level of the deck enable a performance of what might be fancifully referred to as a 'fish's eye view'. In his discussion of 'inhuman' perspectives offered by the film, Ohad Landesman writes: 'when the camera floats on the wet deck alongside dead fish, it takes the perspective of one of them, bumping into the others'.[85] In suggesting that the camera adopts the perspective of a dead fish, Landesman inadvertently highlights a logic of appropriation underpinning the film's performance of embodied, 'inhuman' vision, and the indifference of that performance to the status of the fish as living or dead, as flesh or meat.[86] By refusing to single out individual animals and their particular deaths, *Leviathan* not only contributes to the Heideggerian logic whereby the animal is seen to be 'incapable of proper death'[87] but exploits that logic in the service of its fantasies of technologically enabled posthuman embodiment. What Sobchack describes as technophilic fantasies of 'beating the meat'[88] are given literal force in *Leviathan*, as the fleshed perspective of the animal-as-meat is invoked in order to be transcended by cyborgian, GoPro vision.[89]

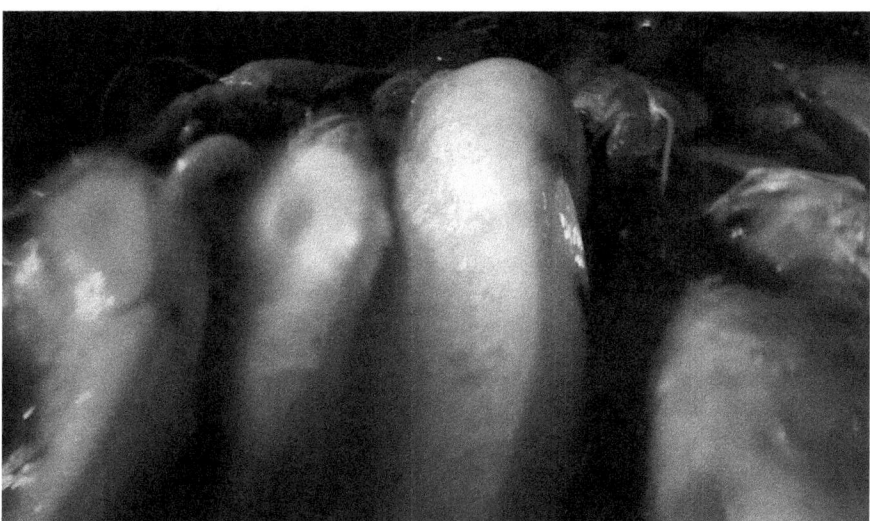

Figure 4.4 Indistinct realms of life and death (*Leviathan*).

These indistinctions between singularities, and between life and death, necessarily work against the film's envisaging of animal worlds. *Leviathan*'s deathly, fusional logic refuses what Jean-Luc Nancy calls the 'spacing' of the world and the intervals that exist between singular plural beings, shaping modes of coexistence. In *The Creation of the World or Globalization*, Nancy understands spacing as that which allows the world to unfold, dispersing the fusional, totalising impulse of the global, extending as the condition of justice.[90] Injustice arises from any (violent) attempt to obscure distinction, to collapse the spacing of coexistence. In *Corpus*, Nancy links this question of spacing and justice specifically to the body:

> Bodies are evident – and that's why all justice and justness [*justesse*] start and end with these. Injustice is the mixing, breaking, crushing, and stifling of bodies, making them indistinct (gathered up in a dark centre, piled up to eliminate the space between them, within them – assassinating even the space of their just death).[91]

For Nancy, justice denotes justness – a marking of clarity, distinction or exactitude, a distinct tracing of a space between bodies, between beings. Yet it is 'the mixing, breaking, crushing, and stifling of bodies, making them indistinct' that is at stake in *Leviathan* – both in the act of slaughter itself and in the way in which that act is presented by the film. Just as the fish on the trawler are 'piled up to eliminate the space between them', so the film, in its inattentiveness to singularities, and in its indifference to the fish as living or dead, finds itself 'assassinating even the space of their just death'. Nancy's implicit reference to holocaustic violence speaks to *Leviathan*'s scenes of mass killing and to the annihilation of the spacing of bodies and worlds with which it colludes.

However, *Leviathan* might be approached from a different, more generous perspective, particularly if we bear in mind Deleuze and Guattari's reflections on worlding in *A Thousand Plateaus*. The film's technique of 'distributed embodiment', its restless dispersal of vision, might be read in terms of the 'desubjectified' affective assemblages discussed in Chapter 1. Along these lines, *Leviathan* could be seen in fact as the perfect embodiment of Deleuze and Guattari's model of worlding: 'becoming-everybody/everything, making the world a becoming, is to world, to make a world or worlds, in other words, to find one's proximities and zones of indiscernibility'.[92] Moreover, in *Cinema 2*, reflecting on Melville's *Moby-Dick*, Deleuze sees the ship, in its division between above and below deck, as a privileged vector of the coexistence of the actual and the virtual:

> the ship is caught between its two crystalline faces: a limpid face which is the ship from above, where everything should be visible, according to order; an opaque face which is the ship from down below, and which occurs underwater [. . .] This is the circuit of two virtual images which continually become actual in relation to each other, and are continually revived.[93]

Leviathan's restless moves above and below deck, and in particular above and below the water's surface (as the GoPro camera attached to a stick dips in and out of the water) animate this continual exchange between the actual and the virtual, pointing to a coexistence of different durations that is also suggested by the film's dispersal of embodied perspective. There are certainly ways of reading *Leviathan* more sympathetically, and it is possible to do so via the Deleuzian framework that I outline in this study. This alternative reading of *Leviathan* also allows us to note a possible point of tension between Deleuze and Guattari's celebration of 'zones of indiscernibility' and Nancy's critique of indistinction.[94] Yet as we saw above, in the specific context of animal life converted into meat, this 'zone of indiscernibility' for Deleuze is infused with a recognition of pain and suffering. And it is this which seems overlooked by *Leviathan*, in spite of possibilities of reading the film more generously. For as noted above, its aesthetic of 'distributed embodiment' – that which might be seen on one level as a 'becoming-everybody/everything' – is predicated at least in part on the affective charge of animal death and on the foreclosure of any liberating kind of becoming for the animal. All that each fish becomes is undifferentiated meat, in a form of dead end that denotes anything but the emergence of worlds.

Yet, recalling Deleuze's reflection, in his engagement with Foucault, that '[l]ife becomes resistance to power when power takes life as its object'),[95] there *is* a certain resistance of life to biopower here – that much is registered by the giant machinery of the trawler and the gruelling labour of the fishermen, bearing witness to the ability of fish to evade capture and the immense effort required to catch them.[96] As Pick puts it in her reading of Elizabeth Bishop's poem 'The Fish', 'the activity of fishing itself confirms animal resistance'.[97] And when we watch *Leviathan*, we do not see the ones that get away, the fish that escape the trawler's reach. But within the film's own logic of presentation, its relentless conversion of animal death into aesthetic labour, the 'potentially creative, aleatory element that inheres in the very gambit of biopower, one not wholly subject to the thanatological drift of a biopolitics'[98] is arguably closed down. Within the film's sovereign, thanatological vision, the only lines of flight are those open to the birds above but not to the dying fish on the deck.

ANIMALISATION

Unmoored from the rest of the world, life and death in *Leviathan* are presented as both anonymous and exceptional. We only ever see the space of the trawler and the immediate surrounding waters in the film. We know this to be somewhere off the coast of New Bedford, but, as one review observes, '[l]ocation and context are unimportant [. . .] because *Leviathan* does not "take place" anywhere, apart from somewhere aboard, overboard, aloft, and below a fishing trawler'.[99] Thus we see the practice of industrial fishing – including the events of killing – in isolation.[100] This resistance to placing the practice in a wider context – for example, by following the product, as in *Food, Inc.* (Kenner, 2008), or by combining scenes of slaughter with the mundane realities of sales and trade union negotiations, as in Frederick Wiseman's *Meat* (1976) – works against attempts to understand the process of industrial fishing as part of broader biopolitical regimes. To some extent, the attention to industrialised production, expenditure and waste in *Leviathan* automatically places the film in a broader context: against the backdrop of ecological concerns about overfishing and species extinction, these scenes assume a particular charge, heightened by the film's apocalyptic imagery. In interview, Castaing-Taylor has commented on the depletion of fish stocks, and on the governmental mismanaging of fishing in this area.[101] A form of salvage ethnography, the film is shaped by a desire to record an industry on the verge of disappearance or irreversible change. But, as Catherine Russell suggests, *Leviathan* 'walks a fine line between aesthetic spectacle and historical specificity'.[102] As 'sumptuous visuals, enhanced by the hyper-real colors' are 'displaced from their documentary sources', 'the geo-political specificity of the footage tends to be subsumed within a mythic abstraction in which the spectacle is emptied of its radical energies'.[103] The exceptional, apocalyptic space of the trawler – marked out as such by the mythico-religious name of the film itself[104] and by the film's nod to Melville – is unmoored from any explicit articulation of broader historical and political concerns.

What are the implications of refusing to flesh out such concerns in a film featuring industrialised killing? Reflecting on 'revelatory' images of processes of animal slaughter in documentary film, Burt suggests:

> Few films [. . .] actually explore the relationship between this revelatory imagery and other aspects of culture, preferring instead to reinforce its sense of separateness. Magnetised as the eye might be to the act of animal killing, whether through fascination, repulsion or a combination of the two, the sense of isolation that the act has behind the walls of the abattoir is in fact reinforced.[105]

For Burt, *Blood of the Beasts* is an exception to this rule – in Franju's film, we see both inside and outside the slaughterhouse: shots of postwar Paris prompt us to understand the animals as part of the lifeblood, the material resources, of the city.[106] And thus for Burt: 'by moving between the invisible practice of slaughter and the highly visible city', Franju's film 'follows a more transgressive course by making killing more than merely a confined act. I would say that his less "sadistic eye" reveals a far greater and more pervasive sadism.'[107] For Burt, the sadism disclosed by *Blood of the Beasts* is that of a systemically violent instrumentalisation of animal life that reaches far beyond the slaughterhouse, demonstrating 'the extent to which the systems of modernity are built around the figure of the animal'.[108] By contrast, *Leviathan* visually confines its representation of slaughter, reinforcing the separateness to which Burt refers. *Leviathan* offers no broader view of the (unsustainable) circuits of production and commerce in which the industrial process of fishing is bound up. Following Burt's argument, this makes the film more 'sadistic' than *Blood of the Beasts*: *Leviathan* 'magnetises' the eye to acts of killing without channelling that vision towards a broader reflection on the social, political and economic contexts of these acts.

In an essay, 'Abattoir', which appeared in the journal *Documents*, accompanied by Eli Lotar's photographs of La Villette in Paris (one of the slaughterhouses filmed in *Blood of the Beasts*),[109] Georges Bataille writes of the sequestration of the slaughterhouse:

> Nowadays the slaughterhouse is cursed and quarantined like a boat with cholera aboard . . . The victims of this curse are neither the butchers nor the animals, but those fine folk who have reached the point of not being

able to stand their own unseemliness, an unseemliness corresponding in fact to a pathological need for cleanliness.[110]

The imagery of the 'boat with cholera aboard' resonates in particular with *Leviathan*'s own slaughterhouse at sea, isolated in its abjection. For Bataille, such quarantining, and its disavowal of sacrifice and the sacred, is related to questions of class – 'those fine folk' – and bourgeois alienation from the dirt and mess of slaughter.[111] While Bataille's assertion that 'neither the butchers nor the animals' are victims is overstated, his emphasis on class allows for a further dimension of *Leviathan* to come into view. In *Leviathan*, the dirt and abjection of slaughter is confined not only to a particular space but to a particular class – a social identity never made explicit, but signalled by the context (and in this respect, relatively little has changed since Upton Sinclair's *The Jungle* (1906):[112] the labour of industrial slaughter is still typically carried out by the working class and immigrants, often in dangerous working conditions). Moments in *Leviathan* such as the lingering focus on one worker's mermaid tattoo – and the ethnographic curiosity that the film devotes to this, recalling a history of anthropological interest in tattooing – seem telling, suggesting that the film mines the 'fetishistic potency' not only of its animals but also its humans.

In an implicit manner, *Leviathan*'s simultaneous abjection and fetishisation of its 'butchers', shored up by class difference (against the backdrop of the cultural capital of the Harvard Lab), contributes to its positioning of the human within a realm of anonymous animality that echoes, to a certain extent, that of the nonhuman animals in the film.[113] As Wolfe argues, 'the animality of the human' arises 'when the human becomes something anonymous, either through massification (as in Foucault's studies of the mechanisms of biopolitics, such as population sciences and medicalization) or by being reduced to an equally anonymous condition of "bare life"'.[114] While *Blood of the Beasts* demonstrates an interest in the lives of individual workers, revealing (through the voiceover) details of their personal histories, *Leviathan* generally refuses any individualising details, not only through the lack of verbal commentary but through its visual forms. Though there are some rare particularising moments (for example, through close-ups), *Leviathan*'s 'butchers' are mostly presented as interchangeable, their singularities denied by their uniform clothing and by the framing that frequently decapitates them or hides them in shadow. To return to Lippit's logic of inversion, here in a violation of singularity, the human is forced 'to become, like an animal, multiple'. This also recalls Murphet's reading of the 'animalisation of man' in the films of Bresson, effected by forms of visual fragmentation and a 'defacialized approach to the human form'.[115] Indeed, the red gloves on which *Leviathan* repeatedly focuses uncannily recall images in Bresson's *Money* (1983), and the dehumanising violence of economics and class privilege documented by that film. *Leviathan*'s visual strategies suggest a self-conscious attentiveness to the alienating, anonymising dimensions of industrialised labour – to the reduction of the fishermen to another kind of 'biomass' or 'bare life'. This levelling effect might be seen to play into the film's self-positioning as a posthumanist 'relativising' of the human. However, *Leviathan*'s aesthetic approach also risks simply confirming and quarantining, rather than questioning, this animalisation of its human subjects. This then leaves intact the humanisation, through contrast, of the viewers, 'those fine folk' permitted to keep a hygienic distance from this decontextualised vision of slaughter producing the meat they consume.

There is one particular scene in which the human is ambiguously 'redeemed' from animalisation – a scene in which a fisherman falls asleep in front of the television, filmed in a static, extended long take. Russell compares this scene with the film's earlier focus on a decapitated fish: 'Nameless and voiceless, this man is stared at as we have earlier stared at the head of a dead fish. Both man and fish return the gaze without returning the gaze: they look back at the camera without seeing it.'[116] Russell's observations imply that the human, like the fish, has been drawn into a realm of anonymous animality. But *contra* Russell's assertion, this scene does not function in parallel with the earlier scene of the fish – not only because one being is alive, and one is not, but because in the television-watching scene an individual human is granted significantly more time and attention than that given to any of the fish throughout the film. This static long take, striking within the context of *Leviathan*'s generally chaotic, restless motion, works to undercut the film's apparently 'distributed' or non-discriminating mode of attention. The scene's 'facialisation' and identificatory potency[117] further its redemption of the human from anonymous animality – an ambiguous redemption, of course, as the scene still gestures to a certain fascination with a particular kind of abject human state.

As Westmoreland and Luvaas note in their 'Introduction', this particular scene arises repeatedly in the collected essays in the *Visual Anthropology Review*'s special issue on *Leviathan*, becoming the focus of theoretical reflections on the real or on self-reflexivity (an episode of *The Deadliest Catch*, the Discovery channel's reality show about fishing, is on the TV that the man is watching). Westmoreland and Luvaas point suggestively to the critical bias at work here: 'In contrast to the abstract, posthumanist fishing world that dominates the film, the contributors privileged the only scene in the film that provides an isolated human subject, composed in a recognizable manner, and rendered accessible to our observational gaze.'[118] For Westmoreland and Luvaas, this suggests that *Leviathan* points to the disciplinary limits of anthropology and visual ethnography, as critical readings cling to the most recognisable (that is, human) content. What the predominance of this scene in critical commentary suggests further to me is a preference for engaging with the fisherman when he is falling asleep in front of the TV rather than when he is killing – a preference for questions that are more familiar to visual culture studies rather than those that might challenge its anthropocentric assumptions. This points further to blindspots around questions of slaughter, biopolitics and animal capital that I have sought to address here.

Cast adrift in a sea of immersive, apocalyptic aesthetics, the slaughtered animal in *Leviathan* is converted into an 'overly free-floating signifier' – the privileged resource for, and conductor of, the film's 'bestial' performance of prediscursive affect. Though *Leviathan* makes viscerally visible the act of killing, its abstract, indiscriminate vision reduces the fish to undifferentiated matter, refusing to grant each animal death the possibility of eventhood and singularity. In its quest to produce a cinematic vision that gives us, as the film's directors put it, 'a much more corporeal representation of reality', a vision that 'restores us [. . .] to the fabric of the world', *Leviathan* disavows the aesthetic and affective labour done by animal death. The film's indifference to the fish as singular beings reveals a fusional logic – a vision of undifferentiated meat, a harvesting of biomass by the film itself – that closes down the possibility of any envisaging of animal worlds.

To a certain extent, then, the film's aesthetic regime inadvertently mimes the logic of the fishing trade itself, in its biopolitical rendering of disposable lives. Troubling the non-anthropocentrism through which *Leviathan*'s sensory ethnography is commonly framed, such a reading awakens us to the lives and deaths from which the film's technophilic assemblages are extracted, while sensitising us to the 'material politics of animal capital'[119] at work in cinema more broadly. The question of the political has been extended here to include the film's problematic decontextualisation of slaughter and its attendant 'animalisation' of the human. The material politics of industrialised slaughter has emerged as a particular limit point – its substance often elided by critical commentary on *Leviathan* and often resistant to the theories of cinematic representation (Bazin, Lippit, Castaing-Taylor) invoked here. But the slaughterhouse is a key site – materially, ideologically – for any understanding of our relations to animal life. In continuing to develop the field of animals and film, we will need to learn how to look at the slaughterhouse, in the cinema and beyond, with critical rather than blinded or magnetised vision.

NOTES

1. Bousé, *Wildlife Films*, p. 42. Bousé uses this term specifically in relation to wildlife film, but it can be applied to cinema's instrumentalisation of animal life more broadly.
2. Sobchack, *Carnal Thoughts*, p. 245; original emphasis.
3. Shukin, *Animal Capital*, p. 6.

4. See Jaremko-Greenwold, 'Véréna Paravel and Lucien Castaing-Taylor by Anya Jaremko-Greenwold'.
5. De Luca and Jorge, 'Introduction', p. 6.
6. Sobchack, *Carnal Thoughts*, p. 246.
7. On documentary cinema's extraction of aesthetic labour from human protagonists, see Panse, 'The Work of the Documentary Protagonist: The Material Labor of Aesthetics'.
8. See Shukin and O'Brien, 'Being Struck'.
9. On images of animal death as 'a particularly complex kind of rupturing, of both an aesthetic tradition and slaughter's physical and psychical sequestration', see Lawrence, 'Haneke's Stable', p. 69.
10. Siegfried Kracauer, *Theory of Film: The Redemption of Physical Reality* (Princeton: Princeton University Press, 1997), p. 306. On connections between *Leviathan* and Franju's film, see, for example, Cyril Neyrat, 'Blood of the Fish, Beauty of the Monster', translated by Nicholas Elliott, *Leviathan* DVD booklet, *Dogwoof* (2013), pp. 2–5.
11. On conflicted relations of (in)visibility in *Blood of the Beasts*, see McMahon, 'Franju's Animals: Stains, Traces, Histories', in Zoe Angeli and Blake Gutt (eds), *Stains/Les Taches: Communication and Contamination in French and Francophone Literature and Culture* (Bern: Peter Lang, forthcoming).
12. Burt, *Animals in Film*, p. 27.
13. Shukin emphasises 'the double sense of *rendering*' as both mimetic representation and the material 'recycling of animal remains'. *Animal Capital*, p. 20; original emphasis.
14. Though the term is wide-ranging, I understand posthumanism here as necessarily involving interrogation of a humanist logic that, whether intentionally or not, 'grounds discrimination against nonhuman animals'. Wolfe, *What is Posthumanism?* (Minneapolis: University of Minnesota Press, 2010), p. xvii.
15. Selmin Kara and Alanna Thain, 'Sonic Ethnographies: *Leviathan* and New Materialisms in Documentary', in Holly Rogers (ed.), *Music and Sound in Documentary Film* (London: Routledge, 2015), pp. 186–98.
16. For useful critiques of the celebration of 'immersion' that dominates commentary on *Leviathan*, see Ohad Landesman, 'Here, There, and Everywhere: *Leviathan* and the Digital Future of Observational Ethnography', *Visual Anthropology Review*, 31:1 (2015), 12–19, and Christopher Pavsek, '*Leviathan* and the Experience of Sensory Ethnography', *Visual Anthropology Review*, 31:1 (2015), 4–11.
17. As Smaill writes of *Leviathan* and *Sweetgrass*: 'Both films self-consciously appeal to the senses of the viewer and play to phenomenological understandings of cinema.' *Regarding Life*, p. 25.
18. Mark R. Westmoreland and Brent Luvaas, 'Introduction: *Leviathan* and the Entangled Lives of Species', *Visual Anthropology Review*, 31:1 (2015), 1–3 (p. 2).
19. Lisa Stevenson and Eduardo Kohn, '*Leviathan*: An Ethnographic Dream', *Visual Anthropology Review*, 31:1 (2015), 49–53 (p. 49).
20. See Malin Wahlberg on 'the submissive attitude of the critics and scholars towards the intentions of the filmmakers and the scientific lab in question [. . .]'. Wahlberg, '*Leviathan*: From Sensory Ethnography to Gallery Film', *NECSUS: European Journal Of Media Studies*, Autumn 2014. Available at http://www.necsus-ejms.org/leviathan-sensory-ethnography-gallery-film/ (last accessed 14 September 2018).
21. See the Sensory Ethnography Lab website. Available at http://sel.fas.harvard.edu (last accessed 14 September 2018).
22. Stevenson and Kohn, '*Leviathan*', p. 49.
23. Jaremko-Greenwold, 'Véréna Paravel and Lucien Castaing-Taylor'.

24. Kara and Thain, 'Sonic Ethnographies', p. 195.
25. Foucault, *Society Must Be Defended*, p. 241; original emphasis.
26. For example, Stevenson and Kohn refer to 'our shared bodily vulnerability' in their reading of parallels between the human and the animal in the film ('*Leviathan*', p. 51).
27. Pick, 'Reflexive Realism in René Clément's *Forbidden Games*', p. 216.
28. Pick, 'Why Not Look at Animals'.
29. Carol J. Adams, *The Sexual Politics of Meat: A Feminist-Vegetarian Critical Theory*, 20th anniversary edition (New York: Continuum, 2010), p. 66.
30. Rosemary Deller, 'When Flesh Becomes Meat: Encountering Meaty Bodies in Contemporary Culture', PhD thesis, University of Manchester, 2015, p. 29; Jane Bennett, *Vibrant Matter*, p. 47.
31. Bennett, *Vibrant Matter*, pp. 46–7.
32. Deller, 'When Flesh Becomes Meat', p. 31. For a related critique of new materialism, see also Sara Ahmed, 'Imaginary Prohibitions: Some Preliminary Remarks on the Founding Gestures of the "New Materialism"', *European Journal of Women's Studies*, 15 (2008), 23–9; cited by Deller, p. 31n73.
33. Deller, 'When Flesh Becomes Meat', p. 31.
34. Ibid., p. 31.
35. Ibid., p. 31.
36. Deleuze, *Francis Bacon*, p. 23.
37. On pity and animals, see Murphet, 'Pitiable or Political Animals?', and my discussion of this in Chapter 3. Reflecting on this question in both Deleuze and Derrida, Mullarkey suggests: 'Pity, of course, would be a reactive relation that does neither the dying animal nor thinking philosopher any good. Derrida's pity for the animal is a morbid response that Deleuze's vitalist thinking cannot stomach.' Mullarkey, 'Animal Spirits', p. 15.
At the same time, the attentiveness to cross-species vulnerability in both Deleuze and Derrida suggests an important point of intersection.
38. Deleuze, *Francis Bacon*, p. 25.
39. Deleuze, *Cinema 2*, p. 2.
40. Shukin, *Animal Capital*, p. 7, emphasis original.
41. Jaremko-Greenwold, 'Véréna Paravel and Lucien Castaing-Taylor'.
42. Rick Juzwiak, '*Leviathan*: A Documentary Made by People Who Hate Documentaries', *Gawker*, 3 January 2013; cited in Landesman, 'Here, There, and Everywhere', p. 18n5.
43. Shukin, *Animal Capital*, p. 102.
44. Pick, *Creaturely Poetics*, p. 137.
45. Mark Peter Wright, 'Ernst Karel', *Ear Room*, 14 February 2013. Available at https://earroom.wordpress.com/2013/02/14/ernst-karel/ (last accessed 14 September 2018).
46. Kara and Alanna Thain, 'Sonic Ethnographies', p. 187.
47. Lippit, *Electric Animal*.
48. Shukin, *Animal Capital*, p. 141. On the 'flattening of animals' worlds' into a thin layer of animal world as a life on the surface of things', see Broglio, *Surface Encounters*, p. xvii.
49. Shukin, *Animal Capital*, p. 141.
50. Ibid., p. 141.
51. Lippit, *Electric Animal*, pp. 184–7.
52. Shukin, *Animal Capital*, p. 133.
53. Ibid., p. 104.
54. Ibid., p. 6.
55. Lippit, *Electric Animal*, p. 191.
56. Shukin, *Animal Capital*, p. 138.

57. Castaing-Taylor, 'Iconophobia', *Transition*, 69 (1996), 64–88 (p. 86).
58. Ibid., p. 86; original emphasis.
59. The scene functions as a brutal revisiting and reversal of Marey's study of the movement of a skate's fins in water, recorded in his photographic series *Aquatic Locomotion: Sequential Study of the Movements of a Swimming Skate* (1892).
60. Lippit, *Electric Animal*, p. 187.
61. Shukin, *Animal Capital*, p. 88.
62. Kara and Thain, 'Sonic Ethnographies', p. 195.
63. Ibid., p. 188.
64. Neyrat, 'Blood of the Fish, Beauty of the Monster'.
65. Lippit, 'The Death of an Animal', p. 11.
66. As Burt observes, 'A cultural oversensitivity to the treatment of animals on screen appears to sit at odds with a culture that is also heavily dependent on animal exploitation [. . .]'. Burt, *Animals in Film*, p. 14.
67. Lippit, 'The Death of an Animal', p. 11.
68. Jaremko-Greenwold, 'Véréna Paravel and Lucien Castaing-Taylor'.
69. Ibid.
70. Castaing-Taylor notes: 'We were interested in [. . .] in a reductive and absurd way – the actual fish's experience of the world' (Ibid.). Yet his disclaimer here and the film's approach itself seem in tension with this avowed interest.
71. Derrida, *The Animal That Therefore I Am*, p. 9.
72. On envisioning animal multiplicity beyond anthropocentrism, see McHugh, 'Unknowing Animals: Wild Bird Films and the Limits of Knowledge', in Lawrence and McMahon (eds), *Animal Life and the Moving Image*, pp. 271–87.
73. Adam O'Brien, 'Fishwater: *The Bay* and its hyperobject', *Screen* annual conference, University of Glasgow, 27 June 2015.
74. Deleuze and Guattari, *A Thousand Plateaus*, p. 239.
75. As Shukin argues, the thinking of animal intensities proposed by Deleuze and Guattari 'may inadvertently resonate with market forces likewise intent on freeing animal life into a multiplicity of potential exchange values'. *Animal Capital*, p. 42.
76. Sajay Samuel and Dean Bavington, 'Fishing for Biomass', in Joan B. Landes, Paula Young Lee and Paul Youngquist (eds), *Gorgeous Beasts: Animal Bodies in Historical Perspective* (University Park: Pennsylvania State University Press, 2012), pp. 137–50 (p. 142).
77. See Derrida, *Aporias*, especially pp. 74–8.
78. Wahlberg, '*Leviathan*'.
79. Derrida, *The Animal That Therefore I Am*, p. 34.
80. This particular dislocation of death is a function of specific operations of fishing. On the strategic and symbolic distribution of the act of killing in the slaughterhouse, see Noëlie Vialles, *Animal to Edible*, translated by J. A. Underwood (Cambridge: Cambridge University Press, 1994), p. 45.
81. Bazin, 'Death Every Afternoon', p. 30.
82. This relation between animal monstration, death and eventhood is complicated further by the field of biosemiotics and its study of signs that are not primarily 'for' the human. On the ethological aspects of this, see, for example, William J. Rowland, 'Studying Visual Cues in Fish Behaviour: A Review of Ethological Techniques', *Environmental Biology of Fishes*, 56 (1999), 285–305.
83. Bazin, 'Death Every Afternoon', p. 30; original emphasis.
84. In an argument informed by Bazin's essay, and by theorisations of on-screen death by Sobchack, Doane and others, C. Scott Combs argues that, given the temporal unfolding

of film, '[c]inema death takes place somewhere between a precise moment and a complex progression in time'. Combs, *Deathwatch*, p. 5. Though I invoke the elephant's fall in Edison's film as a visible event, it should be noted that here too – as Combs suggests – the exact moment of death is rendered radically indeterminate by elements such as editing (pp. 48–59). On time, death and eventhood in Edison's film, see also Doane, *The Emergence of Cinematic Time*, pp. 140–71, and Pick, '"Sparks Would Fly"', and my discussion of this in the Introduction.
85. Landesman, 'Here, There, and Everywhere', p. 16.
86. For an excellent discussion of haptic visuality in relation to meatiness, drawing on Sobchack's analysis of 'beating the meat', see Deller, 'When Flesh Becomes Meat'.
87. Lippit, 'The Death of an Animal', p. 12.
88. Sobchack, *Carnal Thoughts*, pp. 165–78. Sobchack addresses such fantasies in her critique of Jean Baudrillard's celebratory reading of J. G. Ballard's *Crash* (1973).
89. This fantasy of inhabiting the embodied perspective of the fish and then 'beating the meat' via technology seems to inform the filmmakers' thinking about the film's soundtrack as well. In interview Castaing-Taylor observes: 'The sound is super-compressed and had lots of digital artefacts that we thought were really interesting. They sounded, simultaneously or by turns, bizarrely super-machinic, super-cyborgian, and then really organic, as if they themselves were gasping for air, as if they themselves were drowning.' Allan MacInnis, 'The Aesthetics of Slaughter: *Leviathan* in Context', *CineAction*, 91 (2013), 58–64 (p. 64).
90. Jean-Luc Nancy, *The Creation of the World or Globalization*, translated with an introduction by François Raffoul and David Pettigrew (New York: SUNY Press, 2007). See also McMahon, 'Jean-Luc Nancy and the Spacing of the World', *Contemporary French and Francophone Studies*, 15:5 (2011), 623–31.
91. Nancy, *Corpus*, translated by Richard A. Rand (New York: Fordham University Press, 2008), p. 47.
92. Deleuze and Guattari, *A Thousand Plateaus*, p. 280.
93. Deleuze, *Cinema 2*, p. 71.
94. Yet we also recall Deleuze and Guattari's emphasis on the 'individuated'; see Chapter 1.
95. Deleuze, *Foucault*, p. 77. See my discussion of this in Chapter 1.
96. I draw here on a connection made by Pick between the resistance of the fish and the machinery and effort required to catch them in her reading of *Leviathan*. Pick, 'Why Not Look at Animals', Plenary, *Screen* annual conference, University of Glasgow, 26 June 2015. See also Wadiwel, writing in the context of the mechanised slaughter of chickens: 'it seems difficult to avoid the way in which animal resistance (even if this resistance is "futile") plays a part in the process of slaughter. [. . .] Although it might be easy to imagine animals as passive in this process [. . .] the reality involves a more intense and intimate engagement in a violent power relation, in which humans and machines "struggle" against chickens who would prefer not to die' (Wadiwel, *The War against Animals*, p. 10).
97. Pick, 'Vulnerability'.
98. Wolfe, *Before the Law*, p. 32.
99. Hunter Snyder, '*Leviathan*', *Visual Anthropology Review*, 29:2 (2013), 176–9 (p. 176).
100. Paravel's presence behind the camera aside, this is also an exceptionally masculine space, lending a particular virility to the film and invoking the carnophallogocentrism critiqued by Derrida. See Derrida, *The Animal That Therefore I Am*, p. 104.
101. Jaremko-Greenwold, 'Véréna Paravel and Lucien Castaing-Taylor'.

102. Catherine Russell, '*Leviathan* and the Discourse of Sensory Ethnography: Spleen et idéal', *Visual Anthropology Review*, 31:1 (2015), 27–34 (p. 33).
103. Ibid., p. 33.
104. Ibid., p. 32. The film's title references the Book of Job 41 ('Canst thou draw out leviathan with a hook?'), a connection made explicit by the film's opening epigraph: 'He maketh the deep to boil like a pot: he maketh the sea like a pot of ointment [. . .]'. The title also gestures inescapably to Thomas Hobbes's *Leviathan* (1651), inviting connections between the film and Hobbes's reflections on brute nature and sovereign power.
105. Burt, *Animals in Film*, p. 175.
106. Ibid., pp. 175–6.
107. Ibid., p. 176.
108. Ibid., p. 176.
109. For a reading of *Blood of the Beasts* in relation to Bataille, see Adam Lowenstein, 'Films Without a Face: Shock Horror in the Cinema of Georges Franju', *Cinema Journal*, 37:4 (1998), 37–58.
110. Georges Bataille, 'Abattoir', *Documents*, 6 (November 1929), 32. Published in English in Denis Hollier, *Against Architecture: The Writings of Georges Bataille*, translated by Betsy Wing (Cambridge, MA: MIT Press, 1995), p. xiii.
111. See Lawrence, 'Haneke's Stable', pp. 68–9.
112. Upton Sinclair, *The Jungle* [1906] (London: Penguin, 1985).
113. In her reading *Leviathan*, Smaill also points to a narrowing of the gap between the human and the animal: 'while the humans here are not slaughtered or filleted, and so clearly not subjected to the same processes as the animals, the retreat from dialogue, affect, and other humanizing qualities contributes to the heightened portrayal of life as one that is systemized and optimized in the interests of productivity' (*Regarding Life*, p. 42).
114. Wolfe, *Before the Law*, p. 5.
115. Murphet, 'Pitiable or Political Animals?', p. 109.
116. Russell, '*Leviathan* and the Discourse of Sensory Ethnography', p. 31.
117. Speculating on the potential for spectatorial identification here, MacInnis writes: 'The scene is presented in a lengthy, static shot which itself may lull viewers towards sleep, only to suddenly realize that they have become a mirror image for the blinking, nodding, exhausted fisherman slumped on the opposite side of the screen.' MacInnis, 'The Aesthetics of Slaughter', p. 59.
118. Westmoreland and Luvaas, '*Leviathan* and the Entangled Lives of Species', p. 3.
119. Shukin, *Animal Capital*, p. 88.

CHAPTER 5

Actual/Virtual: *Bovines ou la vraie vie des vaches*

As Julian Murphet has argued, cinema has historically been 'grounded in a project of remorseless amortisation of the animal's most striking characteristic, its ability to move'.[1] Emmanuel Gras's *Bovines ou la vraie vie des vaches* (*A Cow's Life*, 2011), a contemplative reflection on a herd of Charolais cows, both continues and interrupts this history: it is interested in bovine movement, but a ruminating movement that lingers, pauses and generally leads nowhere.[2] Refusing to place cinematic time in the service of an anthropomorphic narrative of psychologically motivated action, *Bovines*'s delayed, wandering images of animal life unfold forms of duration that resist incorporation into a 'sensory-motor schemata' of cause and effect.[3] Like *Leviathan*, *Bovines* is also interested in animals that are killed for food, but we do not witness the act of slaughter in this film, and its slow, distended approach is very different from *Leviathan*'s chaotic, restless motion. Here, as in *Bestiaire* and *The Turin Horse*, 'situations no longer extend into action or reaction in accordance with the requirements of the movement-image'.[4] The durational aesthetic of *Bovines*'s directionless meanderings is arguably the most sustained of all the films explored in this book, the film's torpor seeming fully attuned to the general inaction of the cows themselves.[5]

As Bellour notes in *Le Corps du cinéma*, Deleuze elaborates accounts of the animal and of cinematic time quite separately, without addressing potential links between these accounts.[6] In this chapter I read *Bovines* as a film that, on one level, invites us to seek out further fertile connections between Deleuze's cinema books and his reflections, with Guattari, on the animal, particularly as they are developed in *A Thousand Plateaus* and *What is Philosophy?*. *Bovines* prompts us to address the gaps in Deleuze's writings to which Bellour points, while enabling further interrogation of various dynamics – of worlding, (de)territorialisation and becoming – that I have been tracing throughout the book. Yet in this final chapter I also want to test out the possible limitations of

Figure 5.1 The inextricability of aesthetics and capital (*Bovines ou la vraie vie des vaches*).

this Deleuzo-Guattarian model in relation to the question of politics. Set on a farm, depicting – and, crucially, being dependent on – a regime of animal instrumentalisation, *Bovines* highlights these political limitations, yet inadvertently so, within and against its own sustained attentiveness to animal life. In risking a privileging of what Peter Hallward calls 'virtual creations' over 'actual creatures',[7] *Bovines*'s time-images might be seen to propose, implicitly, a celebration of biovitality rather than an interrogation of biopolitics. While *Bovines* thus reveals a set of contradictions at the heart of its durational aesthetic, it also points to the limitations – as well as the persistent possibilities – of a Deleuzo-Guattarian framework in our consideration of cinema's animal worlds.

TIME AND RUMINATION

Bovines focuses on a herd of Charolais cattle, a beef breed originating in the Charolais region of France. Through a series of predominantly long takes, the 62-minute documentary presents the herd without any voiceover commentary or music. As in the other films explored in previous chapters, *Bovines* resists the expository approach of the conventional wildlife documentary. But in contrast to some of the films discussed thus far, *Bovines* commits itself to focusing exclusively on one particular species. Resisting the episodic movement from one species to another that we find in *Bestiaire*, *Bovines* sustains a mode of attentiveness to one particular group of animals and the rhythms of their everyday lives. While cows have been present throughout the history of cinema in rich and fascinating ways, from Buster Keaton's *Go West* (1925), to Dariush Mehrjui's *The Cow* (1969) and Djibril Diop Mambéty's *Touki Bouki* (1973), they have tended to remain narrative or visual props to the human: it is rare for extensive cinematic attention to be devoted to the animals themselves.[8] But as one review puts it: '*Bovines* is an hour of cows.'[9]

In interviews, Gras reveals a sensitive, philosophically oriented approach to the film's subject.[10] Speaking of his decision to focus on a herd of cows, he says: 'I realised that the question of animals was always posed in relation to wild animals as though we didn't recognise the animality of farmed animals or pets [. . .].'[11] Rather than filming an 'exotic species', Gras explains that he wanted 'to film animals that we see all the time without usually devoting time to looking at them'. In a sense, the project becomes one of estranging the familiar, of reframing our vision of the domesticated cow. Gras recounts that when choosing a title for the film, he wanted to avoid terms like *vaches*, which would be too 'direct', or *bétail* (livestock), which would 'reduce the animal to its function'. To present *bovines* as a noun in French, as in the film's title, is grammatically incorrect: as Gras notes, one would usually refer to either 'des bovins' or 'des races bovines' (but not 'des bovines'). But for Gras, 'the fact of feminising it and transforming it allowed for the creation of something other than just the name of a species'.[12] Gras positions the film as seeking to see the cow anew, as envisaging the lives of cows in ways that reach beyond zoological detail or agricultural function.

Key to the film's project of recasting our vision is its almost exclusive focus on the cows themselves: we wait twenty-five minutes before seeing any humans (the farmers who appear in the second half of the film). Gras explains that this is why he wanted to film beef cows rather than dairy cows (who are milked regularly and therefore have much more contact with humans): 'I wanted to film animals who have their own life, who don't spend that much time with human beings.'[13] In this sense, *Bovines* represents an attempt to address the animals – as much as possible – on their own terms; the film seeks to move beyond an anthropocentric frame of reference, in a bid to disclose *la vraie vie* of its title. The camera is often positioned to be level with the cows, as though invoking their perspective, yet without framing these images as subjective or point-of-view shots. As Gras notes, this visual perspective 'corresponds with a universe that is slightly lower than that of a human'; when humans come into view, they are framed at a lower angle than would usually be the case. Gras explains that he tried not to focus on the faces of the farmers too much: he wanted the humans to appear fairly 'anonymous' (though his approach is more individualising than the logic of interchangeability at work in *Leviathan*'s framing of its humans). He describes these cinematographic strategies as an attempt to relegate the human to a 'secondary' position, and to place himself 'more on the side of the herd'.[14]

But *Bovines* unfolds its alignment with the herd above all through a dynamics of patient looking, attentiveness and duration.[15] Gras explains: 'I absolutely wanted to avoid a story with plot-like events';[16] 'I was interested in entering into a different time, which is that of the cow: they graze and graze and graze [. . .]'.[17] This is time which may seem empty and repetitive at first: in *Bovines*, nothing much appears to happen. Yet Gras speaks of being interested in tracking 'minuscule things evolving within one shot'. He cites the example of a cow grazing in short grass and then coming across a thicker area of grass: 'it becomes a little event', and this becomes a way of 'being in the temporality of the animal, in the sensorial universe of the animal', of 'discovering new things stage by stage'.[18] And thus, Gras recounts: 'I realised that it was a cinematographic question which interested me: [. . .] how should one film something that appears empty to us, and to show in fact – because we move into a different time and space – that it exists, and that it is full of existence.' In terms that resonate with Bailly (*'there are those hearts*, those existences [. . .]'),[19] Gras captures here the philosophical stakes of his film. In its patient observation and temporal distension, *Bovines* seeks out not only a different way of looking at cows but a different model of cinematic eventhood.

The film privileges above all the time of rumination, witnessed in multiple scenes of cattle 'chewing the cud'. In the scene that follows the film's titular credits, we see images of cows grazing in extreme close-up, their heads partially visible, buried in grass. One image then frames, again in extreme close-up, the nostrils and muzzle of a cow grinding food, breathing heavily and burping – a noisy scene of rumination. Hannah Velten outlines the process: 'When cattle are resting, they voluntarily regurgitate some of the rumen content, chew a while, and then swallow it again, where it passes on to the reticulum.'[20] Although these scenes of noisy eating invite possible identificatory responses from spectators (!) and the visceral flickerings of corporeal affinities across species lines, the film's fixation on this process of 'second chewing', which 'may occur for eight hours out of twenty-four in cattle',[21] emphasises bovine time as radically different from human time. *Bovines*'s visual and auditory attention to such scenes discloses a particular sensitivity to the rhythms and reticulations of bovine life. And as the film returns repeatedly to these non-spectacular, non-narrative scenes of rumination, it adopts its own rhythm of 'second chewing', regurgitating material that it then recycles.

Indeed, *Bovines* allows events to repeat and time to drift, as the cows rest or meander through the fields, mooing, grazing or dozing. Presented as a series of tableaux, punctuated by fades, the film works 'in blocs, with deliberately weak connections and floating events',[22] building a Deleuzian series of *opsigns* and *sonsigns*. As one review puts it: '[Gras's] camera tends to remain stationary for long periods of time, as his lumbering subjects move in and out of sight of their own volition.'[23] The apparently unmotivated dimension of the images allows for the soundtrack to come to the fore: the film amplifies sounds of mooing, chomping and breathing, emphasising bovine *sonsigns* that seem to serve no particular expository purpose. If, in the realm of the time-image, characters are 'found less and less in sensory-motor "motivating" situations, but rather in a state of strolling, of sauntering or of rambling which define[s] *pure optical and sound situations*',[24] then *Bovines* uses the extreme slowness of cows – the bovine rhythms of ruminating, sauntering and rambling – to exacerbate this non-extension of perception into action.

Significantly, cows momentarily accompany Deleuze's theorisation of the shift from movement-image to time-image. In *Cinema 2*, Deleuze designates two kinds of recognition in Bergson: '*[a]utomatic or habitual recognition*' and '*attentive recognition*'. Elaborating on the first kind of recognition, in which 'perception extends itself into the usual movements', Deleuze uses two examples: 'the cow recognises grass, I recognise my friend Peter'.[25] The example of the cow is prompted by Bergson's own discussion, in *The Creative Mind*, of the cow eating grass: 'a cow that is being led stop[s] before a meadow, no matter which, simply because it enters the category that we call grass or meadow'.[26] Here Bergson describes the cow's motor response to a habitual source of interest, reading this as indicative of an 'automatic or simple animal existence'.[27] For Deleuze, this signals the domain of the movement-image, of automatic progression, of 'sensory-motor recognition' extending into action, in which 'we pass from one object to *another one*': 'the cow moves from one clump of grass to another, and, with my friend Peter, I move from one subject of conversation to another'.[28] Deleuze's movement-image is thus aligned with a mode of animal automatism that extends to the human – evocatively captured by D. N. Rodowick's description of the movement-image as 'behaviourist'.[29] By contrast, the time-image aligns itself with the second order of recognition in Bergson, 'attentive recognition', in which 'I abandon the extending of my perception': 'My movements – which are more subtle and of another kind – revert to the object, return to the object, so as to emphasise certain contours and take "a few characteristic features" from it.'[30] Thus the cinema of the time-image is one of attentive, lingering attachment and return, in which 'we constitute a pure optical (and sound) image of the thing, we make a description'.[31] Interestingly, though, at this point in Deleuze's discussion, the cow disappears, apparently excluded from this realm of 'attentive recognition' and the time-image.

On one level, *Bovines* might be seen as simply confirming the idea of an 'automatic or simple animal existence'. In cultural representation more broadly, cows are traditionally caricatured as slow and even 'stupid', as the embodiment of *bêtise* (*la bête*, the animal, being the etymological root of this word). To describe a human as 'bovine' is to point to the ways in which that person may be '[i]nert, sluggish; dull, stupid'.[32] Gras's film certainly draws out the physical qualities of inertness and sluggishness often associated with cows, while also allowing these animals, at certain points, to seem psychologically absent, indifferent or slow. As Daniel Walber writes in his review of the film: 'They really do mull about and stare off into the distance, capable of ignoring just about any natural occurrence. Initially it seems almost eerie, the bovines gaping directly into the camera without an ounce of expression.'[33] In early scenes focusing on the cows grazing, their eyes are glazed, seemingly unfocused; such images of apparently unreflective repetition evoke a Cartesian conception of the animal as machine or Bergson's idea of automatic animal behaviour. Yet these glimpses of unreflective repetition – and their gestures to automatism – may not be as far away from the human as we might like to think. And they certainly do not cancel out the manifestation of perception, intelligence and curiosity also in evidence in the film. In one sequence, for example, we witness a cow resourcefully pulling at the branches of a tree, causing apples to fall to the ground in order to eat them. Gras explains that he was interested in how this scene revealed a different, perhaps surprising aspect of bovine behaviour, something beyond the habitual, the automatic: 'we see the intelligence of the animals in this moment'.[34]

This particular scene can arguably be read as a set of movement-images: perception extends into action. Yet other moments in the film evoke a relation between time and perception (both bovine and human) that seems more akin to the time-image. We see this, for example, in a sequence that announces the arrival of a plastic bag. We first notice the bag as a blurred, abstract object on the horizon. Refocusing, the camera then eerily attends to the bag as it has done to the cows, tracking its motion as it quivers across the field. One cow sniffs at it; other cows approach – though they will eventually decide to move on, these are gestures of curiosity that seem far from the bovine 'indifference' described by Walber or the 'automatic or simple animal existence' that Grosz locates in Bergson. At the same time, the scene itself unfolds a time-image: floating into the field of vision – disrupting both the pastoral aesthetic (for the viewer) and 'automatic recognition' (for the viewer, for the cows) – the plastic bag signals a moment in which perception does not extend into action, both diegetically and spectatorially. Time-images also gradually accrue in the film through repetition: *Bovines* takes the apparently mechanistic action of a cow eating grass – that which exemplifies the movement-image for Deleuze – and in repeatedly returning to this, emphasising 'certain contours', extracts this image from the realm of automatic recognition, and from a history of connections between animal automatism, technology and cinematic images,[35] reorientating it towards the realm of attentive recognition. Thus while Deleuze, following Bergson, consigns the cow to the behaviourist, automatic domain of the movement-image, *Bovines* re-envisages cows in the attentive, lingering terrain of the time-image.

The film's privileging of perception over action – and the question of how we 'read' the perceptual worlds of these animals – comes to the fore in the scene of a calf's birth. The cow giving birth seems relatively expressionless; she does not utter a sound. On one level, it might be tempting to read the scene as Walber does: 'It seems that cows hardly notice the act of giving birth. She abides, silent, mostly just waiting for her child to tumble out.' Walber sees this as exemplifying the 'bland outlook' of the cows in general.[36] Yet the scene is not so much about a supposed vacancy of response but rather the opacity of that response, resisting precisely the kind of anthropomorphic reading that Walber wishes to bring to it. A later observation that he makes seems closer to the mark: 'If she is in pain we have no clear way of knowing it.'[37] For what *Bovines* presents in this scene is a perceptual and sensorial world that does not easily correspond with our own.

The cinematography emphasises the contours of this world by focusing on the mother rather than the calf. Gras explains that he didn't want to film from the angle of the calf emerging (the supposed centre of action); rather, the visual focus is on the cow who is giving birth, statically framed in profile. The long take documents her labour, her 'endurance':[38] we see the rise and fall of her belly, 'we feel the effort of the animal and see her expressions, her gaze'.[39] Thus as Gras suggests, 'I filmed not the action but the perception of the animal.'[40] Again, a different logic of eventhood is at stake. The sequence then shows other cows gathering around and sniffing at the newborn calf, apparently curious about this new arrival – gestures of interest, expressivity and collectivity that further resist a reading in terms of bovine 'indifference'. These are

Figure 5.2 Calling the calves (*Bovines*).

time-images in the sense described by Deleuze, in that they 'prevent perception being extended into action in order to put it in contact with thought, and [. . .] to subordinate the image to the demands of new signs which would take it beyond movement'.[41] Through an aesthetic of temporal distension, of lingering attachment, *Bovines* unfolds perceptual worlds marked by 'new signs' that resist straightforward legibility, while ushering in 'contact with thought'.

FROM TERRITORY TO PENSIVITY

Yet just as Deleuze in his thinking of the time-image emphasises a shift from subject to world (as seen in Chapter 1), so *Bovines* opens beyond a focus on the cows themselves to the territories that they construct.[42] In this sense, the film resonates with Deleuze and Guattari's discussion of animal territories in *What is Philosophy?*:

> Perhaps art begins with the animal, at least with the animal that carves out a territory and constructs a house [. . .] the territory implies the emergence of pure sensory qualities, or sensibilia that cease to be merely functional and become expressive features, making possible a transformation of functions.[43]

These 'pure sensory qualities' are arguably akin to the '*pure optical and sound situations*' that shape the time-image, foregrounding potential intersections between animal territory (as conceived by Deleuze and Guattari in *What is Philosophy?*) and the account of cinematic time given by Deleuze in *Cinema 2*. Both animal territory and the time-image entail the liberation of sensory, expressive qualities beyond the purely functional.[44] While Deleuze himself leaves such potential links unarticulated in his work, the shift from 'functional milieu' to 'expressive' territory mapped by *What is Philosophy?*[45] is arguably mirrored by the shift from the movement-image to the time-image in his cinema books – a connection that *Bovines* helps us to see.

Bovines establishes a sense of animal territory in the opening sequence: indeed, Gras speaks of wanting the opening shots to 'give the sensation of arriving at the territory of the cows'.[46] We see a fence, a spider's web glistening with dew, and a field in the background; in the second shot, a close-up, in sharp focus, of barbed wire and the spider's web, quivering slightly in the breeze. Gras explains that he wanted the shots to be marked by the presence of human traces (fence, barbed wire) but the absence of human figures: 'One is with the animals not with human beings.'[47] Yet, significantly, the first two shots place us in a territory not only without humans but also – predominantly – without cows.⁴⁸ While a group of cows can just about be discerned, out of focus, in the background of the second shot, it is only via the third image, a long distance shot of the field, that we encounter the first obvious markers of bovine presence: we see cows more clearly in the background this time, and we hear a moo, but the exact source of the sound is not immediately located for us. In resonance with the idea of a 'being of sensation' beyond the flesh evoked in *What is Philosophy?*,⁴⁹ the film traces this expanse of territory first and foremost as a space that extends beyond the immediate bodily presence of the cows.

Here, as Deleuze and Guattari suggest, '[a]rt begins not with the flesh but with the house',⁵⁰ as *Bovines* opens with territory rather than bodies. *Bovines*'s perception is immediately 'acentred', displacing not only the human, as Gras suggests, but also the film's titular animal species. Indeed, the central territory announced by the opening shot is arguably that of the spider rather than the cow, underlined by the first two shots featuring the web.⁵¹ If 'every territory encompasses or cuts across the territories of other species', 'forming interspecies junction points',⁵² then from the opening of the film we are made aware of what Deleuze and Guattari, drawing on Uexküll, describe as 'a composite system rich in points and counterpoints'.⁵³ The time-image slowly unfolds these collective assemblages, these expressive territories. (At the same time, the visual emphasis on the barbed wire keeps in view a particular territorialisation of the animal by the human, to which I return below.)

Bovines foregrounds the role of sound in this initial construction of territory. One cow moos continuously – a sound that, as noted above, we hear before the film locates the source visually (it is 'acousmatic' in Michel Chion's terms).⁵⁴ Drawing a territory, as though unharnessed from the body, the mooing acts as a 'refrain', a 'sonorous bloc' of sensation.⁵⁵ After the film has located the source of the sound (centrally framing the cow under a tree), the following shot moves in closer and tracks the cow's lumbering movement from screen left to right. The sequence emphasises the duration of the cow's mooing, filming it over a number of minutes, as it becomes more insistent, strident and hoarse. Gras explains that he was interested in how the sound opens the film with a question rather than the kind of pedagogical exposition that often accompanies animal images in wildlife documentary: 'we see an animal that we usually consider as very placid [. . .] and her moo is very expressive. Something is happening for her, but we don't know what it is.'⁵⁶ Gras reveals that the cow walked around mooing for about half an hour; the film edits and condenses this (while also intermittently cutting to another cow, looking on). The scene is thus made up of fragments, reminding us that it is not so much a Bazinian integrity of time and space that is at stake here but rather a set of *opsigns* and *sonsigns* unharnessed from any clear logic of cause and effect. It might be tempting to characterise *Bovines* as a film in which 'nothing much happens', and perhaps to evoke the kind of anxiety around unstructured time diagnosed by Doane (as discussed in the Introduction). But as Gras notes, *something is happening* for this cow, though it is an event that remains opaque to the viewer.

After a few minutes, the cow, still mooing, gradually turns and begins walking towards the camera. The camera tracks her movement. The cow then halts, face-to-face with the camera, centrally framed. The effect is electrifying, recalling the force of the direct looks to camera in *Bestiaire*. Tags visible in both ears, flies on her face, she turns her head and moos again. She turns back and looks directly at the camera again. We hear her breathing. The sequence is assigned a particular significance by its position: fading to black, it leads into the announcement of the film's title. Gras says that he wanted to open the film with the idea of an 'exchange of looks' (*regards croisés*): 'we've just been looking at animals but they also look at us; they are conscious of our presence. The experience of being looked at by a cow . . . well, it's quite troubling . . .'.[57] Gras's comments recall Bailly's emphasis on the animal look: 'no object and no plant [. . .] can do what any animal can do: see us, and make us understand that we are seen.'[58] (Of course, we the viewers are not actually seen here, but the film encourages us to feel, to have a sense of, the cow's gaze upon us.) For Bailly, such looks remind us of the ways in which '[a]nimals are spectators in the world. We are spectators in the world alongside them and simultaneously. This community of the sense of sight makes us alike and relates us; it posits between us the possibility of a threshold [. . .]'.[59]

Yet, as Bailly recognises, such commonalities are also shot through by asymmetries of power. As in *Bestiaire*, the animal gaze is shaped by an uneasy set of tensions: we are reminded of the ways in which the force of the look, captured on film, is enabled by the captivity of the animal (its domestication on the farm underlined by the tags in the cow's ears and by the barbed wire made prominent in these opening scenes). Yet as we saw in relation to *Bestiaire*, the animal look might also be said to exceed this set of biopolitical coordinates. For as Bailly suggests:

> The gaze gazes, and the unformulated is, in it, the pathway of thought, or at least of a thinking that is not uttered, not articulated, but that takes place and sees itself, holds itself in this purely strange and strangely limitless place which is the surface of the eye. [. . .] In the face of that which is and can only be for us neither question nor response, we experience the feeling of being in the presence of an unknown force, at once supplicating and calm, that in effect traverses us. This force may not need to be named, but where it is exercised it is as though we were in the presence of a different form of thought, a thought that could only have ahead of it, and overwhelmingly, the *pensive* path.[60]

As we saw in Chapter 2, Bailly tends to ground the 'pensivity' of animals in the look. But *Bovines* moves beyond this privileging of the optical, suggesting that 'pensivity' – 'the presence of a different form of thought' – is also made manifest through animal sound. The strident moo that haunts this sequence insistently gestures to 'the *pensive* path' indicated by Bailly here.

Thus *something is happening*. But in its apparent opacity, its resistance to legibility, pensivity has the potential to interrupt narrative drive. In *S/Z*, Barthes points to the ways in which the final sentence of Honoré de Balzac's *Sarrasine* (1830) – 'The marquise remained pensive' – suspends the text's conclusion.[61] As Rancière puts it, reflecting on Barthes's reading: 'Pensiveness [. . .] arrives to thwart the logic of the action'; 'What is interrupted is the relationship between narration and expression.'[62] Though seemingly far away from the narrative world of Balzac's *Sarrasine*, the pensive paths opened up by animal looks and sounds in *Bovines* similarly 'suspend narrative logic in favour of an indeterminate expressive logic'.[63] In its non-extension of perception into action, the time-image tends towards such moments of narrative suspension. *Bovines* uses its time-images to dwell on animal pensivity in all its 'indeterminate expressive logic'.

Yet *Bovines* is a film that is not just about thinking; it is also a film about feeling. We sense this in particular in the film's close-up engagement with the cows. The images which first introduce the mother cow in labour are shot at night: in extreme close-up, the camera focuses on the contours of her body – the expanse of skin, the hairy surface, the rise and fall as she breathes heavily. Rendered in intensely affective terms, these are the first contractions of the cow that we will later see giving birth.[64] But, given the isolation of these images, and their dislocation from the scene of birth itself (which arrives a few scenes later), the viewer would only make this connection retrospectively, if at all.[65] The images and sounds propose a 'logic of sensation'[66] rather than an economy of narrative representation. The close-up scale, the darkness of the shot and the lack of clear coordinates evoke Laura U. Marks's theory of 'haptic visuality' (itself shaped by Deleuzian thought) – a mode of embodied spectatorship that responds to images and sounds in sensory, tactile terms before they are pulled into regimes of signification; a form of looking, hearing and feeling without knowing.[67] For Gras, the film foregrounds the sound of the cows breathing so that 'we physically feel their mass, almost their interiority', 'so that without intellectualisation, without explanation of what an animal is, we put ourselves in their universe and suddenly almost feel among them'.[68] He speaks of this emphasis on a 'very material sensation' as a way of establishing a connection with 'the animal world'.[69] *Bovines* uses its images and sounds to feel its way – in tactile, affective terms – into the worlds of these animals, while simultaneously marking the opacity, the 'indeterminate expressive logic' of these worlds.

DETERRITORIALISATION, BECOMING

Yet while such moments might seem to privilege individualised expressions of animal pensivity and affect (with the focus, for example, on one cow mooing, or another cow giving birth), *Bovines* is also interested in forms of multiplicity, becoming and deterritorialisation – an interest that is in line with the moves beyond the 'house' of the flesh, the phenomenologically lived body that we have already seen above. Rather than setting up protagonists ('I didn't want to make a film where there were heroines', Gras says), the film seeks to exploit 'the fact that [the cows] are all white, and it's difficult to distinguish one from the other'; '[i]f there's an individual who becomes prominent, it's just for the length of a scene'.[70] In this sense, *Bovines* is different from the prolonged focus on one particular horse in *The Turin Horse*. By refusing to privilege any one animal in particular, *Bovines* creates what Deleuze and Guattari would read as forms of becoming-animal, 'a pack, a gang, a population, a peopling, in short multiplicity'.[71] This kind of becoming is foregrounded in scenes such as the one in which the cows gather under a tree for shelter during a storm. At one point, the shot focuses on the mingling of their legs (with some heads lowering into view), highlighting the herd as 'a pack' – not subjects but assemblages, not molar identities but molecular collectivities.

But in *Bovines* becoming also reaches beyond the herd itself, as the film allows us to sense the becoming of the world more broadly. As Michel Ciment writes: 'in an almost tactile manner', the film 'makes us feel nature [. . .], the early morning fog, the torrential rain, the green pastures, the heat of the sun'.[72] During the sequence of the storm, an extreme close-up of the surface of a puddle fills the screen with ripples forming concentric circles. The flatness of the camera angle, and the liquidity of image and sound, release a set of percepts and affects, unharnessed from any one viewing position, human or bovine. Here, as in *What is Philosophy?*, 'one is not in the world, one becomes with the world, one becomes in contemplating it. All is vision, becoming. One becomes universe. Becomings animal, vegetable, molecular, becoming zero.'[73] The sensory assemblage of the storm sequence, its liquid percepts and affects, are indicative of the kind of 'non-human becoming' or worlding that, for Deleuze and Guattari, the artwork can bring into being.[74] As noted in Chapter 1, this mode of worlding embraces intensive processes of *haecceity* and a logic of the non-subjective, the impersonal and the virtual that reaches beyond the circumscribed subjective worlds of Uexküll's theory of the *Umwelt*. For Deleuze and Guattari, as we have seen, worlding is a form of conjugation 'with others': 'becoming-everybody/everything, making the world a becoming, is to world, to make a world or worlds, in other words, to find one's proximities and zones of indiscernibility'.[75]

Thus, in a general movement of deterritorialisation, *Bovines* encourages us to see multiple worlds coexisting and becoming. An early sequence opens with the sounds of insects over a black screen and then a close-up of grass, shot from directly overhead, tracking ever so slowly from left to right. The blades of grass are magnified, revealing drops of dew and holes in leaves left behind by insects. In the director's commentary, Gras speaks of wanting to emphasise the 'life' of the grass; again, there is a sense in which the film is interested in exploring territories, assemblages and life-worlds that reach across different realms. The tracking shot does not mime the movement of either cow or human; in Deleuze's terms, it is a movement-image unharnessed from any embodied point of anchorage, offering an 'acentred' form of perception and sensation.[76] (And here again, *Bovines* highlights the usefulness of thinking across and between the work of Deleuze and Guattari and Deleuze's cinema books.) As Deleuze and Guattari suggest in *A Thousand Plateaus*, in terms that are particularly apt for this sequence:

> One is then like grass: one has made the world, everybody/everything, into a becoming, because one has made a necessarily communicating world, because one has suppressed in oneself everything that prevents us from slipping between things and growing in the midst of things.[77]

When the film cuts to the next shot, the camera is at ground level, the grass sharply in focus in the foreground, the head of a cow grazing out of focus in the background. A further cut, and the camera is amid the grass, as a static close-up focuses on a crane fly scrambling across blades of grass (we hear the quivering sound of the insect). In the following shot, also at ground level, the crane fly flits across the frame; the grazing cow remains out of focus. Yet the cow's image is gradually pulled into focus, becoming more distinct. In its shifting planes of visual and auditory focus – moving between grass, insect and cow – one senses the 'necessarily communicating world' of the film, its manner of 'slipping between things and growing in the midst of things'. Modulating attention in different directions, *Bovines* unfolds a general logic of becoming, worlding and deterritorialisation.

As part of this logic of becoming, the film expresses an interest in deterritorialising effects through which the image of the cow might be recast or indeed cast off. At around nine minutes, one shot of a cow's mouth buried in grass is framed in such extreme close-up that it generates a *décadrage*, a composition of 'disjointed, crushed or fragmented planes',[78] a concept that Deleuze and Guattari borrow from Bonitzer. The shot focuses on the cow's mouth, lingering until 'something else happens'.[79] In conjunction with the amplified sounds of feeding, snuffling and munching, the image works to blur species lines, temporarily suggesting something more akin to canine rather than bovine movement, or rather something in between: a 'zone of indetermination'.[80] Here the cinematic frame opens to a deframing, a line of flight, by which the cow cinematically escapes his/her own being, becoming other – a deterritorialisation shared by the viewer, once more propelled beyond the domain of 'automatic recognition'. The film then cuts directly to a long shot of the grass field, generating further disorientations of scale. Here the close-up is 'traversed by a deframing power that opens it onto a plane of composition or an infinite field of forces'.[81] Deterritorialising the cow, this deframing power constructs a set of liberated affective vectors and resonances, of virtuality, of lines of flight.

BOVINE CAPITAL

Yet within and against this general logic of deterritorialisation, *Bovines* also keeps in view the space of the farm as a set of territorialising forces that instrumentalise animal being. In the first scene of herding, one cow is led to a van bearing the sign 'CHAROLAIS MEAT – DIRECT SALE'. In the same shot, we see a cow with a tagged ear, looking on. Such moments bluntly remind us of the cow's status as a form of capital.[82] As Velten notes, the history of the cow is one of domestication and commodification: 'the domestic cow and oxen became a form of mobile wealth', ushering in 'the early stratification of society'.[83] While the uses to which cows have been historically put suggest their perpetual objectification, recent work in critical animal studies has sought to argue that such histories reveal forms of cross-species 'collaboration', opening up possibilities for considering the agency of animals, including farmed animals.[84] But *Bovines* intimates a set of more rigid power asymmetries – when humans arrive on the scene, the cows are immediately positioned as passive.

In the film's final scene of herding, we see a tractor emerging along a road through trees in darkness; as it approaches, the camera tracks backwards, revealing a sudden pace and mobility that seems out of place in the context of the general torpor of the film. The tractor is then shown removing a group of calves from the herd, presumably to be sent to market. Nicolas Azalbert underlines the dramatic change in the film's register marked by these scenes: 'the idyllic life brusquely reveals that which lies outside the frame, and the animals turn back into livestock'.[85] Through a brisk montage of activity, the film (re)enters the realm of anthropocentric action, and of the movement-image. The drive for speed is emphasised by the constant command of the farmers as they herd the cows – 'Allez! Allez!' – to which the strident mooing of the cows appears to respond (in protest?). If sound marks the possibility of bovine resistance or agency, that possibility is quickly closed down: the cattle are forced to move rapidly (from right to left) in a manner that invites contrast with their slow lumberings earlier in the film (mostly from left to right). The logic of sensory-motor connections takes hold, and human speech and rapid camera movement mark a shift from wandering bovine time to the accelerated dynamics of agricapital – bovine bodies and time are reterritorialised by the farm, and by the film. The calves driven onto the truck are squashed in, forced to jostle together; though there is not enough space, still the command of 'Allez! Allez!' persists. As Velten suggests, the separation of cows from the herd is a painful, distressing experience for cattle, who are intensely social creatures.[86] *Bovines* intimates this in its prolonged engagement with these final events, cutting to the cows left behind, who constantly moo and look on in the direction of the tractor as it departs. As the scene of separation draws to a close, the camera focuses on one cow, groaning, nose pressed to the barbed wire. In envisaging something that looks like animal mourning,[87] such images and sounds counter Nietzsche's figure of the amnesiac cow living blissfully in the present moment.[88] This sequence also invites us to reconsider, in hindsight, the persistent moo with which the film opens (was that also an utterance of pain and protest?).[89]

Bovines's sequences of herding recall a scene in which cattle cross the bridge to the slaughterhouse in Franju's *Blood of the Beasts* (1949). *Bovines* differs markedly from *Blood of the Beasts* by refusing to visualise death, but like the allegorical impulse of Franju's film, and its bloody invocation of the death camps, Gras's focus on herding, separation and barbed wire ensures that the film finds itself haunted by a human history of extermination, and, specifically, by 'the cattle-cars bearing human loads to Dachau, Treblinka and Auschwitz'.[90] An image focusing on barbed wire, preceding the storm sequence, threatens to invoke the opening of Alain Resnais's *Night and Fog* (1955). These palimpsestic glimpses of a history beyond the present are fleeting in *Bovines*, but the invocation of such image repertoires, unearthed from postwar French cinema, implicitly complicates a reading of the film as being uniquely about cows, tentatively extending the film's consideration of organised slaughter to the human.[91]

Yet *Bovines*'s recognition of organised killing, and of life as capital, seems conflicted. For the film invests in a certain bucolic romanticisation of the cows (even if Gras suggests in interview that this is not the case) – a film about beef cattle in intensive farming conditions, such as a CAFO (concentrated animal feeding operation), would certainly look very different. *Bovines*'s striking long shots of Charolais cattle alone in misty pastures corresponds to a certain aesthetic history: such images have long been used to connote a pastoral ideal – a tendency prevalent in the genre of cattle painting which developed from the mid-1600s onwards, particularly in the Netherlands.[92] Yet that pastoral ideal has always been underwritten by the inextricability of aesthetics and capital: as Velten notes, the dairy cow in painting became 'an emblem of Dutch prosperity' against the backdrop of land-reclamation programmes in the Netherlands leading to a proliferation of cattle rearing,[93] with networks of capital shaping animals in both life and art. In *Bovines*, the image of the Charolais cow functions in similar terms, recalling the work of the French painter Jacques

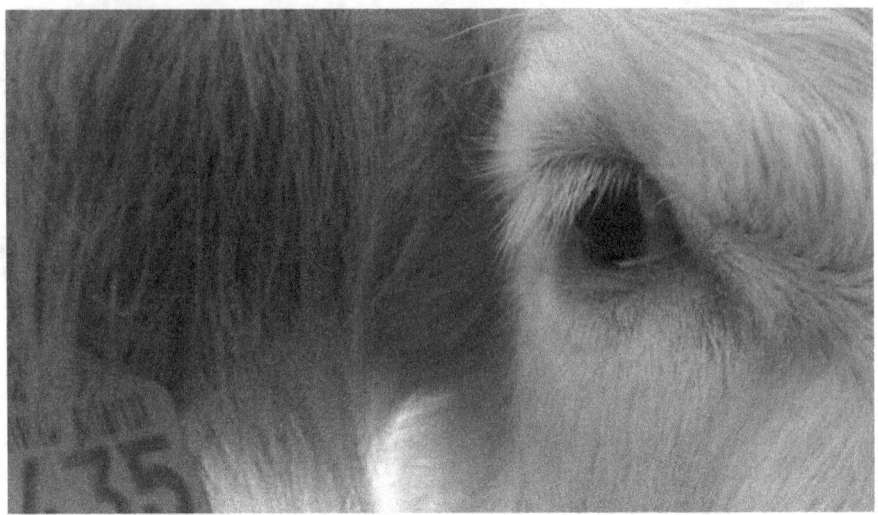

Figure 5.3 Animal capital (*Bovines*).

Raymond Brascassat (1804–69), and evoking links between animal capital and national identity explored by Shukin: the image of the Charolais breed, recalling its biological origins in France,[94] functions fetishistically as both life form and 'iconic symbol' to connote 'organic national unity'.[95] As the film lingers in close-up over the colours and textures of bovine coats and muscles, visual fetishism becomes inextricable from commodification. The language of cattle-breeding companies similarly foregrounds the fetishistic function of the Charolais icon – as one website puts it: 'The added bonus for Charolais crossbred progeny is their distinct colour and markings which gives added confidence to store cattle buyers.'[96] Thus what attracts and assures the agricultural market – the aesthetic of the cows' striking appearance – is also capitalised on by Gras's film. The materiality of animal capital shapes the film's aesthetic, revealing the commodity fetishism underlying its bucolic investments.

RENDERING

Such entanglements of animal material, capital and the aesthetic are explored by Shukin in the particular context of the cinematic medium, as she points to the use of gelatin ('a protein extracted from the skin, bones, and connective tissues of cattle, sheep, and pigs') in the production of celluloid film stock.[97] Cows play a particular role in this photochemical history – as Shukin documents, emulsion scientists worked to refine details of cow diets in order to produce optimum quality gelatin. Such insights reveal a set of visceral entanglements between the biopolitical production of cows and of images.[98] In the age of celluloid, gelatin 'marks a "vanishing point" where moving images are both inconspicuously and *viscerally* contingent on mass animal disassembly, in contradiction with cinema's framing semiotic of "animation"'.[99] Animals are fetishised simultaneously onscreen as 'naturally photogenic figures in motion' and offscreen as 'the emulsion industry's most photosensitive substance', revealing what Shukin describes as a 'double logic of rendering': 'The rendered material [. . .] archives an "unconscious" death wish on animal life that is radically, yet productively, at odds with the fetishistic signs of life.'[100]

Bovines is structured by this 'double logic of rendering'. The film fetishises life, as signalled both by the lingering attention paid to the photogenic Charolais cows and by its titular promise to reveal to us a hitherto unseen perspective – the 'true life' of cows. Yet, for beef cows, this 'true life' consists of more than just grazing in a field: it also involves the experience of being separated from the herd and killed in a slaughterhouse. Though *Bovines* shows us something of the former, it hides from us the latter, averting its gaze, and ours, from the realities of slaughter. The film's own process of rendering – its investment in 'fetishistic signs of life'– reveals a double logic, a set of tensions between an affectionate celebration of bovine vitality and the pathological conditions of death-driven production that make this cinematic celebration possible. As the film's credits tellingly acknowledge: 'A big thanks to the farmers, without whom this film could not have existed.' Farming makes this film possible; killing is the ground of aesthetic production. The film's visual attention to animal life inadvertently 'archives an "unconscious" death wish'. And *Bovines* is haunted not only by off-screen scenes of slaughter but by a photochemical history in which cows destined for gelatin give life to photographic images. The film's scenes of rumination regurgitate the material links between bovine diet, gelatin and film, unwittingly working to bring these biopolitical histories to light.

There is another deathly history that *Bovines* inadvertently regurgitates here as well. For in reflecting on this film, it is difficult to ignore a more recent history of cattle, one particularly pertinent to France – that of BSE (bovine spongiform encephalopathy), or 'mad cow disease'. While the BSE crisis was first identified in Britain in 1986 and widely reported and acted upon through a mass slaughter plan, it was severely underreported in France.[101] Indeed, it has been argued that 'the French BSE epidemic in the late 1980s was completely undetected, and only the second wave, after 1990, was observed'.[102] *Bovines* makes no explicit reference to BSE, but this repressed history arguably haunts the film, there to be detected in particular in the film's investment in the iconicity of the white Charolais cow, in its connotations not only of 'organic national unity' but also perhaps a particular kind of uninfected purity.[103]

The BSE outbreak revealed a pathological history of rendering, as Shukin suggests: the disease resulted from the circular (or 'tautological') practice of feeding 'rendered brains, spinal cords, and nervous tissues' – that is, the waste products of slaughter – back to livestock, in order to fatten animals more quickly and 'facilitate the rapid turnover of animal capital'.[104] In an eruptive disclosure of the ways in which animal 'material' passes not only from the farm to the slaughterhouse but back again, the BSE epidemic laid bare this vicious loop of rendering and the pathologies of modern agriculture's reproductions of animal life. But in the form of its human variant, Creutzfeldt-Jakob disease, the BSE outbreak also revealed the threat of zoonotic diseases that pass from animals to humans. For Shukin, the contemporary threat of such species-crossing epidemics (which also include diseases such as the H5N1 avian flu virus) forms part of a broader cultural nexus of anxiety and longing in relation to animal life: 'the crossing of species lines is produced not only as a pathological object of fear but also an object of intense desire'.[105] Contemporary representations of animal life are structured, Shukin contends, by this paradoxical logic: 'if human–animal intimacy is pathologised in the cultural discourse of pandemic, it is contradictorily fetishised as an object of desire in concurrent cultural discourses'.[106] *Bovines* seems profoundly shaped by this contradictory structure. In its close-up engagement with bovine life, in its promise to unveil the 'true life' of cows, the film responds to a contemporary longing for revitalised forms of cross-species kinship. Yet read in relation to the viral loops of modern agricapital, what haunts the fantasy of human–bovine intimacy offered up by *Bovines* is a disavowed history of BSE and the persistent threat of 'biomobility'. If for Deleuze and Guattari, becoming-animal entails modes of 'contagion', then *Bovines* both represses and unwittingly recalls the pathological dimensions of a contagious dynamic of becoming-animal. Intersecting with various contexts of bovine rendering (from the photochemical to the zoonotic), Gras's film inadvertently articulates the deadly loops of animal capital that reach from the farm to the slaughterhouse to the cinema and back again.

TIME AND POLITICS

Yet the rhythms of the Deleuzian time-image might be viewed on one level as a form of aesthetic resistance to rendering, and to the efficient conversion of animal into capital. Reflecting on the slaughterhouses of Chicago's 'bovine city' that would provide Henry Ford with a model of industrial efficiency, Shukin writes: 'In the time-motion efficiencies on display in the vertical abattoirs of Packingtown, cattle were forced to walk up chutes to an elevated landing so that the gravitational pull of their own bodies would propel them down the disassembly line.'[107] The accelerated movement of animals, alive and dead, along the disassembly line signals an efficient conversion of life into capital, while establishing, Shukin argues, protocinematic structures of serialised representation and visceral viewing (through turn-of-the-century practices of slaughterhouse spectatorship). The meandering animal time documented by *Bovines* intervenes in this history, slowly subverting capitalism's time-motion ideologies of speed, spectacle and efficiency. This is underlined by the film's attention to rumination, no doubt an inefficient process by Fordist and Taylorist standards. Reflecting on an unmanageable surplus, idleness or waste, *Bovines* privileges the time of bovine rumination over that of human or mechanical efficiency. In a non-linear, meandering mode, *Bovines* shifts bovine time away from the seriality of the disassembly line and the workings of industrial capitalism. In this sense, cinematic slowness is on the side of the animal.

However, cinematic slowness might have another effect here, particularly when read in extradiegetic terms. Bearing in mind Shukin's analysis of animals as 'metaphors and brands mediating new technologies, commodities, and markets',[108] one could read the burgeoning presence of animals in slow art films such as *Bovines*, *Bestiaire* and *Le Quattro Volte* as another form of branding serving to circulate capital. In this sense, the slow animal art film functions as a further instance of neoliberal cultures speculating in 'signs of noncapitalized life even as they effectively render it incarnate capital'.[109] An exploitation of animal life is not new to art cinema (or to cinema in general), as indicated, for example, by the documentary deaths of pigs in Jean-Luc Godard's *Weekend* (1967) and Michael Haneke's *Benny's Video* (1992).[110] Though *Bovines* frames the animal as a bearer of lived time rather than as an index of a deathly, annihilating instant, its attentive, durational aesthetic arguably signals how modern biopower 'denounces physical violence and operates, instead, through sympathetic investments in animal communication'.[111] Here the possibility of an ethical form of cross-species communication enabled by cinema becomes disturbingly compromised by the structures of instrumentalisation on which it relies.

Bovines's inextricability from the workings of capitalism – both diegetically and extradiegetically – places pressure on the model of animal time, becoming and affect that emerges from reading the film in conjunction with Deleuze and Guattari. Moreover, if capitalism is also rhizomatic, as thinkers such as Slavoj Zizek suggest, becomings – including becoming-animal – may not be as subversive as Deleuze and Guattari wish them to be.[112] Such a critique can also be applied, Shukin suggests, to the related concept of affect: 'Far from being politically motivated, the micropolitical force of affect described by Deleuze and Guattari [. . .] is cast as a "nonvoluntary" force springing from the irrepressible multiplicity of heterogeneous nature.'[113] Clearly this idea of affect as 'nonvoluntary' is particularly problematic when connected to a regime of production capitalising on animal powerlessness. As Shukin argues, '[i]n the context of animal capital, there is a great deal at stake in romanticising affect as a rogue portion of pure energy linked to animality as a state of virtual rather than actual embodiment'.[114] Given that animal energy is so predominantly conceived as a virtual, deterritorialised economy, not least through the often invisible processes of animal disassembly and rendering discussed above, the thinking of animal intensities and affects proposed by Deleuze and Guattari 'may inadvertently resonate with market forces likewise intent on freeing animal life into a multiplicity of potential exchange values'.[115]

Such reservations point to the political limitations of the reading of *Bovines* – in terms of affects, becomings and lines of flight – that I have outlined above. As Hallward writes of Deleuze's thought more broadly: 'A philosophy based on deterritorialisation, dissipation and flight can offer only the most immaterial and evanescent grip on the mechanisms of exploitation and domination that continue to condition so much of what happens in our world.'[116] Hallward further contends, citing Deleuze: 'Once "a social field is defined less by its conflicts and contradictions than by the lines of flight running through it", any distinctive space for political action can only be subsumed within the more general dynamics of creation or life.'[117] If *Bovines* sketches its 'social field' in terms of lines of flight, virtuality and affect, it also arguably subsumes 'any distinctive space for political action [. . .] within the more general dynamics of creation or life', as underlined by the film's fetishisation of animal vitality discussed above. In refusing to show the slaughterhouse, the film arguably largely sidesteps political conflict, replacing this with a system of deterritorialising *opsigns* and *sonsigns*. And thus, despite certain gestures to the fate of the cows onscreen, *Bovines* remains a celebration of biovitality rather than an interrogation of biopolitics.

This politically limiting move may in fact be exacerbated by *Bovines*'s investment in the Deleuzian time-image, despite my more affirmative reading of the film's durational aesthetic above. In privileging the non-extension of perception into action, *Bovines* foregrounds the realm of the virtual; in line with the workings of the time-image, the cows are presented as 'seers' rather than 'agents'.[118] Reflecting on how the 'disqualification of actuality concerns the paralysis of the subject or actor' in Deleuze's thought, Hallward writes:

> Since what powers Deleuze's cosmology is the immediate differentiation of creation through the infinite proliferation of virtual creations, the creatures that actualise these creatings are confined to a derivative if not limiting role. A creature's own interests, actions or decisions are of minimal or preliminary significance at best: the renewal of creation always requires the paralysis and dissolution of the creature per se.[119]

This framework of actual creatures and virtual creatings, formulated here by Hallward to emphasise a general 'subjection' of the human 'to the imperatives of creative life or thought' within Deleuze's philosophy,[120] invites transposition to *Bovines*'s own creatures. Gras's cows are 'confined to a derivative if not limiting role' – the actualised yet *politically paralysed* ground upon which the film's own virtual creatings might take place. If in Deleuze's model, as Hallward suggests, 'power is not that of the individual itself', and 'an individual only provides a vessel for the power that works through it',[121] then this divestment of power is precisely what the time-image celebrates, and what *Bovines* foregrounds: power working through the animal as 'seer' rather than 'agent'; cinematic time given over, in the end, to virtual creatings rather than actual creatures.

BEYOND THANATOPOLITICS

Yet what might be recuperated, politically, from a reading of *Bovines* with Deleuze and Guattari? It is possible to argue, as I have done above, that by refusing to show the slaughterhouse, the film sidesteps political conflict. Such conflict is faced head-on, to excoriating effect, by filmmakers such as Franju and by artists such as Sue Coe.[122] Yet, as seen in the previous chapter on *Leviathan*, visceral visions of slaughter can also eclipse political critique. One is tempted to assert that there must be modes of engaging politically that do not necessarily involve a visual literalisation of the thanatological drive of the slaughterhouse. There may still be ways of reading *Bovines* in which political critique – and a critique of the farm and the slaughterhouse in particular – is not foreclosed.

One possibility lies in the scene of the calf's birth discussed above. *Bovines* devotes a significant amount of time to the birth, and to images of the mother attending to the calf. As the mother licks, washes and feeds her new-born, the film emphasises the intimacy of their bond. Gras explains that he wanted to show this relationship in 'a present manner, by spending time with them': at this point in the film, 'we don't know it yet but it's the beginning of the story'; 'there will be an end which is going to concern the relation between the cow and the calf'.[123] *Bovines* sets up the relation between mother and calf in the first half of the film in order for the separation of the calves from the herd to be felt all the more forcefully in the second half. During the scene of separation, in which the cattle can be heard constantly mooing, apparently in protest, we hear one female farmer say (her voice only just audible amid the general noise): 'They're calling their calves. It's the mothers.' A fleeting comment, but it is particularly significant in a film that all but evacuates human speech. Gras said that he wanted to keep this comment in the film because it testifies to the

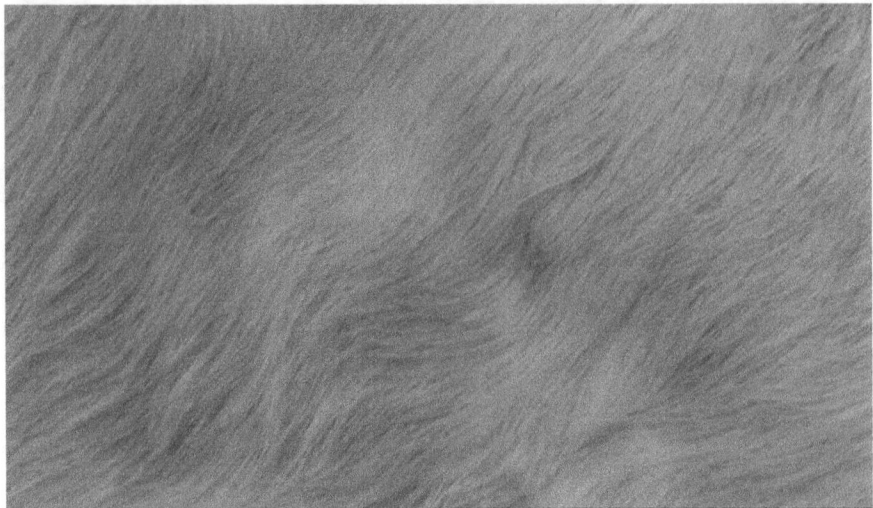

Figure 5.4 Becoming other (*Bovines*).

suffering of the cows. The responses of the cows here, he says, are like a form of 'evidence': these are 'mothers who have raised their calves'; 'they are reacting to, subjected to, what is happening'.[124]

In this sense, we might say that *Bovines* is also a film about motherhood, and about the pain of enforced separation between mother and child. For some viewers, this reading will seem too 'sentimental', too close to a *Bambi*-esque anthropomorphism.[125] But others will find in these scenes of bonding and separation a latent critique of the world of the farm (a world in which pregnancy amounts to the generation of capital). It seems particularly powerful that the film's most explicit recognition of animal suffering is placed in the mouth of a farmer. And it also seems significant that these words are uttered by a woman. It is as though her gender forms the basis of a solidarity that temporarily promises to cross species lines. And in this sense, *Bovines* might be read as a feminist film – a reading encouraged further by its own 'feminised' title.[126] In one sense these scenes of separation might be seen to play out Hallward's model of politically paralysed creatures. Yet the relation of these scenes to the rest of the film also allows for precisely the kind of political 'conflicts and contradictions' that Hallward is looking for to come into view.

For the critical force of these contradictions is strengthened by the film's structure. In the first half of the film, as we have seen, *Bovines* takes the time to establish, gradually, worlds of perception, sentience and intelligence beyond the category of *bêtise* or placid indifference to which the cow is usually consigned. The scene revealing the cow's resourceful approach to apple eating is positioned just before the arrival of the tractor and the dispatch of the calves to market.¹²⁷ Such glimpses of bovine thoughtfulness build on previous scenes, such as the one in which one cow patiently licks another with such attention that it seems impossible not to read it as a gesture of care.¹²⁸ Gras explains: 'I wanted to show the living creatures behind what we put on our plates [. . .] I am not a vegetarian, but I would like people to see that cows, usually considered as rather stupid and rough animals, have feelings and sensations too.'¹²⁹ Rather like the unfolding of animal worlds in *Bestiaire*, *Bovines* reveals realms of perception and pensivity that work to question the biopolitical regimes in which these animals are forced to live. But *Bovines* has to work 'harder' than *Bestiaire*: its animals are less exotic, less charismatic, and, according to conventional wisdom, less 'obviously' intelligent. They belong to the lowest rung of the hierarchy of mammals drawn up by the human: beef cows, destined for the slaughterhouse. But *Bovines* reveals them to be much more than this.

Yet the film also allows a further political argument to unfold here, one that arguably exceeds the director's intentions, as well as Hallward's model of political action. Hallward's critique of power working through, rather than belonging to, the individual nods to the distinction between *puissance* and *pouvoir* that Deleuze draws from Spinoza. And while this is at the root of Hallward's problem with Deleuze (because it upholds a non-relational logic of 'internal and self-differing power'),¹³⁰ it is nevertheless here, perhaps, that we might still detect possible lines of aesthetico-political resistance, however fragile and contested they remain.¹³¹ As Elena del Río suggests, 'Spinoza's affirmative idea of power as a potential or capacity for existence (*potentia/puissance*) provides a necessary supplement to the negative model of power as domination or circumscription (*potestas/pouvoir*).'¹³² As noted in previous chapters, Deleuze and Guattari's thinking of *puissance*, following Spinoza, insists that there is something other than the saturated field of power as sovereignty or domination. As del Río puts it: 'Insofar as each body displays its own capacities for existence (*potentia/puissance*), its possibilities for action, thought, and becoming are not entirely disabled by the operations of cultural and social systems.'¹³³ This chimes with Wolfe's emphasis in his reading of Foucault, as we have seen, on 'a potentially creative, aleatory element that inheres in the very gambit of biopower, one not wholly subject to the thanatological drift of a biopolitics subordinated to the paradigm of sovereignty'. As Wolfe continues: 'there is a chance – and this marks in no small part Foucault's debt to Nietzsche [. . .] – for life to burst through power's systematic operation in ways that are more and more difficult to anticipate'.¹³⁴ In these final remarks on *Bovines*, then, I seek to move beyond an all-encompassing frame of sovereign power (exemplified by Shukin's 'double logic of rendering') while keeping the question of biopolitics in view. I am interested in pursuing the political via precisely the dimensions of 'virtual [. . .] embodiment' and 'virtual creatings' critiqued respectively by Shukin and Hallward.

As del Río observes, the distinction between *puissance* and *pouvoir* corresponds in Deleuze and Guattari to the distinction between molar (identitarian) and molecular (impersonal) modalities. Yet a recognition of the material realities of animal lives arguably places particular pressure on the political potential of molecular *puissance* as opposed to molar *pouvoir*. Though for del Río 'possibilities for action, thought, and becoming are not entirely disabled by the operations of cultural and social systems', it is clear that in the domain of the farmed animal, these possibilities *are* in fact very much disabled. The molar identities of agricapital imposed on 'meat animals' in particular are arguably all-consuming. However, the opening of a space in which to consider the powers and capacities of the body otherwise, beyond the operations of *pouvoir* (following Deleuze and Guattari, and also Foucault), remains helpful, particularly in the realm of the aesthetic; it may be this very space – of envisaging *otherwise* – that *Bovines* occupies. Yet it is also the closing down of this space – in the omnivorous workings of animal capital – that *Bovines* inadvertently diagnoses.

Following the removal of the calves to be sent to market – a scene that highlights, as we have seen, the devastating workings of *pouvoir* – the film's final sequence opens with a close-up of the face of a ruminating cow; the eye is prominent, recalling Burt's analysis, drawing on Bergson and Deleuze, of 'the eye-image itself as point of origin for the attention to life'.[135] The close-up shifts slightly, so as to include the numbered tag attached to the cow's ear. The shot then reframes to exclude the tag. As the cow's head turns, the close-up moves slowly away from the eye so that the side of the face fills the screen. The contours of what we see shift, transform, becoming abstract, becoming other. What is foregrounded is a tactile focus on the undulating surfaces of the face, accompanied by amplified sounds of ruminating and breathing: forces of life, sentience, pensivity. The close-up reframes again to focus on the mouth (chewing) and then the nose (rough surfaces visible, nostrils dribbling a little), emphasising further the material presence of a sensing, perceiving being. Yet as Deleuze and Guattari remind us, such affective forces also extend beyond the phenomenologically lived body, designating 'a more profound and almost unlivable power [*puissance*]'.[136] Through an act of *décadrage* (a deframing of the tag), a line of flight, a layer of virtuality opens up: we have moved from the territorialising drive of agricapital's claim on this cow to the deterritorialising force of *puissance*.

This final sequence encapsulates the tensions at the heart of *Bovines*: capital vs life, *pouvoir* vs *puissance* – or rather, following the monistic impulse in Deleuze and Guattari, a continual exchange between these realms, in a mode of assemblage rather than 'dualist opposition'.[137] In the line of flight opened up here, the film gestures to a virtual – aesthetically carved out – space of resistance to capital.[138] Yet this final scene of rumination also figures a repetition (with difference) – a regurgitation – of earlier scenes of rumination. There is a

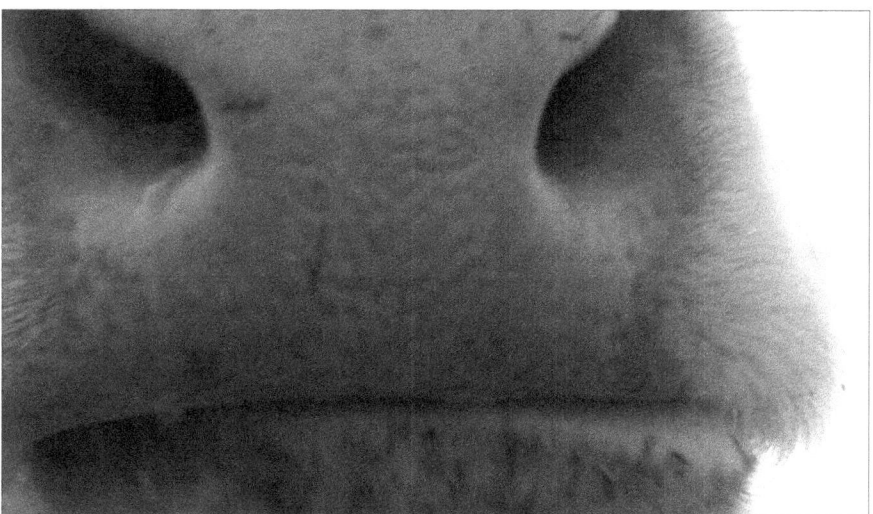

Figure 5.5 Rumination, life, *puissance* (*Bovines*)

certain circularity here, and a sense in which the film, like the farm, is caught up in a process whereby the conditions of production, as Shukin suggests, are endlessly reproduced.[139] What seems like the glimmer of an ethical cinematic attention to life risks being reconverted into the undying, interminable nature of agricapital. Perhaps the film's investment in life cycles – encompassing birth onscreen and death offscreen – simply affirms these processes of (re)production and the infernal survival of capital. Perhaps Hallward is right – and the thought of Deleuze (and of Guattari), like *Bovines*, offers little in the way of a critique of regimes of exploitation, particularly in the domain of animals. And yet, against the farm's territorialisation of docile, domesticated bodies, the film opens up 'a potentially creative, aleatory element'. *Bovines* takes these 'meat animals' and allows them – even if only temporarily – to move beyond the 'house' of the flesh. It shows how the virtual – that category critiqued by Shukin and Hallward – can still be political. In reflecting on modes of becoming and flights beyond the functional, *Bovines*, like Deleuze and Guattari, considers expressive, sentient worlds in excess of capitalism's hold on life. However 'evanescent' or 'immaterial' these glimpses, surely they still matter.

NOTES

1. Murphet, 'Pitiable or Political Animals?', p. 102.
2. Although strictly the word 'cow' specifies the female animal, I follow common usage of the term as gender non-specific.

3. Deleuze, *Cinema 2*, p. 3.
4. Ibid., p. 261.
5. For a fascinating recent literary reflection on the meandering habits of cows, see Lydia Davis, *The Cows* (Louisville: Sarabande Books, 2011).
6. Bellour, *Le Corps du cinéma*, p. 431.
7. Hallward, *Out of this World*, p. 163.
8. In Tarr's *Sátántangó*, the wanderings of the herd of cows in the film's opening long take will be recuperated in narrative terms: the cows are, as Rancière puts it, 'the last stock of a collective farm [. . .] being liquidated'; 'it is the money from this sale that will be the centre of the intrigue'. Rancière, *Béla Tarr, The Time After*, p. 37.
9. Walber, 'Pastoral: Emmanuel Gras's *Bovines* at Rooftop Films'.
10. I engage in depth with Gras's comments on *Bovines*, particularly his director's commentary, because he offers especially thoughtful, pertinent insights. There is potential irony here, in that Gras's commentary might end up functioning as precisely the kind of expository voiceover that is characteristic of the wildlife documentary and that Gras seeks to refuse in his film. Yet while I draw on the director's comments, I seek to privilege what the film communicates on its own terms.
11. Anne Tézenas du Montcel, '"Faire vivre au spectateur une vie d'animal": rencontre avec Emmanuel Gras', 2012, *Bovines* DVD, Blaq Out/UniversCiné Collection.
12. Ibid.
13. Ibid.
14. Ibid.
15. While Gras expected the shoot to take just a month or so, he ended up filming over a year – an indication of the patient approach that shapes the film. Ibid.
16. Ibid.
17. Gras, 'Director's Commentary', 2013, *Bovines* DVD, Blaq Out/UniversCiné Collection.
18. Ibid.
19. Bailly, *The Animal Side*, p. 5; original emphasis.
20. Hannah Velten, *Cow* (London: Reaktion, 2007), p. 12.
21. Ibid., p. 12.
22. Deleuze, *Cinema 2*, p. 1.
23. Walber, 'Pastoral'.
24. Deleuze, *Cinema 2*, p. 124; original emphasis.
25. Ibid., p. 42.
26. Bergson, *The Creative Mind*, translated by Mabelle Andison (Westport, CT: Greenwood, 1946), p. 62.
27. Elizabeth Grosz, *The Nick of Time: Politics, Evolution, and the Untimely* (Crows Nest: Allen & Unwin, 2004), p. 181.
28. Deleuze, *Cinema 2*, p. 42; original emphasis.
29. D. N. Rodowick, *Gilles Deleuze's Time Machine* (Durham, NC: Duke University Press, 1997), p. 70.
30. Deleuze, *Cinema 2*, p. 42.
31. Ibid., p. 42.
32. *Oxford English Dictionary*. Available at http://www.oed.com/view/Entry/22176 (last accessed 14 September 2018).
33. Walber, 'Pastoral'.
34. Gras, 'Director's Commentary'.
35. See Lippit's *Electric Animal*.
36. Walber, 'Pastoral'.

37. Ibid.
38. See my discussion of animal labour and 'endurance' in *The Turin Horse* (Chapter 3).
39. Gras, 'Director's Commentary'.
40. Ibid.
41. Deleuze, *Cinema 2*, p. 1.
42. On cows in Deleuze and attendant links to animal territory and becoming in literature, see Ryan, '"The Reality of Becoming": Deleuze, Woolf, and the Territory of Cows', *Deleuze Studies*, 7:4 (2013), 537–61.
43. Deleuze and Guattari, *What is Philosophy?*, p. 183. Deleuze and Guattari build this argument with reference to a particular species, the bower bird, or 'stagemaker' (*Scenopoetes dentirostris*), a bird that decorates its nest through elaborate, colourful constructions of leaves, branches and flowers, constructing 'a stage for itself', primarily in order to attract a mate, but in a manner that also reveals an expressivity beyond functionality. The bower bird's territory is not only visual but auditory too: the bird also 'sings a complex song made up from its own notes and, at intervals, those of other birds that it imitates: it is a complete artist.' And thus:

> This is not a synaesthesia of the flesh but blocs of sensations in the territory – colors, postures, and sounds that sketch out a total work of art. These sonorous blocs are refrains; but there are also refrains of posture and color, and postures and colors are always being introduced into refrains: bowing low, straightening up, dancing in a circle and a line of colors. The whole of the refrain is the being of sensation. Monuments are refrains. In this respect, art is continually haunted by the animal. (*What is Philosophy?*, p. 184)

44. For an emphasis on the sensory dimensions of Deleuze and Guattari's conception of territory, see Grosz, *Chaos, Territory, Art: Deleuze and the Framing of the Earth* (New York: Columbia University Press, 2008), p. 12.
45. As Buchanan suggests, a territory for Deleuze and Guattari 'is extracted from a milieu because its expressivity breaks away from the coding specific to its milieu'. Buchanan, *Onto-Ethologies*, p. 178.
46. Gras, 'Director's Commentary'.
47. Ibid.
48. As we saw in Chapter 2, this pattern of the delayed 'reveal' of the animal is echoed in *Bestiaire*; Côté's film is arguably in dialogue with *Bovines* at this point.
49. Deleuze and Guattari, *What is Philosophy?*, p. 184.
50. Ibid., p. 186.
51. Deleuze and Guattari mention the spider's web in their discussion of animals, art and territory, drawing on Uexküll: 'The spider's web contains "a very subtle portrait of the fly", which serves as its counterpoint' (*What is Philosophy?*, p. 185). In Uexküll's 'melodic, polyphonic, and contrapuntal conception of Nature', as Deleuze and Guattari describe it, the spider's web is attuned to the fly – it evokes the presence, the *Umwelt*, not only of the spider but also, contrapuntally, of the fly.
52. Deleuze and Guattari, *What is Philosophy?*, p. 185.
53. Ibid., p. 187.
54. Michel Chion, *Audio-Vision: Sound on Screen*, edited and translated by Claudia Gorbmann (New York: Columbia University Press, 1994).
55. Deleuze and Guattari use these terms to describe the sounds and territory of the 'stagemaker' bird in *What is Philosophy?*; see the note on this above.
56. Gras, 'Director's Commentary'.

57. Ibid.
58. Bailly, *The Animal Side*, p. 16.
59. Ibid., p. 16.
60. Ibid., pp. 14–15.
61. Barthes, *S/Z*, translated by Richard Miller (Oxford: Basil Blackwell, 1990); Honoré de Balzac, *Sarrasine* [1830], reprinted in Barthes, *S/Z*, pp. 221–54.
62. Rancière, *The Future of the Image*, p. 122.
63. Ibid., p. 122.
64. Revealed in Gras, 'Director's Commentary'.
65. Commenting on this scene, Gras speaks of looking for a 'level of abstraction'; 'what we are seeing is not clearly defined'. Montcel, '"Faire vivre au spectateur une vie d'animal"'.
66. Deleuze, *Francis Bacon*.
67. Laura U. Marks, *The Skin of the Film: Intercultural Cinema, Embodiment and the Senses* (Durham, NC and London: Duke University Press, 2000).
68. Montcel, '"Faire vivre au spectateur une vie d'animal"'.
69. Ibid.
70. Ibid.
71. Deleuze and Guattari, *A Thousand Plateaus*, p. 239.
72. Michel Ciment, 'Bovines ou la vraie vie des vaches', *Positif*, 613 (March 2012), 40.
73. Deleuze and Guattari, *What is Philosophy?*, p. 169.
74. As Deleuze and Guattari propose: '*Affects are precisely these nonhuman becomings of man*' (*What is Philosophy?*, p.169; original emphasis). See also Patricia Pisters's reading of becoming-animal in relation to Deleuze's reflections on art and cinema: 'A "logic of sensations" and affection-images seem important to express and sense the passive and active affects that are involved in becoming-animal.' Pisters, *The Matrix of Visual Culture: Working with Deleuze in Film Theory* (Stanford: Stanford University Press, 2003), p. 142.
75. Deleuze and Guattari, *A Thousand Plateaus*, p. 280.
76. Deleuze, *Cinema 1*, p. 60.
77. Deleuze and Guattari, *A Thousand Plateaus*, p. 280.
78. Bonitzer cited in Deleuze and Guattari 1994: p. 187n28.
79. Gras, 'Director's Commentary'. Gras is actually speaking here in relation to another close-up of a cow's mouth in the film, but his comment also resonates with this scene.
80. Deleuze and Guattari, *A Thousand Plateaus*, p. 257. Discussing this scene, Gras speaks of how, by focusing first on the grass, and then on fragments of the animal's face, he wanted to evoke the aesthetics of a thriller or horror, echoing the delayed 'reveal' of the alien or monster in its entirety (Gras, 'Director's Commentary'). The apparently vacant stare of the cow while grazing seems to invoke this 'alien' quality too.
81. Deleuze and Guattari, *What is Philosophy?*, p. 188.
82. Velten, *Cow*, p. 22. This is underlined by the etymology of the word cattle, '[d]erived from the Middle English and Old Northern French *catel*, the late Latin *captale* and the Latin *capitale*, meaning "capital" in the sense of chattel or chief property'. Ibid., p. 22.
83. And as Jamie Lorimer and Clemens Driessen note: 'There is a long and distinguished history of bovine biotechnology through which the bodies, ethologies and ecologies of cattle have been modernised' – a history that includes domestication, selective breeding and 'contemporary interventions in bovine genetics'. Lorimer and Driessen also include consideration of a 'Deleuzian biophilosophy' that offers '"lines of flight" for "becoming-otherwise"' – in the context of rewilding cattle, they focus on the figure of the 'monster'

and its 'potential to provide a shock to thought, to "actualise" the "virtual" into new formations full of difference'. Jamie Lorimer and Clemens Driessen, 'Bovine Biopolitics and the Promise of Monsters in the Rewilding of Heck Cattle', *Geoforum*, 48 (2013), 249–59 (pp. 251–2; p. 257; p. 251).
84. On cross-species collaboration, see Haraway, *When Species Meet*. On collaborating (with) cows in particular, see Fudge, 'Farmyard Choreographies: Or, Reading Invisible Cows in Early Modern Culture', *Reading Animals* Conference, University of Sheffield, 20 July 2014, and also the work of Porcher (for example, Porcher, 'The Work of Animals', and Porcher and Tiphaine Schmitt, 'Dairy Cows: Workers in the Shadows?', *Society and Animals*, 20:1 (2012), 39–60). It is significant, though, that in all of these examples, the focus is on dairy cows. Meat animals, and particularly the stage at which they enter the slaughterhouse, figure as a certain limit point or blindspot in these theories of cross-species collaboration.
85. Nicolas Azalbert, 'Bovines', *Cahiers du cinéma*, 675 (February 2012), 52.
86. As Velten puts it: 'Cattle are gregarious creatures and, as such, will always live in herds and become exceedingly anxious when separated from their group.' Velten, *Cow*, pp. 20–1.
87. Reflecting on Piero di Cosimo's *A Satyr Mourning over a Nymph* (1495), Bailly notes the presence of the dog in the scene: 'What we see, here again, is a gaze, the insistent presence of a gaze, and through this gaze, in an obviously silent register, the deep, flat brilliance of mourning.' As Bailly suggests, it is 'as if that sadness were accessible [. . .] only at the price of a distress that a perfectly normal and norm-governed human being cannot feel'. Bailly, *The Animal Side*, p. 36. *Bovines* refuses to silence its animals, but it similarly asks us to recognise the presence of animal mourning beyond that which might be 'normally' or 'normatively' attributed to the animal.
88. 'Consider the cattle, grazing as they pass you by: they do not know what is meant by yesterday or today, they leap about, eat, rest, digest, leap about again, and so from morn till night and from day to day, fettered to the moment and its pleasure or displeasure, and thus neither melancholy nor bored.' Nietzsche, *Untimely Meditations*, translated by R. J. Hollingdale and edited by Daniel Breazeale (Cambridge: Cambridge University Press, 1997), p. 60.
89. In the director's commentary, Gras raises the possibility that she is mooing 'perhaps for the calf she is looking for'.
90. Murphet, 'Pitiable or Political Animals?', p. 111.
91. On the fraught and complex links between mass animal slaughter and the Holocaust, in the context of a reflection on mortality and suffering shared across species lines, see Derrida, *The Animal That Therefore I Am*; on the biopolitical implications of this, see Wolfe, *Before the Law*.
92. Velten, *Cow*, p. 86. In his review of *Bovines*, Ciment cites the seventeenth-century Dutch painter Paulus Potter, describing Gras as 'his worthy successor'. Ciment, 'Bovines ou la vraie vie des vaches', 40.
93. Velten, *Cow*, pp. 86–7.
94. In Michel Houellebecq's *Submission*, the Charolais cow is evoked as a clichéd image of the French countryside. At a service station somewhere near Châteauroux, the narrator flatly observes: 'The parking lot dominated the surrounding countryside, which was deserted except for a couple of cows – Charolais, probably.' Houellebecq, *Submission*, translated by Lorin Stein (New York: Farrar, Straus and Giroux, 2015), p. 102.
95. Shukin, *Animal Capital*, p. 3; p. 227.
96. The British Charolais Cattle Society. Available at http://www.charolais.co.uk/society/breed-description/ (last accessed 14 September 2018).

97. Shukin, *Animal Capital*, p. 104.
98. One breakthrough at Kodak in 1925 revealed the importance of mustard seeds: as the head of Kodak's research laboratory later recalled, 'we found out that if cows didn't like mustard there wouldn't be any movies at all' (cited in Shukin, *Animal Capital*, p. 109).
99. Ibid., p. 91; original emphasis.
100. Ibid., p. 111; p. 91.
101. Kim Wilsher, 'France in Denial as BSE-Infected Beef Entered Food Chain', *The Telegraph*, 5 July 2004. Available at http://www.smh.com.au/articles/2004/07/04/1088879375088.html (last accessed 14 September 2018).
102. Virginie Supervie and Dominique Costagliola, 'The Unrecognised French BSE Epidemic', *Veterinary Research*, 35:3 (2004), 349–62. Available at http://www.vetres.org/articles/vetres/abs/2004/03/V4008/V4008.html (last accessed 14 September 2018).
103. The (French) farming industry's investment in the relative 'whiteness' of the pure-breed Charolais cow might be read in terms of its racialising hierarchies as well. On intersections between animality and race, see, for example, Wolfe, *Animal Rites*, Christopher Petersen, *Bestial Traces: Race, Sexuality, Animality* (New York: Fordham University Press, 2013), and Chen and Luciano (eds), 'Queer Inhumanisms'.
104. Shukin, *Animal Capital*, p. 86; p. 226.
105. Ibid., p. 188.
106. Ibid., p. 46.
107. Ibid., p. 93.
108. Ibid., p. 24.
109. Ibid., pp. 225–6.
110. See Lawrence, 'Haneke's Stable'.
111. Shukin, *Animal Capital*, p. 156.
112. Slavoj Zizek, *Bodies without Organs: On Deleuze and Consequences* (London: Routledge, 2004), p. 184; cited in Shukin, *Animal Capital*, p. 32.
113. Shukin, *Animal Capital*, p. 31.
114. Ibid., p. 31.
115. Ibid., p. 42.
116. Hallward, *Out of this World*, p. 162.
117. Ibid., p. 162.
118. Deleuze, *Cinema 2*, p. xi.
119. Hallward, *Out of this World*, p. 163.
120. Ibid., p. 163.
121. Ibid., p. 163.
122. On Sue Coe's art, see: Baker, *The Postmodern Animal*; Wolfe, *What is Posthumanism?*, pp. 145–67; Baker, *Artist Animal*, pp. 144–79; Stephen F. Eisenman, *The Ghosts of Our Meat* (Carlisle: The Trout Gallery, 2013).
123. Gras, 'Director's Commentary'.
124. Ibid.
125. Léo Soesanto gestures to this in his review of *Bovines*: 'when the farmer arrives, we're not far from *Bambi*'. Soesanto, 'Portraits de ruminants en futurs steaks: un pur trip en compagnie des vaches', *Les Inrockuptibles*, 21 February 2012. Available at http://www.lesinrocks.com/cinema/films-a-l-affiche/bovines/ (last accessed 14 September 2018).
126. On intersections between animal politics and feminism, see Adams, *The Sexual Politics of Meat*.
127. This juxtaposition is very consciously drawn: in the director's commentary, Gras underlines the significance of the position of the apple-eating scene.

128. As one review notes: 'Among a herd, cows establish bonds of friendship and even "chum up" in pairs, where each cow takes care of the other. They often share gestures of tenderness and affection' ('*Bovines*, the reinvention of a genre', *Down to Earth*, 30 July 2012. Available at http://downtoearth.danone.com/2012/07/30/bovines-the-reinvention-of-a-genre/ (last accessed 14 September 2018)). This moment in *Bovines* resonates with the scene in *Bestiaire* in which one chimp grooms another (discussed in Chapter 2).
129. Gras in '*Bovines*, the reinvention of a genre'.
130. Hallward, *Out of this World*, p. 153.
131. On recuperating a political Deleuze in the wake of Hallward's reading, see, for example, John Protevi, 'Peter Hallward, *Out of this World: Deleuze and the Philosophy of Creation*', *Notre Dame Philosophical Reviews*, 3 August 2007. Available at http://ndpr.nd.edu/news/23058/?id=10564 (last accessed 14 September 2018). Protevi argues that Deleuze's thought resists the dualism of the virtual and the actual on which Hallward's critique relies. Grosz rejects Hallward's 'hierarchical organisation' of philosophy as the 'less materialised counterpart of art' (Grosz, *Chaos, Territory, Art*, p. 5n5). Broadly both responses defend the material dimensions of Deleuze's thought against Hallward's otherworldly version.
132. Elena Del Río, *Deleuze and the Cinemas of Performance: Powers of Affection* (Edinburgh: Edinburgh University Press, 2008), pp. 8–9.
133. Ibid., pp. 8–9.
134. Wolfe, *Before the Law*, pp. 32–3.
135. Burt, 'Morbidity and Vitalism', p. 171.
136. Deleuze, *Francis Bacon*, p. 44.
137. Deleuze and Guattari, *A Thousand Plateaus*, p. 4.
138. See Crowley's important analysis of Deleuze's reflections on 'the capacity of works of art to channel energetic forces that can help us battle all manner of constraints'; Crowley refers to this as a process of '"combative extraction", in which contingent negativity is, despite itself, opened on to the affirmation of something positive. Such affirmation is always, for Deleuze, on the side of vitality: combative extraction opens a channel beyond any local misery towards the welcome, lively possibility of something else that can help us fight or escape this misery.' In this sense, for Deleuze, 'the effectivity of the artwork derives from the ability to channel those forces of differentiation through which life as such affirms itself.' Crowley, 'Deleuze on Painting', *French Studies*, 67:3 (2013), 371–85, pp. 371–2.
139. Shukin, *Animal Capital*, p. 17; p. 231.

Conclusion: Cinematic Worlds and Beyond

Bailly's *The Animal Side* opens with an account of catching a glimpse of a deer crossing the path of his car one night. The journey is consciously framed as a cinematic scene: 'Even if one is not speeding, there is a pure cinematic sensation of irreversible thrust [. . .].'[1] Suddenly a deer jumps out of the undergrowth by the road, runs ahead in fright and then disappears. On the one hand, Bailly describes the moment as 'ordinary', an everyday occurrence; on the other hand, the vision has 'the clarity, the violence, of an image in a dream'.[2] He writes:

> it was as if with my eyes, in that instant, for the duration of that instant, I had touched some part of the animal world. Touched, yes, touched with my eyes, despite the impossibility. In no way had I entered that world; on the contrary, it was rather as if its strangeness had declared itself anew, as if I had actually been allowed for an instant to see something from which as a human being I shall be forever excluded [. . .] it has always seemed to me that this strangeness ought to be considered on its own terms, as a different posture, a different impetus, and quite simply a different modality of being.[3]

Here Bailly comes into contact, momentarily, with 'some part of the animal world', a 'different modality of being'. The deer is viewed from behind (the animal's hindquarters are seen rising and falling). Bailly's account thereby resists falling into the overdetermined pathos of an exchange of looks between the animal and the human. Yet there is still a form of contact-at-distance here – a mode of impossible 'touching' that preserves a gap, a strangeness, a difference, interrupting appropriation.[4] Bailly recognises his exclusion from this fleetingly encountered 'animal world' – he seeks only to register the presence of this world, to allow it to be apprehended on its own terms. He continues:

> The strangeness did not lie in the fact that the deer burst forth or that it fled [. . .] the strangeness lay in the opportunity I was given to follow the animal for a while: that is, at bottom, the chance to accompany it in spite of itself, thus prolonging a contact that as a general rule is much briefer.[5]

This is something that cinema can do (which is perhaps why Bailly frames this as a cinematic scene) – it can 'follow the animal for a while'. And as we have seen throughout this study, through particular forms of durational attentiveness, cinema can prolong, sustain and deepen 'a contact that as a general rule is much briefer'.

And yet, despite the apparent relinquishing of appropriation at stake here, the encounter that Bailly describes is haunted by the thrill of the hunt: 'I found myself back in the position of pursuer, a dog in a pack, or a hunter.'[6] What Bailly glimpses in his transitory encounter with the deer is also 'a world filled with terror, frightened movements, silent gaps'[7] – a world of fear and vulnerability, overshadowed by the threat of violence, by the asymmetries of power between the human and the animal.

Reflecting on the '*unprecedented* proportions' of 'subjection of the animal' that shape contemporary biopolitical regimes, Derrida writes of the specific ways, through processes such as mass industrialised meat production, in which animal life is constantly reproduced in order to be killed. What is occurring, he writes, is

> the organization and exploitation of an artificial, infernal, virtually interminable survival, in conditions that previous generations would have judged monstrous, outside of every presumed norm of a life proper to animals that are thus exterminated by means of their continued existence or even their overpopulation.[8]

No one 'can [. . .] seriously deny the disavowal that this involves',[9] Derrida writes. Indeed:

> Everybody knows what terrifying and intolerable pictures a realist painting could give to the industrial, mechanical, chemical, hormonal, and genetic violence to which man has been submitting animal life for the past two centuries. Everybody knows what the production, breeding, transport, and slaughter of these animals has become.[10]

These are the material realities of the ways in which animal lives are rendered in our biopolitical present. Derrida sets out the details clearly. But in the next sentence he writes: 'Instead of thrusting these images in your faces or awakening them in your memory, something that would be both too easy and endless, let me simply say a word about this "pathos".'[11] It is here that he then develops his reflections on pathos, pity and compassion, and 'the sharing of this suffering among the living'.[12]

For Burt, there is a certain failure in Derrida's argument here. Derrida's claim that '[e]verybody knows' this, and that it 'would be both too easy and endless' to develop the details seems to point, for Burt, to 'a knowledge of the massacre of animals, which has no need of a philosophy'.[13] As Burt observes further: 'Faced with an image of this scale of horror, he prefers to substitute a word' – that is, the word 'pathos'.[14] For Burt, this is indicative of the ways in which '[t]he permutations of language and death form, unform, and reform around the figure of the animal [. . .]';[15] '[t]he animal is [. . .] a writing effect that latches onto a more generalised and inflated concept of otherness'.[16] Yet while this may be the case at certain points in *The Animal That Therefore I Am*, in the pages that focus on the material realities of the biopolitical 'organization and exploitation' of animal lives, we sense something else at work. Despite Derrida's apparent turning away from 'these images', the material facts are clearly stated – 'the reduction of the animal not only to production and overactive reproduction (hormones, genetic crossbreeding, cloning, etc.) of meat for consumption, but also of all sorts of other end products [. . .]'.[17] And the sense of outrage that courses through these pages is difficult to ignore, all the more so perhaps because of its striking directness – something of an incongruity in Derrida's oeuvre as a whole, and a further index of what he sees as the ethical and political urgency of the situation that he describes.

Like Bailly, Derrida follows the animal here (recalling the motif of 'following' that threads through the latter's text).[18] Perhaps Derrida doesn't go far enough, as Burt suggests. Perhaps he might have followed the animal further, into those 'terrifying and intolerable pictures' that he evokes. Yet in this posthumously published text, Derrida still leaves us with a powerful indictment of the '*unprecedented*' subjection that shapes our everyday relations with animal lives and deaths. And he leaves us with a call for political change, a call for something that might 'awaken us to our responsibilities and our obligations vis-à-vis the living in general, and precisely to this fundamental compassion that, were we to take it seriously, would have to change even the very cornerstone [. . .] of the philosophical problematic of the animal'.[19]

Deleuze too evokes the question of responsibility in his reflections on animal death. Referring to Karl Philipp Moritz's *Anton Reiser* (1785–90), in which the protagonist (Moritz's alter ego) contemplates a calf destined for slaughter, Deleuze and Guattari write: 'Karl Philipp Moritz feels responsible not for the calves that die but before the calves that die [. . .]'.²⁰ To feel responsible *for* would be to relegate the animal to the passive position of victim; to feel responsible *before* is to be called to account, and to feel summoned to respond in a way that opens up an exchange between human and animal realms. Deleuze returns obsessively to Moritz's dying calf. For not only does this scene appear here in *A Thousand Plateaus*, but it returns in his text on Francis Bacon and also in *What is Philosophy?*. In the former, the reference to Moritz occurs in the middle of Deleuze's reflection on Bacon's fascination with butcher shops (which I discussed in Chapter 4). Noting the 'convulsive pain and vulnerability' to which meat attests, Deleuze suggests: 'Meat is the common zone of man and the beast, their zone of indiscernibility [. . .]: the man who suffers is a beast, the beast that suffers is a man. This is the reality of becoming.'²¹ He continues:

> What revolutionary person – in art, politics, religion, or elsewhere – has not felt that extreme moment when he or she was nothing but a beast, and became responsible not for the calves that died, but *before* the calves that died?²²

The notion of being responsible not for but 'before' the slaughtered animal returns here, and this is imagined as a deeply transformative process – a radical form of becoming. And in *What is Philosophy?*, we find a further return to the slaughtered calf:

> We think and write for animals themselves. We become animal so that the animal also becomes something else. The agony of a rat or the slaughter of a calf remains present in thought not through pity but as the zone of exchange between man and animal in which something of one passes into the other. This is the constitutive relationship of philosophy with non-philosophy. Becoming is always double, and it is this double becoming that constitutes the people to come and the new earth.²³

While there are points of intersection between Deleuze and Derrida here (particularly in relation to the recognition of pain and vulnerability that Deleuze invokes), for Deleuze and Guattari, in contradistinction to Derrida, this is not a question of pity, for this would risk being only 'reactive'²⁴ and relegating the animal to a position of passivity.²⁵ Deleuze and Guattari emphasise rather a zone of affective exchange between the human and the animal, an active process of mutual becoming. Bailly too is also fascinated by the scene with the calf in *Anton Reiser*: he finds there 'the most poignant narrative of the possible community – through thought – between man and beast'.²⁶ And there is a call for political change in Bailly's text too – as we saw in the Introduction, he invokes Derrida and writes of a world 'shared among creatures, and that a politics could be invented on this basis, if it is not too late'.[27] As we have seen, Deleuze links this awakening of responsibility to a form of revolution ('What revolutionary person [. . .] has not felt that extreme moment when he or she [. . .] became responsible not for the calves that died, but *before* the calves that died?') and to a political future, a radical becoming, a 'people to come'.

This question of animal suffering, and of forms of vulnerability through which animal and human lives are differentially exposed, runs through the films explored in this study, from the reflections on 'enduring' and death-in-life states in *Bestiaire* and *The Turin Horse*, to the scenes of slaughter in *Leviathan* and the powerlessness explored by *Bovines*. Indeed, Deleuze's notion of a responsibility '*before* the calves that died' is literalised in *Bovines* in the scene in which the calves are separated from the rest of the herd in order to be sent to market. The female farmer's acknowledgement of the mooing protest of the cows – 'They're calling their calves. It's the mothers' – testifies to the suffering at stake there, opening up, beyond the reign of agricapital, a fleeting recognition of bovine worlds of sentience, perception, pain and possibly mourning too. By bearing witness in this way, the farmer becomes responsible '*before* the calves that died', with the kinds of political, even revolutionary, implications that Deleuze envisages. There is clearly a tension here, however: she is 'responsible *for*' these deaths – not necessarily in the sense of feeling pity but certainly in the sense of being complicit in sending these animals to their deaths. But, at the same time, an opening to a different form of human–animal relation, beyond the biopolitical rendering of life by the farm, flickers into view. As I suggested in Chapter 5, it seems significant that this recognition of maternal animal suffering is uttered by a woman, as though her gender forms the basis of a solidarity that temporarily promises to cross species lines. There is, in Deleuze's sense, a form of political *becoming* at work here, and a gesturing to a 'people to come'. At the same time, the film itself becomes responsible '*before* the calves that died', by indicating – however fleetingly – a world in which cows might count as something more than simply their agricultural 'use value'. And, in the focus on the sounds of protest coming from the herd, there is also an opening here to the ways in which animals become responsible *before* other animals, thereby extending beyond Deleuze's assumption that the 'revolutionary person' called to respond is always necessarily human.

In this study, cinematic duration, and its propensity for dilation and delay, has been key to reflections on animal worlds. The non-extension of perception into action characteristic of the Deleuzian time-image, and cinema's attendant moves between the actual and the virtual, have been seen to bear witness to animal realms of pensivity, sentience and meaning-making. Resisting the all-too-efficient reduction of life to resource that characterises biopolitical structures, the seemingly uneventful wanderings of the slow animal film has allowed for the 'use value' of the animal (as entertainment, labour or food) to be probed and questioned by a 'wasting' of cinematic time. At the same time, cinematic duration has been crucial to reflections on suffering and biopolitical force. *Bestiaire* focuses on animals enduring time, on 'a limbo economy of interminable survival',[28] and the relentless duration of being made to live in captivity. *The Turin Horse* also engages, through extreme modes of temporal dilation, with the issue of enduring, the film's focus on precarity and fatigue-as-survival being implicitly shaped by contemporary contexts of labour insecurity and environmental crisis. In both films, as in *Bovines*, durational attentiveness works to foreground forms of suffering under biopolitical regimes while opening up, from within those regimes, the meaning-making dimensions of variegated animal (and human) worlds.

Indeed, in all of the films in this study, there appear to be two different concepts of life at stake: the 'bare life' produced by biopolitical regimes and the worlds that unfurl, and make meaning, beyond this (though in the case of *Leviathan*, as I have argued, such worlds are closed down by the film itself). This corresponds to the two different orders of power that I have traced throughout this study, following Deleuze (particularly in his readings of Spinoza and Foucault) – power as domination (*pouvoir*) and power as potential (*puissance*), understood as being in a relation of continual exchange (rather than dichotomous opposition). While the films in this study document the workings of *pouvoir* through the biopolitical management of animal lives – at the zoo, on the farm – they also envisage lines of flight through the biopolitical matrix of 'bare life', gesturing to a mode of 'becoming-other' that, for Deleuze and Guattari, is open to animals.[29] This is reminiscent too of Haraway's 'creatures of fierce and ordinary reality' who are also 'creatures of imagined possibility'.[30] In the sequence with the chimps in *Bestiaire*, the image birfurcates into the actual and the virtual, evoking worlds of sentience, thought and intraspecies care that exceed and challenge the reduction of animal being to carceral life. In *The Turin Horse*, we witness the resistance of life to power (recalling the Nietzschean potential 'for life to burst through power's systematic operation'[31]), as the horse's withdrawal from labour – and from the visual regime of the film itself – opens up a line of flight. The final image of *Bovines* – the tactile close-up of the ruminating cow, ear tagged, body appropriated – captures an ongoing tension between the territorialising drive of agricapital and the deterritorialising force of *puissance* articulated via the scene's attentiveness to rhythms of life, sentience and perception. We do see acts of animal resistance in these films – some fleeting (the lion rattling the cage in *Bestiaire*; the cattle mooing in protest in *Bovines*), and one particularly sustained act (the refusal to labour in *The Turin Horse*). But my focus has been above all on the lines of resistance opened up aesthetically by the forms of the films themselves – in their patient attentiveness to animal worlds, their moves between the actual and the virtual, and their implicitly political openings to imagining animal lives otherwise.

Yet these films also remain inextricably bound up with networks of 'animal capital'. As I have indicated, they acknowledge – often in their end credits – the debts that they owe to the biopolitical regimes that have enabled their portrayals of animal life: *Bestiaire* expresses gratitude for the 'permission and generosity' of Parc Safari, *Leviathan* names and honours its fishermen, and *Bovines* offers '[a] big thanks to the farmers, without whom this film could not have existed'. *The Turin Horse* is similarly implicated in relays of animal capital, relying on the labour and possible retraumatisation of a horse who brings with her a history of suffering and abuse. The long take with which Tarr and Hranitzky's film opens not only exploits but actively produces the vulnerability that it registers. Similar tensions are also at work in other 'slow animal films' such as Frammartino's *Le Quattro Volte* and Philibert's *Nénette*. *Le Quattro Volte*'s on-screen celebration of the agency of goats is haunted by the fact that offscreen these goats are farmed for their meat (a traditional dish of Calabria, where the film is set).[32] And as Barbara Creed writes of *Nénette*: the film creates 'a form of interspecies cinema' and 'a form of human/animal communication', but 'this comes at a terrible cost – not for the zoo visitor, but for the animal captive in the zoo'.[33] In all these films, the ethical and political potential of a form of cross-species contact enabled by cinema is in tension with the instrumentalising structures of animal capital on which it depends. The biopolitical spaces of the zoo, the farm and the trawler make these films possible – unavoidably so – reminding us that the appearance of these animals onscreen is also an index of their vulnerability to human control and domination.

And as Shukin reminds us, addressing what she sees as a blindspot in Derrida's account of the biopolitics of animal life, 'the reproductive value of animals is by no means only biological [. . .] animal signs and metaphors are also key symbolic resources of capital's reproduction'.[34] In this light, we might wonder, as I suggested in Chapter 5, whether the recent proliferation of slow animal art films can be read as symptomatic of what Shukin describes as 'the soaring speculation in animal signs as a semiotic currency of market culture'.[35] The films in this study are contradictorily implicated in the operations of 'rendering' diagnosed by Shukin, instrumentalising animal being, to a certain extent, as 'raw material' for their own symbolic operations – from *Bestiaire*'s interest in cinematic self-reflexivity (articulated via the fetishistic motifs of zoo display and taxidermy), to *Bovines*'s tendency, at times, to aestheticise the photogenic Charolais cow (the striking appearance of this particular species being also a key guarantor, in the cattle industry, of market value). The critical successes of this emergent wave of filmmaking might even be seen to rely on a form of 'branding' (as 'contemplative' art cinema about animals), accruing 'semiotic currency', aesthetic capital and philosophical credentials in the wake of the animal turn in the humanities. Nowhere is this more the case than in *Leviathan*, which, under the guise of 'sensory ethnography' and the 'posthumanist' self-positioning of that methodology, efficiently converts animal death into the electrifying charge of its hallucinatory, immersive vision. However philosophically articulate and politically astute, *Bestiaire*, *Bovines* and *The Turin Horse* thus remain subtly implicated in the material and symbolic economies of what Shukin calls 'animal capital', signalling a set of ambiguities and tensions that I have traced throughout the book. But it is in *Leviathan* where we see the extraction of animal capital reach its violent apotheosis.

Indeed, the contrast between *Leviathan*'s restlessly flitting vision and the sustained, durational attentiveness of the other films returns us to this study's central claim about the relation between cinematic time and animal worlds. *Bestiaire*, *Bovines* and *The Turin Horse* deploy forms of temporal distension and delay in order to feel their way – in sensorial, material, affective terms – into animal worlds, while simultaneously gesturing to the opacity or unknowability of those worlds. Through their paring away of narrative plot and overtly symbolising frameworks, these films attend to what Bailly describes as 'a threshold that precedes all interpretation'. However, we might also bear in mind Pick's critique of Bailly here – that 'the designation of animals as our radical others can at times feel like willful enchantment, at the expense of more worldly relations'.[36] Pick's insight helps us to locate the particular contribution of these films to a developing body of philosophical thought about animal life. It is not only that, by virtue of their basis in 'live action', they engage with 'actual animals' in indexical, material, situated ways (as I suggested in the Introduction). In their patient, lingering modes of durational engagement, these films register the unknowability of animal worlds while remaining grounded in, and politically attentive to, the material conditions of animal lives and deaths, the 'more worldly relations' that Pick describes here. As we have seen, the 'worldly relations' addressed by these films have included practices such as farming, slaughter and meat-eating, zoo exhibition, taxidermy and animal labour. While I have suggested that animal labour constitutes a particular blindspot within the continental tradition's engagement with animals (including the work of Derrida and Bailly), it is addressed at length by Tarr and Hranitzky's *The Turin Horse*, indicating further ways in which cinema might be seen to exceed the reach of certain philosophical accounts of animals.

Yet the work of Deleuze has been key to this study's exploration of the relation between cinematic time and animal worlds. Drawing on Deleuze's precise engagements with animal life (in his own work and with Guattari), alongside and also beyond the usual invocations of 'becoming-animal' that tend to dominate Deleuzo–Guattarian readings of animal 'texts', I have sought to foreground the value of Deleuze's thought for critical animal studies, while expanding the range of conceptual resources that can be usefully derived from his work. I have also emphasised what Deleuze's theory of cinematic time – and attendant reflections on the actual/virtual and the plurality of worlds – can add in particular to the developing body of scholarship on animals and film. In so doing, I have sought to build on, yet also diverge from, the recourse to Bazinian models of realism that have often dominated the field, in order to make a particular case for a Deleuzian thinking of cinematic time that reaches beyond subjectively lived time, and beyond the circumscribed 'bubbles' of animal worlds in Uexküll's model, to something more open – to realms of differing, becoming, deterritorialisation and flight.

In its pluralisation of worlds, and in its opening to the virtual from within rigid structures of biopolitical domination, cinema has emerged here as a privileged realm for that 'potentially creative, aleatory element that inheres in the very gambit of biopower' (as identified by Wolfe in his engagement with Foucault). It is through modes of durational attentiveness in particular that animals on our screens might be perceived, as Bailly puts it, 'in their pure singularity, as distinct beings that participate in the world of the living'. Films such as *Bestiaire*, *Bovines* and *The Turin Horse* offer a subtle diagnosis of our biopolitical present and its seemingly relentless 'subjection of the animal'. Yet these films also hold out the promise of something else, gesturing to possible lines of flight and political futures, in which our relations with animal worlds – both onscreen and off – might be reconfigured otherwise.

NOTES

1. Bailly, *The Animal Side*, p. 1.
2. Ibid., p. 2.
3. Ibid., p. 2.
4. One thinks here of Nancy's work on touch as a form of contact-at-distance, explored in texts such as *Corpus*, and of the collaboration between Nancy and Bailly in their co-authored work, *La Comparution* (Paris: Christian Bourgois, 1991).
5. Bailly, *The Animal Side*, p. 7.
6. Ibid., p. 7.
7. Ibid., p. 1.
8. Derrida, *The Animal That Therefore I Am*, pp. 25–6; original emphasis. He goes on to draw a comparison with the extermination of the Jews – an extremely conflicted connection but one that is arguably not meant to suggest equivalence.
9. Ibid., p. 25
10. Ibid., p. 26.
11. Ibid., p. 26.
12. Ibid., p. 26.
13. Burt, 'Morbidity and Vitalism', p. 160.
14. Ibid., p. 160.
15. Ibid., p. 158.

16. Ibid., p. 159. This is part of Burt's critique of the 'morbid' dimensions of Derrida's reflections on animals, with which he contrasts Deleuze's vitalist approach (although Burt also notes of Derrida's text that 'despite an archaicising trend within his analysis of the history of philosophy, his position is richer than my critique might suggest' (p. 162)). I have sought to hold both threads – Derrida and Deleuze, morbidity and vitalism – together in my analyses. It is also worth noting here, as Matthew Calarco argues, that Derrida's thought 'does not limit the interruptive capacity of the animal simply to its vulnerability and susceptibility to wounding and suffering' (Calarco draws here on the 'event' of Derrida's interruptive encounter with his cat; Calarco, *Zoographies: The Question of the Animal from Heidegger to Derrida* (New York: Columbia University Press, 2008), p. 120).
17. Derrida, p. 25. His list is cited in full in my Introduction.
18. As initially set in motion via the play on *suis* in the title in French, *L'Animal que donc je suis* being translatable as 'The Animal That Therefore I Am/I Follow'.
19. Derrida, p. 27.
20. Deleuze and Guattari, *A Thousand Plateaus*, p. 240; Karl Philipp Moritz, *Anton Reiser* [1785–90] (London: Penguin, 1997).
21. Deleuze, *Francis Bacon*, p. 25.
22. Ibid., p. 25; original emphasis.
23. Deleuze and Guattari, *What is Philosophy?*, p. 109. As Mullarkey suggests, 'nonphilosophy' here might be understood as 'an ineliminable remainder' beyond philosophy, as that which 'escape[s] Theory altogether'. Mullarkey, 'Animal Spirits', p. 12.
24. Ibid., p. 15.
25. Though as I suggested in Chapter 3, one would hope that pity and political change are not necessarily mutually exclusive; indeed, Derrida argues for the role of pity, and compassion for animal suffering, in transformations 'to the law, ethics, and politics'). Derrida, *The Animal That Therefore I Am*, p. 26.
26. Bailly, *The Animal Side*, p. 23.
27. Ibid., p. 15.
28. Shukin, *Animal Capital*, p. 39.
29. Deleuze and Guattari, *A Thousand Plateaus*, p. 238.
30. Haraway, *When Species Meet*, p. 4.
31. Wolfe, *Before the Law*, pp. 32–3.
32. Michelangelo Frammartino, 'Michelangelo Frammartino talks to Jonathan Romney', *Le Quattro Volte* DVD, New Wave Films, 2011.
33. Barbara Creed, '*Nénette*: Film theory, animals and boredom', *NECSUS: European Journal of Media Studies*, Spring 2013. Available at http://www.necsus-ejms.org/nenette-film-theory-animals-and-boredom/ (last accessed 14 September 2018).
34. Shukin, *Animal Capital*, p. 12.
35. Ibid., p. 12.
36. Pick, 'Some Small Discrepancy', p. 183.

Bibliography

Acampora, Christa Davis and Ralph R. Acampora (eds), *A Nietzschean Bestiary: Becoming Animal Beyond Docile and Brutal* (Lanham, MD: Rowman & Littlefield, 2004).
Adams, Carol J., *The Sexual Politics of Meat: A Feminist-Vegetarian Critical Theory*, 20th anniversary edition (New York: Continuum, 2010).
Agamben, Giorgio, *Homo Sacer: Sovereign Power and Bare Life*, translated by Daniel Heller-Roazen (Stanford: Stanford University Press, 1998).
Agamben, Giorgio, *The Open: Man and Animal*, translated by Kevin Attell (Stanford: Stanford University Press, 2004).
Ahmed, Sara, 'Imaginary Prohibitions: Some Preliminary Remarks on the Founding Gestures of the "New Materialism"', *European Journal of Women's Studies*, 15 (2008), 23–9.
Aloi, Giovanni, *Art and Animals* (London: I. B. Tauris, 2011).
Anderson, Melissa, '*Bestiaire* Ponders What Transpires When We Look at Animals', *The Village Voice*, 17 October 2012. Available at www.villagevoice.com/2012-10-17/film/bestiaire-ponders-what-transpires-when-we-look-at-animals/ (last accessed 14 September 2018).
Ansell-Pearson, Keith, 'The Reality of the Virtual', *MLN*, 120:5 (2005), 1112–27.
Azalbert, Nicolas, 'Bovines', *Cahiers du cinéma*, 675 (February 2012), 52.
Badiou, Alain, *The Century*, translated by Alberto Toscano (Cambridge: Polity, 2007).
Bailly, Jean-Christophe, *The Animal Side*, translated by Catherine Porter (New York: Fordham University Press, 2011).
Bailly, Jean-Christophe, *Le Parti pris des animaux* (Paris: Christian Bourgois, 2013).
Bailly, Jean-Christophe, with Éric Poitevin, *Le Puits des oiseaux* (Paris: Seuil, 2016).
Bailly, Jean-Christophe and Jean-Luc Nancy, *La Comparution* (Paris: Christian Bourgois, 1991).
Baker, Steve, *The Postmodern Animal* (London: Reaktion, 2000).
Baker, Steve, 'What Does Becoming-Animal Look Like?', in Nigel Rothfels (ed.), *Representing Animals: Theories of Contemporary Culture* (Bloomington: Indiana University Press, 2002), pp. 67–98.
Baker, Steve, *Artist Animal* (Minneapolis: University of Minnesota Press, 2013).
Balzac, Honoré de, *Sarrasine* [1830], reprinted in Roland Barthes, *S/Z*, translated by Richard Miller (Oxford: Basil Blackwell, 1990), pp. 221–54.
Barthes, Roland, *S/Z*, translated by Richard Miller (Oxford: Basil Blackwell, 1990).
Barthes, Roland, *Camera Lucida: Reflections on Photography*, translated by Richard Howard (London: Vintage, 1993).
Bataille, Georges, 'Abattoir', *Documents*, 6 (November 1929), 32.

Bazin, André, 'Les Films d'animaux nous révèlent le cinéma', *Radio Cinéma Télévision*, 285: 2–3, 8.
Bazin, André, 'The Virtues and Limitations of Montage', in *What is Cinema?*, Vol. 1, edited and translated by Hugh Gray (Berkeley: University of California Press 1967), pp. 41–52.
Bazin, André, 'Death Every Afternoon', translated by Mark A. Cohen, in Ivone Margulies (ed.), *Rites of Realism* (Durham, NC: Duke University Press, 2003), pp. 27–31.
Bazin, André, 'De Sica: Metteur en scène', in *What is Cinema?*, Vol. 2, edited and translated by Hugh Gray (Berkeley: University of California Press, 2005), pp. 61–78.
Bazin, André, 'Umberto D: A Great Work', in *What is Cinema?*, Vol. 2, edited and translated by Hugh Gray (Berkeley: University of California Press, 2005), pp. 79–82.
Beasley-Murray, Jon, 'Whatever Happened to Neorealism? Bazin, Deleuze and Tarkovsky's Long Take', *Iris*, 23 (Spring 1997), 37–52.
Bednarek, Joanna, 'The Oedipal Animal? Companion Species and Becoming', in Colin Gardner and Patricia MacCormack (eds), *Deleuze and the Animal* (Edinburgh: Edinburgh University Press, 2017), pp. 52–74.
Béghin, Cyril, 'L'animal sans image', *Cahiers du cinéma*, 701 (June 2014), 74–7.
Bellour, Raymond, *Le Corps du cinéma: hypnoses, émotions, animalités* (Paris: POL, 2009).
Bellour, Raymond, 'From Hypnosis to Animals', edited and translated by Alistair Fox, *Cinema Journal*, 53:3 (2014), 8–24.
Bennett, Jane, *Vibrant Matter: A Political Ecology of Things* (Durham, NC and London: Duke University Press, 2010).
Berger, John, 'Why Look at Animals?', in *About Looking* (London: Bloomsbury, 1980), pp. 3–28.
Bergson, Henri, *The Creative Mind*, translated by Mabelle Andison (Westport, CT: Greenwood, 1946).
Bergson, Henri, Creative Evolution, translated by Arthur Mitchell (New York: Dover, 1998).
Bichet, Yves, *La Part animale* (Paris: Gallimard, 1994).
Bordwell, David, 'Intensified Continuity: Visual Style in Contemporary American Film', *Film Quarterly*, 55:3 (2002), 16–28.
Bousé, Derek, *Wildlife Films* (Philadelphia: University of Pennsylvania Press, 2000).
'Bovines, the reinvention of a genre', *Down to Earth*, 30 July 2012. Available at http://downtoearth.danone.com/2012/07/30/bovines-the-reinvention-of-a-genre/ (last accessed 14 September 2018).
Bozak, Nadia, *The Cinematic Footprint: Lights, Camera, Natural Resources* (New Brunswick: Rutgers University Press, 2012).
Braidotti, Rosi, *The Posthuman* (Cambridge: Polity, 2013).
Braun, Maria, *Eadweard Muybridge* (London: Reaktion Books, 2010).
Broglio, Ron, *Surface Encounters: Thinking with Animals and Art* (Minneapolis: University of Minnesota Press, 2011).
Buchanan, Brett, *Onto-Ethologies: The Animal Environments of Uexküll, Heidegger, Merleau-Ponty, and Deleuze* (New York: SUNY Press, 2008).
Budiansky, Stephen, *The Nature of Horses: Their Evolution, Intelligence and Behaviour* (London: Phoenix, 1997).
Burke, Andrew, 'ZooTube: Streaming Animal Life', in Michael Lawrence and Karen Lury (eds), *The Zoo and Screen Media: Images of Exhibition and Encounter* (Basingstoke: Palgrave Macmillan, 2016), pp. 65–83.
Burt, Jonathan, *Animals in Film* (London: Reaktion, 2002).
Burt, Jonathan, 'John Berger's "Why Look at Animals?": A Close Reading', *Worldviews*, 9:2 (2005), 203–18.

Burt, Jonathan, 'Morbidity and Vitalism: Derrida, Bergson, Deleuze and Animal Film Imagery', *Configurations*, 14:1–2 (2006), 157–79.
Cahill, James, 'A YouTube Bestiary: Twenty-six Theses on a Post-cinema of Animal Attractions', in Paul Flaig and Katherine Groo (eds), *New Silent Cinema* (New York: Routledge, 2015), pp. 263–93.
Calarco, Matthew, *Zoographies: The Question of the Animal from Heidegger to Derrida* (New York: Columbia University Press, 2008).
Castaing-Taylor, Lucien, 'Iconophobia', *Transition*, 69 (1996), 64–88.
Chen, Mel Y. and Dana Luciano (eds), 'Queer Inhumanisms', *GLQ: A Journal of Lesbian and Gay Studies*, 21:2–3 (2015).
Chion, Michel, *Audio-Vision: Sound on Screen*, edited and translated by Claudia Gorbmann (New York: Columbia University Press, 1994).
Chris, Cynthia, *Watching Wildlife* (Minneapolis: University of Minnesota Press, 2006).
Chrulew, Matthew and Dinesh Joseph Wadiwel (eds), *Foucault and Animals* (Leiden and Boston: Brill, 2017).
Ciment, Michel, 'Bovines ou la vraie vie des vaches', *Positif*, 613 (March 2012), 40.
Cocker, Mark, 'Death of the Naturalist: Why is the "New Nature-Writing" So Tame?', *The New Statesman*, 17 June 2015. Available at http://www.newstatesman.com/culture/2015/06/death-naturalist-why-new-nature-writing-so-tame (last accessed 14 September 2018).
Coetzee, J. M., *The Lives of Animals*, edited by Amy Gutmann (Princeton: Princeton University Press, 1999).
Colebrook, Claire, *Gilles Deleuze* (London: Routledge, 2002).
Combs, C. Scott, *Deathwatch: American Film, Technology, and the End of Life* (New York: Columbia University Press, 2014).
Comolli, Jean-Louis, 'Mechanical Bodies, Ever More Heavenly', translated by Annette Michelson, *October*, 83 (Winter 1998), 19–24.
Comolli, Jean-Louis, *Voir et pouvoir. L'innocence perdue: cinéma, télévision, fiction, documentaire* (Lagrasse: Verdier, 2004).
Conley, Tom, 'The Film Event: From Interval to Interstice', in Gregory Flaxman (ed.), *The Brain is the Screen: Deleuze and the Philosophy of Cinema* (Minneapolis: University of Minnesota Press, 2000), pp. 303–25.
Cooper, Sarah, *Chris Marker* (Manchester: Manchester University Press, 2008).
Côté, Denis, 'The Animal Equation', *Cinema Scope*, 14 (2012), 10–12.
Côté, Denis, 'Interview with the Filmmaker Denis Côté', 12 October 2012, *Bestiaire* DVD, The KimStim Collection.
Creed, Barbara, 'Nénette: Film theory, animals and boredom', *NECSUS: European Journal Of Media Studies*, Spring 2013. Available at http://www.necsus-ejms.org/nenette-film-theory-animals-and-boredom/ (last accessed 14 September 2018).
Crowley, Martin, 'Deleuze on Painting', *French Studies*, 67:3 (2013), 371–85.
Crowley, Martin, 'No Futures (Duras 72/77)', *Qui parle*, 24:2 (2016), 109–36.
Crowley, 'The Many Worlds of Jean-Luc Nancy', *Paragraph*, 42:1 (2019), 22–36.
Cubitt, Sean, *EcoMedia* (Amsterdam and New York: Rodolfi, 2005).
Daney, Serge, 'The Screen of Fantasy (Bazin and Animals)', translated by Mark A. Cohen, in Ivone Margulies (ed.), *Rites of Realism* (Durham, NC: Duke University Press, 2003) pp. 32–41.
Daston, Lorraine and Gregg Mitman (eds), *Thinking with Animals: New Perspectives on Anthropomorphism* (New York: Columbia University Press, 2006).
Davis, Lydia, *The Cows* (Louisville: Sarabande Books, 2011).
Del Amo, Jean-Baptiste, *Règne animal* (Paris: Gallimard, 2016).

Deleuze, Gilles, *Spinoza: Practical Philosophy*, translated by Robert Hurley (San Francisco: City Lights Books, 1988).
Deleuze, Gilles, 'Postscript on the Societies of Control', *October*, 59 (1992), 3–7.
Deleuze, Gilles, 'The Exhausted', translated by Anthony Ullman, *SubStance*, 24:3, 78 (1995), 3–28.
Deleuze, Gilles, *Negotiations 1972–1990*, translated by Martin Joughin (New York: Columbia University Press, 1995).
Deleuze, Gilles, *Francis Bacon: The Logic of Sensation*, translated by Daniel W. Smith (London and New York: Continuum, 2003).
Deleuze, Gilles, *Cinema 1: The Movement-Image*, translated by Hugh Tomlinson and Barbara Habberjam (London and New York: Continuum, 2005).
Deleuze, Gilles, *Cinema 2: The Time-Image*, translated by Hugh Tomlinson and Robert Galeta (London and New York: Continuum, 2005).
Deleuze, Gilles, *Foucault*, translated and edited by Seán Hand (London and New York: Continuum, 2006).
Deleuze, Gilles, 'A is for Animal', *L'Abécédaire de Gilles Deleuze/Gilles Deleuze from A to Z* [television documentary], with Claire Parnet (directed by Pierre-André Boutang, 1988–9). Available at https://vimeo.com/108004617 (last accessed 14 September 2018).
Deleuze, Gilles and Félix Guattari, *Anti-Oedipus: Capitalism and Schizophrenia*, translated by Robert Hurley, Mark Seem and Helen R. Lane (Minneapolis: University of Minnesota Press, 1983).
Deleuze, Gilles and Félix Guattari, *Kafka: Toward a Minor Literature*, translated by Dana Polan (Minneapolis: University of Minnesota Press, 1986).
Deleuze, Gilles and Félix Guattari, *A Thousand Plateaus: Capitalism and Schizophrenia*, translated by Brian Massumi (Minneapolis: University of Minnesota Press, 1987).
Deleuze, Gilles and Félix Guattari, *What is Philosophy?*, translated by Graham Burchell and Hugh Tomlinson (London and New York: Verso, 1994).
Deller, Rosemary, 'When Flesh Becomes Meat: Encountering Meaty Bodies in Contemporary Culture', PhD thesis, University of Manchester, 2015.
Delorme, Stéphane and Céline Gailleurd, '"Mes films de vengeance": Entretien avec Denis Côté', *Cahiers du cinéma*, 687 (March 2013), 49–51.
Del Río, Elena, *Deleuze and the Cinemas of Performance: Powers of Affection* (Edinburgh: Edinburgh University Press, 2008).
De Luca, Tiago, 'Natural Views: Animals, Contingency and Death in Carlos Reygadas's *Japón* and Lisandro Alonso's *Los Muertos*', in Tiago De Luca and Nuno Barradas Jorge (eds), *Slow Cinema* (Edinburgh: Edinburgh University Press, 2015), pp. 219–30.
De Luca, Tiago and Nuno Barradas Jorge, 'Introduction: From Slow Cinema to Slow Cinemas', in Tiago De Luca and Nuno Barradas Jorge (eds), *Slow Cinema* (Edinburgh: Edinburgh University Press, 2015), pp. 1–21.
Dequen, Bruno, 'Mécanique animale', *24 images*, 157 (2012), 42.
Derrida, Jacques, '"Eating Well," or the Calculation of the Subject: An Interview with Jacques Derrida', translated by Peter Connor and Avita Ronell, in Eduardo Cadava, Peter Connor and Jean-Luc Nancy (eds), *Who Comes After the Subject?* (New York: Routledge, 1992), pp 96–119.
Derrida, Jacques, *Aporias*, translated by Thomas Dutoit (Stanford: Stanford University Press, 1993).
Derrida, Jacques, *Memoirs of the Blind: The Self Portrait and Other Ruins*, translated by Pascale-Anne Brault and Michael Naas (Chicago: University of Chicago Press, 1993).
Derrida, Jacques, *The Animal That Therefore I Am*, translated by David Wills and edited by Marie-Louise Mallet (New York: Fordham University Press, 2008).

Derrida, Jacques, *The Beast and the Sovereign, Vol. 1*, translated by Geoffrey Bennington (Chicago: University of Chicago Press, 2009).
Derrida, Jacques, *The Beast and the Sovereign, Vol. 2*, translated by Geoffrey Bennington (Chicago: University of Chicago Press, 2011).
Despret, Vinciane, 'Do Animals Work? Creating Pragmatic Narratives', in Matthew Senior, David L. Clark and Carla Freccero (eds), 'Animots: Postanimality in French Thought', *Yale French Studies*, 127 (2015), 124–42.
Diamond, Cora, 'The Difficulty of Reality and the Difficulty of Philosophy', *Partial Answers: Journal of Literature and the History of Ideas*, 1:2 (2003), 1–26.
Di Santo, Michael John, '"Dramas of Fallen Horses": Conrad, Dostoevsky and Nietzsche', *Conradiana*, 42:3 (2010), 45–68.
Doane, Mary Ann, *The Emergence of Cinematic Time: Modernity, Contingency, the Archive* (Cambridge, MA: Harvard University Press, 2002).
Dostoyevsky, Fyodor, *Crime and Punishment* [1866], translated by David McDuff (London: Penguin, 2003).
Dostoyevsky, Fyodor, *The Idiot* [1874], translated by David McDuff (London: Penguin, 2004).
Engélibert, Jean-Paul, Lucie Campos, Catherine Coquio and Georges Chapouthier (eds), *La Question animale: entre science, littérature et philosophie* (Rennes: Presses Universitaires de Rennes, 2011).
Eisenman, Stephen F., *The Ghosts of Our Meat* (Carlisle: The Trout Gallery, 2013).
Evans, Georgina, 'A Cut or a Dissolve? Insects and Identification in Microcosmos', in Michael Lawrence and Laura McMahon (eds), *Animal Life and the Moving Image* (London: BFI, 2015), pp. 108–20.
Fay, Jennifer, 'Seeing/Loving Animals: André Bazin's Posthumanism', *Journal of Visual Culture*, 7:1 (2008), 41–64.
Flanagan, Matthew, 'Towards an Aesthetic of Slow in Contemporary Cinema', *16:9*, 29 (November 2008). Available at http://www.16-9.dk/2008-11/side11_inenglish.htm (last accessed 14 September 2018).
Flaxman, Gregory, 'Cinema Year Zero', in Gregory Flaxman (ed.), *The Brain is the Screen: Deleuze and the Philosophy of Cinema* (Minneapolis: University of Minnesota Press, 2000), pp. 87–108.
Foer, Jonathan Safran, *Eating Animals* (London: Penguin, 2009).
Fontenay, Élisabeth de, *Le Silence des bêtes: La Philosophie à l'épreuve de l'animalité* (Paris: Fayard, 1999).
Foucault, Michel, *The History of Sexuality, Vol. 1*, translated by Robert Hurley (New York: Vintage, 1980).
Foucault, Michel, *Discipline and Punish: The Birth of the Prison*, translated by Alan Sheridan (New York: Vintage, 1995).
Foucault, Michel, *Society Must Be Defended: Lectures at the Collège de France, 1975–76*, translated by David Macey and edited by Mauro Bertani and Alessandro Fontana (New York: Picador, 2003).
Frammartino, Michelangelo, 'Michelangelo Frammartino talks to Jonathan Romney', *Le Quattro Volte* DVD, New Wave Films, 2011.
Freud, Sigmund, 'Analysis of a Phobia of a Five Year Old Boy' [1909], in *The Pelican Freud Library* (Harmondsworth: Penguin, 1977), Vol. 8, Case Histories 1, pp. 169–306.
Fudge, Erica, *Animal* (London: Reaktion, 2002).
Fudge, Erica, 'A Left-Handed Blow: Writing the History of Animals', in Nigel Rothfels (ed.), *Representing Animals: Theories of Contemporary Culture* (Bloomington: Indiana University Press, 2002).

Fudge, Erica, 'Farmyard Choreographies: Or, Reading Invisible Cows in Early Modern Culture', Reading Animals Conference, University of Sheffield, 20 July 2014.

Gailleurd, Céline, 'Mécanique de l'absurde', *Cahiers du cinéma*, 687 (March 2013), 48.

Galt, Rosalind, 'Cats and the Moving Image: Feline Cinematicity from Lumière to Maru', in Michael Lawrence and Laura McMahon (eds), *Animal Life and the Moving Image* (London: BFI, 2015), pp. 42–57.

Garcia, Tristan, *Mémoires de la jungle* (Paris: Gallimard, 2010).

Gardner, Colin and Patricia MacCormack (eds), *Deleuze and the Animal* (Edinburgh: Edinburgh University Press, 2017).

Gester, Julien, 'Ovni documentaire sans parole entre élégie zoologique et fantastique clinique', *Libération*, 27 February 2013.

Ginn, Franklin, 'When Horses Won't Eat: Apocalypse and the Anthropocene', *Annals of the Association of American Geographers*, 105:2 (2015), 351–9.

Gorfinkel, Elena, 'The Body's Failed Labor: Performance Work in Sexploitation Cinema', in Elena Gorfinkel (ed.), 'The Work of the Image: Cinema, Labor, Aesthetic', *Framework: The Journal of Cinema and Media*, 53:1 (Spring 2012), 79–98.

Gorfinkel, Elena, 'Weariness, Waiting: Endurance and Art Cinema's Tired Bodies', *Discourse*, 34: 2/3 (2012), 311–47.

Gras, Emmanuel, 'Bovines: trois extraits commentés par Emmanuel Gras, réalisateur', *Télérama*, 2012. Available at http://www.telerama.fr/cinema/trois-extraits-commentes-de-bovines-par-emmanuel-gras, 78310.php (last accessed 14 September 2018).

Gras, Emmanuel, 'Director's Commentary', 2013, *Bovines* DVD, Blaq Out/UniversCiné Collection.

Greene, Ann Norton, *Horses at Work: Harnessing Power in Industrial America* (Cambridge, MA and London: Harvard University Press, 2008).

Grosz, Elizabeth, *The Nick of Time: Politics, Evolution, and the Untimely* (Crows Nest: Allen & Unwin, 2004).

Grosz, Elizabeth, *Chaos, Territory, Art: Deleuze and the Framing of the Earth* (New York: Columbia University Press, 2008).

Gruen, Lori, *The Ethics of Captivity* (New York: Oxford University Press, 2014).

Grugeau, Gérard, 'L'enfermement', *24 images*, 157 (2012), 43.

Hallward, Peter, *Out of this World: Deleuze and the Philosophy of Creation* (London and New York: Verso, 2006).

Hames, Peter, 'The Melancholy of Resistance: The Films of Béla Tarr', *Kinoeye*, 1:1, 3 September 2001. Available at http://www.kinoeye.org/01/01/hames01.php (last accessed 14 September 2018).

Haraway, Donna, *Primate Visions: Gender, Race and Nature in the World of Modern Science* (New York: Routledge, 1989).

Haraway, Donna, *When Species Meet* (Minneapolis: University of Minnesota Press, 2007).

Haraway, Donna, *Staying with the Trouble: Making Kin in the Chthulucene* (Durham, NC and London: Duke University Press, 2016).

Hardt, Michael and Negri, Antonio, *Empire* (Cambridge, MA: Harvard University Press, 2000).

Harries, Rhiannon, 'The Future of Documentary: Time, Ethics and Politics in Recent European Documentary Film', PhD thesis, University of Cambridge, 2016.

Heidegger, Martin, *Being and Time*, translated by John Macquarrie and Edward Robinson (New York: Harper, 1962).

Heidegger, Martin, *The Fundamental Concepts of Metaphysics: World, Finitude, Solitude*, translated by William McNeill and Nicholas Walker (Bloomington: Indiana University Press, 1995).

Hockenhull, Stella, 'Horseplay: Equine Performance and Creaturely Acts in Cinema', *NECSUS: European Journal of Media Studies*, Spring 2015. Available at http://www.necsus-ejms.org/horseplay-equine-performance-and-creaturely-acts-in-cinema/ (last accessed 14 September 2018).
Hollier, Denis, *Against Architecture: The Writings of Georges Bataille*, translated by Betsy Wing (Cambridge, MA: MIT Press, 1995).
Houellebecq, Michel, *Submission*, translated by Lorin Stein (New York: Farrar, Straus and Giroux, 2015).
Howard, Ed, *Only the Cinema* [blog], 13 February 2012. Available at http://seul-le-cinema.blogspot.co.uk/2012/02/s.html (last accessed 14 September 2018).
Hribal, Jason, '"Animals Are Part of the Working Class": A Challenge to Labor History', *Labor History*, 44:4 (2003), 435–53.
Hribal, Jason, 'Animals, Agency, and Class: Writing the History of Animals from Below', *Human Ecology Review*, 14:1 (2007), 101–12.
Hribal, Jason, 'Animals Are Part of the Working Class Reviewed', *Borderlands*, 11:2 (2012), 1–37. Available at http://www.borderlands.net.au/vol11no2_2012/hribal_animals.pdf (last accessed 14 September 2018).
Hribal, Jason, '32 Million Reasons: NYC Horse Carriages vs. Carriage Horses', *Counterpunch*, 24 June 2014.
Hughes, Helen, 'Arguments without words in *Unser täglich Brot* (Geyrhalter 2005)', *Continuum: Journal of Media & Cultural Studies*, 27:3 (2013), 347–64.
Ivakhiv, Adrian, *Ecologies of the Moving Image: Cinema, Affect, Nature* (Waterloo: Wilfred Laurier University Press, 2013).
Jaffe, Ira, *Slow Movies: Countering the Cinema of Action* (New York: Columbia University Press, 2014).
Jaremko-Greenwold, Anya, 'Véréna Paravel and Lucien Castaing-Taylor by Anya Jaremko-Greenwold', *BOMB Magazine*, 1 March 2013. Available at https://bombmagazine.org/articles/verena-paravel-and-lucien-castaing-taylor (last accessed 14 September 2018).
Jeong, Seung-hoon and Dudley Andrew, 'Grizzly Ghost: Herzog, Bazin and the Cinematic Animal', *Screen*, 49:1 (2008), 1–12.
Jeong, Seung-hoon, 'Animals: An Adventure in Bazin's Ontology', in Dudley Andrew (ed.), *Opening Bazin* (New York: Oxford University Press, 2011), pp. 177–86.
Juzwiak, Rick, 'Leviathan: A Documentary Made by People Who Hate Documentaries', *Gawker*, 3 January 2013.
Kara, Selmin and Alanna Thain, 'Sonic Ethnographies: *Leviathan* and New Materialisms in Documentary', in Holly Rogers (ed.), *Music and Sound in Documentary Film* (London: Routledge, 2015), pp. 186–98.
Kelemen, Fred, 'The Last Dance', *Sight and Sound*, June 2012, p. 39.
King, Barbara J., *How Animals Grieve* (Chicago: University of Chicago Press, 2014).
Koehler, Robert, 'Agrarian Utopias/Dystopias', *Cinema Scope*, 40 (2009), 12–15. Available at http://cinema-scope.com/features/features-agrarian-utopiasdystopias-the-new-nonfiction/ (last accessed 14 September 2018).
Kracauer, Siegfried, *Theory of Film: The Redemption of Physical Reality* (Princeton: Princeton University Press, 1997).
Krasznahorkai, László, *Animalinside*, translated by Ottilie Mulzet, illustrated by Max Neumann (London: Sylph Editions, 2012).
Krasznahorkai, László, *The Last Wolf & Herman*, translated by George Szirtes and John Batki (New York: New Directions, 2016).

Krasznahorkai, László, 'At the Latest, in Turin', in *The World Goes On*, translated by John Batki, Ottilie Mulzet and George Szirtes (London: Tuskar Rock Press, 2017), pp. 21–3.

Kundera, Milan, 'The Tragedy of Central Europe', translated by Edmund White, *New York Review of Books*, 31:7 (26 April 1984).

LaCapra, Dominick, *History and Its Limits: Human, Animal, Violence* (Ithaca and London: Cornell University Press, 2009).

Ladino, Jennifer F., 'Working with Animals: Regarding Companion Species in Documentary Film', in Stephen Rust, Salma Monani and Sean Cubitt (eds), *Ecocinema Theory and Practice* (New York: Routledge, 2012), pp. 129–48.

Lam, Stephanie, 'It's About Time: Slow Aesthetics in Experimental EcoCinema and Nature Cam Videos', in Tiago De Luca and Nuno Barradas Jorge (eds), *Slow Cinema* (Edinburgh: Edinburgh University Press, 2015), pp. 207–18.

Landesman, Ohad, 'Here, There, and Everywhere: *Leviathan* and the Digital Future of Observational Ethnography', *Visual Anthropology Review*, 31:1 (2015), 12–19.

Latour, Bruno, *Reassembling the Social: An Introduction to Actor-Network-Theory* (Oxford: Oxford University Press, 2005).

Lawrence, Michael, 'Haneke's Stable: the Death of an Animal and the Figuration of the Human', in Brian Price and John David Rhodes (eds), *On Michael Haneke* (Detroit: Wayne State University Press, 2010), pp. 63–84.

Lawrence, Michael, 'Muybridgean Motion/Materialist Film: Malcolm Le Grice's *Berlin Horse*', in Michael Lawrence and Laura McMahon (eds), *Animal Life and the Moving Image* (London: BFI, 2015), pp. 72–91.

Lawrence, Michael and Laura McMahon (eds), *Animal Life and the Moving Image* (London: BFI, 2015).

Lazzarato, Maurizio, 'Immaterial Labor', translated by Paul Colilli and Ed Emory, in Paolo Virno and Michael Hardt (eds), *Radical Thought in Italy: A Potential Politics* (Minneapolis: University of Minnesota Press, 1996), pp. 132–47.

Lim, Song Hwee, *Tsai Ming-liang and a Cinema of Slowness* (Honolulu: University of Hawai'i Press, 2014).

Lippit, Akira Mizuta, *Electric Animal: Toward a Rhetoric of Wildlife* (Minneapolis: University of Minnesota Press, 2000).

Lippit, Akira Mizuta, 'The Death of an Animal', *Film Quarterly*, 56:1 (2002), 9–22.

Lorimer, Jamie and Driessen, Clemens, 'Bovine Biopolitics and the Promise of Monsters in the Rewilding of Heck Cattle', *Geoforum*, 48 (2013), 249–59.

Lowenstein, Adam, 'Films Without a Face: Shock Horror in the Cinema of Georges Franju', *Cinema Journal*, 37:4 (1998), 37–58.

Lübecker, Nikolaj and Daniele Rugo (eds), *James Benning's Environments: Politics, Ecology, Duration* (Edinburgh: Edinburgh University Press, 2017).

MacDonald, Scott, *The Garden in the Machine: A Field Guide to Independent Films About Place* (Berkeley: University of California Press, 2001).

MacDonald, Scott, 'Toward an Eco-Cinema', *ISLE: Interdisciplinary Studies in Literature and Environment*, 11:2 (2004), 107–32.

MacInnis, Allan, 'The Aesthetics of Slaughter: *Leviathan* in Context', *CineAction*, 91 (2013), 58–64.

Mackay, Robin and Avanessian, Armen, 'Introduction', in Robin Mackay and Armen Avanessian (eds), *#Accelerate: The Accelerationist Reader* (Falmouth: Urbanomic, 2014), pp. 1–46.

Malamud, Randy, *An Introduction to Animals and Visual Culture* (Basingstoke: Palgrave Macmillan, 2012).

Margulies, Ivone, *Nothing Happens: Chantal Akerman's Hyperrealist Everyday* (Durham, NC and London: Duke University Press, 1996).
Marks, Laura U., 'Signs of the Time: Deleuze, Peirce, and the Documentary Image', in Gregory Flaxman (ed.), *The Brain is the Screen: Deleuze and the Philosophy of Cinema* (Minneapolis: University of Minnesota Press, 2000), pp. 193–214.
Marks, Laura U., *The Skin of the Film: Intercultural Cinema, Embodiment and the Senses* (Durham, NC and London: Duke University Press, 2000).
Marvin, Garry and Mullan, Bob, *Zoo Culture* (London: Weidenfeld & Nicolson, 1987).
Martin-Jones, David, *Cinema Against Doublethink: Ethical Encounters with the Lost Pasts of World History* (New York: Routledge, 2018).
Marx, Karl, *Capital: A Critique of Political Economy, Vol. 1*, translated by Ben Fowkes (New York: Penguin, 1990).
Massumi, Brian, *What Animals Teach Us about Politics* (Durham, NC: Duke University Press, 2014).
Mazierska, Eva, 'What Happened to the Polish Multitude? Representation of Working People in Polish Postcommunist Cinema', in Eva Mazierska (ed.), 'Working Life Now and Then', *Framework*, 53:1 (Spring 2012), 207–27.
Mazierska, Eva (ed.), *Work in Cinema: Labor and the Human Condition* (New York: Palgrave Macmillan, 2013).
McCance, Dawn, *Critical Animal Studies: An Introduction* (New York: SUNY Press, 2013).
McHugh, Susan, *Animal Stories: Narrating Across Species Lines* (Minneapolis: University of Minnesota Press, 2011).
McHugh, Susan, 'Unknowing Animals: Wild Bird Films and the Limits of Knowledge', in Michael Lawrence and Laura McMahon (eds), *Animal Life and the Moving Image* (London: BFI, 2015), pp. 271–87.
McKay, Robert, 'James Agee's "A Mother's Tale" and the Biopolitics of Animal Life and Death in Postwar America', in Alastair Hunt and Stephanie Youngblood (eds), *Against Life* (Evanston, IL: Northwestern University Press, 2016), pp. 143–60.
McLaughlin, Emily, 'The Practice of Writing and the Practice of Living: Michel Deguy's and Philippe Jaccottet's Ecopoetics', *Fixxions*, 11 (2015). Available at http://www.revue-critique-de-fixxion-francaise-contemporaine.org/rcffc/issue/view/21 (last accessed 14 September 2018).
McMahon, Laura, 'Jean-Luc Nancy and the Spacing of the World', *Contemporary French and Francophone Studies*, 15:5 (2011), 623–31.
McMahon, Laura, 'Introduction', in Laura McMahon (ed.), 'Screen animals dossier', *Screen*, 56:1 (2015), 81–7.
McMahon, Laura, 'Franju's Animals: Stains, Traces, Histories', in Zoe Angeli and Blake Gutt (eds), *Stains/Les Taches: Communication and Contamination in French and Francophone Literature and Culture* (Bern: Peter Lang, forthcoming).
Melville, Herman, *Moby-Dick* [1851] (London: Penguin, 2003).
Mengue, Philippe, 'The Idiot in Societies of Control', *Theory & Event*, 16:3 (2013).
Mills, Brett, 'Television Wildlife Documentaries and Animals' Right to Privacy', *Continuum: Journal of Media & Cultural Studies*, 24:2 (2010), 193–202.
Misek, Richard, 'Dead Time: Cinema, Heidegger and Boredom', *Continuum: Journal of Media and Cultural Studies*, 24:5 (2010), 777–85.
Mitman, Gregg, *Reel Nature: America's Romance with Wildlife on Film*, 2nd edition (Cambridge, MA: Harvard University Press, 2009).
Montcel, Anne Tézenas du, '"Faire vivre au spectateur une vie d'animal": rencontre avec Emmanuel Gras', 2012, *Bovines* DVD, Blaq Out/UniversCiné.

Moritz, Karl Philipp, *Anton Reiser* [1785–1790] (London: Penguin, 1997).
Morton, Timothy, *Hyperobjects: Philosophy and Ecology After the End of the World* (Minneapolis: University of Minnesota Press, 2013).
Mroz, Matilda, *Temporality and Film Analysis* (Edinburgh: Edinburgh University Press, 2012).
Mullarkey, John, *Refractions of Reality: Philosophy and the Moving Image* (New York: Palgrave Macmillan, 2009).
Mullarkey, John, 'Animal Spirits: Philosomorphism and the Background Revolts of Cinema', *Angelaki: Journal of the Theoretical Humanities*, 18:1 (2013), 11–29.
Murphet, Julian, 'Pitiable or Political Animals?', *SubStance*, 37:3, Issue 117 (2008), 'The Political Animal', 97–116.
Nancy, Jean-Luc, *The Creation of the World or Globalization*, translated with an introduction by François Raffoul and David Pettigrew (New York: SUNY Press, 2007).
Nancy, Jean-Luc, *Corpus*, translated by Richard A. Rand (New York: Fordham University Press, 2008).
Nealon, Jeffrey, *Foucault Beyond Foucault: Power and Its Intensifications since 1984* (Stanford: Stanford University Press, 2007).
Nessel, Sabine, 'The Media Animal: On the Mise-en-scène of Animals in the Zoo and Cinema', in Nessel *et al.* (eds), *Animals and the Cinema: Classifications, Cinephilias, Philosophies* (Berlin: Bertz and Fischer, 2012), pp. 33–48.
Neyrat, Cyril, 'Blood of the Fish, Beauty of the Monster', translated by Nicholas Elliott, *Leviathan* DVD booklet, Dogwoof (2013), pp. 2–5.
Nichols, Bill, *Representing Reality: Issues and Concepts in Documentary* (Bloomington: Indiana University Press, 1991).
Nietzsche, Friedrich, 'The Dawn', in Walter Kaufmann (ed.), *The Portable Nietzsche*, translated by Kaufmann (New York: Penguin, 1977), pp. 76–92.
Nietzsche, Friedrich, *Untimely Meditations*, translated by R. J. Hollingdale and edited by Daniel Breazeale (Cambridge: Cambridge University Press, 1997).
Oleszczyk, Michal, 'Sundance Film Festival 2012: *Bestiaire*', *The House Next Door*, 24 January 2012. Available at http://www.slantmagazine.com/house/2012/01/sundance-film-festival-2012-bestiaire/ (last accessed 14 September 2018).
O'Brien, Adam, 'Fishwater: *The Bay* and its hyperobject', *Screen* annual conference, University of Glasgow, 27 June 2015.
O'Meara, Radha, 'Do Cats Know They Rule YouTube? Surveillance and the Pleasures of Cat Videos', *M/C Journal: A Journal of Media and Culture*, 17:2 (2014). Available at http://journal.media-culture.org.au/index.php/mcjournal/article/view/794 (last accessed 14 September 2018).
O'Shaughnessy, Martin, 'French Film and Work: The Work Done by Work-Centered Films', in Eva Mazierska (ed.), 'Working Life Now and Then', *Framework*, 53:1 (Spring 2012), 155–71.
Panse, Silke, 'The Work of the Documentary Protagonist: The Material Labor of Aesthetics', in Alexandra Juhasz and Alice Lebow (eds), *A Companion to Contemporary Documentary Film* (Chichester: Wiley Blackwell, 2015), pp. 155–75.
Parc Safari website. Available at https://www.parcsafari.com/en/ (last accessed 14 September 2018).
Pavsek, Christopher, '*Leviathan* and the Experience of Sensory Ethnography,' *Visual Anthropology Review*, 31:1 (2015), 4–11.
Petersen, Christopher, *Bestial Traces: Race, Sexuality, Animality* (New York: Fordham University Press, 2013).
Petkovic, Vladan, 'Simple and Pure' [interview with Tarr], *Cineuropa*, 4 March 2011. Available at: http://www.cineuropa.org/en/interview/198131/ (last accessed 14 September 2018).

Pick, Anat, *Creaturely Poetics: Animality and Vulnerability in Literature and Film* (New York: Columbia University Press, 2011).
Pick, Anat, 'Some Small Discrepancy: Jean-Christophe Bailly's Creaturely Ontology', *Journal of Animal Ethics*, 3:2 (2013), 176–87.
Pick, Anat, 'Three Worlds: Dwelling and Worldhood on Screen', in Anat Pick and Guinevere Narraway (eds), *Screening Nature: Cinema Beyond the Human* (Oxford: Berghahn, 2013), pp. 21–36.
Pick, Anat, 'Animal Life in the Cinematic Umwelt', in Michael Lawrence and Laura McMahon (eds), *Animal Life and the Moving Image* (London: British Film Institute, 2015), pp. 221–37.
Pick, Anat, 'Reflexive Realism in René Clément's Forbidden Games', in Matthew Senior, David L. Clark and Carla Freccero (eds), 'Animots: Postanimality in French Thought', *Yale French Studies*, 127 (2015), 205–20.
Pick, Anat, 'Why Not Look at Animals', *NECSUS: European Journal of Media Studies*, Spring 2015. Available at http://www.necsus-ejms.org/why-not-look-at-animals/ (last accessed 14 September 2018).
Pick, Anat, 'Why Not Look at Animals', Plenary, *Screen* annual conference, University of Glasgow, 26 June 2015.
Pick, Anat, '"Sparks Would Fly": Electricity and the Spectacle of Animality', in Michael Lundblad (ed.), *Animalities: Literary and Cultural Studies Beyond the Human* (Edinburgh: Edinburgh University Press, 2017), pp. 104–26.
Pick, Anat, 'Vulnerability', in Lori Gruen (ed.), *Critical Terms for Animal Studies* (Chicago: University of Chicago Press, 2018), pp. 410–23.
Pick, Anat and Guinevere Narraway (eds), *Screening Nature: Cinema Beyond the Human* (Oxford: Berghahn, 2013).
Pisters, Patricia, *The Matrix of Visual Culture: Working with Deleuze in Film Theory* (Stanford: Stanford University Press, 2003).
Poliquin, Rachel, *The Breathless Zoo: Taxidermy and the Cultures of Longing* (University Park: Pennsylvania State University Press, 2012).
Porcher, Jocelyne, 'The Work of Animals: A Change for Social Sciences', *Humanimalia: A Journal of Human/Animal Interface Studies*, 6:1 (2014). Available at http://www.depauw.edu/humanimalia/issue%2011/porcher.html (last accessed 14 September 2018).
Porcher Jocelyne and Tiphaine Schmitt, 'Dairy Cows: Workers in the Shadows?', *Society and Animals*, 20:1 (2012), 39–60.
Protevi, John, 'Peter Hallward, Out of this World: Deleuze and the Philosophy of Creation', *Notre Dame Philosophical Reviews*, 3 August 2007. Available at http://ndpr.nd.edu/news/23058/?id=10564 (last accessed 14 September 2018).
Rancière, Jacques, *The Nights of Labor: The Workers' Dream in Nineteenth Century France*, translated by John Drury (Philadelphia: Temple University Press, 1989).
Rancière, Jacques, *The Future of the Image*, translated by Gregory Elliott (London: Verso, 2007).
Rancière, Jacques, *Béla Tarr, The Time After*, translated by Erik Beranek (Minneapolis: Univocal, 2013).
Rancière, Jacques, 'Béla Tarr: The Poetics and Politics of Fiction', in Tiago De Luca and Nuno Barradas Jorge (eds), *Slow Cinema* (Edinburgh: Edinburgh University Press, 2015), pp. 245–60.
Raspiengeas, Jean-Claude, 'En cage, au zoo', *La Croix*, 27 February 2013.
Revaz, Noëlle, *With the Animals*, translated by W. Donald Wilson (Champaign, Dublin and London: Dalkey Archive Press, 2012).
Ridout, Nicholas, 'Animal Labour in the Theatrical Economy', *Theatre Research International*, 29:1 (2004), 57–65.
Rodowick, D. N., *Gilles Deleuze's Time Machine* (Durham, NC: Duke University Press, 1997).

Roffe, Jon and Hannah Stark (eds), *Deleuze and the Non/Human* (New York: Palgrave Macmillan, 2015).
Roffe, Jon and Hannah Stark, 'Introduction: Deleuze and the Non/Human', in Jon Roffe and Hannah Stark (eds), *Deleuze and the Non/Human* (New York: Palgrave Macmillan, 2015), pp. 1–16.
Romney, Jonathan, 'Gone with the Wind', *Sight and Sound*, June 2012, 34–6.
Rosen, Philip, *Change Mummified: Cinema, Historicity, Theory* (Minneapolis: University of Minnesota Press, 2001).
Rothermel, Dennis, 'Becoming-Animal Cinema Narrative', in Colin Gardner and Patricia MacCormack (eds), *Deleuze and the Animal* (Edinburgh: Edinburgh University Press, 2017), pp. 266–74.
Rowland, William J., 'Studying Visual Cues in Fish Behaviour: A Review of Ethological Techniques', *Environmental Biology of Fishes*, 56 (1999), 285–305.
Russell, Catherine, '*Leviathan* and the Discourse of Sensory Ethnography: Spleen et idéal,' *Visual Anthropology Review*, 31:1 (2015), 27–34.
Rust, Stephen, Salma Monani and Sean Cubitt (eds), *Ecocinema Theory and Practice* (New York: Routledge, 2012).
Rust, Stephen, 'Ecocinema and the Wildlife Film', in Louise Westling (ed.), *The Cambridge Companion to Literature and the Environment* (Cambridge: Cambridge University Press, 2013), pp. 226–40.
Ryan, Derek, '"The Reality of Becoming": Deleuze, Woolf, and the Territory of Cows', *Deleuze Studies*, 7:4 (2013), 537–61.
Ryan, Derek, *Animal Theory: A Critical Introduction* (Edinburgh: Edinburgh University Press, 2013).
Samuel, Sajay and Bavington, Dean, 'Fishing for Biomass,' in Joan B. Landes, Paula Young Lee and Paul Youngquist (eds), *Gorgeous Beasts: Animal Bodies in Historical Perspective* (University Park: Pennsylvania State University Press, 2012).
Sanyal, Debarati, 'Calais's "Jungle": Refugees, Biopolitics, and the Arts of Resistance', *Representations*, October 2016. Available at http://www.representations.org/advance-publications/#_edn30 (last accessed 14 September 2018).
Saxton, Libby, *Haunted Images: Film, Ethics and the Holocaust* (London: Wallflower Press, 2008).
Schoonover, Karl, 'Wastrels of Time: Slow Cinema's Laboring Body, the Political Spectator, and the Queer', *Framework: The Journal of Cinema and Media*, 53:1 (2012), 65–78.
Scott, A. O., 'Facing the Abyss with Boiled Potatoes and Plum Brandy: Béla Tarr's Final Film, "The Turin Horse"', *The New York Times*, 9 February 2012. Available at http://www.nytimes.com/2012/02/10/movies/the-turin-horse-from-bela-tarr.html (last accessed 14 September 2018).
Selyem, Zsuzsa, 'How Long and When: Open Time Interval and Dignified Living Creatures in *The Turin Horse*', *Acta Universitatis Sapientiae: Film and Media Studies*, 10 (2015), 105–20.
Senior, Matthew, David L. Clark and Carla Freccero, 'Editors' Preface: Ecce animot: Postanimality from Cave to Screen', in Matthew Senior, David L. Clark and Carla Freccero (eds), 'Animots: Postanimality in French Thought', *Yale French Studies*, 127 (2015), 1–18.
Sensory Ethnography Lab website. Available at http://sel.fas.harvard.edu (last accessed 14 September 2018).
Shafer, Leah, 'Cat Videos and the Superflat Cinema of Attractions', *Film Criticism*, 40:2 (2016). Available at http://dx.doi.org/10.3998/fc.13761232.0040.208 (last accessed 14 September 2018).
Shukin, Nicole, *Animal Capital: Rendering Life in Biopolitical Times* (Minneapolis: University of Minnesota Press, 2009).

Shukin, Nicole and Sarah O'Brien, 'Being Struck: On the Force of Slaughter and Cinematic Affect', in Michael Lawrence and Laura McMahon (eds), *Animal Life and the Moving Image* (London: BFI, 2015), pp. 187–202.
Simon, Anne, 'Animality and Contemporary French Literary Studies: Overview and Perspectives', in Louisa MacKenzie and Stephanie Posthumus (eds), *French Thinking about Animals* (East Lansing: Michigan State University Press, 2015), pp. 75–88.
Sinclair, Upton, *The Jungle* [1906] (London: Penguin, 1985).
Singer, Peter, *Animal Liberation* (New York: Avon Books, 1975).
Smaill, Belinda, 'Documentary Film and Animal Modernity in Raw Herring and Sweetgrass', *Australian Humanities Review*, 57 (2014), 61–80.
Smaill, Belinda, 'Tasmanian Tigers and Polar Bears: The Documentary Moving Image and (Species) Loss', *NECSUS: European Journal of Media Studies*, Spring 2015. Available at http://necsus-ejms.org/tasmanian-tigers-and-polar-bears-the-documentary-moving-image-and-species-loss/ (last accessed 14 September 2018).
Smaill, Belinda, *Regarding Life: Animals and the Documentary Moving Image* (Albany: SUNY Press, 2016).
Snyder, Hunter, '*Leviathan*', *Visual Anthropology Review*, 29:2 (2013), 176–9.
Sobchack, Vivian, *The Address of the Eye: A Phenomenology of Film Experience* (Princeton, NJ and Oxford: Princeton University Press, 1992).
Sobchack, Vivian, *Carnal Thoughts: Embodiment and Moving Image Culture* (Berkeley: University of California Press, 2004).
Soesanto, Léo, 'Portraits de ruminants en futurs steaks: un pur trip en compagnie des vaches', *Les inrockuptibles*, 21 February 2012. Available at http://www.lesinrocks.com/cinema/films-a-l-affiche/bovines/ (last accessed 14 September 2018).
Stevenson, Lisa and Eduardo Kohn, '*Leviathan*: An Ethnographic Dream', *Visual Anthropology Review*, 31:1 (2015), 49–53.
Stojanova, Christina, 'The Damnation of Labor in the Films of Béla Tarr', in Ewa Mazierska (ed.), *Work in Cinema: Labor and the Human Condition* (New York: Palgrave Macmillan, 2013), pp. 169–87.
Supervie, Virginie and Dominique Costagliola, 'The Unrecognised French BSE Epidemic', *Veterinary Research*, 35:3 (2004), 349–62. Available at http://www.vetres.org/articles/vetres/abs/2004/03/V4008/V4008.html (last accessed 14 September 2018).
Szendy, Peter, 'Animal Filmicum', in Corinne Maury and Sylvie Rollet (eds), *Béla Tarr: de la colère au tourment* (Crisnée: Yellow Now, 2016), pp. 97–109.
Tuan, Yi Fu, *Dominance and Affection: The Making of Pets* (New Haven: Yale University Press, 1984).
Uexküll, Jakob von, *A Foray into the Worlds of Animals and Humans, with A Theory of Meaning*, translated by Joseph D. O'Neil (Minneapolis: University of Minnesota Press, 2010).
Velten, Hannah, *Cow* (London: Reaktion, 2007).
Vialles, Noëlie, *Animal to Edible*, translated by J. A. Underwood (Cambridge: Cambridge University Press, 1994).
Wadiwel, Dinesh Joseph, *The War against Animals* (Leiden and Boston: Brill Rodopi, 2015).
Walber, Daniel, 'Pastoral: Emmanuel Gras's Bovines at Rooftop Films', 1 August 2012. Available at http://www.brooklynrail.org/2012/08/film/pastoral-emmanuel-grass-bovines-at-rooftop-films (last accessed 14 September 2018).
Wahlberg, Malin, '*Leviathan*: From Sensory Ethnography to Gallery Film', *NECSUS: European Journal of Media Studies*, Autumn 2014. Available at http://www.necsus-ejms.org/leviathan-sensory-ethnography-gallery-film/ (last accessed 14 September 2018).
Walker, Elaine, *Horse* (London: Reaktion, 2008).

Weil, Kari, *Thinking Animals: Why Animal Studies Now?* (New York: Columbia University Press, 2012).

Westmoreland, Mark R. and Brent Luvaas, 'Introduction: *Leviathan* and the Entangled Lives of Species', *Visual Anthropology Review*, 31:1 (2015), 1–3.

Willoquet, Paula (ed.), *Framing the World: Explorations in Ecocriticism and Film* (Charlottesville: University of Virginia Press, 2010).

Winthrop-Young, Geoffrey, 'Afterword – Bubbles and Webs: A Backdoor Stroll Through the Readings of Uexküll', in *A Foray into the Worlds of Animals and Humans, with A Theory of Meaning*, translated by Joseph D. O'Neil (Minneapolis: University of Minnesota Press, 2010), pp. 209–43.

Wilsher, Kim, 'France in Denial as BSE-Infected Beef Entered Food Chain', *The Telegraph*, 5 July 2004. Available at http://www.smh.com.au/articles/2004/07/04/1088879375088.html (last accessed 14 September 2018).

Wolfe, Cary, *Animal Rites: American Culture, the Discourse of Species, and Posthumanist Theory* (Chicago: University of Chicago Press, 2003).

Wolfe, Cary, 'Introduction', in Cary Wolfe (ed.), *Zoontologies: The Question of the Animal* (Minneapolis: University of Minnesota Press, 2003), pp. ix–xxiii.

Wolfe, Cary, 'Learning from Temple Grandin, or, Animal Studies, Disability Studies, and Who Comes After the Subject', *New Formations*, 64 (2008), 110–23.

Wolfe, Cary, *What is Posthumanism?* (Minneapolis: University of Minnesota Press, 2010).

Wolfe, Cary, *Before the Law: Humans and Other Animals in a Biopolitical Frame* (Chicago: University of Chicago Press, 2013).

Wright, Mark Peter, 'Ernst Karel', *Ear Room*, 14 February 2013. Available at https://earroom.wordpress.com/2013/02/14/ernst-karel/ (last accessed 14 September 2018).

Yacavone, Daniel, *Film Worlds: A Philosophical Aesthetics of Cinema* (New York: Columbia University Press, 2015).

Zizek, Slavoj, *Bodies without Organs: On Deleuze and Consequences* (London: Routledge, 2004).

Filmography

Abendland (Nikolaus Geyrhalter, 2011)
A Man Escaped (Robert Bresson, 1956)
Animals (Nicolas Philibert, 1996)
Apocalypse Now (Francis Ford Coppola, 1979)
Arctic Tale (Adam Ravetch and Sarah Robertson, 2007)
Au hasard Balthazar (Robert Bresson, 1966)
Being Caribou (Leanne Allison, Canada, 2008)
Benny's Video (Michael Haneke, 1992)
Bestiaire (Denis Côté, 2012)
Blackfish (Gabriela Cowperthwaite, 2013)
Blood of the Beasts (Georges Franju, 1949)
Bovines ou la vraie vie des vaches (*A Cow's Life*, Emmanuel Gras, 2011)
Bullfight (Pierre Braunberger, 1951)
Carcasses (Denis Côté, 2009)
C'est quoi ce travail? (Luc Joulé and Sébastien Jousse, 2015)
Cowspiracy: The Sustainability Secret (Kip Andersen and Keegan Kuhn, 2014)
Damnation (Béla Tarr, 1988)
Darwin's Nightmare (Hubert Sauper, 2004)
Earth (Alastair Fothergill and Mark Linfield, 2009)
Electrocuting an Elephant (Thomas Edison, 1903)
Extinct: The Tasmanian Tiger (Channel 4, 2001)
Food, Inc. (Robert Kenner, 2008)
Foreign Parts (Véréna Paravel and J. P. Sniadecki, 2010)
Fowl Play (Adam Durand, 2009)
Freedom (Lisandro Alonso, 2001)
Frozen Planet (BBC, 2011)
Germany, Year Zero (Roberto Rossellini, 1948)
Gilles Deleuze from A to Z [television documentary], with Claire Parnet (directed by Pierre-André Boutang, 1988–9)
Go West (Buster Keaton, 1925)
Grizzly Man (Werner Herzog, 2005)
I Do Not Know What It Is I Am Like (Bill Viola, 1986)
Jeanne Dielman, 23 quai du Commerce, 1080 Bruxelles (Chantal Akerman, 1975)

La Jetée (Chris Marker, 1962)
Le Quattro Volte (Michelangelo Frammartino, 2010)
Les Hommes (Ariane Michel, 2006)
Leviathan (Lucien Castaing-Taylor and Véréna Paravel, 2012)
Life of Pi (Ang Lee, 2012)
March of the Penguins (Luc Jacquet, 2005)
Meat (Frederick Wiseman, 1976)
Microcosmos (Claude Nuridsany and Marie Pérennou, 1996)
Money (Robert Bresson, 1983)
Mouchette (Robert Bresson, 1967)
Nénette (Nicolas Philibert, 2010)
Night and Fog (Alain Resnais, 1955)
Noah (Darren Aronofsky, 2014)
Of Horses and Men (Benedikt Erlingsson, 2013)
Our Daily Bread (Nikolaus Geyrhalter, 2005)
Park Lanes (Kevin Jerome Everson, 2015)
Primate (Frederick Wiseman, 1974)
Rams (Grímur Hákonarson, 2015)
Raw Herring (Leonard Retel Helmrich and Hetty Naaijkens-Retel Helmrich, 2013)
Rocco and His Brothers (Luchino Visconti, 1960)
Rosetta (Jean-Pierre and Luc Dardenne, 1999)
Sátántangó (Béla Tarr, 1994)
Stromboli (Roberto Rossellini, 1950)
Sweetgrass (Ilisa Barbash and Lucien Castaing-Taylor, 2009)
The Birds (Alfred Hitchcock, 1963)
The Cove (Louie Psihoyos, 2009)
The Cow (Dariush Mehrjui, 1969)
The Dead (Lisandro Alonso, 2004)
The Farmer's Horse (Crown Film Unit, 1951)
The Fly (David Cronenberg, 1986)
The Moo Man (Andy Heathcote, 2012)
The Rules of the Game (Jean Renoir, 1939)
The Seasons (Artavazd Pelechian, 1975)
The Turin Horse (Béla Tarr and Ágnes Hranitzky, 2011)
Touki Bouki (Djibril Diop Mambéty, 1973)
Tropical Malady (Apichatpong Weerasethakul, 2004)
Umberto D. (Vittorio De Sica, 1952)
Weekend (Jean-Luc Godard, 1967)
Wendy and Lucy (Kelly Reichardt, 2008)
Werckmeister Harmonies (Béla Tarr, 2000)
Willard (Daniel Mann, 1971)
Winged Migration (Jacques Perrin, Jacques Cluzaud and Michel Debats, 2001)
Workers Leaving the Factory (Louis Lumière, 1895)
Zoo (Frederick Wiseman, 1993)

Index

anthropomorphism, 3, 7, 40, 46, 68, 93, 167, 182
Au hasard Balthazar, 68, 89, 106, 117, 126, 131

Bailly, Jean-Christophe, 2, 11, 13–14, 16, 23–6, 28, 43, 45, 59, 67, 73, 86–9, 105, 164, 170–1, 189, 192–6, 199–200
Bazin, André, 2, 5, 26–7, 42, 50–2, 56, 58, 66, 100, 147–8, 155, 169, 200
becoming-animal, 2, 43, 47–8, 147, 172, 178–9, 199
Bellour, Raymond, 2, 23, 27, 78, 161
Berger, John, 12, 67, 73, 79, 119
Bergson, Henri, 9, 47, 51, 53, 165–6, 184
biopolitics, 1, 3–4, 9, 13–22, 26, 29, 43, 58, 67, 72–6, 83–6, 88, 99, 110, 122, 136–7, 145, 147, 151, 155, 180, 183, 170, 177, 193–4, 196–7, 200
Blood of the Beasts, 50, 135, 140–1, 148, 152–3, 162, 175, 198
Burt, Jonathan, 1, 12, 14, 23, 26, 42, 49, 57–8, 80, 84, 86, 101, 152, 184, 194

cruelty, 49, 57–8, 73, 101–2, 106–7, 115

dead time, 2, 6, 27, 68, 75–6
Deleuze, Gilles, 1–4, 8–9, 11, 16, 20–1, 23–4, 26–9, 42–3, 45–9, 52–9, 66, 75–6, 83–5, 96, 100, 113, 115–16, 118–23, 122–3, 135–7, 139–40, 147, 150–1, 161–2, 164–6, 168–9, 171–4, 178–81, 183–5, 194–7, 199–200
Derrida, Jacques, 2, 7, 11, 13–17, 23–6, 29, 45, 105, 139, 146–7, 193–6, 198–9
deterritorialisation, 9, 20, 27, 47–8, 59, 84, 86, 121–2, 161, 172–4, 180, 184, 197, 200

ecology, 10–12, 22, 102, 108–10, 123, 151
Electrocuting an Elephant, 5–6, 19, 49, 141
exhaustion, 27, 95, 99, 101, 110–14, 121–2

Foucault, Michel, 13–14, 20, 23, 29, 58, 72, 118, 137, 151, 153, 183–4, 197, 200

Guattari, Félix, 2–3, 11, 20, 26, 28–9, 42–3, 45–9, 55, 58–9, 84–5, 116, 120–1, 135–6, 147, 150, 161–2, 168–9, 172–4, 178–81, 183–5, 194–5, 197, 199

haecceity, 48, 172
Haraway, Donna, 11, 15–18, 24, 27, 46, 77, 81–2, 121, 197
Heidegger, Martin, 2, 23, 26, 42, 44–6, 50, 143, 148

indexicality, 12, 16, 49–50, 100, 135, 179, 199

labour, 4, 6, 15–17, 22, 27–8, 70, 77, 82, 95, 97–9, 102–7, 110–12, 114–16, 118–19, 121–3, 134–5, 140, 142, 151, 153–5, 167, 171, 197–9
Le Quattro Volte, 1, 10, 21, 68, 179, 198
line of flight, 1, 9, 18, 27, 29, 37, 49, 59, 85–6, 88, 99, 114–19, 123, 151, 173–4, 180, 184–5, 197, 200
Lippit, Akira Mizuta, 12, 14, 23, 26–7, 42, 49–50, 79–80, 141–3, 145–6, 148, 153, 155
long take, 4, 7, 22, 28, 51, 66, 68, 70, 75, 77, 83–4, 87, 99–102, 105, 115, 118, 122, 135, 154, 162, 167, 198

meat, 3, 13, 22, 138–40, 143, 145–6, 148, 150–1, 154–5, 174, 184–5, 193–5, 198–9

monstration, 19–20, 79–80, 140–5, 148
mourning, 12, 175, 189n87, 196
movement-image, 8–9, 42, 52, 66, 75, 161, 165–6, 168, 173–4
Muybridge, Eadweard, 1, 12, 78, 102, 141

Nancy, Jean-Luc, 11, 28, 149–50
Nénette, 66, 68, 76, 198
Nietzsche, Friedrich, 20, 27, 29, 58, 97, 99, 101, 105, 107, 113, 115, 118–21, 175, 183, 197

pensivity, 2, 24–6, 28, 67, 83, 86–7, 89, 170–2, 183–4, 196
phenomenology, 29, 42, 51–2, 88, 100, 172, 184
Pick, Anat, 2, 23, 25–6, 42, 49–51, 56, 67, 72, 84, 101, 106, 119, 137–41, 151, 199
point of view, 7, 53–4, 56–7, 121–2, 163
posthumanism, 11, 135–7, 140, 144, 148, 154, 199
puissance, 20, 29, 59, 183–5, 197

Rancière, Jacques, 27, 76, 95–8, 100, 105, 108, 112–16, 119, 122, 171
rendering, 18–20, 135, 140–3, 155, 176–80, 183, 194, 196, 198

Shukin, Nicole, 2–4, 11, 13–16, 18–21, 28–9, 49, 72–3, 79–80, 82, 110, 121, 134–5, 140–3, 145, 176–80, 183, 185, 198–9

slaughter, 13–15, 18, 23–4, 28, 116, 135–6, 138, 140–1, 143–4, 147–9, 151–5, 161, 175, 177–81, 183, 193–6, 199
slow cinema, 4–10, 12, 17, 26, 51, 98, 102, 135, 165, 179, 196–8
Sobchack, Vivian, 26, 42, 50, 134, 148
sound, 7, 28, 69–71, 74, 78–9, 83, 100, 110, 120, 134, 143, 159n89, 165, 169–75, 184, 196

taxidermy, 12, 27, 66, 68, 75–8, 81–2, 88, 198–9
The Rules of the Game, 49–50, 134–5
time-image, 2, 8–9, 16, 26–8, 42–3, 52–8, 66–7, 75–6, 83, 88, 96, 122, 162, 165–9, 171, 178, 180–1, 196

Uexküll, Jakob von, 2–3, 24, 26, 42–6, 48, 50, 55–7, 120–1, 169, 172, 200
Umwelt, 2, 26, 42–5, 48, 63, 56, 84, 172

virtuality, 1–2, 9, 17–18, 20–1, 28–9, 34, 42, 45, 48–9, 52–5, 57–8, 85–6, 88, 122–3, 150, 162, 172, 174, 180–1, 183–5, 196–8, 200
vulnerability, 18, 23–4, 49, 77, 101–2, 134, 136, 138–40, 195–6, 198

Wolfe, Cary, 3, 10, 14–15, 20, 22, 118, 153, 183, 200

ZooCam, 7–8, 76

EU representative:
Easy Access System Europe
Mustamäe tee 50, 10621 Tallinn, Estonia
Gpsr.requests@easproject.com

www.ingramcontent.com/pod-product-compliance
Lightning Source LLC
Chambersburg PA
CBHW071840230426
43671CB00012B/2012